URBAN PHOTOGRAPHY

An Hachette UK Company
www.hachette.co.uk

First published in the UK
in 2019 by Ilex, a division of
Octopus Publishing Group Ltd
Carmelite House
50 Victoria Embankment
London EC4Y 0DZ
www.octopusbooks.co.uk
www.octopusbooksusa.com

Distributed in the US by Hachette Book Group
1290 Avenue of the Americas, 4th & 5th Floors,
New York, NY 10104

Distributed in Canada by Canadian Manda Group
664 Annette Street, Toronto, Ontario, Canada M6S 2C8

Publisher: Alison Starling
Commissioner: Frank Gallaugher
Consultant Publisher: Adam Juniper
Managing Editor: Rachel Silverlight
Art Director: Ben Gardiner
Designer: Simon Goggin
Picture Research: Giulia Hetherington
Production Controller: Sarah Kulasek Boyd

ISBN 978-1-78157-612-0

A CIP catalogue record for this book
is available from the British Library.

Printed and bound in China

10 9 8 7 6 5 4 3 2 1

URBAN PHOTOGRAPHY

TIM CORNBILL

ilex

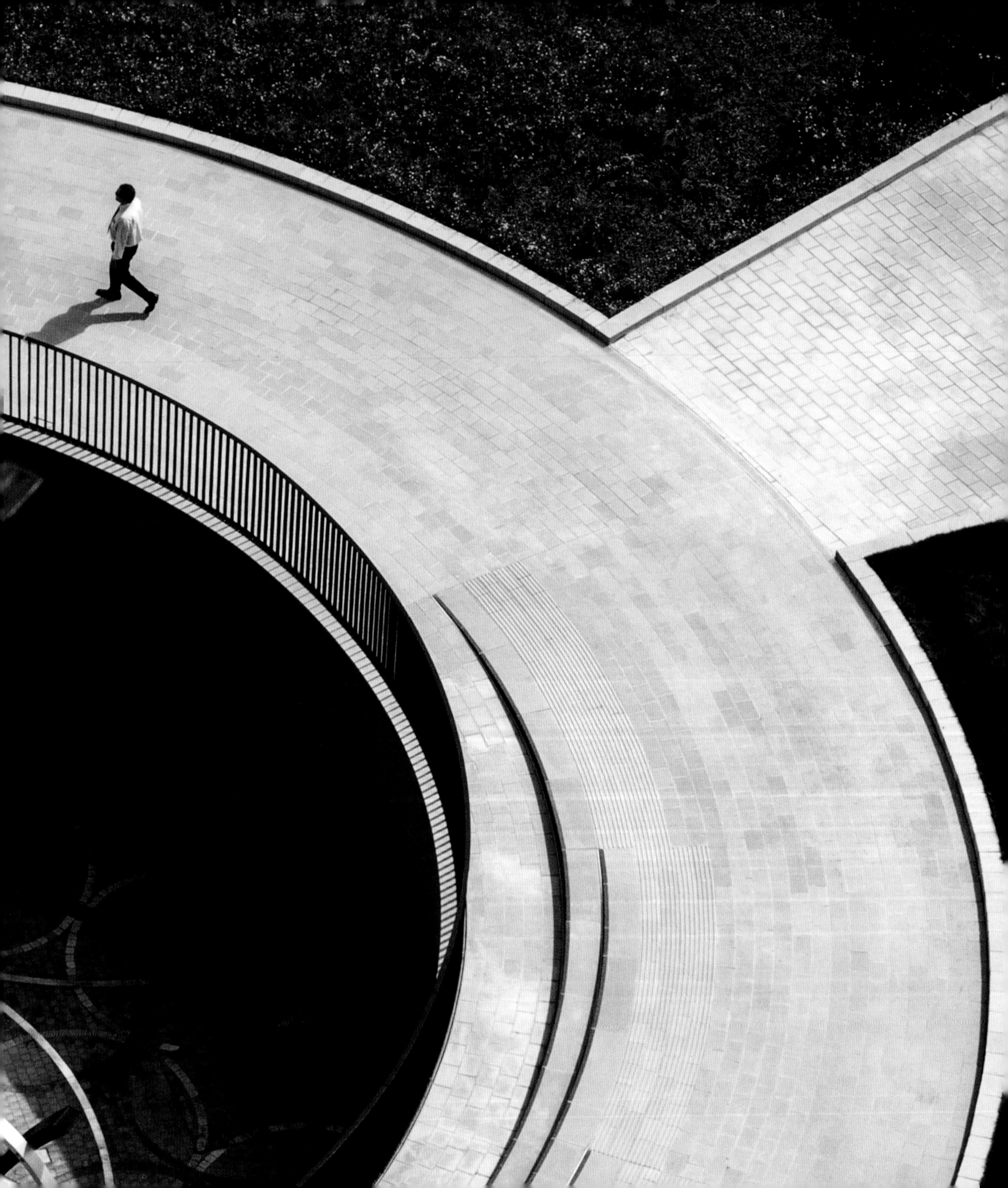

CONTENTS

INTRODUCTION

The urban environment is the perfect setting in which to learn all aspects of the photographic art. The city is a melting pot of society, containing variations on everything, from types of architecture that might be radically different from neighbourhood to neighbourhood – or from one side of the street to the other – to the people you see sitting at cafés and bus stops, enjoying amenities, in groups or on dates. One location can offer a huge array of possibilities depending on where you look, how you frame the shot, the time of day or the weather conditions.

This is a book about urban photography, but it is really a book about all photography. It will give you the essential factors to consider when approaching any subject, and provide inspiration, giving you fresh ideas for subjects and approaches.

Each aspect of urban photography comes with its own set of needs and considerations. Certain focal lengths in lenses, for example, may be better suited to certain types of photography than others, and you won't be able to successfully take a long exposure if you don't have a tripod. We look at the various kinds of cameras and lenses you can use for urban photography in Chapter 1. As others have said before, however, the best camera is the one you have on you, and it's important not to get hung up on the equipment. This book takes the philosophy that, technical limits aside, your phone's camera is just fine, if that's the one you use.

In general, other things are more important to your photography, and I can't overstate the impact that a little preparation can make, as we see in Chapter 2. Scouting the location, knowing what the weather is going to do – this will make a much bigger difference to your photos than the kind of camera you use. Getting to know your city is also crucial to photographic success, and we come to that in Chapter 3. Every urban environment has its own character, as the examples in this chapter will show you.

Architectural photography, which we look at in Chapter 4, is the perfect genre in which to really get to grips with composition, while practising your street photography, covered in Chapter 5, will help you learn to seize the moment and think on your feet. If urban photography is all about the epic skylines for you, Chapter 6 will show you how to get stunning results, even if your own city isn't as tall as New York City. After Dark – Chapter 7 – is when some of the most creative photography can happen, and here we cover everything from brilliant bokeh to beautiful light trails, and even astrophotography.

We close with chapters on Post-Production, which looks at a few simple techniques that can make a big difference to your shots, and The Next Level, which will point you in the right direction if you're looking to take your photography further.

RIGHT
Modern architecture or abstract art? Urban photography offers endless subjects and an infinite variety of approaches. It's the perfect genre to gain a grounding in photographic techniques and develop your own style.

'One location can offer a huge array of possibilities depending on where you look, how you frame the shot, the time of day or the weather conditions.'

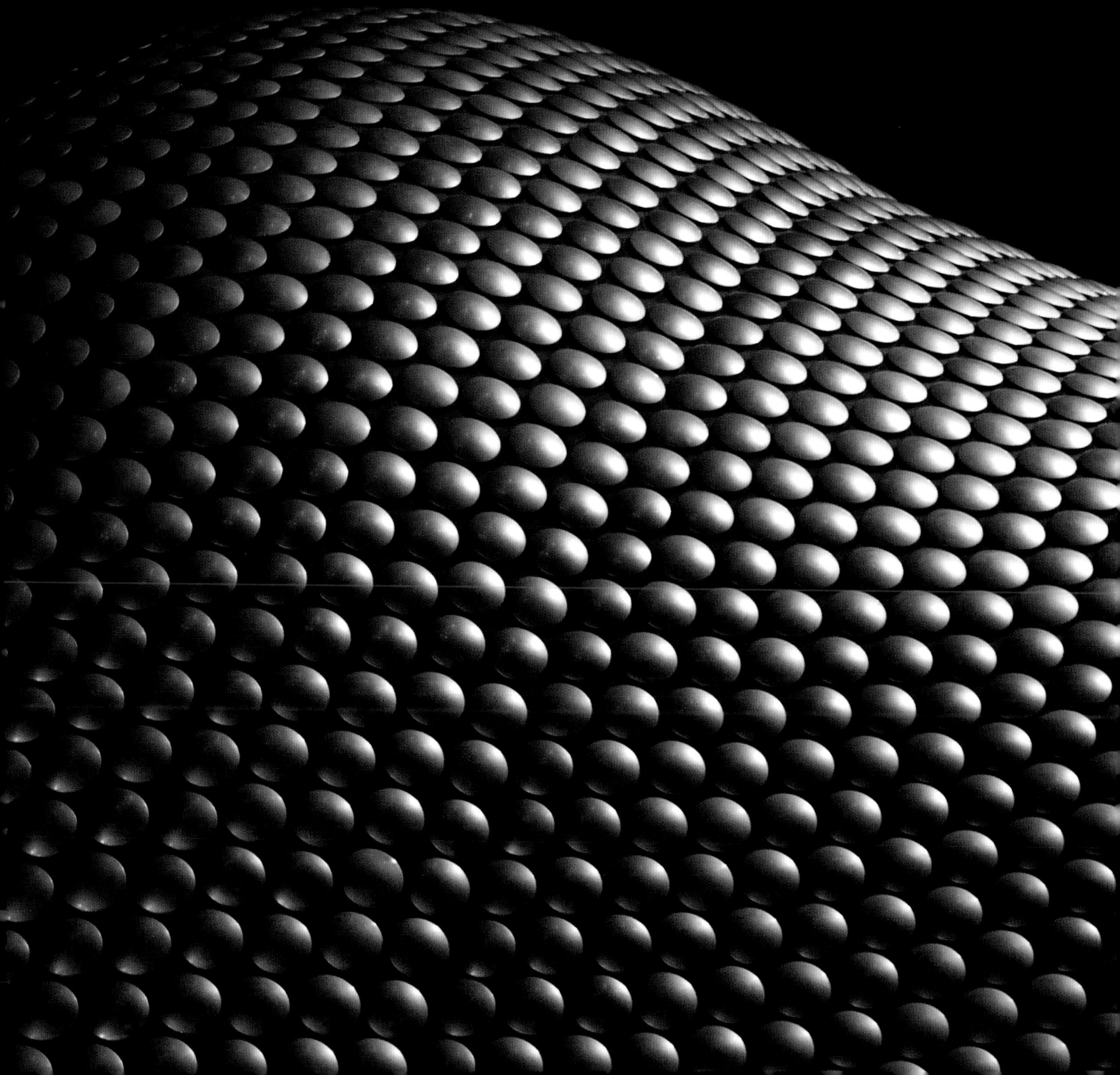

PHOTOGRAPHIC PHILOSOPHY

Throughout this book, I hope to encourage you to explore your urban environment and try your hand at different photographic genres. Trying out different skills and getting out of your comfort zone is the surest way to grow as a photographer and develop your own style. Before we go into information relevant specifically to urban photography, here are a few words of more general advice.

DON'T HOLD BACK

If you want to develop your skills as a photographer, this advice may be obvious, but it's something that a lot of people don't consider. The first piece of advice I want to give is: take loads of photographs. It is not like the days when we were restricted to a maximum of 36 shots on the film. The more photographs you take, the better a photographer you will become, and it really is as simple as that. Coming from the perspective of the digital photographer, there are no limits to how many photos you can take – except for the size of your memory card of course. If you often find that you are running out of room, go and get a larger card, or transfer your photos to your computer or hard drive more frequently. There is nothing worse than running out of space on your memory card, and then hastily having to decide which photographs to discard when there is a spectacular sunset happening behind you.

NEVER DELETE

This brings me to my second recommendation. Never delete a photograph. You never know whether a shot you think is a failure will turn out to be a success until you see it printed or on a larger screen. The small screen on the back of your camera will not present you with an accurate preview of the full exposure. In years to come, you will also thank yourself for keeping all those shots that didn't quite work out. They will become a marker of your development as a photographer, when you can look back and think about how you would approach them differently now.

EXPLORE

I love nothing more than exploring a city, wandering the streets, and seeing architecture anew through photography. I get the most satisfaction from the medium when I am discovering unfamiliar places with my camera, and capturing them as stills. So, travel to new destinations – your camera makes a great companion. Or if you can't do that, explore a place you're very familiar with, and see if looking at it through your photographic eye doesn't transform it. When you set out looking for a strong composition, or for the one detail that sums up the character of a place, you'll be amazed at how new it looks.

But, it's important to remember that 'exploring' doesn't need to be limited to its literal meaning. Exploring can be about trying new techniques, shooting styles or processes. Watch tutorials online or read about a technique you want to try, then go out and try it in the real world. Don't limit yourself by the type or style of photography you shoot: just as getting to grips with urban photography makes you a better all-round photographer, learning one new skill will impact the rest of your photography.

RIGHT, TOP
Architectural and abstract: Birmingham's iconic Cube under construction.

RIGHT, BOTTOM
This shot was shortlisted in the CABE 'Urban Beauty' competition in 2007.

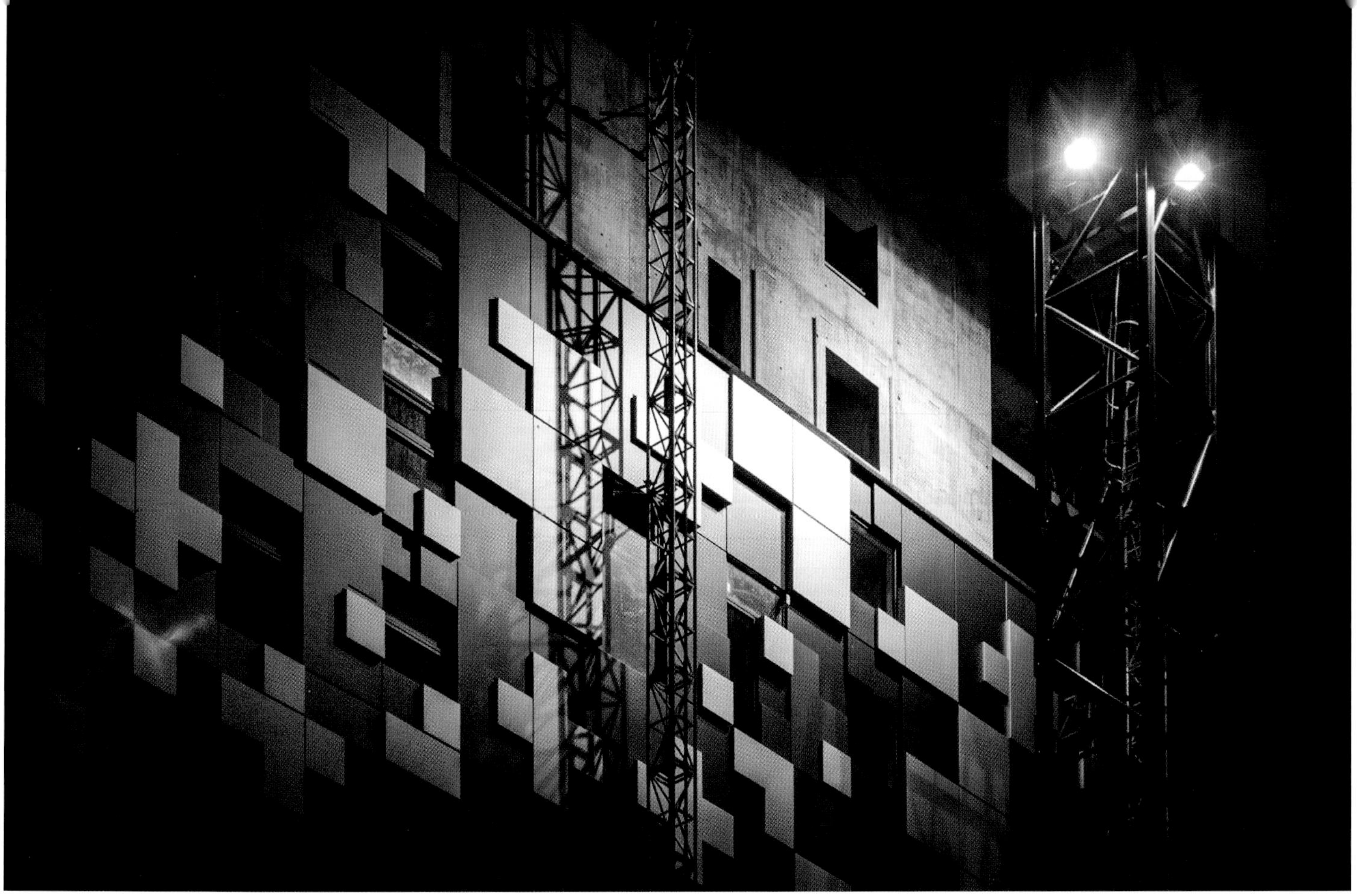

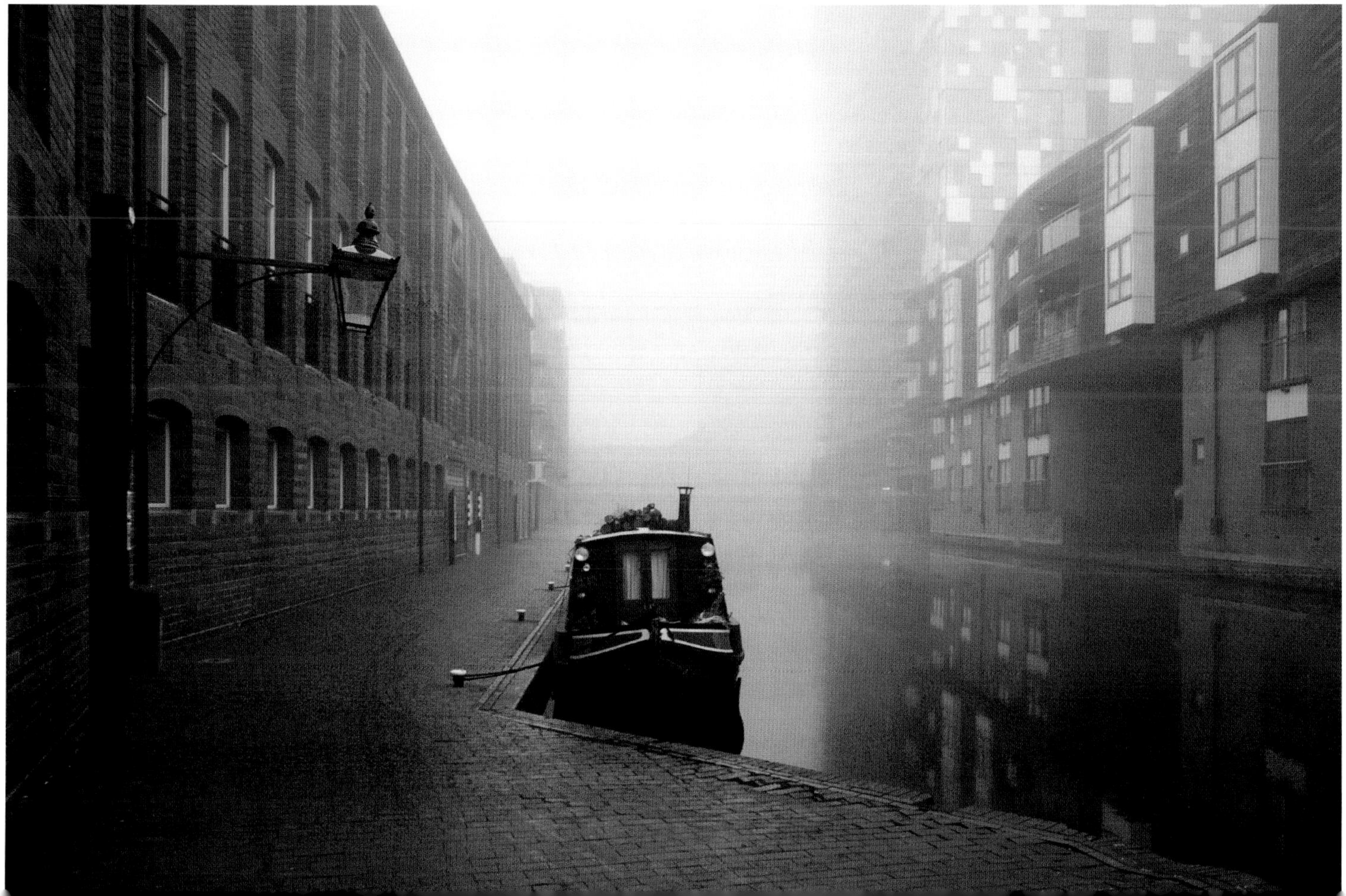

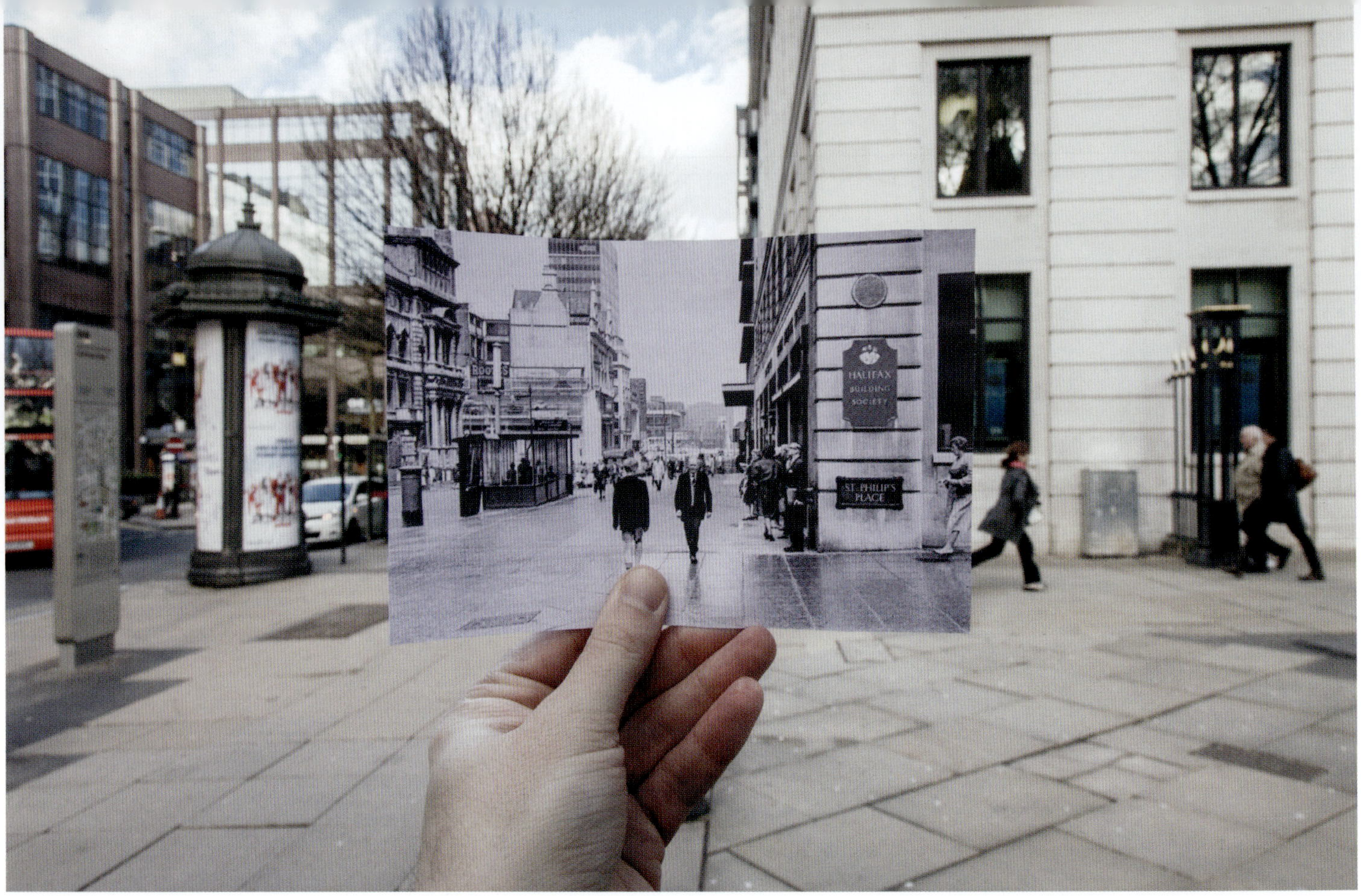
HALIFAX
BUILDING
SOCIETY
ST. PHILIP'S PLACE

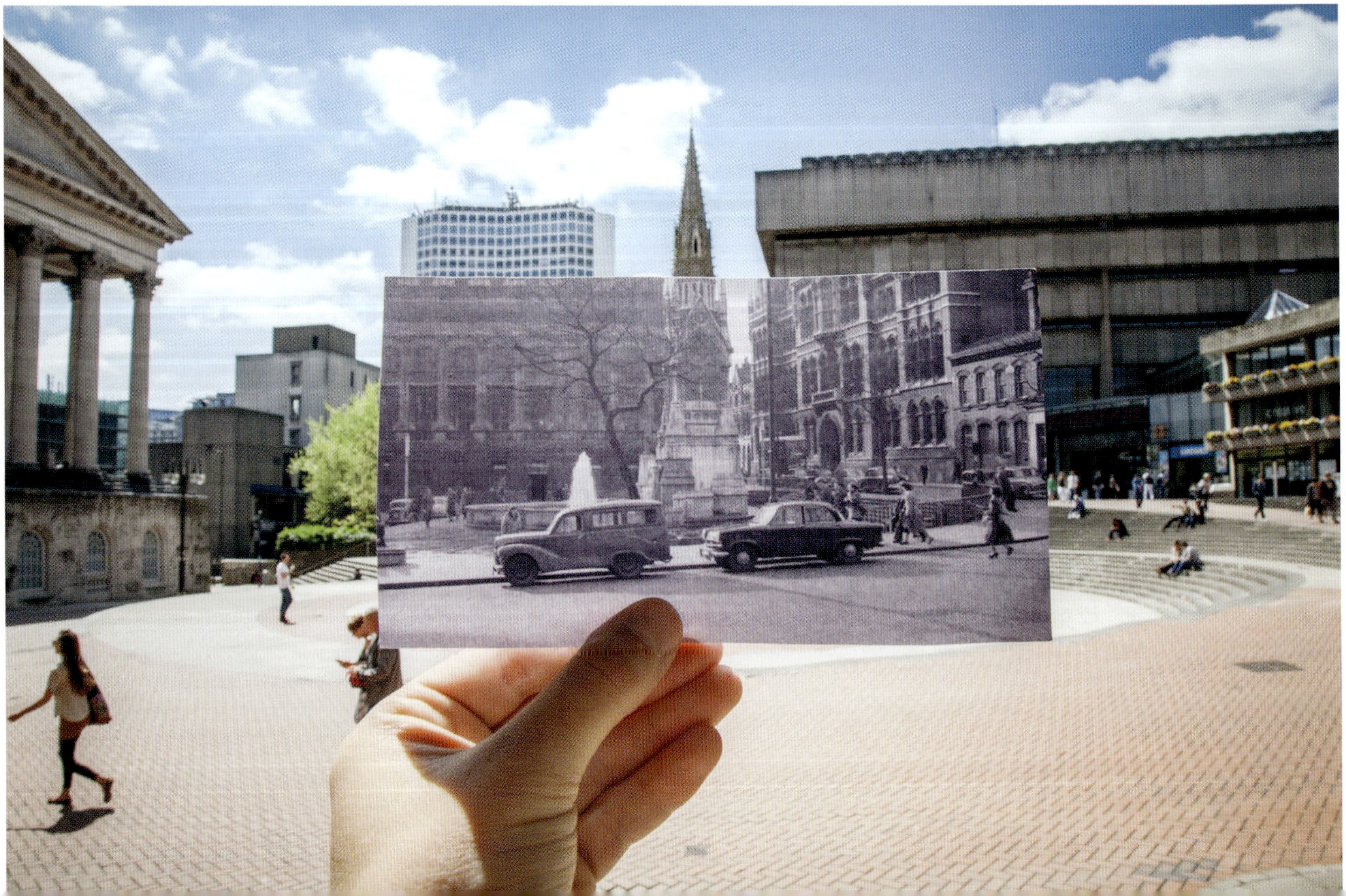

LEFT, TOP & BOTTOM
Urban photography is about connecting with your surroundings, and there are many ways to do this. Here, I compare the city as it appears today with shots taken 50 years before.

REACT

Learn to react to your surroundings. When you've taken enough photographs, you'll probably find that you will have developed 'photographer's intuition.' By experiencing different conditions and environments, you will see what works and what doesn't, and you'll then be able to train your brain to know whether a photograph is going to be any good before you've even taken it. You might be walking around town, for example, when you spot the sun lighting up a building you had never noticed before. The sun might disappear behind the clouds, but when it appears again it might just be the perfect shot–so you wait. An auxiliary piece of advice, therefore, is to always carry a camera with you wherever you go, even if it's just your smartphone. And to develop your photographer's intuition, constantly be searching for shots and looking with your photographer's eye.

THE BEST CAMERA IS THE ONE YOU HAVE ON YOU

Yes, we discuss equipment in the first chapter of this book and yes, I've already given this advice, but it bears repeating. People get too fixated on the equipment they're using. Use whatever camera you have, and learn to work within its limitations and to its strengths. After all, a smartphone might not be great for a low-light, long-exposure shot, but it is fantastic for wide-angle shots of the city in good light conditions. A better investment than kit for your development as a photographer is to join a local photography group, attend a photography workshop, visit a new destination, or meet up with your photography peers and see what you can learn from them.

BE UNIQUE

Create your own style, follow your own path, and be unique. It is difficult to stand out from the crowd in a world where just over one trillion photos are taken each year, but your viewpoint is unique and you can express that through your photography. In fact, you will already be doing this by following the type of photography you are interested in. Your unique take on the particular environment you are in, with whatever light and weather conditions are prevailing at the moment of the shot, is already adding up to a fair level of individuality. And a little knowledge – both in terms of the place you're photographing and your photographic skills – will take you even further. Likewise, try not to recreate other people's work, but instead look at it objectively and use it as inspiration.

LOVE

Most importantly, go out and enjoy yourself. The love and passion you invest in your subject will be recognized by others who view your photographs.

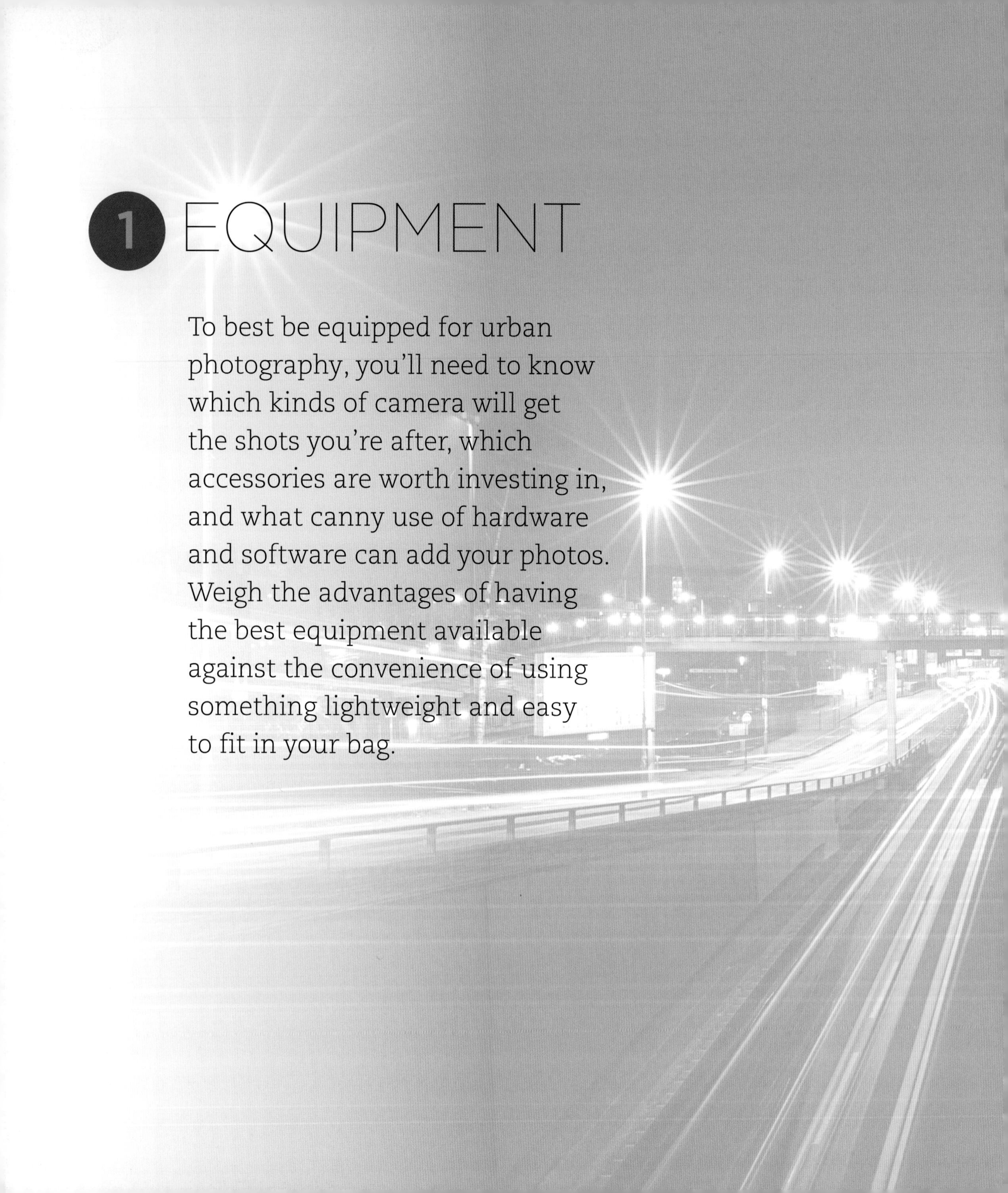

1 EQUIPMENT

To best be equipped for urban photography, you'll need to know which kinds of camera will get the shots you're after, which accessories are worth investing in, and what canny use of hardware and software can add your photos. Weigh the advantages of having the best equipment available against the convenience of using something lightweight and easy to fit in your bag.

CHOOSING A CAMERA

What is the best camera to use for shooting in an urban environment? There is no single answer, but, if you're aspiring to take a certain kind of shot, you may find that one works better than others. This list is by no means exhaustive, but it will give you an idea of what your options are.

SMARTPHONE

Your smartphone may be the single greatest photography tool that can fit in your pocket. Phone cameras have improved enormously over the last few years, producing outstanding photographs with beautiful colour rendition. Some even allow you to manually control the aperture and shutter speed, and offer presets for different types of photography (if your phone doesn't offer this, you may find a compatible app that will give you this capacity). Don't worry too much about the megapixel count because, due to the relative compactness of the phone's sensor, more megapixels may actually result in worse quality. The main draw of the phone camera is its convenience: it can be carried everywhere and used to upload your photos to storage or social media without having to transfer files. You will also draw less attention to yourself when you get out your phone, rather than a hefty DSLR.

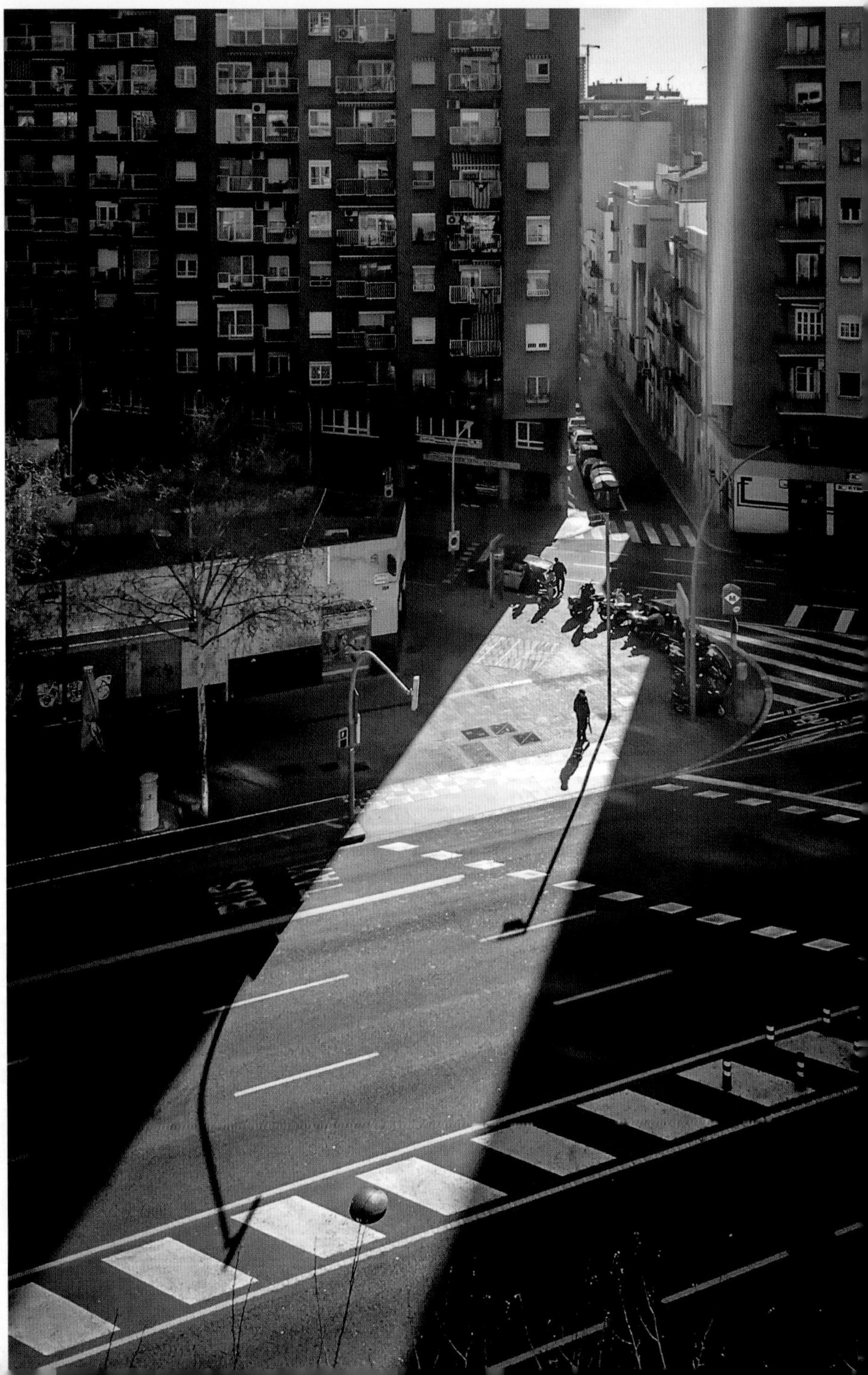

RIGHT
Looking down on the streets of Barcelona with a smartphone.

OPPOSITE
When the weather turns sometimes the best camera is the one in your pocket. This was taken with an iPhone 6s Plus, in 2016.

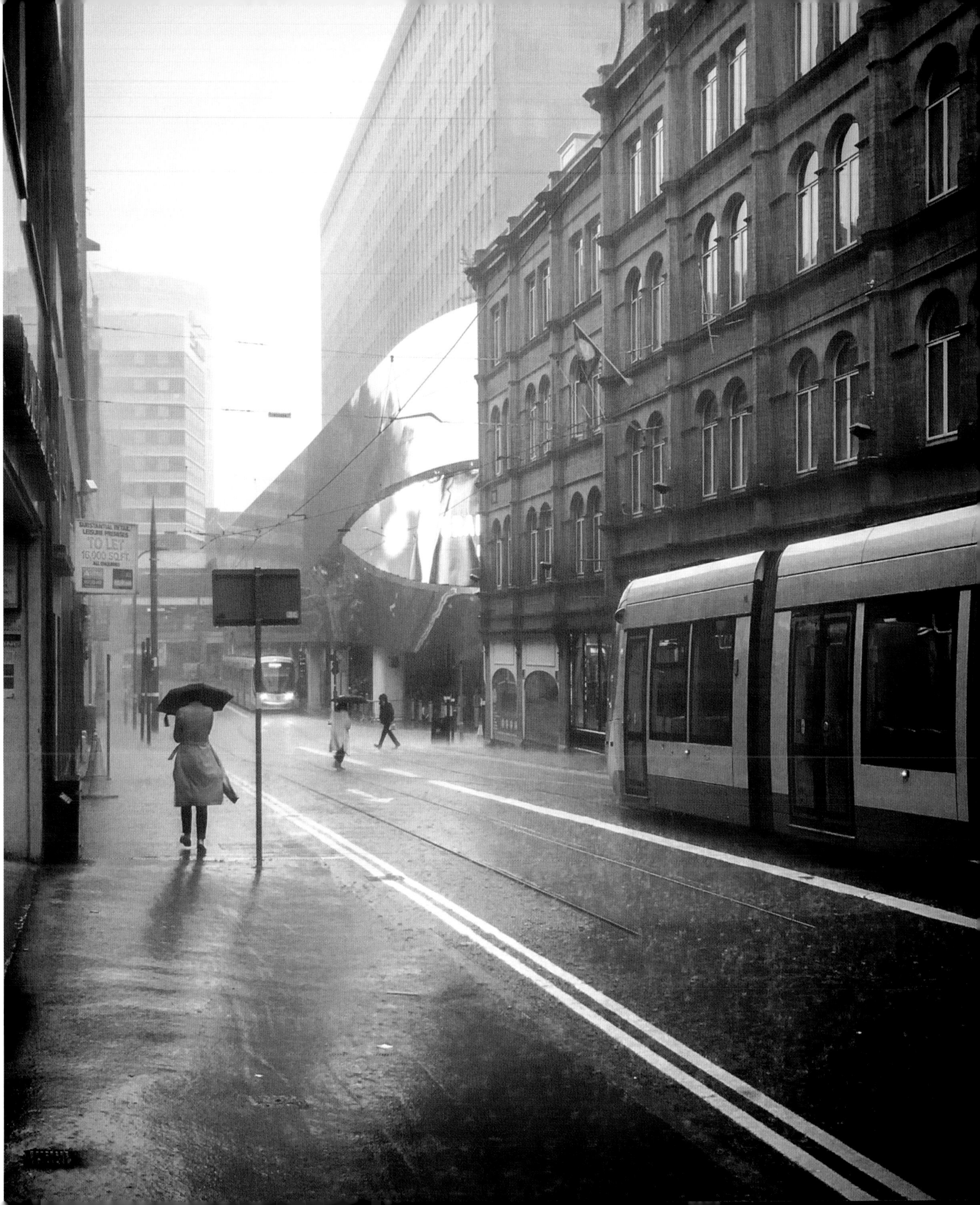
TO LET

POINT AND SHOOT

A point-and-shoot camera is your entry level dedicated camera. As with the smartphone, the sensors and lenses are relatively small, but you will usually see an increase in image quality. They usually offer optical zoom, as opposed to the almost useless digital zoom you are likely restricted to on your phone, and what manual controls are included will generally depend on how much you pay. The majority of models rely on back screens for framing shots, but some at the higher end of the market feature proper viewfinders, letting you see exactly what the camera sees. The majority of current models will have WiFi or Bluetooth so that files can be transferred to your smartphone or computer on the move. Due to the size of these cameras, you are not going to draw too much attention to yourself when taking a photo, but you won't be able to hide behind a pretence of sending a text.

INTERCHANGEABLE-LENS CAMERA

If you want to take your photography to the next level and have complete control over optics and camera functions, then you need a camera with interchangeable-lens functionality. The majority of these have viewfinders, with only the most compact versions relying on the screen on the rear of the camera. They are also likely to have some degree of weather protection, meaning you can take them out in most types of weather without having to worry too much about getting them wet. The main disadvantage of these cameras is that they are quite bulky, so when you get them out it is difficult to not look like a professional photographer – which may restrict your usage. The biggest advantages with these cameras are pretty significant, including but not limited to: the large sensors, the manual controls and the ability to change the lenses on the body. This opens up the opportunity to take much more creative kinds of shots.

OTHER CAMERAS

A couple of specialist cameras are worth a mention: one is the action camera, such as GoPro, which is ideal for amazing viewpoints and live action shots. They often feature wide-angle lenses and are usually shockproof and waterproof, so they will withstand being dropped, or a heavy downpour.

Drones with cameras are also becoming more and more popular for capturing a unique perspective on the urban environment, but be aware of local restrictions using these, including licenses required and limitations on where they can be flown.

BELOW
Sometimes you need a wide-angle lens to be able to convey the sheer scale of a space. Your smartphone already features one of these.

RIGHT
When you know where to stand, you don't need a technical camera – the composition will do the hard work for you.

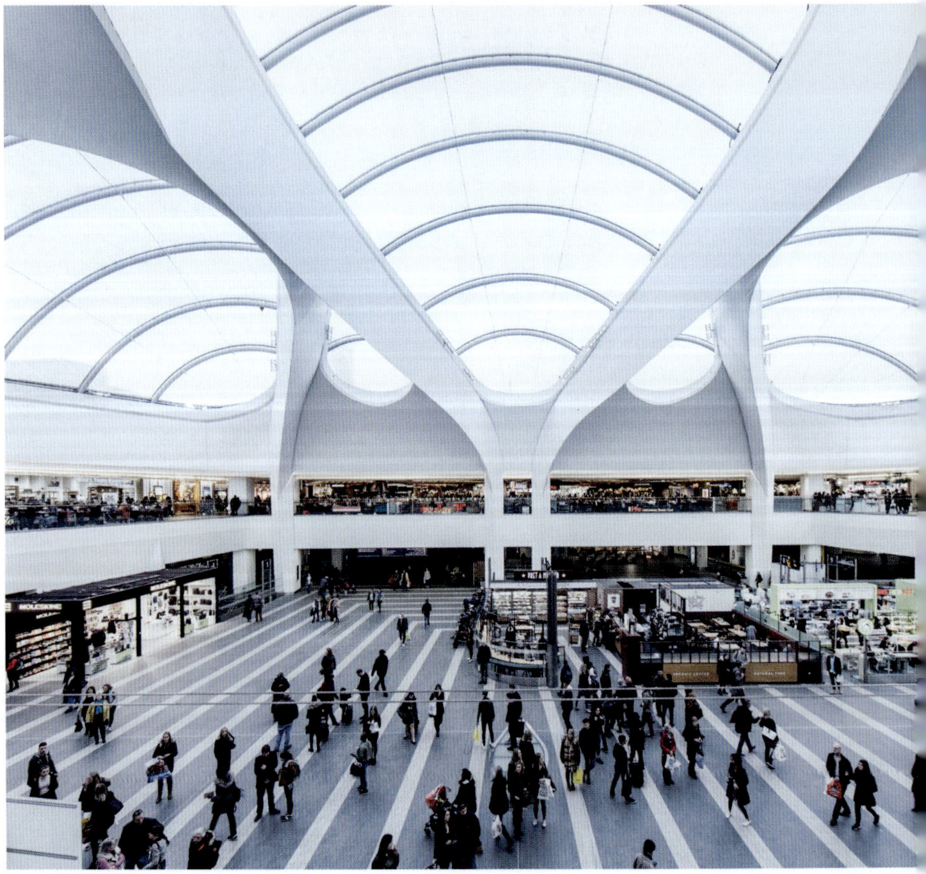

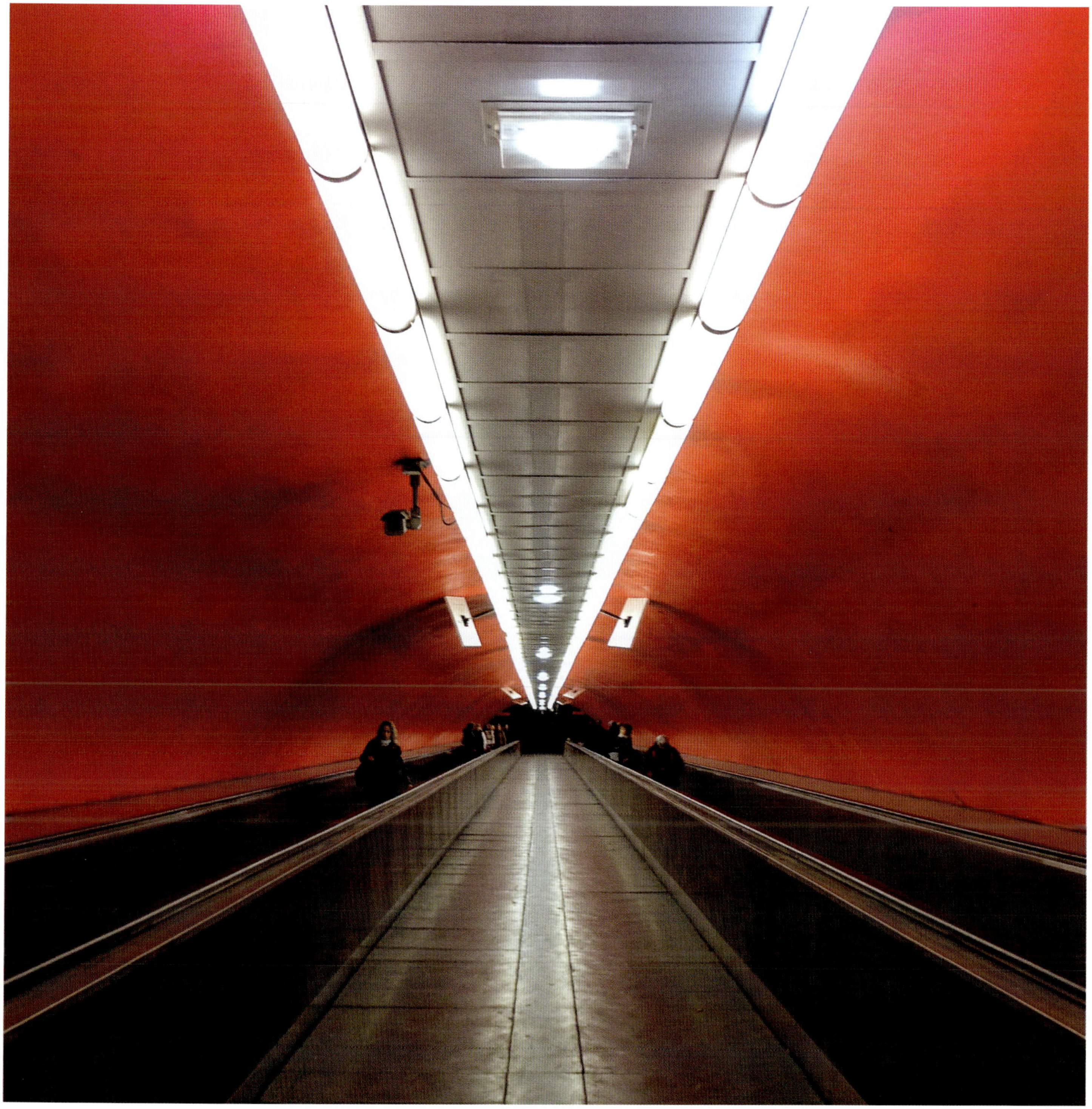

MANUAL FUNCTIONS

It is not essential to have manual functions on your camera, or to use them, but doing so will give you a lot more creative freedom. The following gives a brief rundown of the key manual functions so that if you want to take this step with your photography, you'll have a basic understanding of what these functions do.

AUTO VS MANUAL

All cameras will come equipped with an Auto setting, which basically means that the camera makes all the decisions for you. It will try to figure out what to expose for, what to focus on, and where to set the white balance. Using this mode is helpful when you first get a camera, but on the whole, the photographs are unlikely to excite, and you may get results you weren't expecting. One example of this is when the camera extends the shutter speed when you are in a dark room, because it wants to gather enough light to create a sharp image. This can lead to a blurred shot. Another way Auto mode will ruin your photos is, for example, when you try to shoot a beautiful sunset: the camera will try to balance out the tones it thinks are too warm – removing the very thing you wanted to capture. It's important to remember that a camera is not anywhere near as intelligent as your eyes and will always offer you its 'best guess' when you use Auto mode. If you want your photograph to reflect what your eyes actually see, you may well need to embrace manual.

ISO

So, if you want to take a photo in a dark space (and you don't have a tripod with you), what can you do? You'll notice that your camera may be equipped with a semi-automatic function that is labelled as 'P' next to the automatic 'A' function. This setting essentially does everything that the Auto function does, but allows you to change the ISO on the camera. The ISO relates to the sensitivity of the camera's sensor. By increasing the ISO, the sensor is able to capture more light, making this a quick fix when shooting in environments that are too dark to capture an exposure without blur caused by a too-slow shutter speed. The only problem is that at higher levels (ISO 3200+), increasing the ISO can make photos grainy. The lowest value on the camera of ISO 100 will create a smooth photograph, and the level you can take it to without it affecting the quality of the overall image will vary from camera to camera, but the current breed of top-end mirrorless and DSLR cameras can go much higher without any noticeable effect on picture quality.

SHUTTER SPEED

Shutter speed is the length of time the shutter is open in order to achieve the optimum exposure. When shooting hand-held, it's best to avoid anything slower than 1/60 of a second. Any longer than this and you will start to see blurring, unless you have a very steady hand! The longer your lens, the less you'll get away with slower shutter speeds, too, for the same reason.

At the other end of the spectrum, long exposures can be put to good creative use – capturing car trails at night or moving clouds in the day, for example – with the assistance of a tripod. Some creative ideas are discussed in a later chapter (see pages 132–41).

RIGHT
If you're shooting an internal space at night you'll need to master your camera's manual settings. This is taken hand-held but uses a high ISO to limit the exposure time.

OPPOSITE
When you're working with very little light, you will really test how far you can push the ISO on your camera.

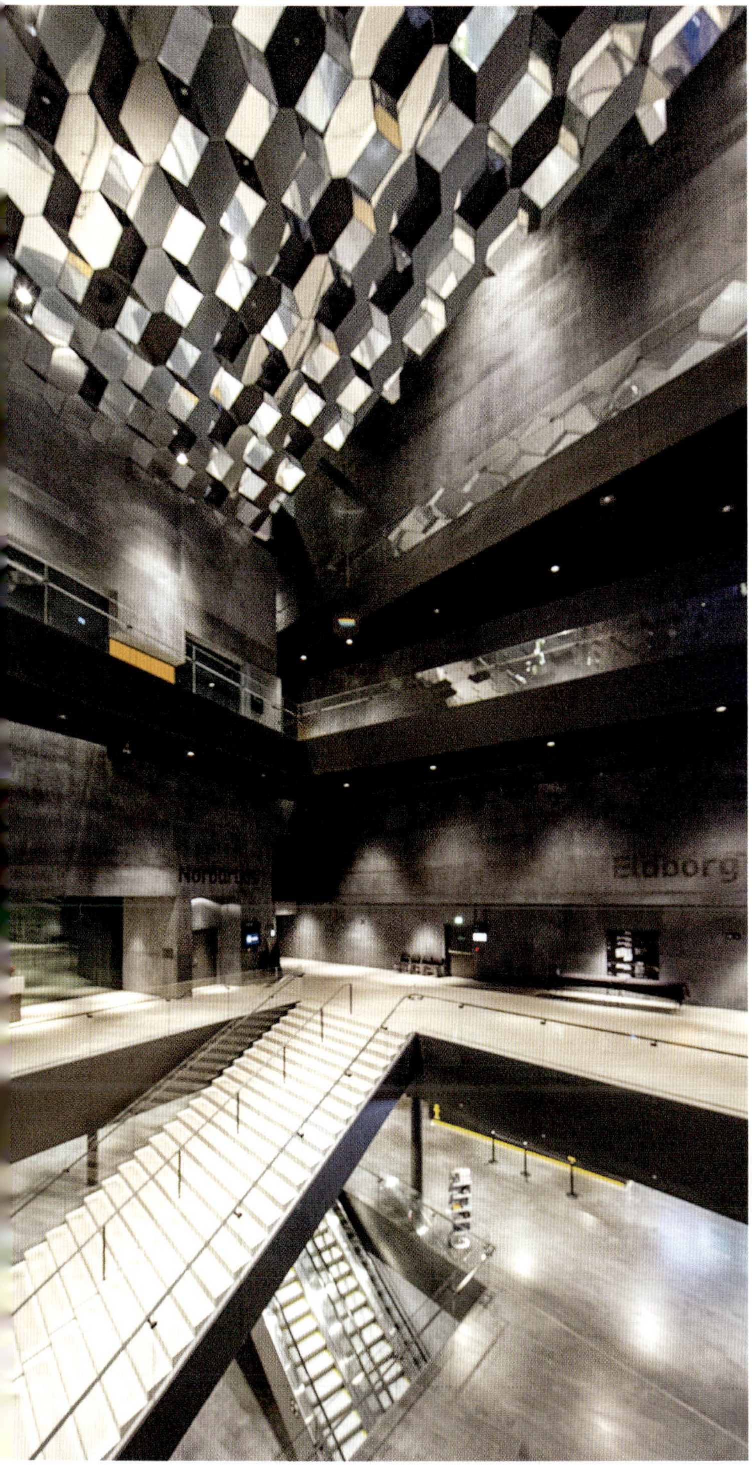
Eldborg

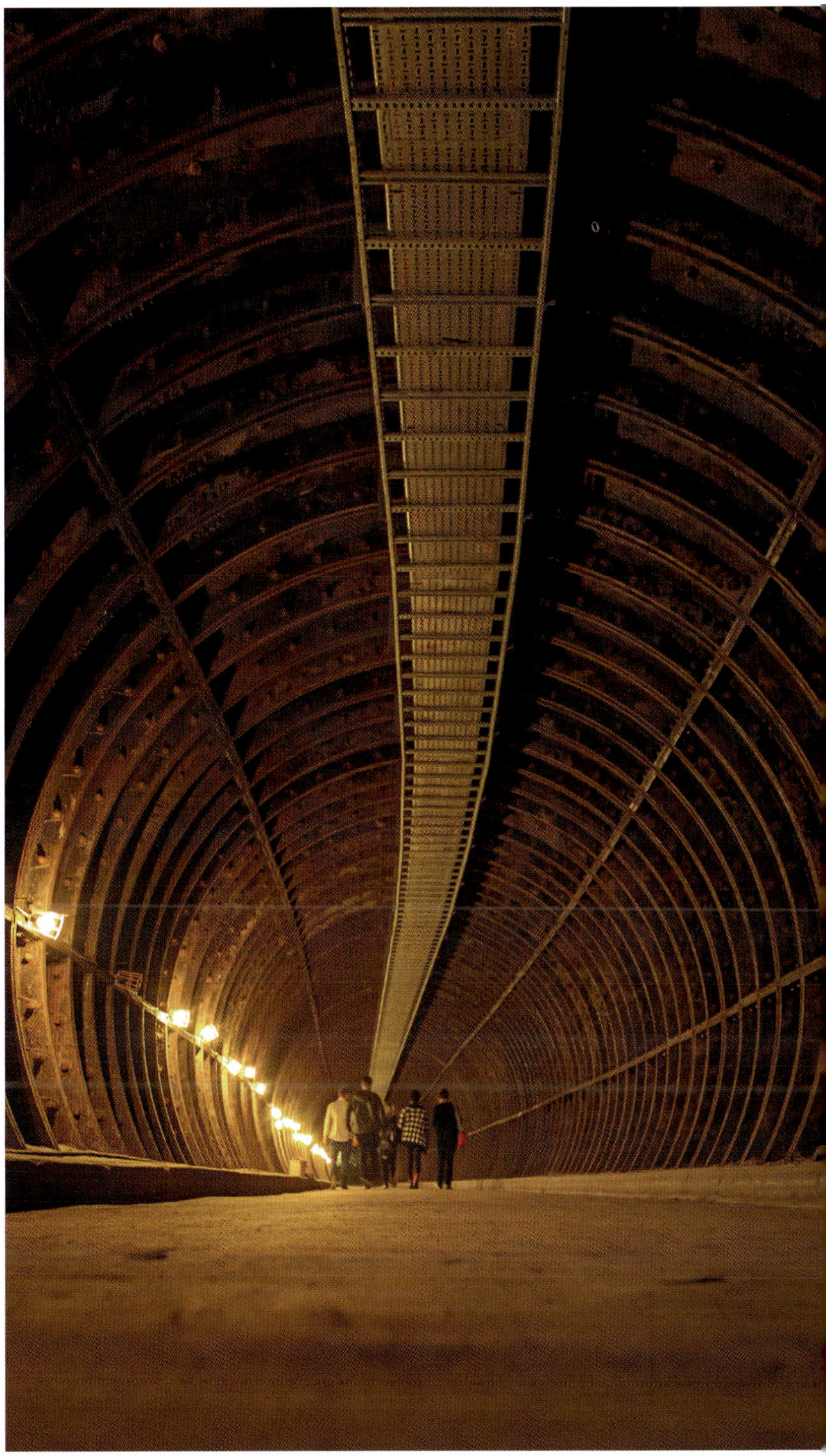

APERTURE

Though it is important to understand ISO and shutter speed, probably the most important setting to control is the aperture. This is the variable opening on the camera through which light passes. The size of the aperture is defined by the f-number of the lens. The lower the f-number, the more the aperture is open, and the more light will hit the sensor/film. The wider the aperture, therefore, the quicker the shutter speed can be to achieve correct exposure. Not all lenses are created equal: some 'quick' lenses can be opened to *f*/1.2, which is about as wide as they come. Lenses that are considered 'slow' will have f-numbers starting at about 5.6. A shot that was possible to take hand-held with the *f*/1.2 lens might require a tripod to achieve the correct exposure using an *f*/5.6 lens, because the narrower aperture requires a longer exposure (slower shutter speed) to let the same amount of light in.

Your aperture setting controls more than just the length of time required for a correct exposure, however; it also has an impact on the depth of field. 'Depth of field' refers to how long the range of focus, from near to far, in a shot is. Typically, the lower the f-number that is used, the shallower the depth of field, so elements in the foreground and/or background will be out of focus, depending on where you choose to set your focus. The farther away from the focus point, the greater the focus drop-off will be. To achieve a greater depth of field – i.e. where everything is in focus from the closest point to a point far away – requires a higher f-number. You might imagine that you'd want everything to be as sharp as possible, but there are times when the ability to blur the background makes the difference between a successful and unsuccessful shot.

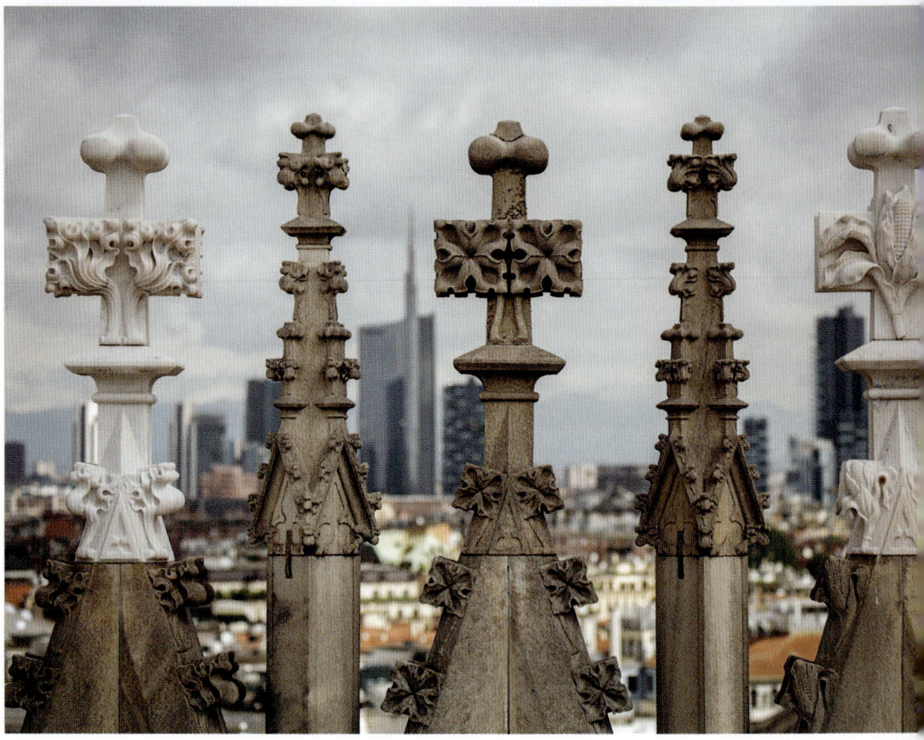

FOCAL LENGTH & DEPTH OF FIELD

This is not technically in the same category as the manual functions on your camera body, but it's useful to know that aperture is not the only thing that can impact depth of field; it is also affected by focal length. Generally, the longer your focal length, the narrower the range of focus. Compare the two photos on these pages. Both have a medium aperture setting, but the photo taken with a focal length of 50mm retains sharpness from the foreground all the way to the plane in the sky. The photo taken with a 100mm lens sees considerable focus dropoff toward the background.

ABOVE
Shot with a medium aperture of f/4 and a focal length of 100mm, we get an impression of the city skyline while focusing on the ornate stonework in the foreground.

RIGHT
An aperture of f/11 and focal length of 50mm keeps everything in focus, from the plane high in the sky to the railings of the building's balconies close at hand.

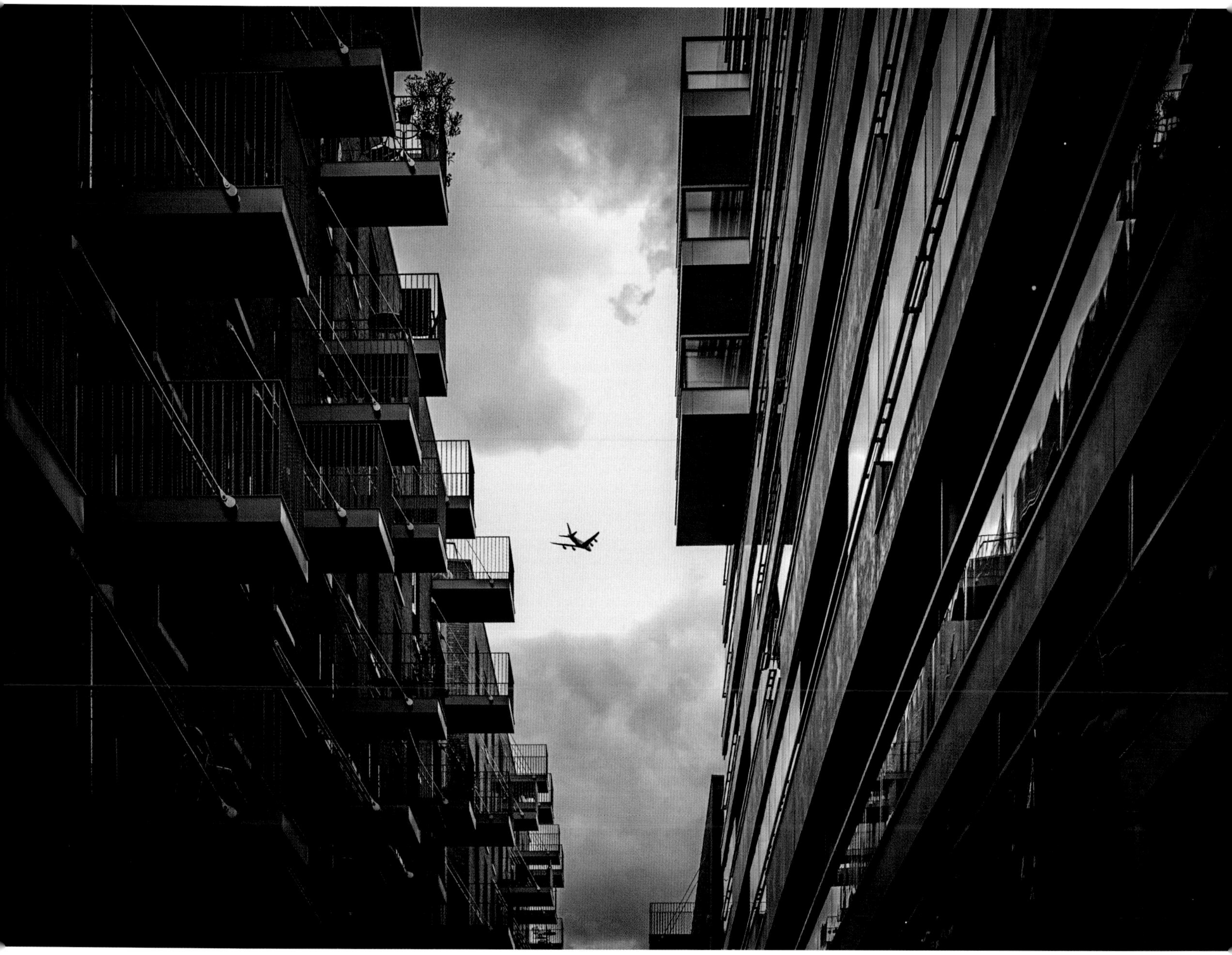

SPECIALIST EQUIPMENT

After getting to know the manual functions on your camera, you may find you want even more creative control, which only a certain kind of lens or bit of kit can give you. Here, I run through a few different types of lenses that are available, how you can use a tripod to best effect, and a few other gadgets that are worth exploring.

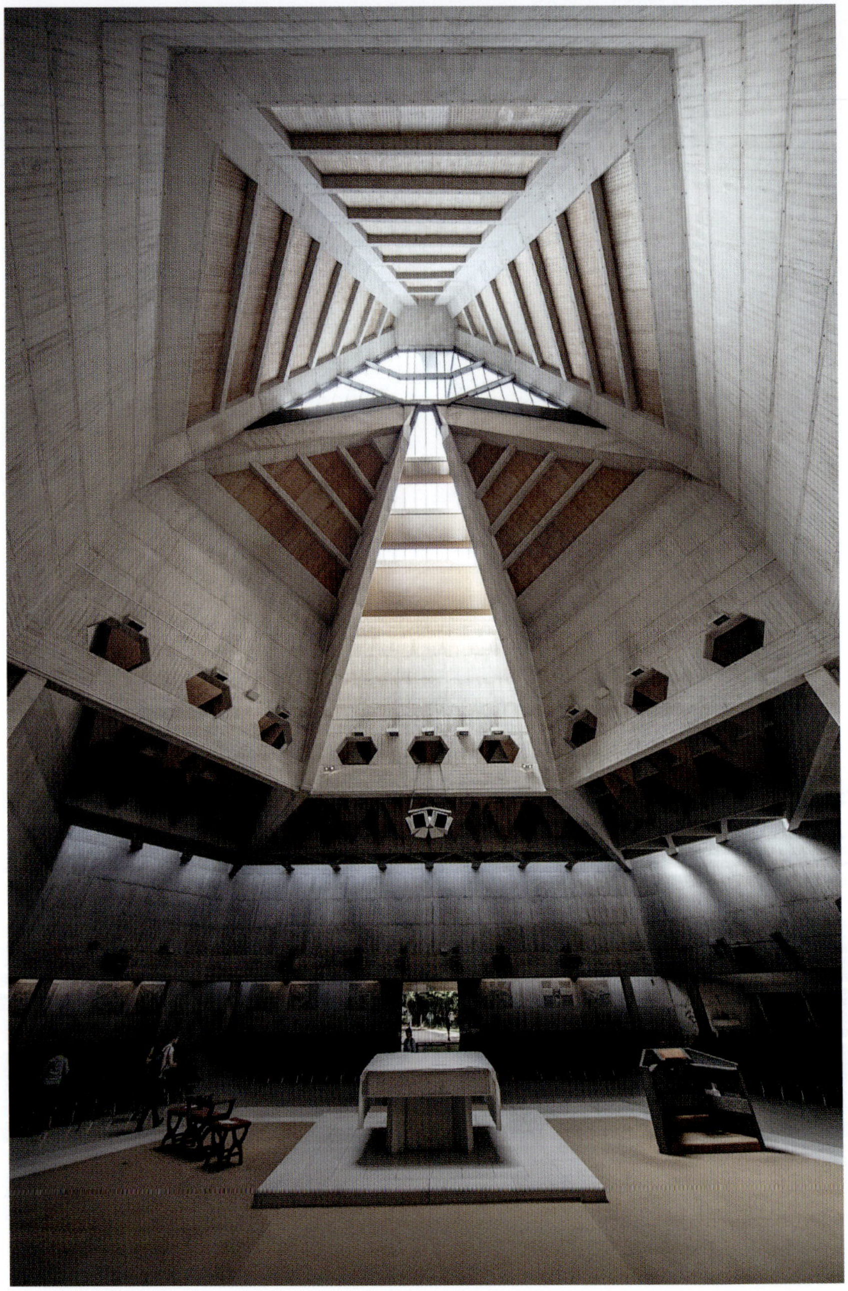

LENSES

As we saw on the previous pages, not all lenses are built the same. Aside from the speed (maximum aperture setting) and the depth of field, the kind of lens you use also affects how much of a scene you can fit into the frame. This depends on the focal length and, typically, the rule is that the shorter the focal length, the wider the field of view. Shorter focal lengths (below 24mm) are usually considered to be 'wide-angle' lenses, at the bottom end of which (11mm and below) are 'fisheye' lenses. Such lenses give you the widest possible angle of view, but you'll start to see distortion that increases as your focal length gets shorter. Take a look at images taken with a fisheye lens for a good demonstration of this.

The other end of the scale is the 'telephoto' lens, starting from a focal length of 70mm but potentially extending beyond 300mm. The longer the focal length, the narrower the lens's field of view, and the greater the magnification. A telephoto lens, then, is good for focusing on things in the distance, but will crop out much of the scene.

Right in the middle is the 35mm lens (50mm on a full-frame camera). This is considered the perfect length for street photographers, since it reportedly gives the field of vision closest to that of the human eye, and usually offers a quick aperture.

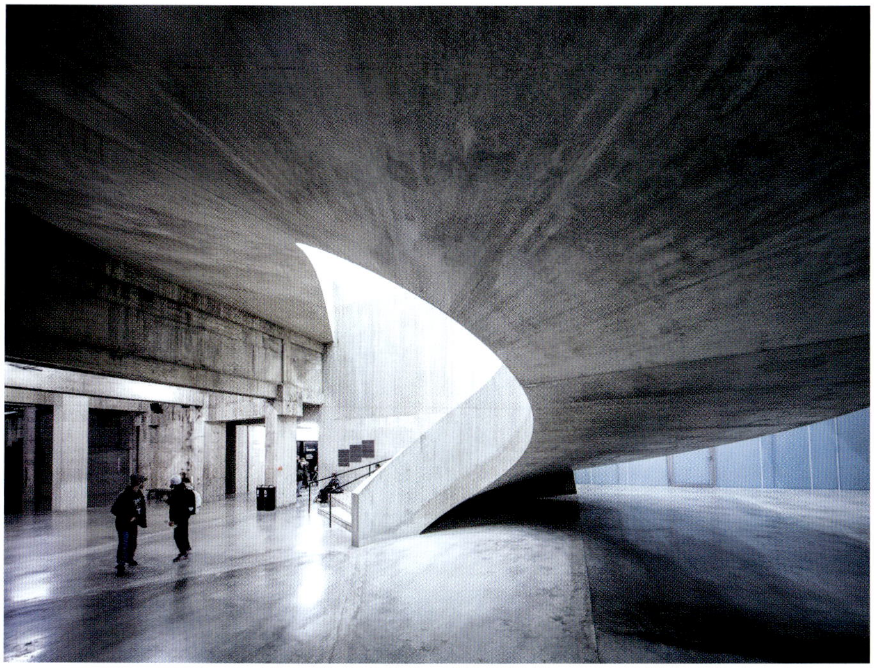

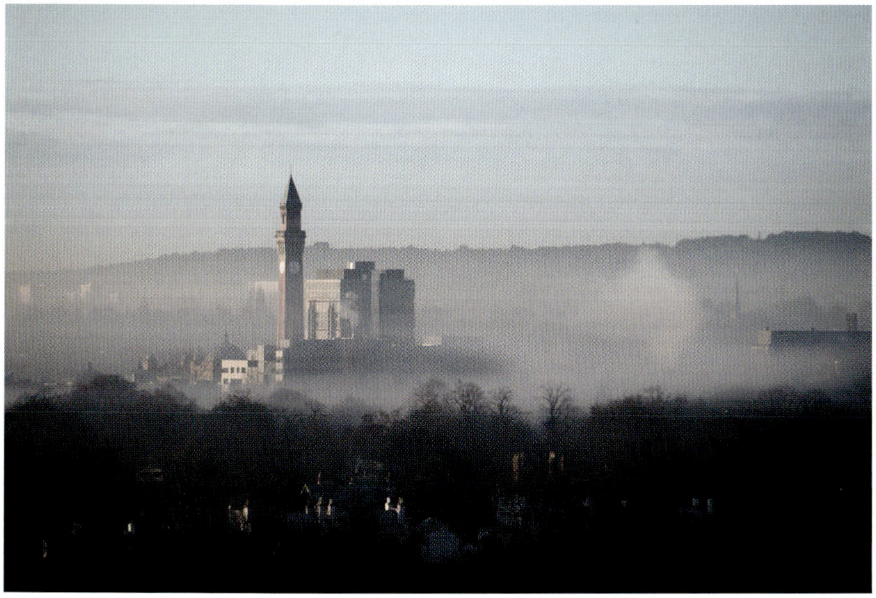

PRIME VS ZOOM

Zoom lenses can be really useful, allowing you a range of focal lengths – i.e. greater control of magnification and crop – without the hassle of swapping lenses or changing your physical distance. A standard zoom lens might give you a focal-length range of 24–55mm, while a fairly standard range for a telephoto zoom lens is 70–200mm. The downside to a zoom lens is that it is made of many more moving parts, which usually results in a smaller maximum aperture. That standard zoom lens, for example, might give you a maximum of *f*/3.5 at 24mm and *f*/5.6 at 55mm. Prime lenses require far fewer elements, meaning less opportunities for imperfections to creep in. When it's quality and speed you're after, you may be better off sticking with your prime lens and moving your feet more to get that perfect shot.

OPPOSITE
An extremely wide-angle 11mm lens is used to capture the whole structure of the roof and the floor of Clifton Cathedral in Bristol.

LEFT, TOP
You can create a dramatic composition by using a wide-angle lens next to a strong architectural feature.

LEFT, BOTTOM
A 400mm telephoto lens is used to pick out the mist rising around the University of Birmingham.

TILT-SHIFT LENSES

A problem architectural photographers come up against when attempting to capture whole buildings is something known as the 'keystone effect.' This is a perspective distortion in which parallel lines seem angled together, so that a square or cuboid building appears trapezoidal. This is fine in some instances, but often, it will just make your lines look wonky. Tilt-shift lenses are specialist lenses featuring two separate optical elements that can be angled within the lens to correct the perspective in a photo, so that the lines appear parallel as they should be. Tilt-shift lenses are very expensive; a good alternative is perspective correction using software such as Photoshop and Lightroom (see pages 164–5).

TRIPODS

If you want to take long exposures (anything over 1/60 second) or you're using a long telephoto lens, you will need to use a tripod to avoid getting blur from camera shake. The key here is to find a tripod that has the right balance between portability and stability. The general rule is that the heavier the tripod, the more stable it will be – but you probably don't want to be carrying a heavy weight around all day, so do some research. Remember that a heavier lens will require a sturdier tripod. When using a tripod, it's also worth looking into remote triggers. If you're going to all that trouble to avoid camera shake, the last thing you want is to introduce it when you're taking the shot. Timers and wired or wireless triggers can be used instead of hands.

FILTERS

Various filters that fit to the front of your lens offer different functions. A polarizing filter helps enhance the colours of the image and reduce reflections, while Neutral Density filters (ND Filters) can be used to force a slower exposure in a bright scene. Graduated ND filters affect only part of the frame, in a gradient, so that the brightest part of a high-contrast scene (usually the sky) doesn't overexpose.

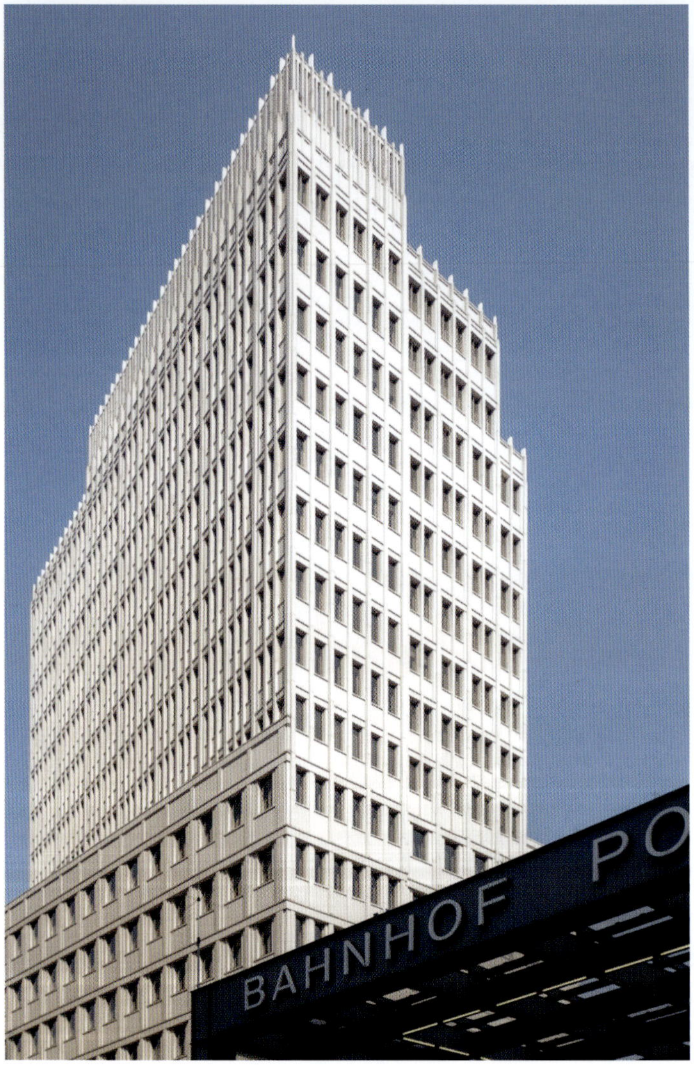

ABOVE
A tilt-shift lens is used to correct the perspective of this building in Potsdamerplatz, Berlin, making the facade vertical.

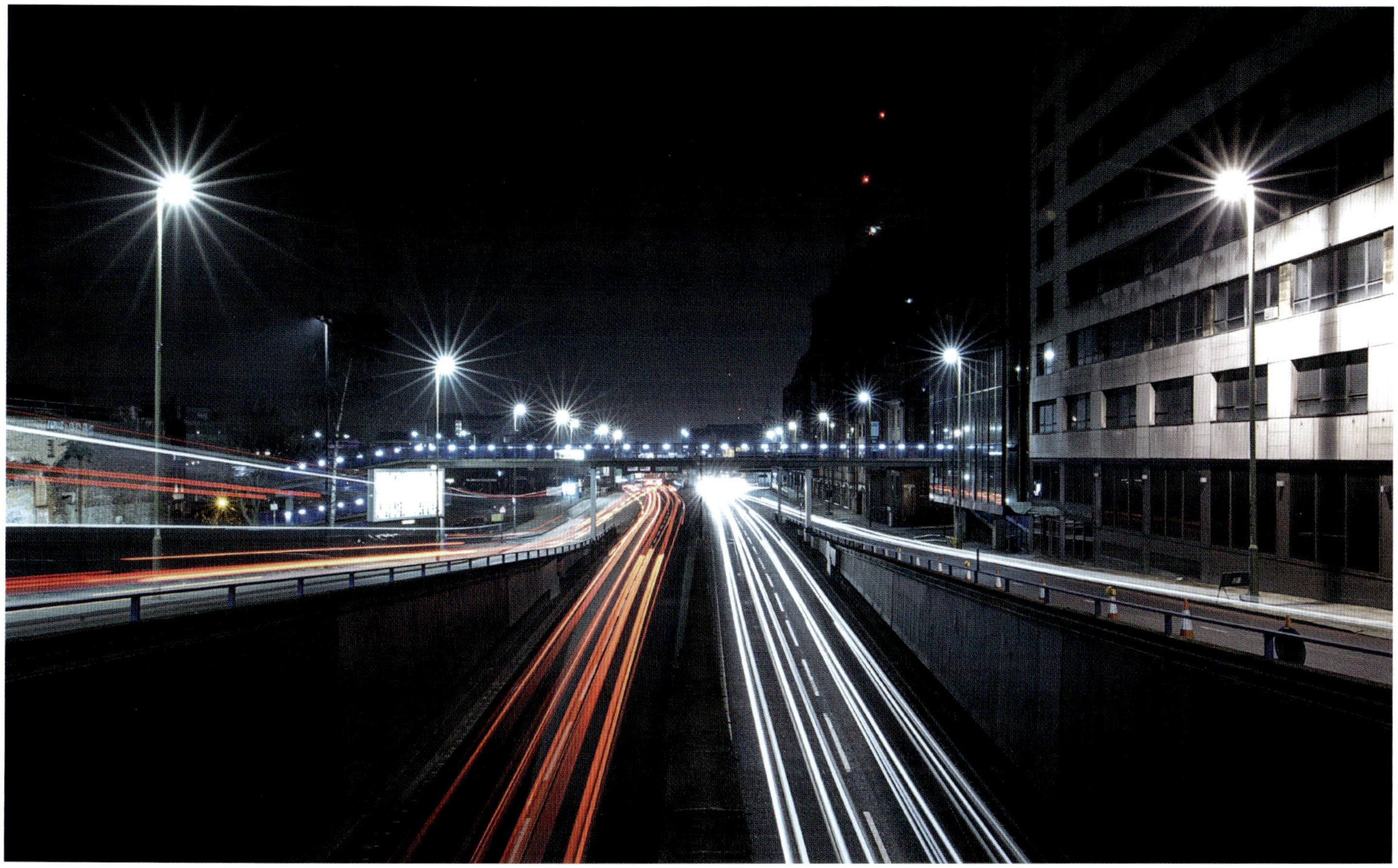

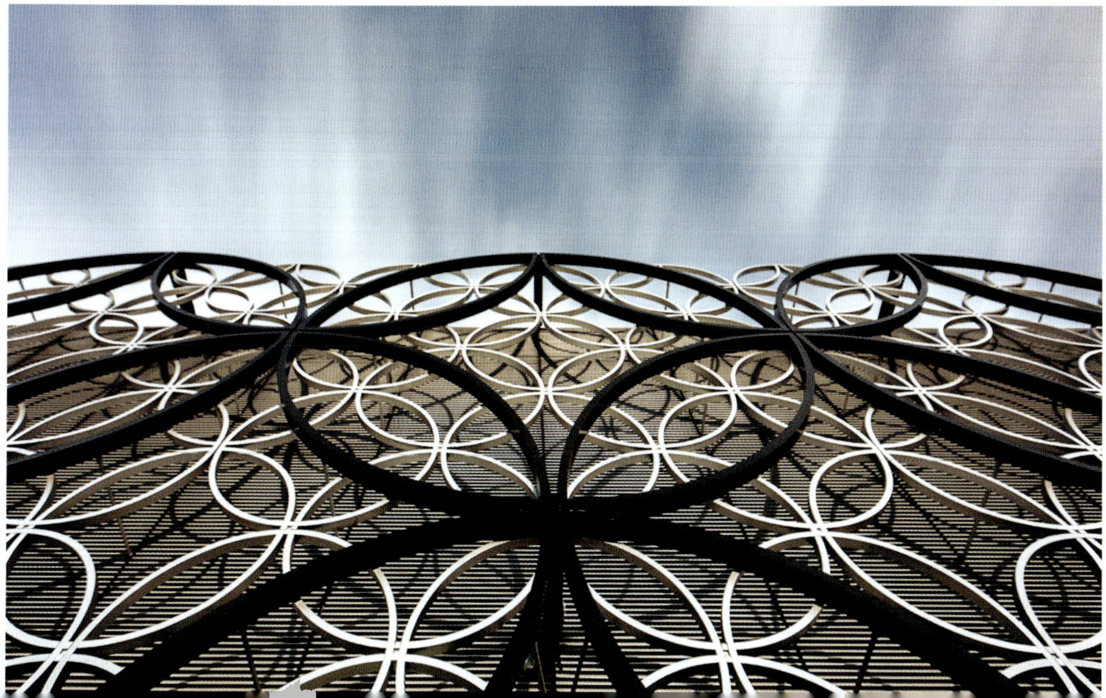

ABOVE
A 13-second exposure to capture the light trails of city traffic definitely requires a tripod.

LEFT
Using an ND Filter allows you to slow the exposure beyond even the smallest aperture setting. Here, it allowed an exposure slow enough (66 seconds) to capture the movement of the clouds in full daylight.

HARDWARE & SOFTWARE

Believe it or not, the majority of the photos you see in commercial contexts have had a certain amount of post-production work. The amount varies from a light touch to the composite image assembled from radically different component parts. However much you believe in getting it right in camera, there's no denying that a little editing can take an adequate photograph to a much higher level, and even a dud shot might yield something you can work with, with the right treatment.

If you are using your smartphone for photography, you probably know that thousands of photography editing applications are available, including those offered by social media platforms such as Instagram. Along with the ability to add filters, text and graphics, they may also allow you to perform more traditional edits, such as cropping, changing the contrast and adjusting the saturation. Social networks are great for those who want to share their work, and possibly build a brand, but if you just want the editing without the sharing, other apps such as Snapseed will serve your purposes.

Computers typically let you perform more detailed edits – they have more memory and processing power than your average mobile phone, and they are simply bigger, so you can see what you're doing better. Depending on the file format and megapixel count of your images, your computer needs to be equipped to handle the file size. Look out for a dedicated graphics card, a decent amount of RAM (at least 16 GB), and a large amount of hard-drive space, because this will get filled quickly. When your catalogue of photos gets larger, you may have to invest in an external hard drive for more storage.

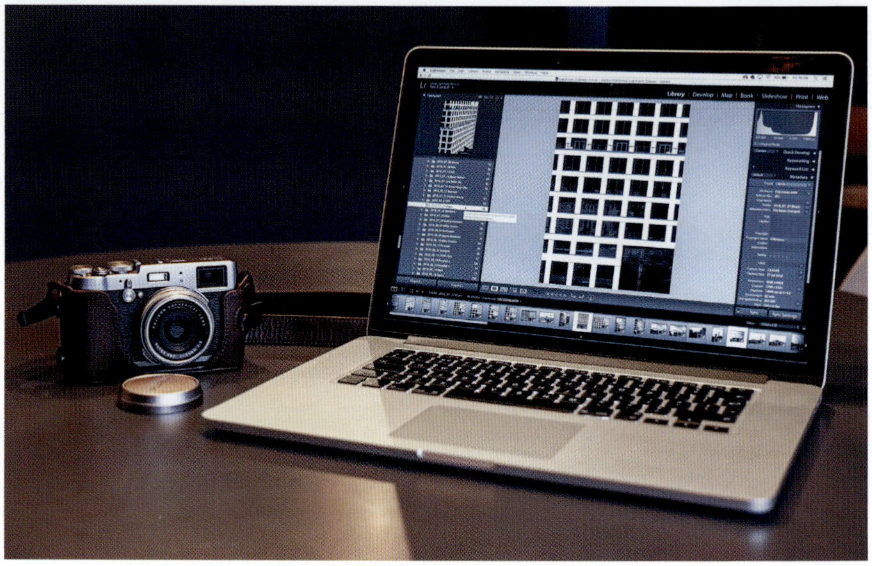

When it comes to image editing packages, the industry standard is Adobe Photoshop. The entry-level version, called Photoshop Elements, is about a sixth of the price of the full program and utilizes just the main functions from Photoshop, and is still an extremely powerful editing tool. Adobe also has a program called Lightroom, which is specifically designed for editing RAW photographic files. This is the perfect choice for the professional photographer, and the tutorials in Chapter 8 (see from page 148) all use Lightroom. As with hardware, there are different software programs and packages to suit all levels of skill and commitment. A beginner who is just enjoying learning about photography might not want to splash out on an expensive software package, and probably won't get that much out of it, but some of the cheapest programs are both powerful and intuitive, so you can get a lot out of them with minimal effort.

ABOVE
My laptop, with Adobe Lightoom installed, is perfect for editing on the go. If you're doing detailed, precision editing, you'll benefit from the addition of a mouse or tablet.

RIGHT
The camera bodies, lenses, flashes, and filters you use determine what kinds of pictures you can take, and how they'll look. But this is only the beginning: learning to use software as skilfully as you do your hardware is, or can be, part of the process.

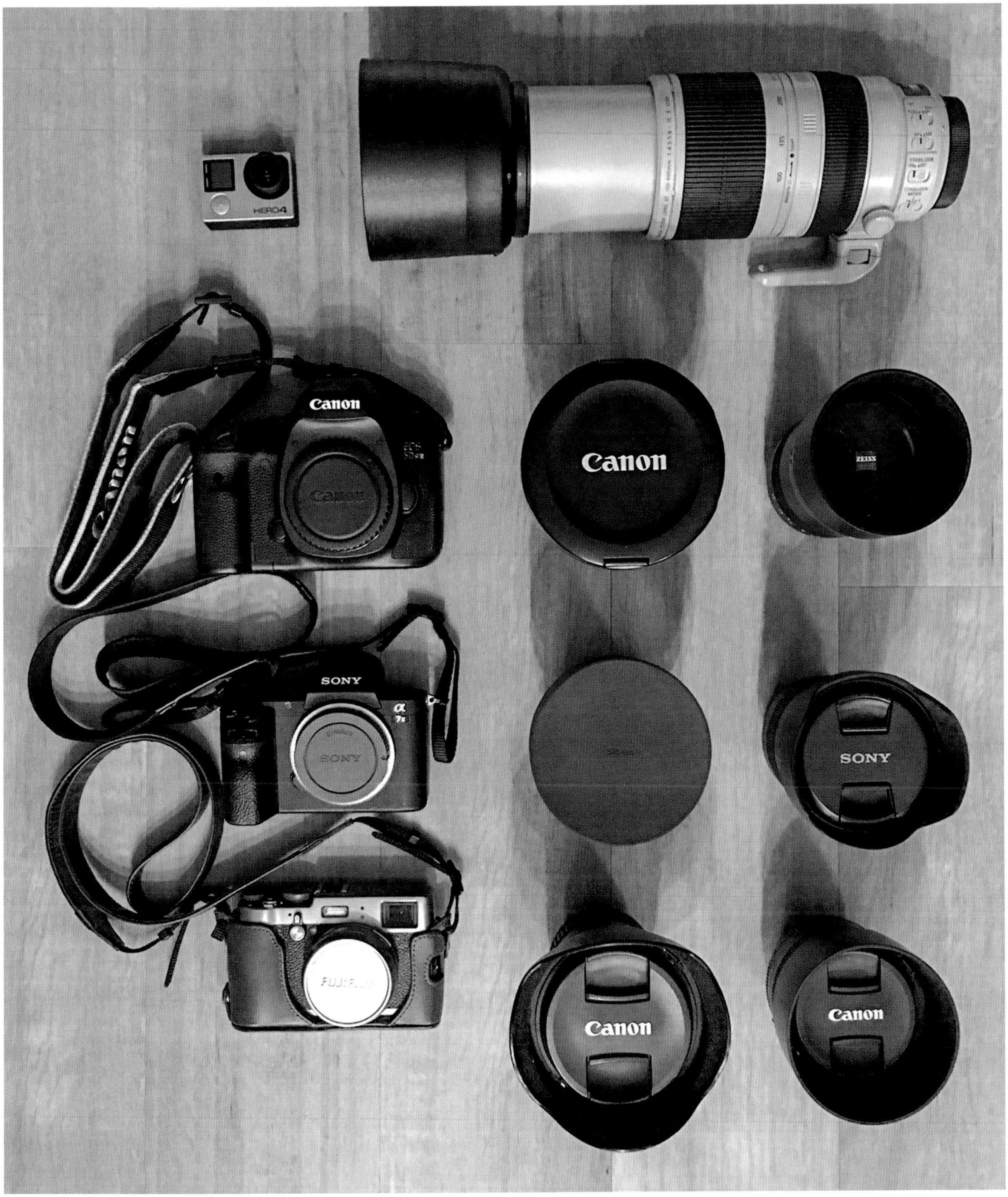
HERO4
Canon
Canon
ZEISS
SONY
SONY
Canon
Canon

2 PREPARATION

Doing your research on the location before setting out on your urban photography trip is useful. Although many people prefer not to know anything about a location before visiting to photograph it, a little research can help you to plan the best time to visit and what equipment to bring, as well as giving you ideas for what to shoot before you get there.

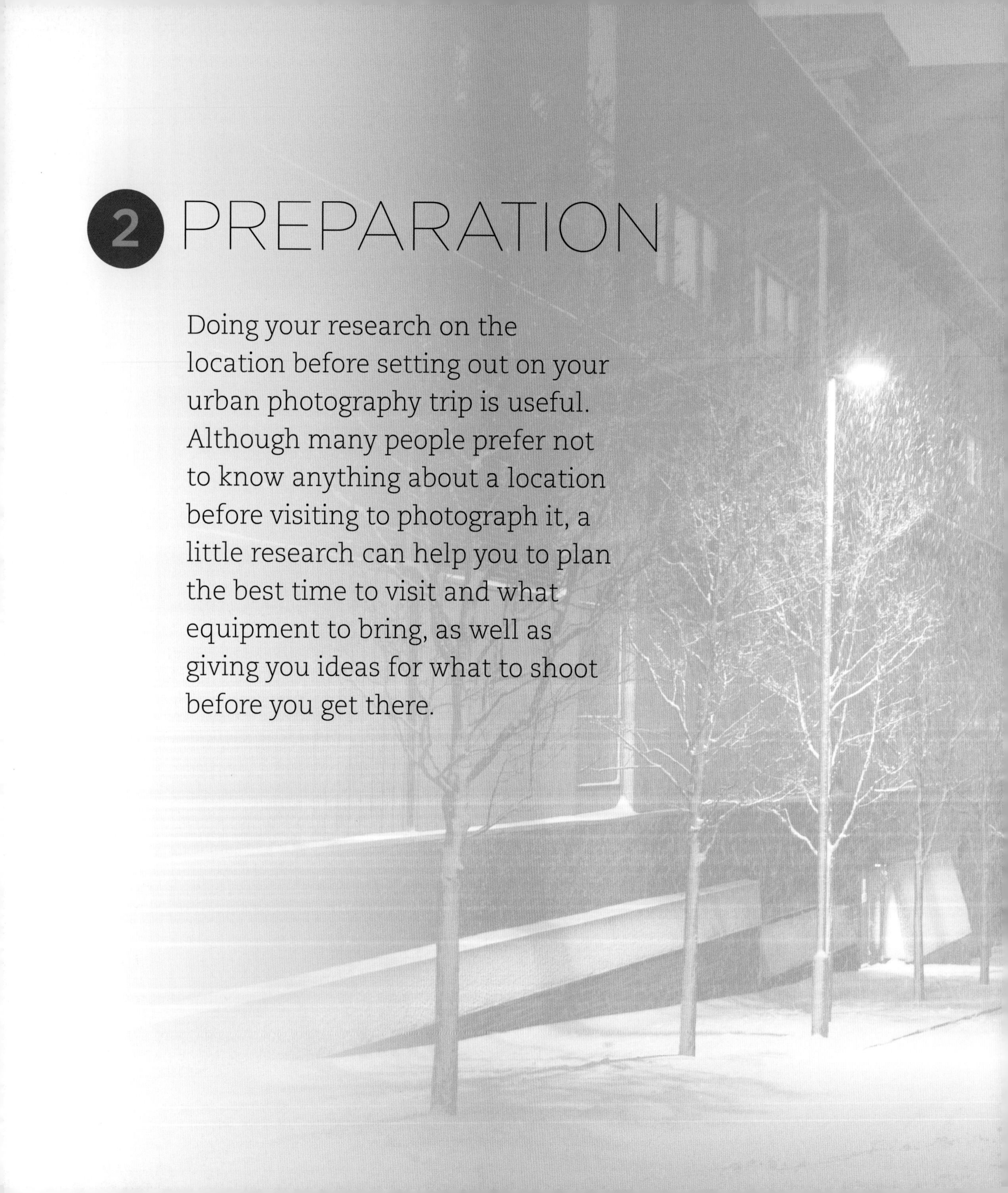

BE PREPARED

Imagine if you arrived at your dream location only to discover that you weren't allowed to access it because a film crew had taken it over for the day. Or if you brought your heavy tripod and most expensive lenses out, hoping to shoot particular architectural details, only to discover that it was a festival day and you'd have been better off with a street photography kit (and attitude). You can make the most of it on the day, sure, but you'd have been better off if you'd known what to expect before you set out.

Time of day, weather, season, public and private events happening, surrounding elements (such as buildings, trees and cranes) and the wider environment can all influence what types of shot are possible and desirable, and you can find out all these things before you get there. Going one step further, visiting your location beforehand can allow you to plan out a shot list, if efficiency is required.

If you're unable to physically visit in advance, do your research on the internet and using social media. A certain building or neighbourhood might catch your eye, there might be some architecture that you might want to check out, or perhaps there's an event – be it protest or party – that should yield some photographic fruits.

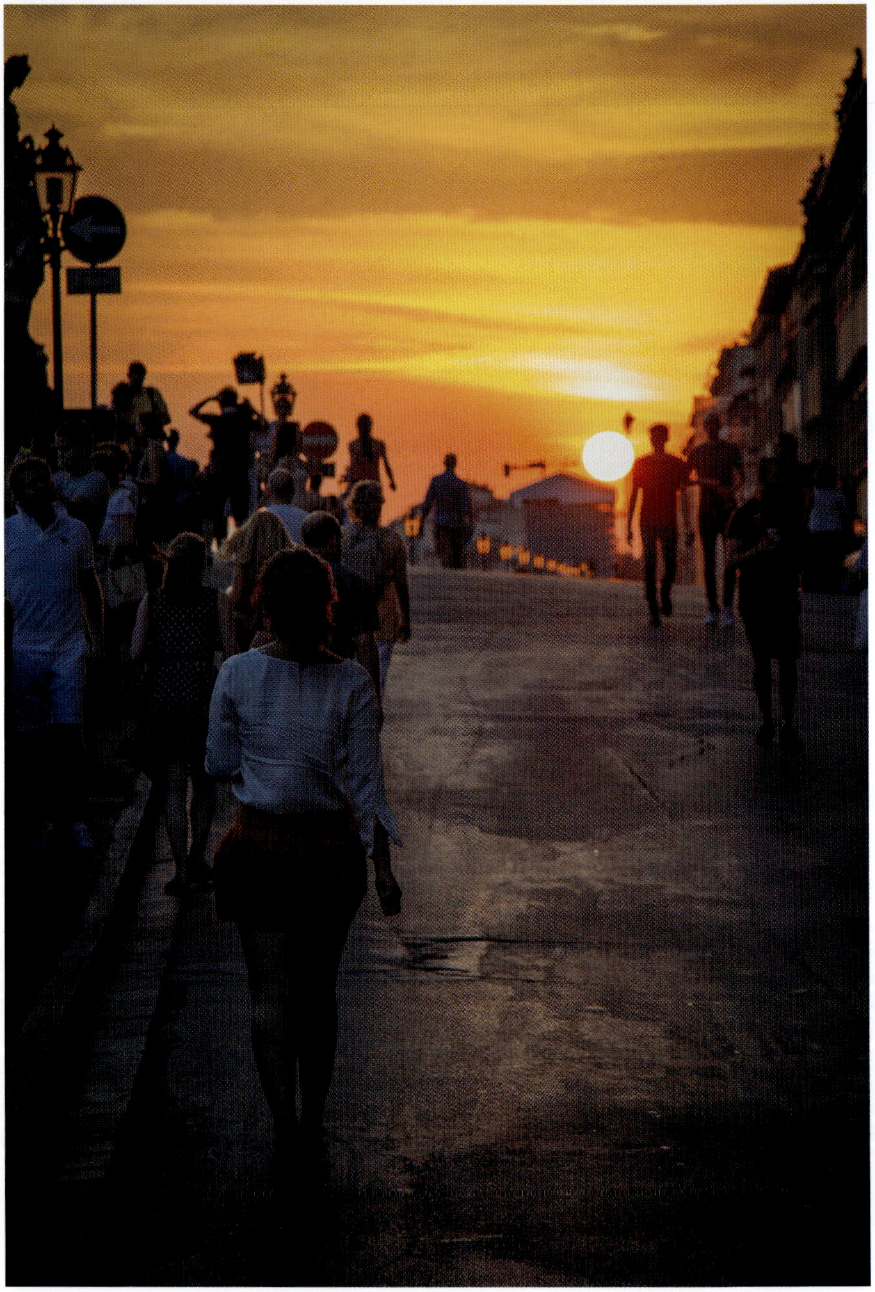

RIGHT
Where and when will the sun set? If you know this in advance, you can be sure to be in a good location to capture it.

OPPOSITE
As much as you want to be prepared, you should also be ready for the unexpected – for example this plume of smoke from a fire, rising over the city, got me out of bed at 4:30 in the morning.

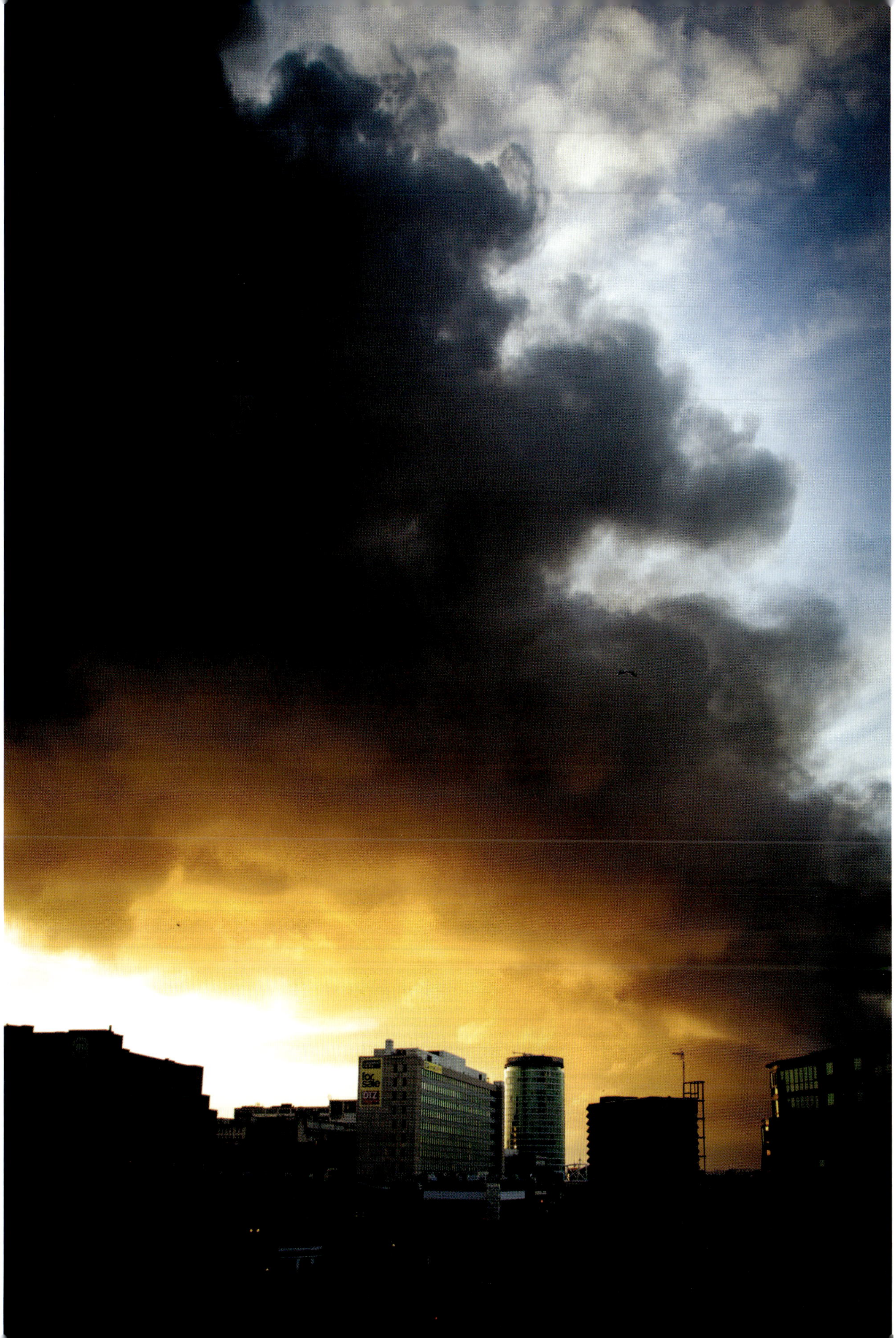
for sale
DTZ

CASE STUDY

THE CUBE, BIRMINGHAM

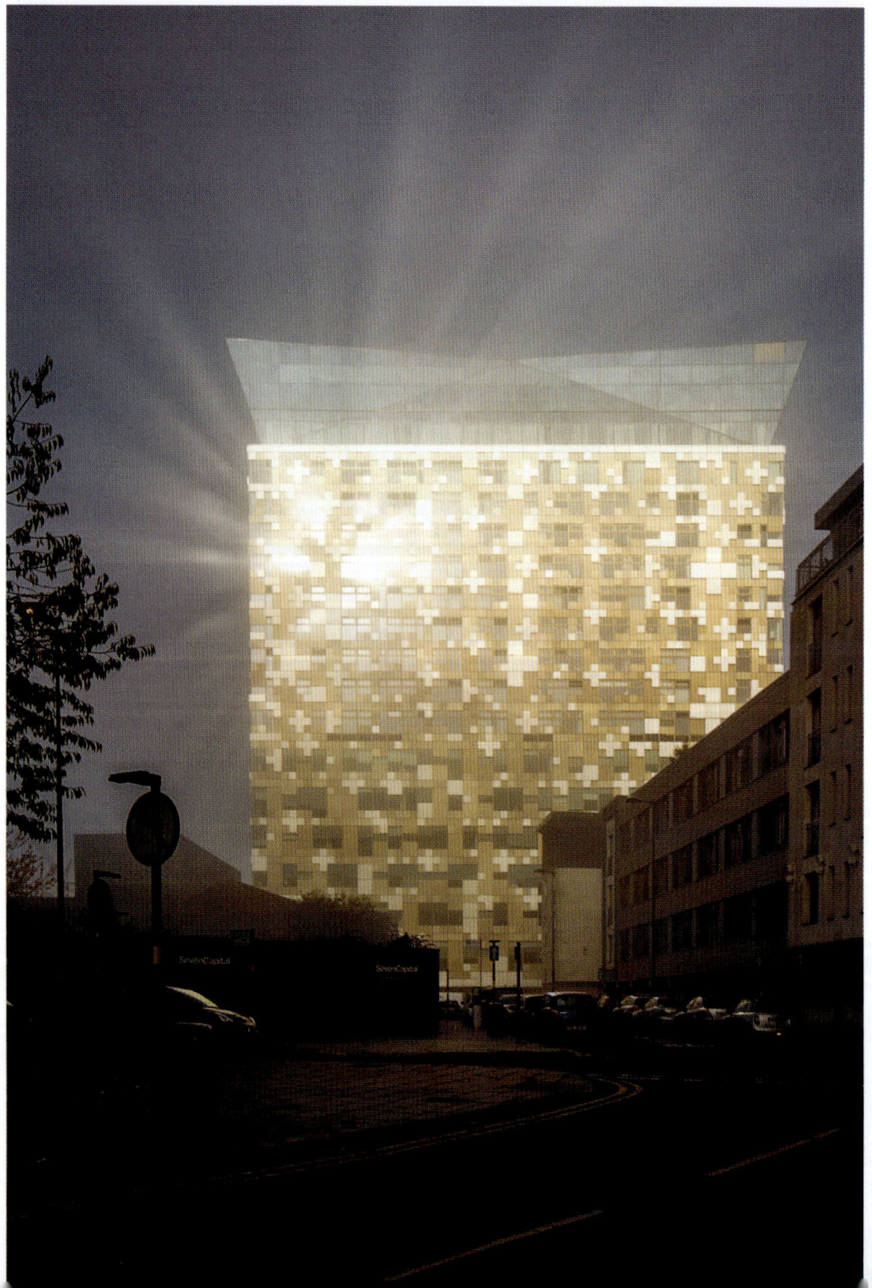

Here is an example of how you might prepare for a visit to a specific location – the kinds of things you will likely want to think about.

Birmingham's iconic Cube is a 25-storey mixed-use development located in the city centre. Built in 2010 and designed by MAKE Architects, it stands out as a unique structure, instantly recognizable on the skyline of the city. The pixel-like facade is one of many features you might want to capture, along with the full-height atrium in the centre of the building, which opens to the elements at the top.

The first thing to do is find out where the building is and which direction it faces, because there will be different opportunities depending on the time of day and year. Then you might consider what aspects of the design you'd like to capture. Is a bigger story hidden in the details of the architecture, or is there something about the building that draws you to it? If other people have shot the building previously, learn from what they did, and think about how you could capture the building in your own way. When you look at the photographs on these pages, also consider what you would need to know, or what it would help to know, to capture them.

LEFT
Flare of the sun through the rising mist, reflecting off the Cube.

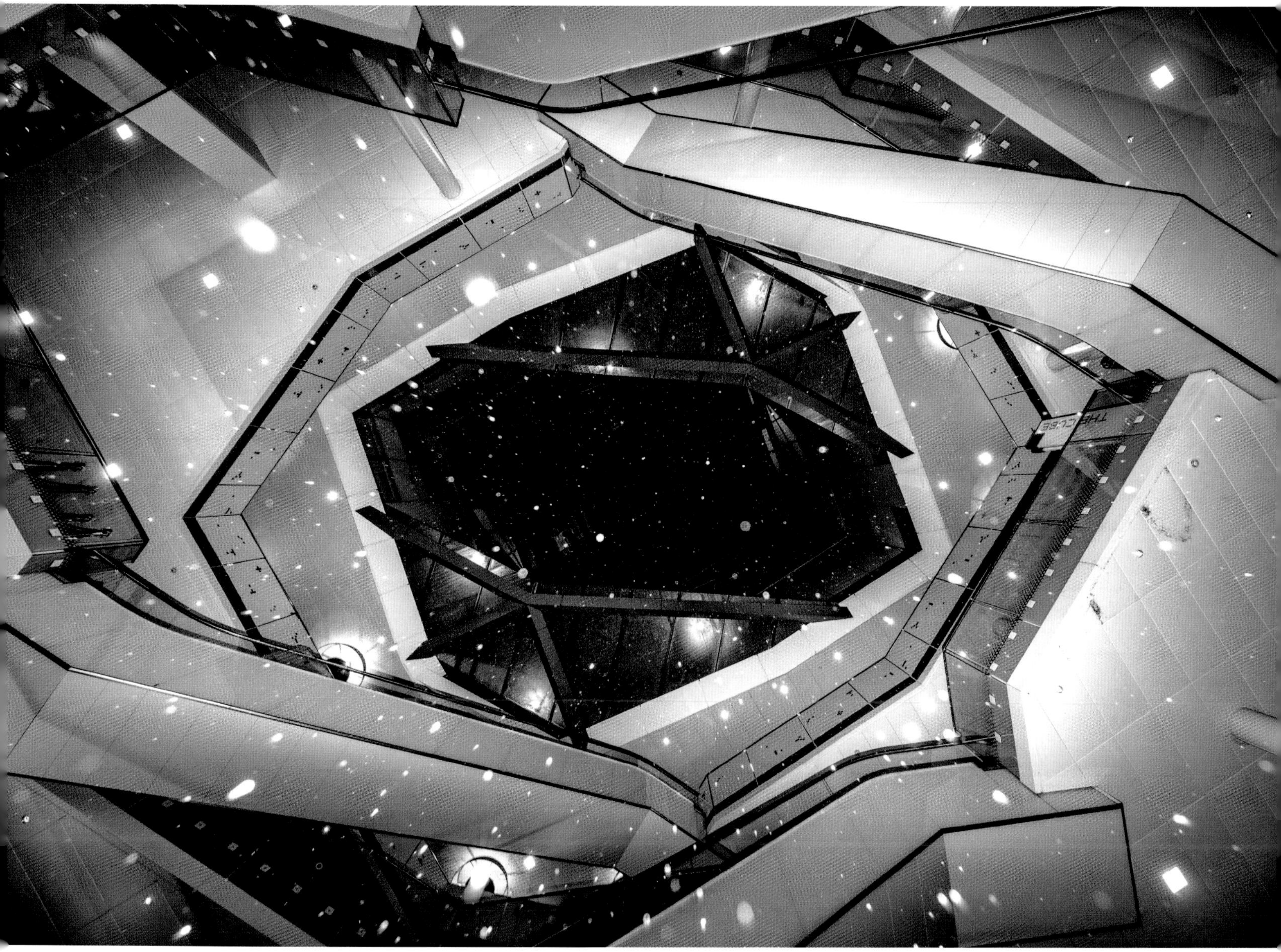

One unique feature of the Cube is the full-height atrium in the centre of the building, with a sculpture of a man holding a balloon suspended in the middle. If you look up through this atrium, it appears as if the sculpture is flying away, which can create a unique focal point. The exposure can be tricky, however, because it is easy to over-expose the sky, and tricky to balance the dynamic range.

ABOVE
This is shot at the base of the atrium, with snow falling all the way down into the building.

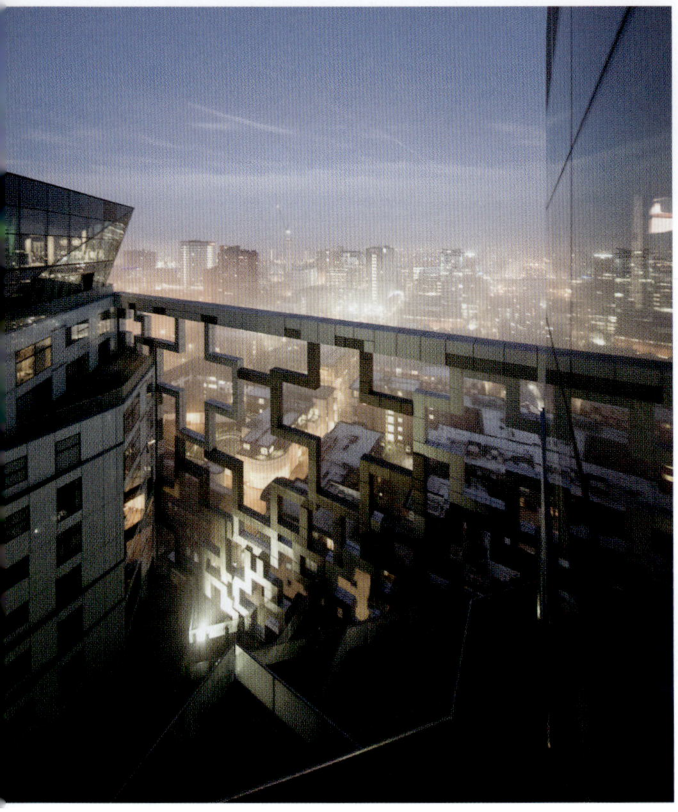

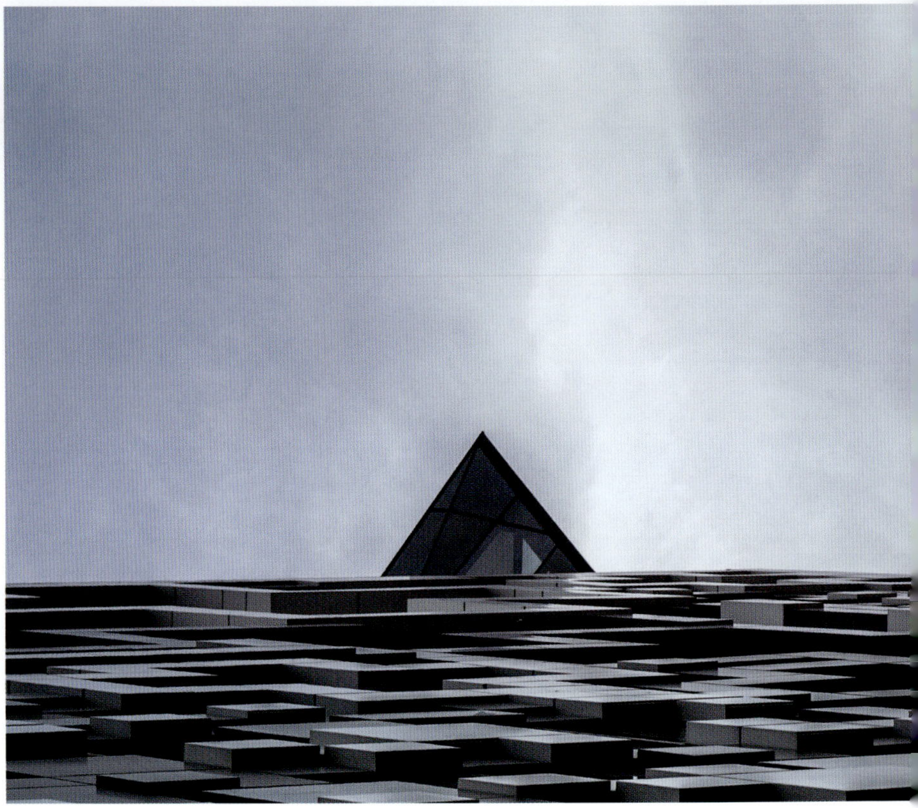

If you view a building on a map, you can judge the typical position of the sun in relation to the way it sits on the site. Then, at certain times of day, you can plan how you'd like to shoot each aspect of the building. The sun rises on the eastern facade of the Cube, so an early morning trip would be ideal if I wanted to capture this lit up, with minimal shadows. The balcony above the atrium looks out to the north and west, so as soon as the sun began setting I would make my way here. From this viewpoint, you can get a photo of the atrium and the fretwork of the northern facade, which is a really unique feature of the building. There are apps available for smartphones which can tell you the exact position of the sun at a certain time of day, which can be very useful for planning where to be and when.

Once you've got the shots based on your ideal scenario (or if, despite all your planning, the weather has something different in mind on the actual day), remember that it can be good to shoot the same thing in different conditions. The Impressionist painter Claude Monet returned to his lily-pond time and time again and found all the inspiration he needed from the changing light and season there. How different might the same feature look in different conditions? The atrium shot on the previous page is a good example of this: in sunshine it might be a good feature for an airy, commercial shot. A snowy day provides the opportunity for a moody, surreal shot.

ABOVE LEFT
A balcony overlooks the city from the top of the atrium.

ABOVE
An abstract view looking up at one of the projecting pieces of glazing on top of the building. This unique perspective shows the building as a landscape, with the glazing forming a pyramid.

RIGHT
In the morning, the low-level sun hits the full facade, lighting up the pixelated features.

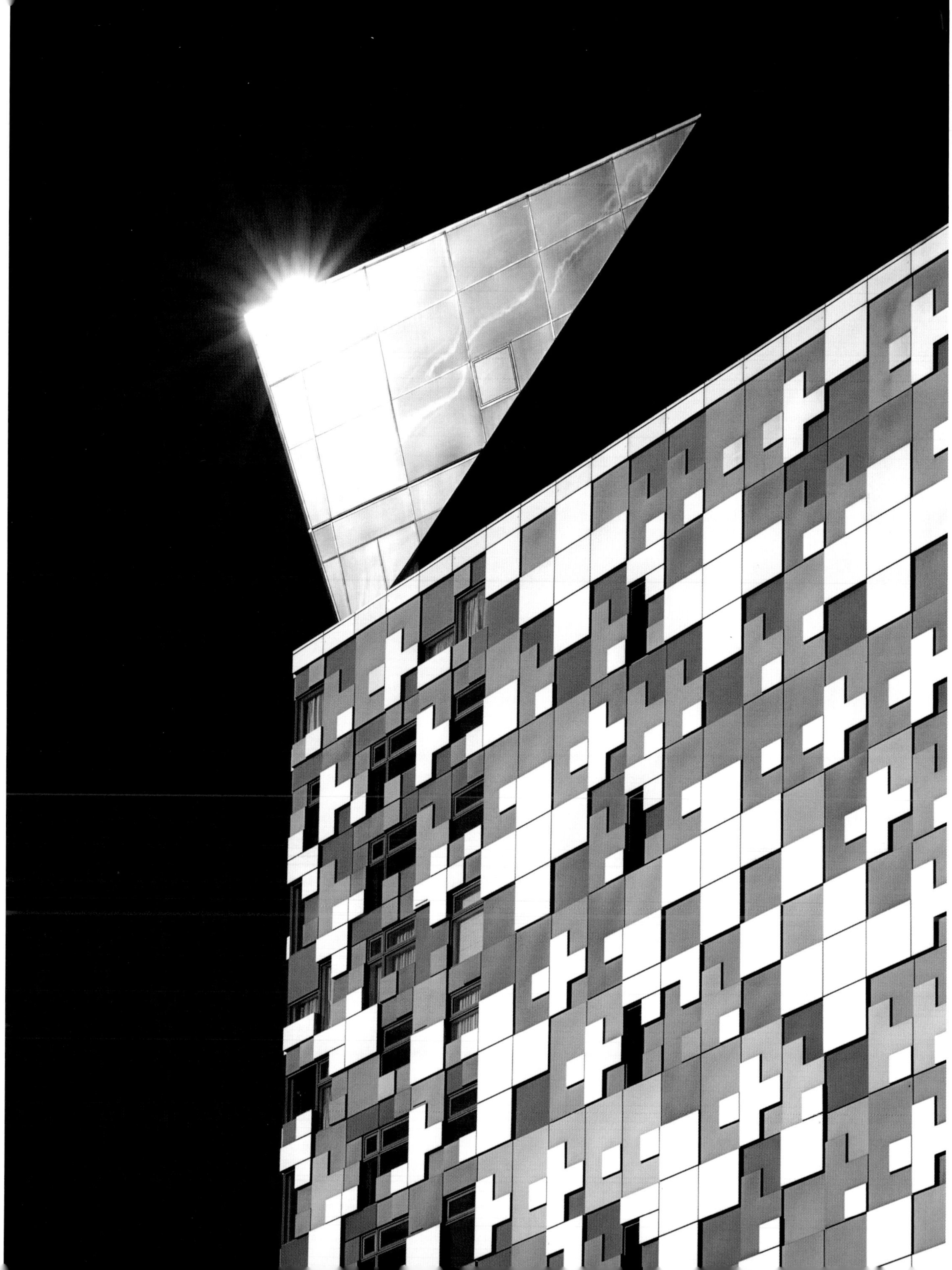

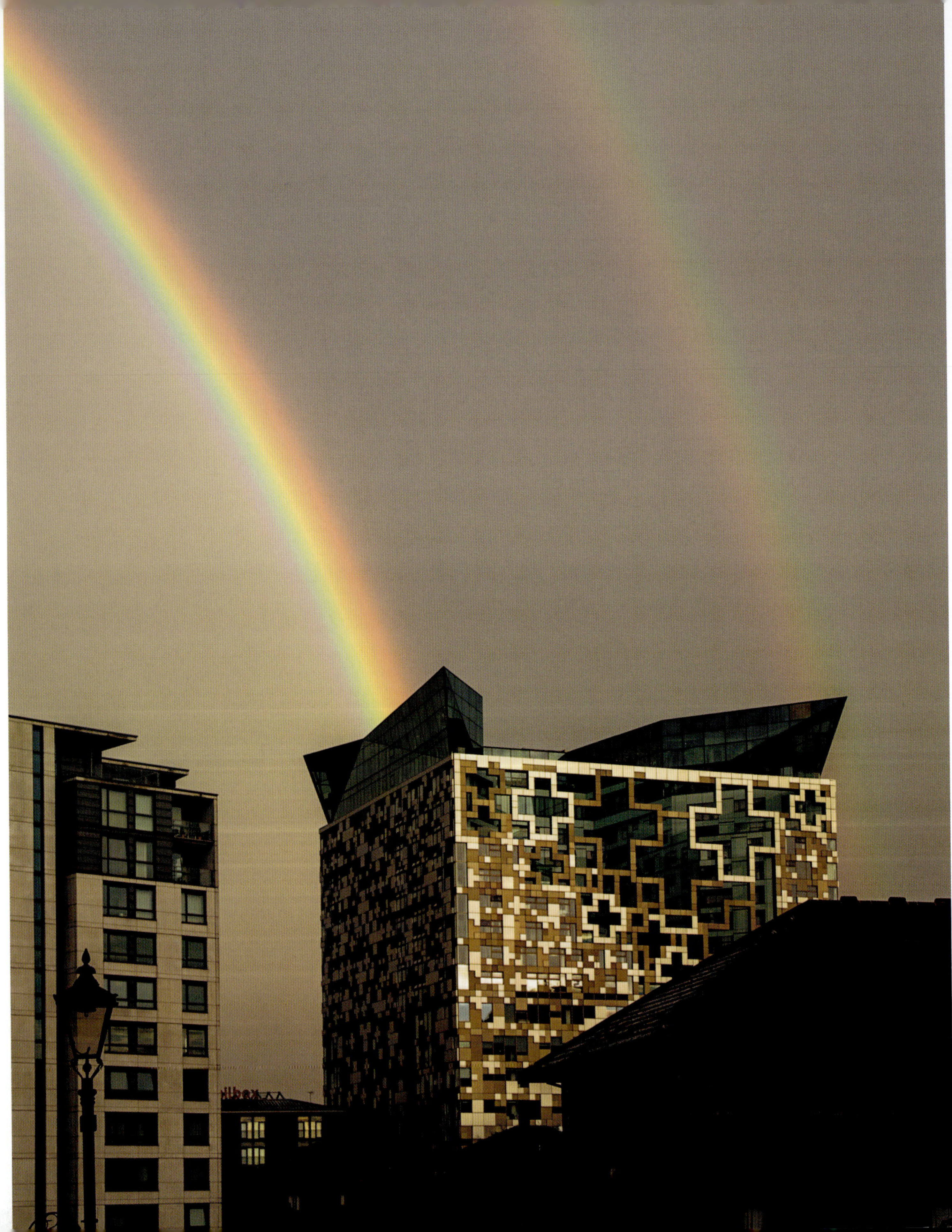

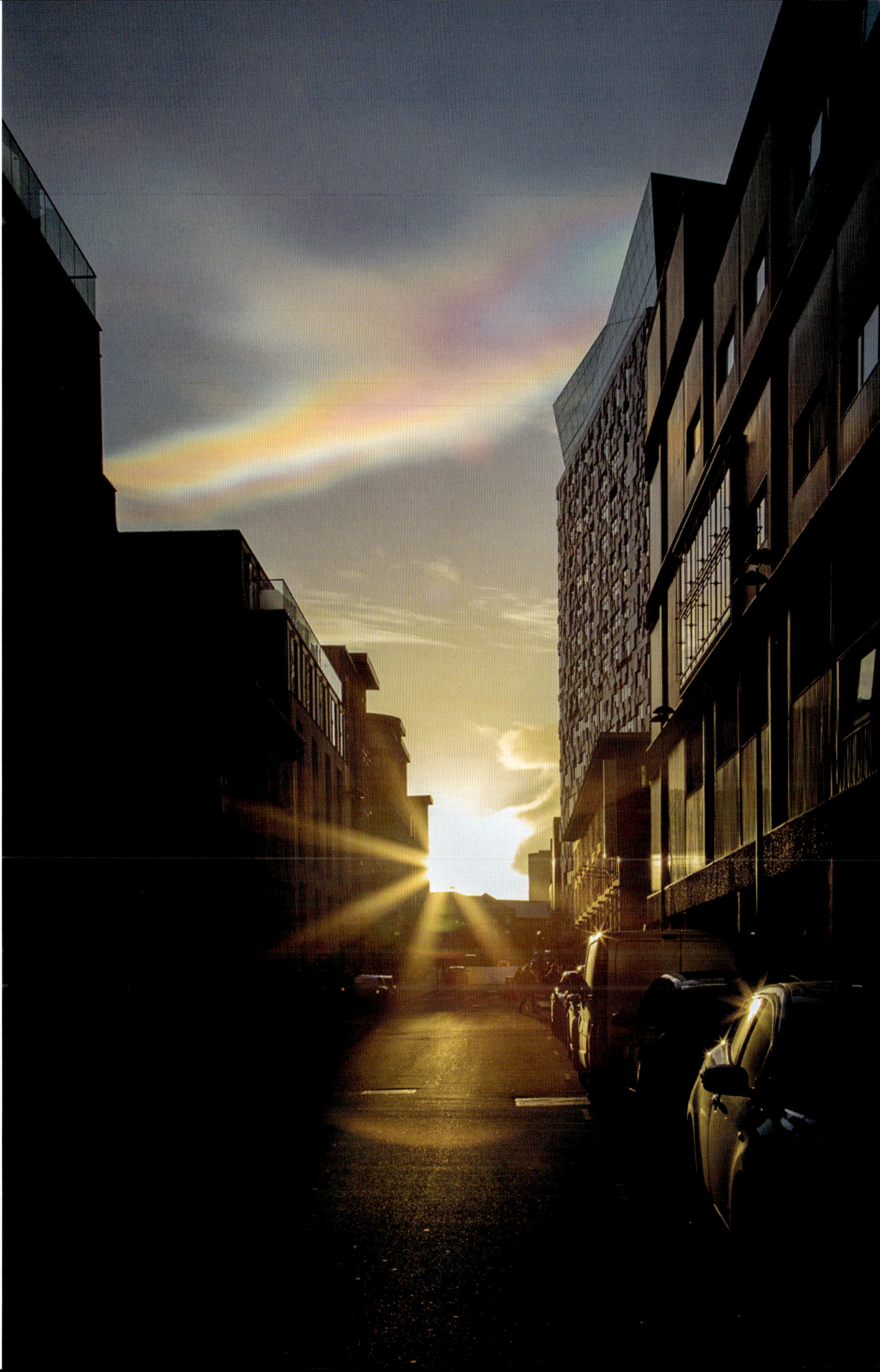

LEFT
Be prepared to act quickly if the weather changes, especially when you're blessed with fleeting phenomena like this double rainbow over the Cube.

RIGHT
The Cube is barely in this shot, which is really all about the rare, rainbow-like nacreous clouds above the city in the last blaze of light before sunset.

IDEAL CONDITIONS

We've touched on how the weather can enhance your photos, and when talking about architectural photography in particular, having the perfect conditions is key to a successful shoot. You need a bit of luck with the weather, then, but you also need to know what you mean by 'perfect conditions,' when they happen, and how to look out for them in the first place. The weather forecast is the first thing to check, but it cannot always be relied on. As a photographer, you also need to learn to react to different conditions and changes in quality of light.

In fact, there is no such thing as 'the best weather' when it comes to urban photography, and I'd be cautious about prescribing rules. But as a guiding principle, certain conditions will help you achieve better results for particular photographs.

ARCHITECTURE

For the classic architectural shot, ideally you want a sunny day with no clouds in the sky. Consider the movement of the sun when you plan which facades to shoot at what time of day, thinking about how you can use shadows to 'sculpt' the architectural detailing. Having the sun in the mid-part of the sky rather than directly above can help with this. Just after sunset, natural lighting conditions often match the lighting within the building, so this is a good time to shoot interior spaces from outside.

PUBLIC SPACES & NETWORKS

The same elements for architecture apply to public spaces, but networks may be photographed at night, using long exposures to show the movement of traffic or trains. The perfect time for this is during twilight, just after sunset, on a clear day. You'll find that even an hour after sunset, when you shoot at

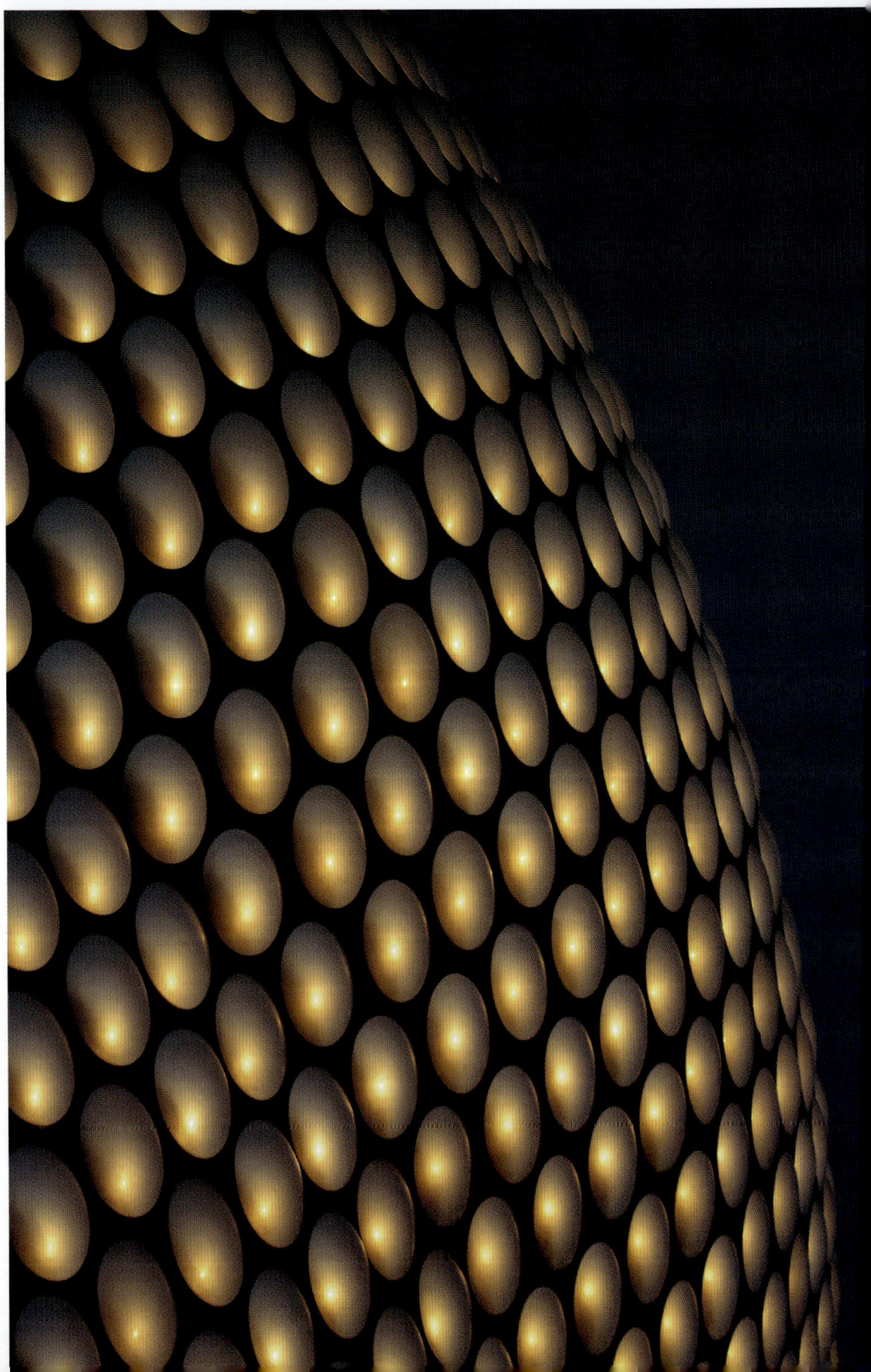

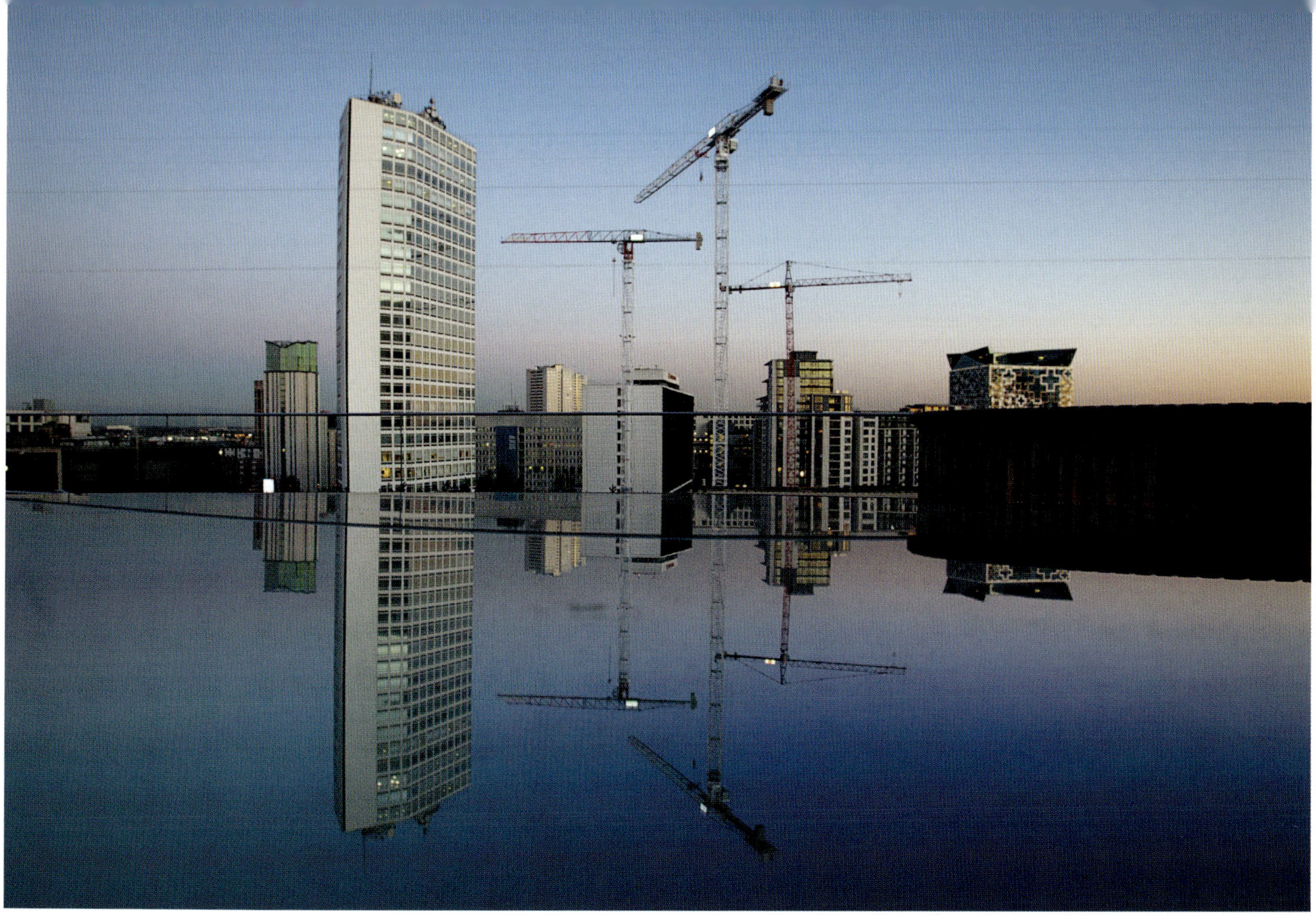

long exposure towards the place the sun set, you'll still get some of the red sky. This creates the perfect backdrop to a long-exposure shot.

STREET PHOTOGRAPHY

Street photography is all about reactions and picking your moment, so this is where the rule about having the perfect weather certainly does not apply. In fact, the most powerful street photography is often produced when it's pouring down with rain or on a freezing-cold morning in winter. It seems that the more extreme the weather, the more dramatic a photo can become.

CITYSCAPES & SKYLINES

The appearance of the city, and the kind of light that falls on it, will change throughout the day, from sunrise to after sunset, so ideally you want a day with few and/or interesting clouds in order to make the most of this. Think about where the sun will be in relation to your view when planning this shot.

WHAT TIME IS IT?

As the above suggests, the time is every bit as important as the type of weather, in terms of the kinds of shot you will produce. The quality of light is determined by the sun's position in the sky, and this will be affected by the time of year, too; in the winter, for instance, the sun stays closer to the horizon, producing intense light and shadow in the mornings and evenings.

As a rule, the higher the sun gets in the sky, the whiter the light and the smaller or fewer the shadows cast. Closer to the horizon, at sunrise or sunset, the 'warmer' the light appears, orange or red, depending on the cloud formation.

LEFT
A thousand tiny suns rise in reflection on the shiny discs of Selfridges in Birmingham.

ABOVE
Here is a good example of why architectural photographers love clear skies. The subtle gradations of the sky at sunset are reflected perfectly on the glass roof.

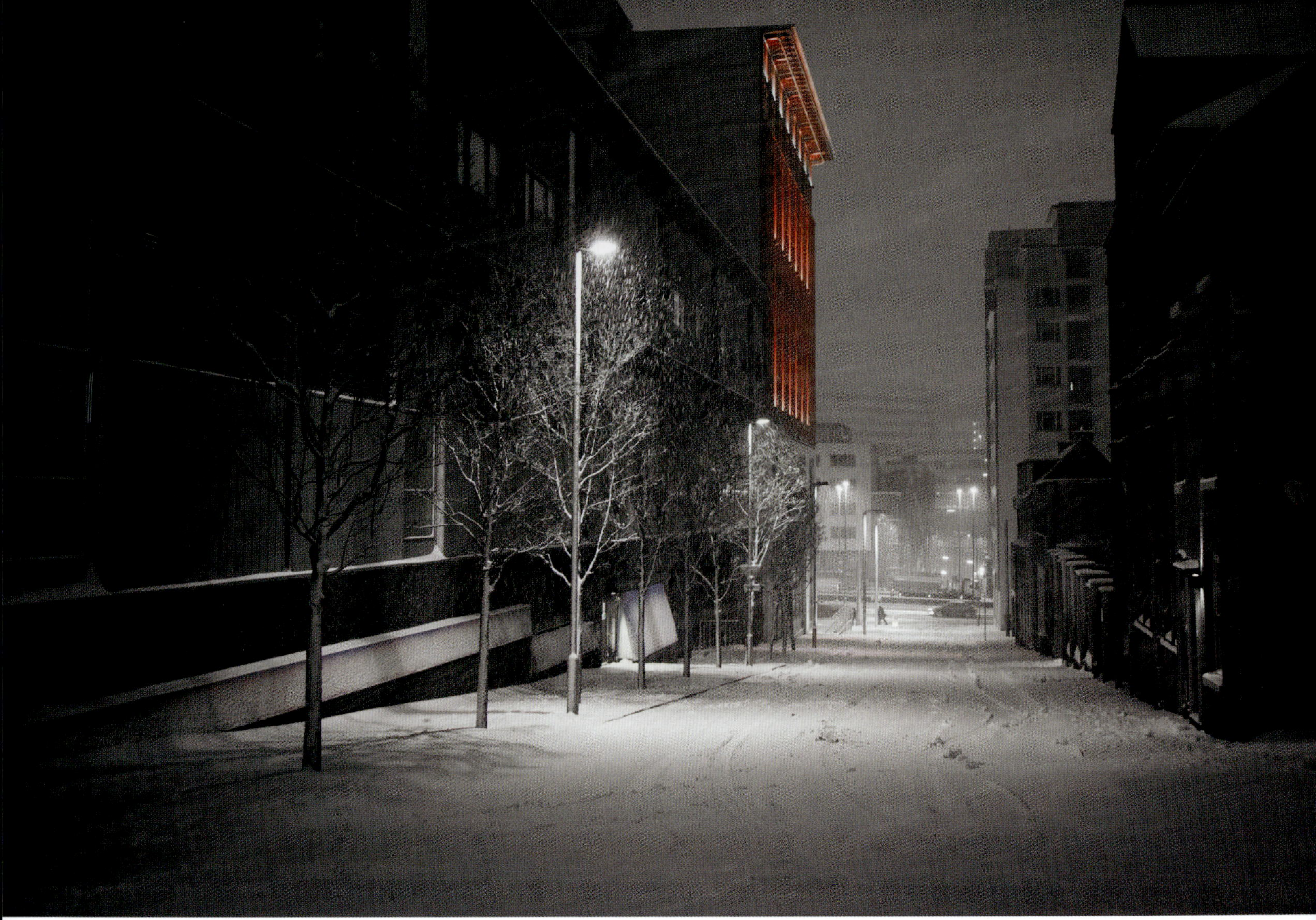

CHASING THE SUN

Three points of twilight, defined as astronomical, nautical and civil, happen before dawn and after dusk. Astronomical twilight starts when the sun is 18 degrees below the horizon, and is a period when there is no colour in the sky. Nautical is when the sun is between 6 and 12 degrees below the horizon, and is so-called because during this period the horizon can be seen by mariners, who use it for navigation. Civil is when the sun is closer than 6 degrees below the horizon and this is otherwise known as dusk, when objects will be clearly visible with the naked eye before dawn. The overlap of the civil and nautical periods is sometimes referred to as 'the blue hour' by photographers, as this is a time when the sun is well below the horizon and the atmosphere takes on a predominantly blue hue.

Due to the changing position of the Earth relative to the sun, the angle at which the sun rises and sets changes from summer to winter – shallower toward the winter solstice, steeper at the summer solstice – meaning that you'll see subtle differences to the light in your city as the seasons change. Start noticing which locations are favoured at different times of the year. The harsh summer sun can flatten out a view that in winter is suddenly dramatically illuminated (if the weather cooperates!).

ABOVE
The time of year affects more than just the sunlight, of course. Seasonal weather can produce very different atmospheres in one location.

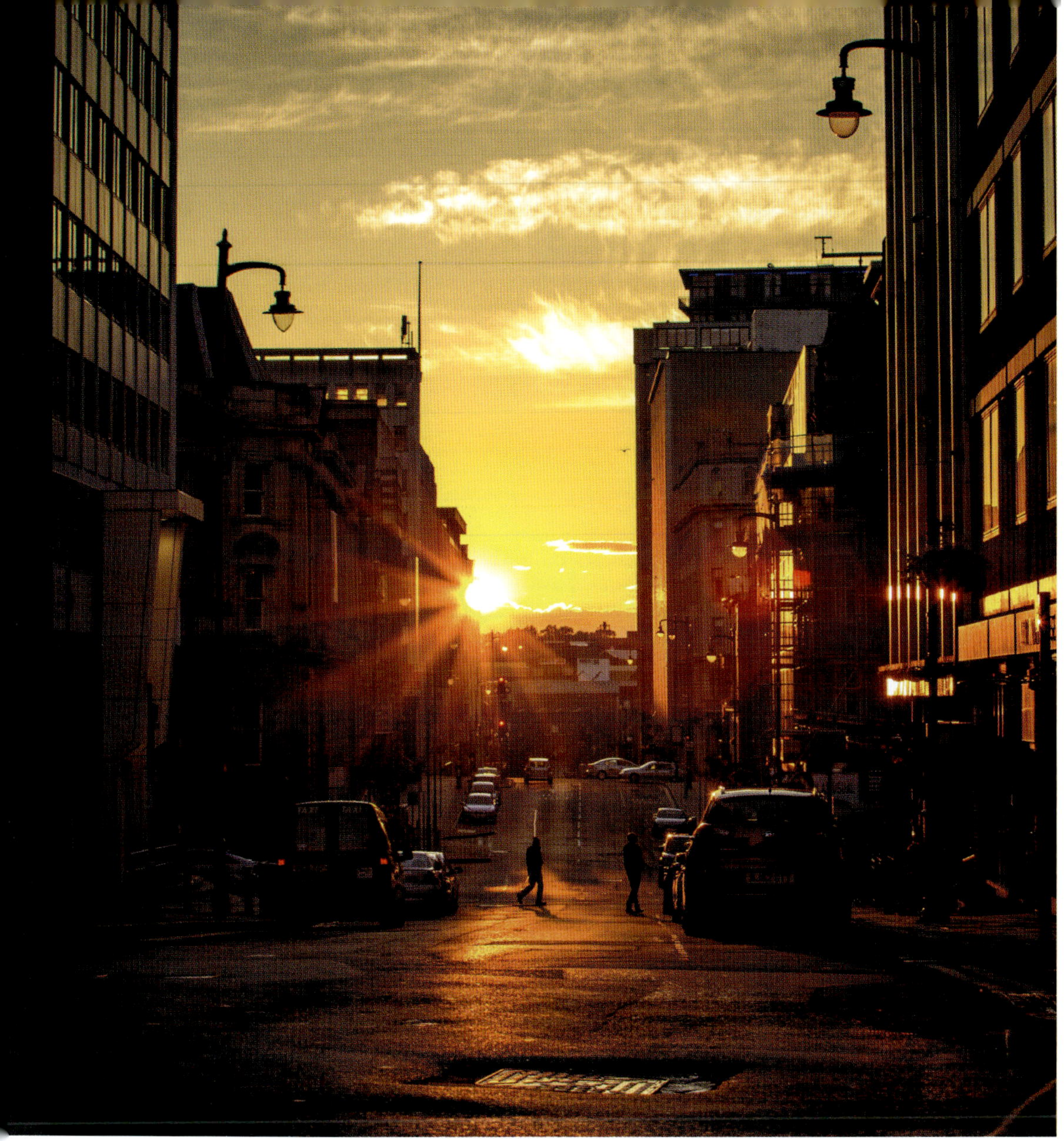

A good example of using your knowledge of the sun's movement to plan a spectacular shoot is a phenomenon that occurs in my city, Birmingham, at the summer solstice, and will occur in many cities at a particular place on a specific day in each year. This is the time when the sunset aligns with a long street or boulevard. Perhaps the most famous example is Manhattanhenge, which occurs twice each year. There is a similar instance in Birmingham in the UK, which has been dubbed Brumhenge, when the sunset on the day of the summer solstice lights up one of the main streets in the city centre. Perhaps a similar occurrence takes place in your local town or city? Explore, research, and follow the sun.

ABOVE
Look out for unique instances where the sun aligns with streets or buildings in the city, like this instance in Birmingham.

KNOW YOUR CLOUDS

Clouds in the sky can add a unique dimension to any type of photography, so it is worth knowing which ones to look out for. With a bit of thought (and luck), they can really add to a composition in the urban environment – softening hard lines, providing an abstract background to a silhouette, modifying the quality of the light, and so on.

CUMULUS

These clouds are the most common in the skies, and they take the fluffy form that is often used to depict clouds by weather forecasters. They hang low in the sky and can accumulate until they completely block the sun. Look out for smaller formations, or the higher-level altocumulus, which often have a lot of blue sky in between them. Something to note here is that white clouds and blue skies will always look great in black and white due to the high contrast between the two.

CIRRUS & MACKEREL

Cirrus clouds are not as common as cumulus, but these are the clouds to look out for if you are looking to add a dynamic background to your shots. These clouds sit high in the atmosphere and look like brush strokes in the sky. They can create amazing shapes, and they are also the ones that capture the redness of the sunset just after the sun has gone down.

The so-called 'mackerel sky' produces an effect not unlike cirrus clouds, though the fish-scale formation tends to be more regular. Mackerel skies are caused by high-altitude atmospheric waves interfering with altocumulus or cirrocumulus clouds. You see a lot of cirrus clouds and mackerel skies in architectural photography because their painterly quality really lifts an image.

RARE CLOUDS

Rarer clouds include cumulonimbus, which are the huge clouds responsible for electrical storms that stretch high up into the atmosphere. If possible, capture these from a distance on a telephoto lens in order to show their immense scales. Even rarer clouds include nacreous, lenticular and mammatus, which all have unique structures. Nacreous clouds are coloured like rainbows, lenticular clouds form shapes like flying saucers, and mammatus clouds look like balls of cotton wool in the sky.

BELOW
The fluffy white form of the common cumulus adds brilliant contrast to the darker, formal architecture below.

RIGHT, TOP
The iridescent nacreous cloud would make a beautiful background for an architectural detail or a low skyline.

RIGHT, BOTTOM
Cirrus clouds being lit by the sun, which has just set below the horizon, make an interesting backdrop for this silhouette shot.

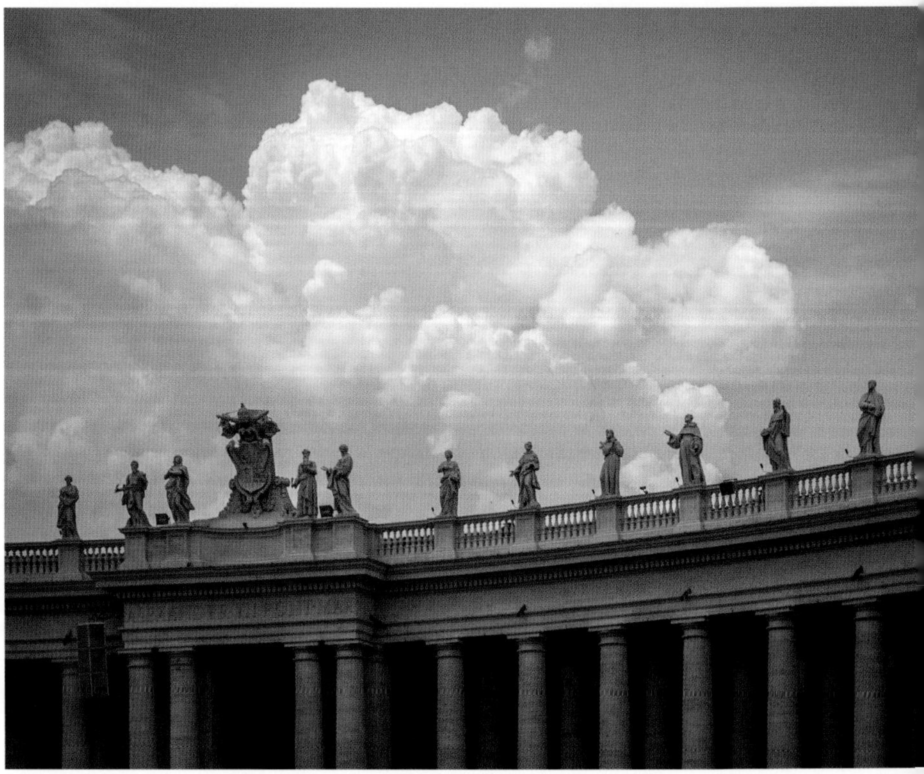

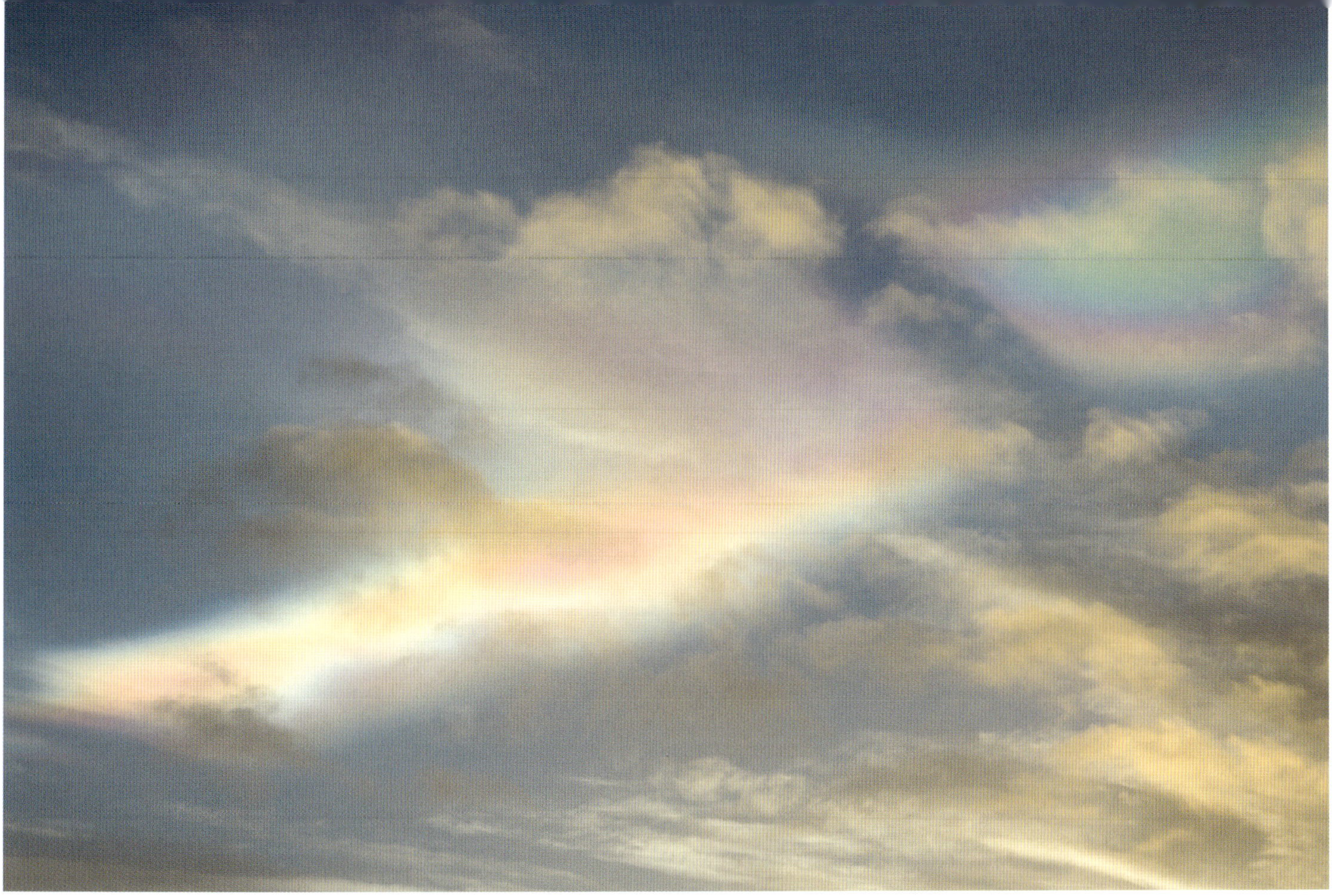

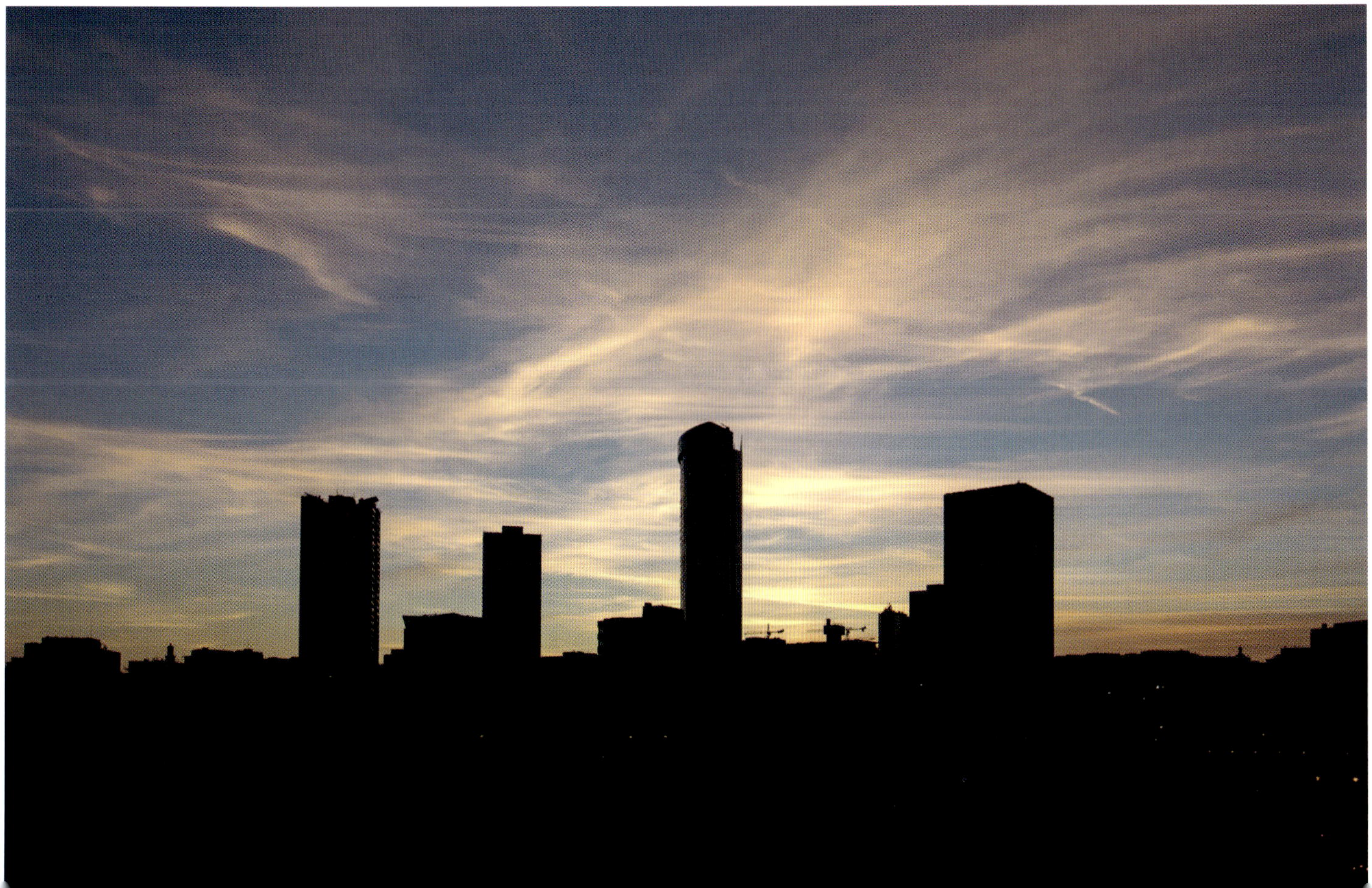

PERMISSIONS

The first thing to consider when it comes to whether or not you need special permission to take or use a photograph is whether it is going to be used for editorial or commercial purposes. Editorial content differs from content produced for commercial use in that it cannot be used to sell, promote, or monetize a business, product or service. If you were to sell your photograph on an image stock site, or to an agency for use in advertising or corporate branding, for example, this would be commercial use. The photographs in this book, on the other hand, fall under editorial use, since they are used for illustrative and explanatory purposes.

When you are out with your camera, chances are you will, from time to time, get asked whether you have permission to take shots in that location. Different laws and restrictions apply in different countries, so you should always do your research for places, both abroad and in your own country, when considering potential shooting locations. You should also be aware of cultural sensitivities, especially when traveling abroad; it's not always appropriate to photograph religious events or political buildings in some countries, for example.

One law that applies in all countries is that on private property you must have permission from the building's owner to photograph there. The classic example of this is in a city shopping centre, where you will almost certainly be on private property. A security guard would be well within their rights to ask you to stop shooting. Many areas in towns and cities are privately owned (including open spaces, such as squares), and it's not always easy to tell. As a rule, if you are unsure, then it is best to ask.

Certain buildings also carry specific copyright conditions. The Sydney Opera House and the Hollywood sign in Los Angeles are two famous examples of this. If you were taking photos of either of these structures for commercial use, you would need to seek permission from the relevant authorities. As another general rule, if you are paying an entrance fee to visit somewhere, then it is likely that there are restrictions on commercial use of any photographs taken there. This also applies to events, where in most cases only accredited photographers would be allowed to use their photographs for commercial purposes, for example at a festival, a play, or a music concert.

In much of the world, you do not need permission to photograph people provided they are in a public place, but if they are recognizable in the photo I'd say you have some moral obligation to gain their permission before using it. For commercial use, you almost always need the permission of the person in the photo and a signed agreement of the terms of the image's use, including any monetary recompense in the form of royalties or a one-off fee that the subject might expect.

The rules vary from country to country, and they may not reflect your expectations. The above should be considered only as general guidelines and not definitive legal advice, but it's easy to find out more with a quick online search.

RIGHT
You may not need any special permission to use photos taken on main public highways such as this, but some spaces, including public squares, are privately owned, and you may need permission to shoot there.

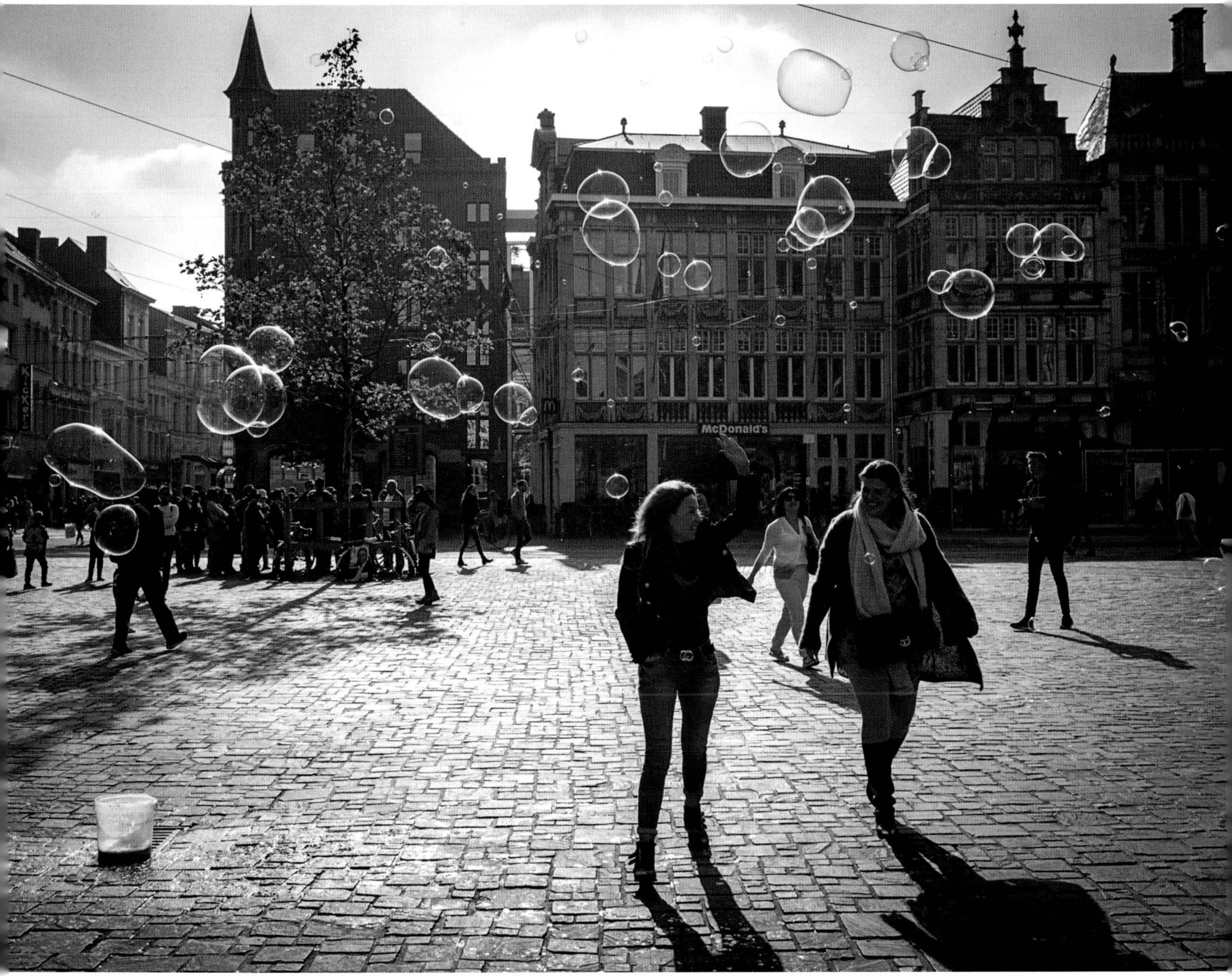
McDonald's

3 THE CITY

In order to explore the theme of urban photography in more detail, here I show a few examples of major cities around the world, and the places and spaces that make them perfect for photographing. My aim is to encourage you to think about how you can apply the advice given in specific examples here to a city near you. Perhaps you'll discover a new landmark or building, or your local architecture. Or perhaps you'll be inspired to travel to one of these places in order to discover them through your own photography.

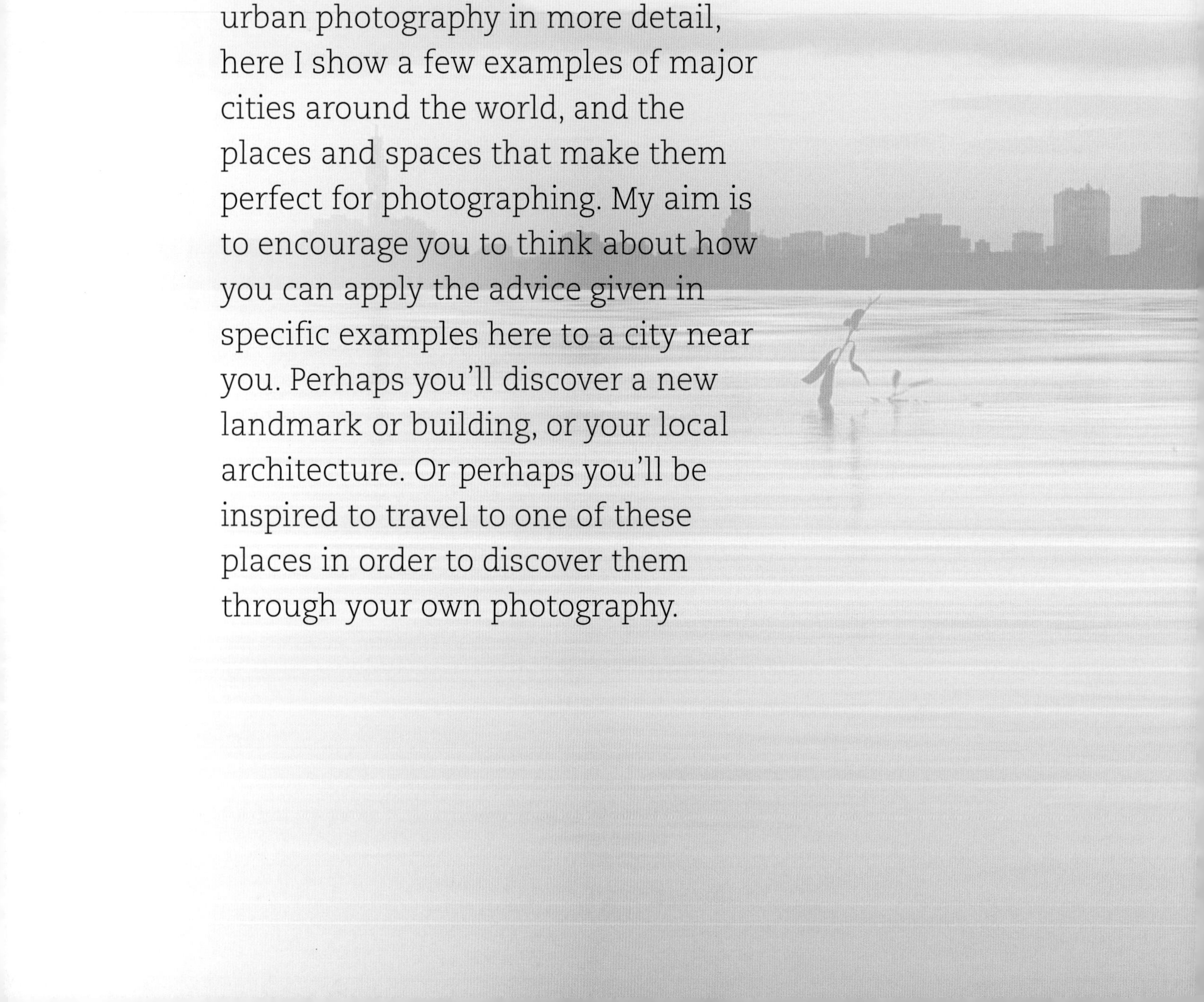

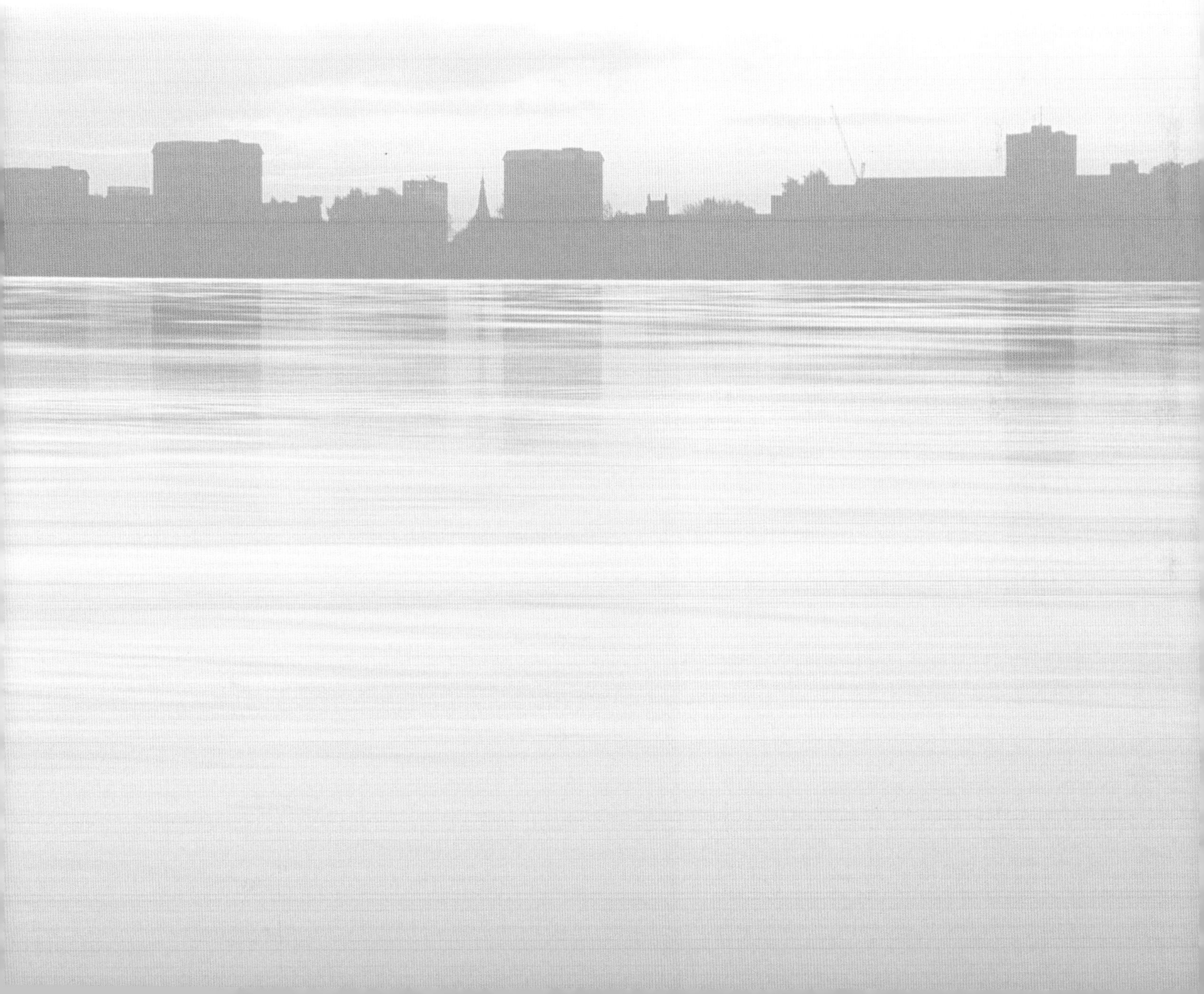

BERLIN

The largest city and capital of Germany, Berlin, is a great example of an urban centre with a huge amount of history. It was split in two at the end of the Second World War by a wall that separated the American and Soviet occupied sides. The wall was taken down in 1989, but parts of it remain, acting as a reminder of different times. Due to the split nature of the city, there is a marked difference in the architecture and planning of the two sides. The Soviet-occupied side was developed in the 1950s and '60s and therefore is well built up with narrow streets and higher-rise buildings. It also features the unique 'Ampelmännchen' – the symbol for 'walk' or 'don't walk' found at pedestrian crossings. The western side was developed less rapidly, but it has had more recent development and houses some fine examples of contemporary architecture. Although completed during the Cold War, one such example is the Niue Nationalgalerie by Ludwig Mies van der Rohe. A minimalist design in steel, glass, and concrete, this is a typical example of Van der Rohe's work. When shooting here, try using a wide-angle lens perpendicular to the entrance, to get the whole building in.

The area around the Reichstag, the seat of the German Parliament, is also worth a visit. Norman Foster renovated the building in 1999 to replace the giant dome that had been destroyed in the war. The new dome offers views across the city and is a fantastic piece of architecture in its own right, with double-helix walkways ascending to its summit. Nearby is the 18th-century Brandenburg Gate, and the Memorial to the Murdered Jews of Europe, which is a series of 2,711 concrete cuboids that rise to varying heights from the ground, over what seems to be an endless area. Designed by

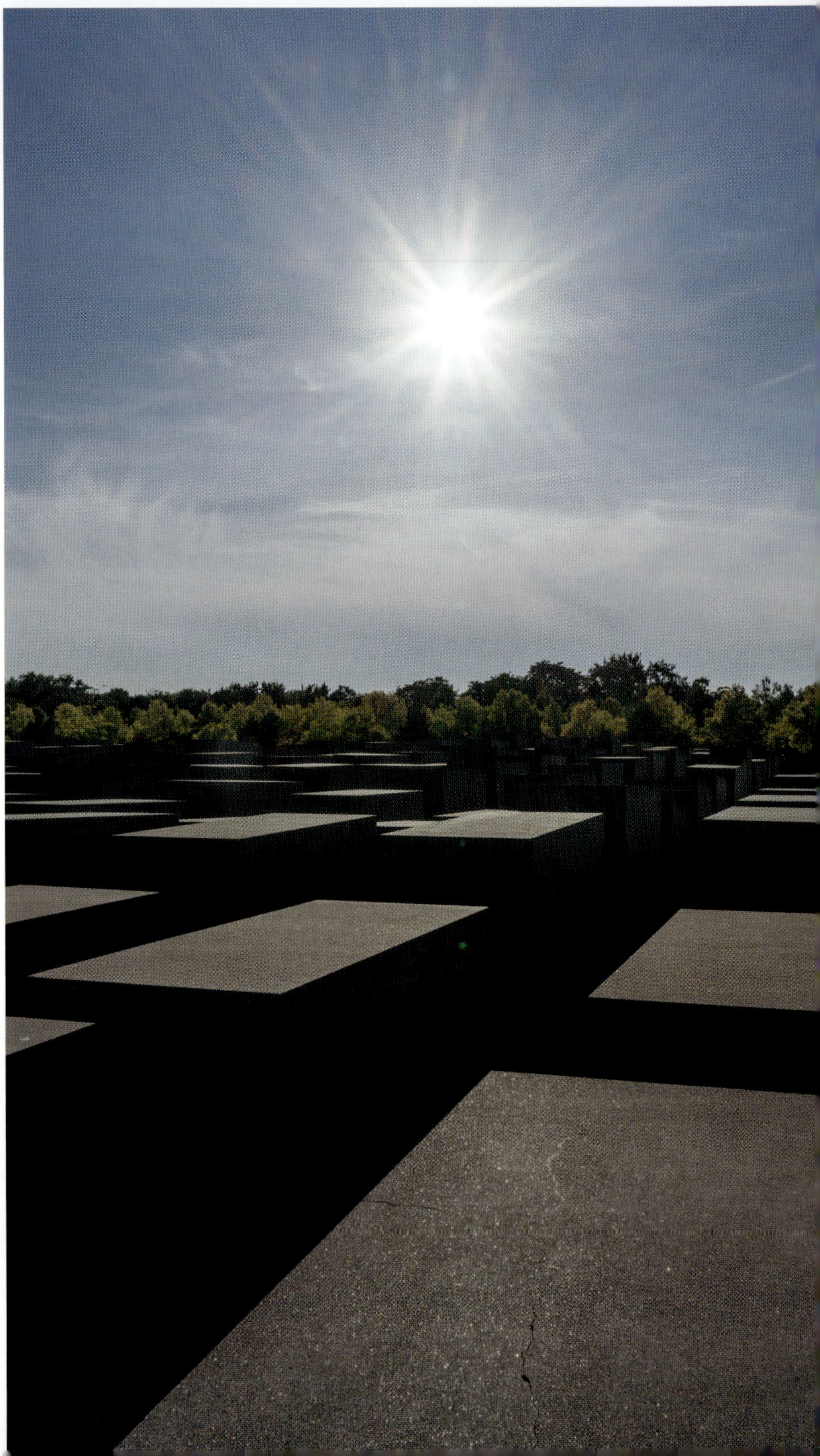

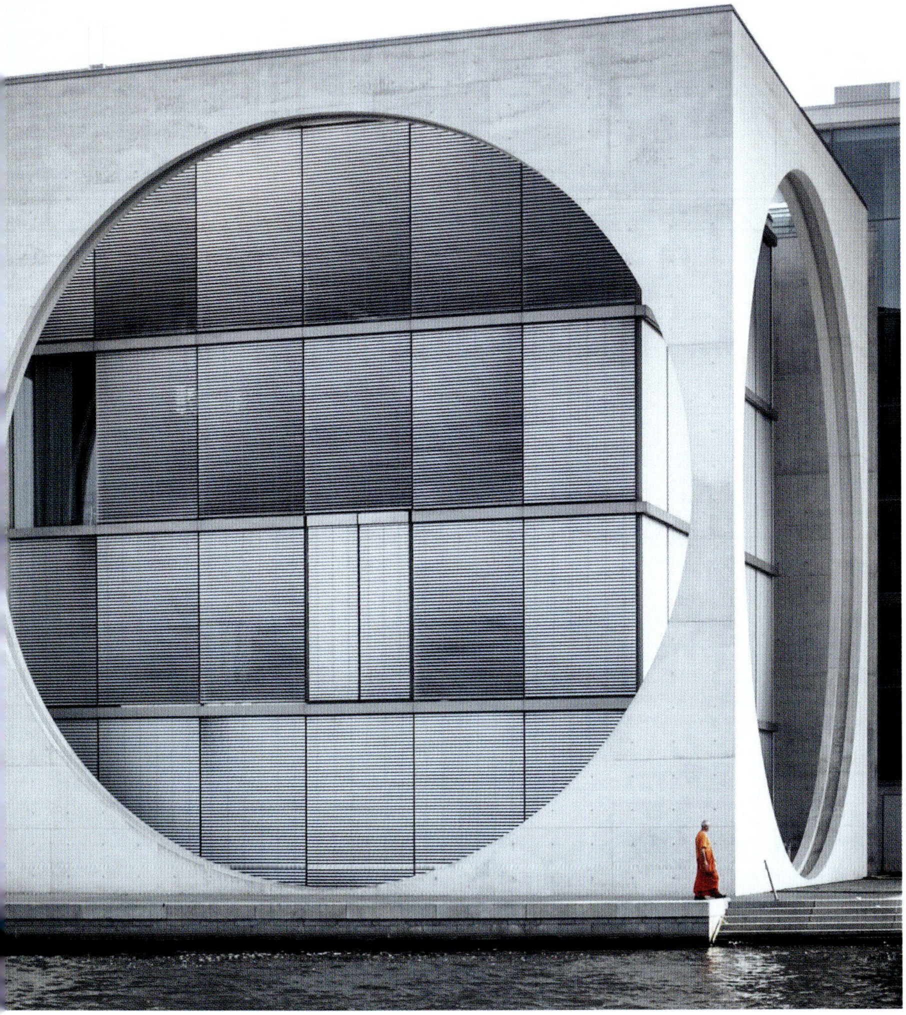

architect Peter Eisenman, it's a quiet, poignant reminder of the history of Berlin's role in the Holocaust. From the sides it doesn't look terribly impressive, but as you wander through it, the ground seems to fall away. Looking down the long passageways that the concrete elements create allows you to discover some great geometric views.

On the other side of the Reichstag is a series of government buildings, including the Chancellory, designed by Schultes Frank Architekten. The facades of these buildings are punched by circular openings in their concrete skin, in a post-modernist style. People walking through your view can ruin a shot in a different setting, but here they will improve it, because the scale of these buildings is amazing in comparison to the people that walk beside them.

The obvious place to go in Berlin to get a view of the city from up high is the Fernsehturm in Alexanderplatz, but there is a Park Inn hotel nearby that offers a better view from its small viewing platform. From here, you can look back at the city and get a shot with the spire of the Fernsehturm in frame.

For more history, there is the Jewish Museum, designed by Daniel Libeskind, which is a spectacular building clad entirely in zinc. For culture, you can visit Museum Island on the River Spree, which is full of Renaissance classical architecture. More modern additions can be found on the west side of Berlin, with the buildings around Potsdammerplatz that were all built in the last decade.

LEFT
A blue sky and sun at a good angle in the sky creates great contrast on the geometric forms of the Memorial to the Murdered Jews of Europe.

ABOVE
Known locally as 'The Washing Machine,' the circles of these government buildings in Berlin make a great dramatic backdrop when anyone is walking past.

BARCELONA

Situated on the south coast of Spain on the Mediterranean Sea, Barcelona mixes a youthful energy with the cultural trimmings of a more traditional Spanish city. Its coastal location, warm climate and eclectic mix of architecture and urban spaces make this an ideal destination for a long photography weekend.

Barcelona is famous for the architecture of Antoni Gaudí, and is where the majority of his work is situated. Construction of his cathedral, the Sagrada Familia, was begun in March 1882 and isn't due for completion until around 2026, when the final central spire will be completely erected. The building is fascinating, with so much intricate sculptural detailing on the facade and internally. Use a telephoto lens to pick out figures in the nativity facade and the details at the top of the spires. Less famous is Park Güell on Carmel Hill, which offers great views of the skyline juxtaposed against Gaudí's vibrant architecture. There are many other Gaudí buildings dotted around the city, which can be a good theme to guide a photographic tour – or just a detail to look out for while you explore.

The city hosted the Olympics in 1992 and the Olympic park is still largely intact on top of Montjuïc, a prominent hill overlooking the harbour, which is also home to a 17th-century fort. The stadium that was used for athletics is at the top of the hill alongside a mast designed by Santiago Calatrava. The diving pool is situated on the side of the cliff, overlooking the city centre, and from here you can make out all of the landmarks on the skyline. The cablecar that links the funicular station to the top of Montjuïc is another great way to see the city from a height.

If you want to shoot the people of Barcelona, the best place to visit is the old town, or even take a trip down Las Ramblas, although the latter is sometimes overrun with tourists due to its location in the heart of the city. In the Gothic Quarter, pay a visit to Plaça Reial, which is lined with restaurants and bars and is always lively in the evening. The surrounding narrow streets of the Gothic Quarter offer some good opportunities for street photography, as well as for capturing a more intimate aspect of the historic city.

You might also want to visit Roger Stick Habour's Las Arenas centre. In this refurbishment of an old bullring, Barcelona's historic cultural and modern commercial sides meet. The top of the building has a full 360-degree platform that elevates you above the rooftops of the locality.

RIGHT
A view across the rooftops of Barcelona, in which you can make out several of the city's historic buildings among its more modern developments. Dominating the skyline is, of course, Gaudí's famous Sagrada Familia.

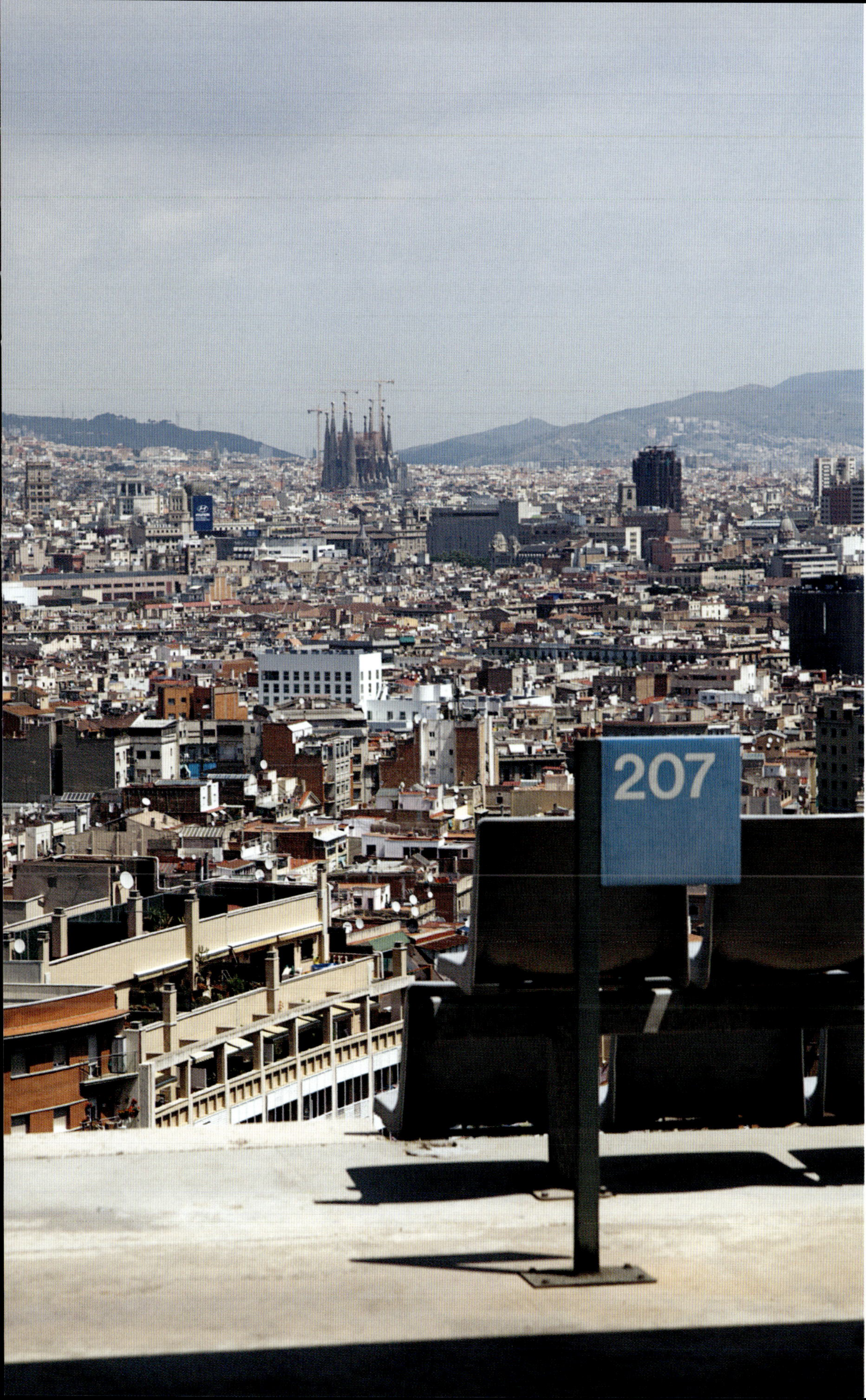
207

NEW YORK CITY

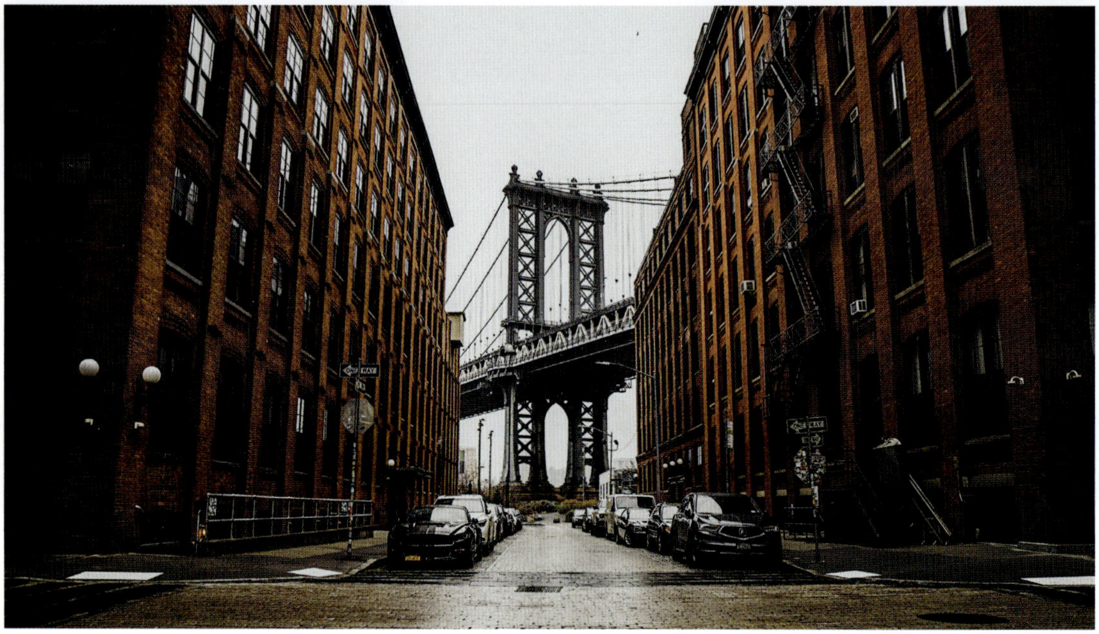

With its mixture of skyscrapers dating from the early 20th century all the way through to the brand new and still under construction, New York's Manhattan has an unarguably incredible skyline. It's also fairly accessible, since many of the buildings have viewing platforms, including the Rockefeller Center, from where you can view the Empire State Building and other landmarks. The city is not limited to the island of Manhattan, though – some of the best views are to be had from the neighbouring districts. A trip across the Brooklyn Bridge will reward you with a great view of Lower Manhattan.

At street level, there are also some amazing spaces to take in and photograph. Central Park, for example, is a unique urban park, surrounded by imposing buildings, including huge skyscrapers on the south side. As with most cities, you'll find that each district has its own character. Greenwich Village, for example, was known throughout the 20th century for being the haunt of artists and writers, and even though it has undergone gentrification, it still carries its history of counter-culture cool with its jazz bars and restaurants. Aside from the iconic buildings and spaces, the 'city that never sleeps' naturally offers plenty of opportunity for chance encounters.

ABOVE
This classic shot of the Brooklyn Bridge goes to show that it's worth exploring beyond Manhattan.

RIGHT
The 1920s-era Art Deco and Neo-Gothic skyscrapers are now dwarfed by their modern, glass cousins, but their intricate detailing and elegant shapes are unsurpassed.

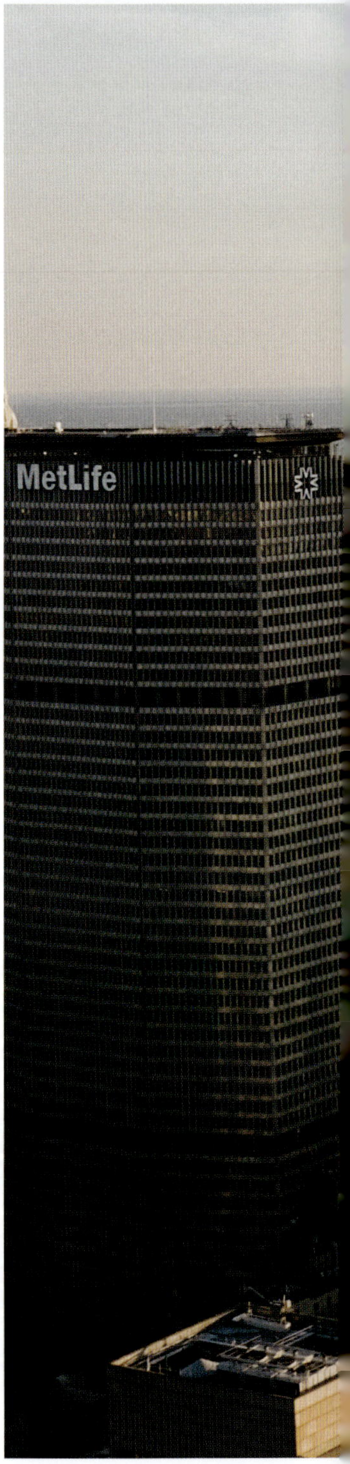

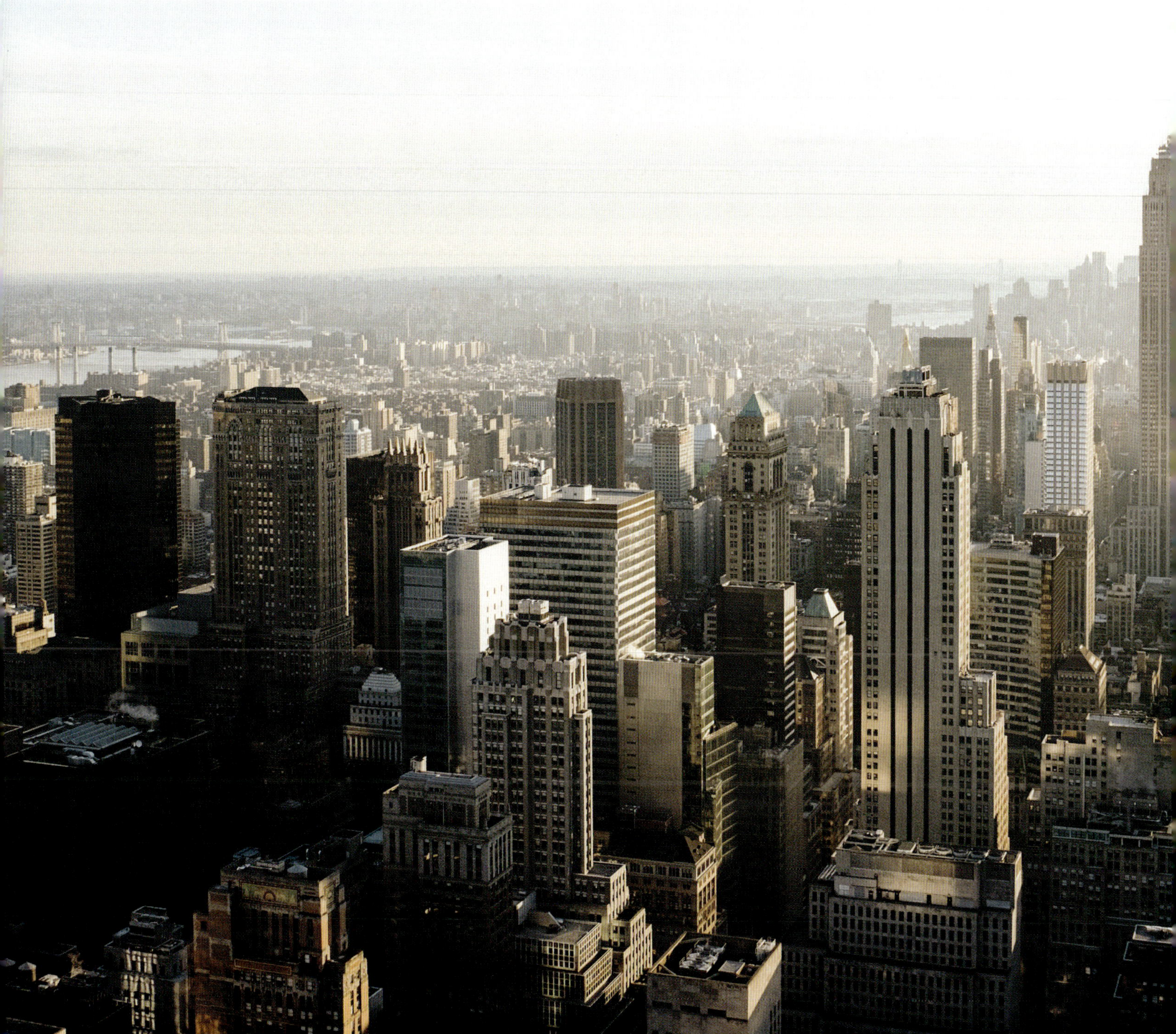

BIRMINGHAM

Although hardly a world-famous city, we look at Birmingham in more detail to show that it is not always the obvious places that are great for urban photography. Birmingham is my home town, and because of that I have explored many of its streets and watched its development over my lifetime. A relatively modern city by European standards, it is interesting because during the 1960s and '70s the city was completely transformed, with much of the unfashionable Victorian architecture demolished in place of modernist structures and the central ring road. It is an example of a city that regenerates every 30 to 40 years, so its face is always changing. The process of redevelopment is now underway to replace much of what was constructed in the decades before.

BELOW
The constant redevelopment of the city is amazing to capture.

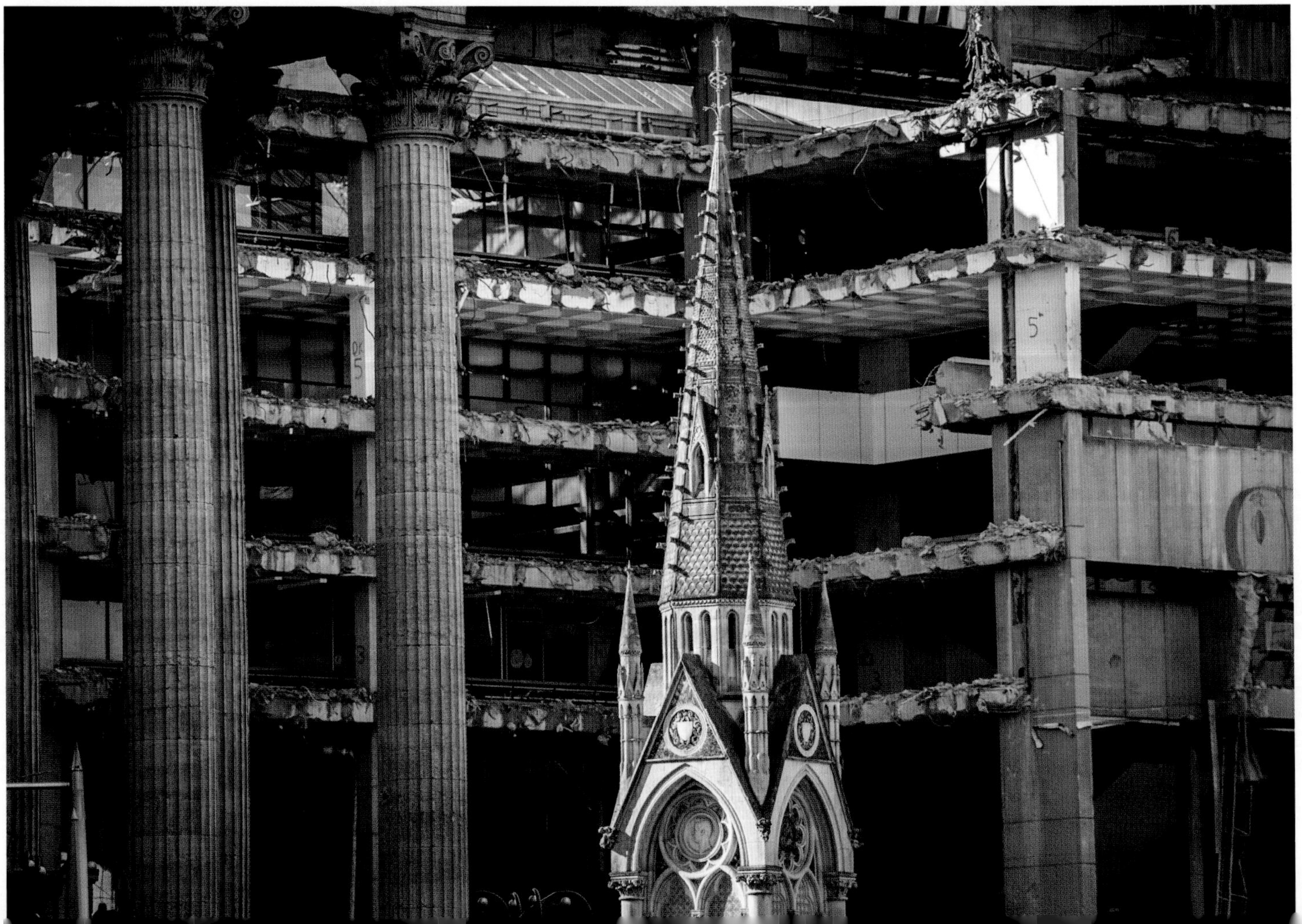

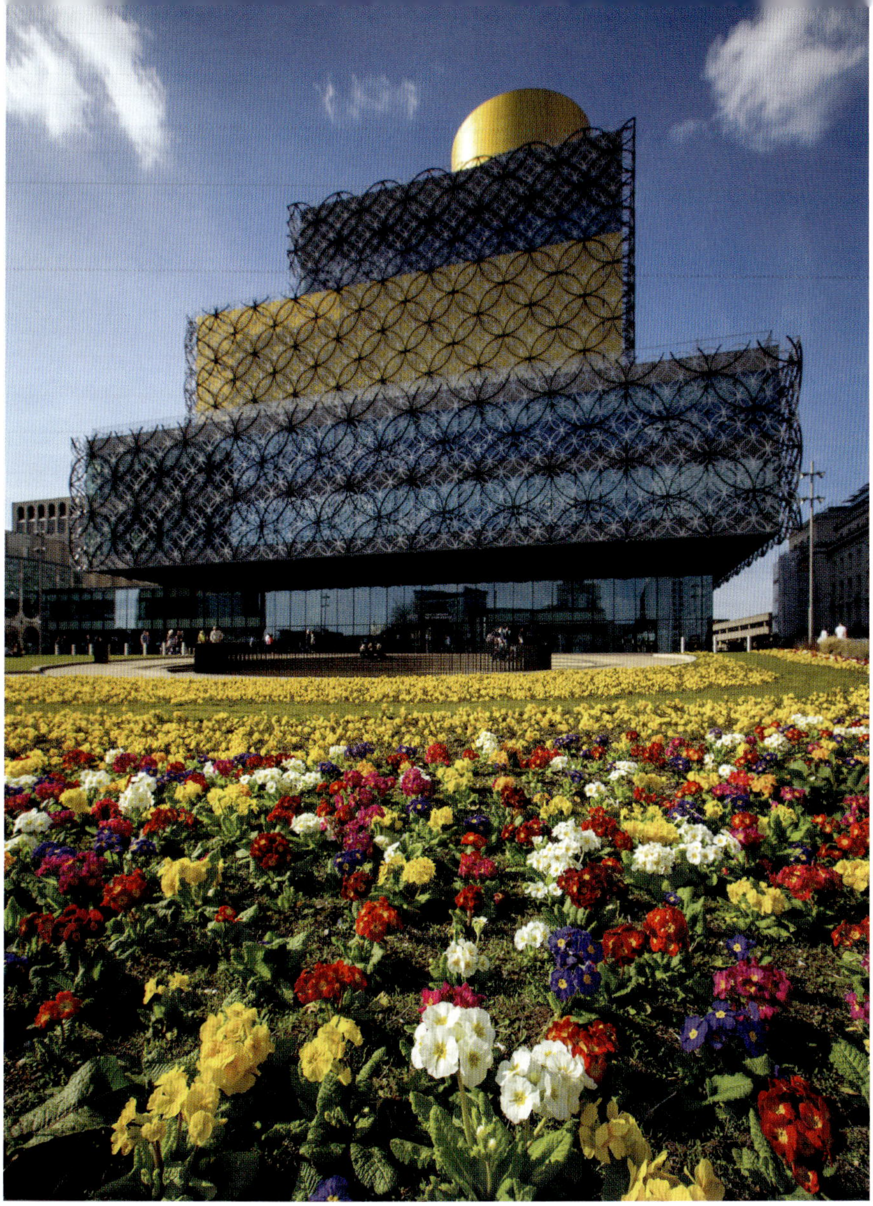

The city has examples of world-class contemporary architecture, typified by the Future Systems Selfridges building, which has a recognizable facade with thousands of silver discs covering its organic form (see pages 7 and 38). Another iconic building in the city centre is the Library of Birmingham, designed by Dutch architecture firm Mecanoo and completed in 2013. Again, it has a unique facade that is comprised of an outer skin of metal filigree in a pattern that represents the city's rich tradition of metalwork in its industrial past. A full-height atrium inside the building takes you all the way to the top, where the Shakespeare Memorial Room is housed. Personally, this is one of my favourite buildings in the world, so to capture it being built and opened on my doorstep was amazing.

With a young, diverse population, Birmingham offers great opportunities for street photography. Take a stroll down New Street and visit the civic squares, Victoria Square and Centenary Square, which regularly hold events such as international dance festivals, food festivals and Christmas markets. Victoria Square is famous for the classical buildings that surround it, including the Council House and the Town Hall – the latter being almost a carbon copy of a Roman temple.

Having lived in Birmingham the majority of my life, it would have been easy to overlook as a destination for photography. Think about your own town or city, and try to observe as you would through the eyes of a tourist visiting a foreign city. Think about when you are on holiday – you might stop and look at an amazing door for five minutes. Try to look at your own city this way, and you'll spot things you hadn't noticed before.

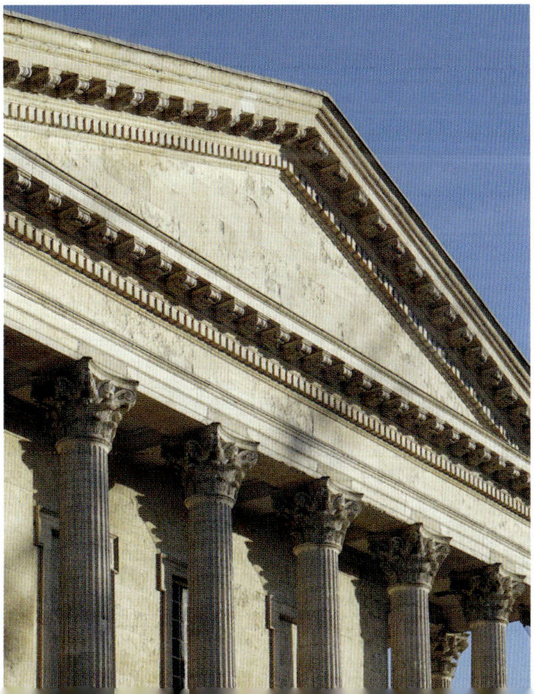

ABOVE
A fine example of Birmingham's contemporary architecture is the Library of Birmingham, built in 2013.

RIGHT
Built in the early 19th century, the Town Hall is a beautiful classical building and an early example of the Roman revival architecture that is widespread in many of the UK's major cities.

DETAILS

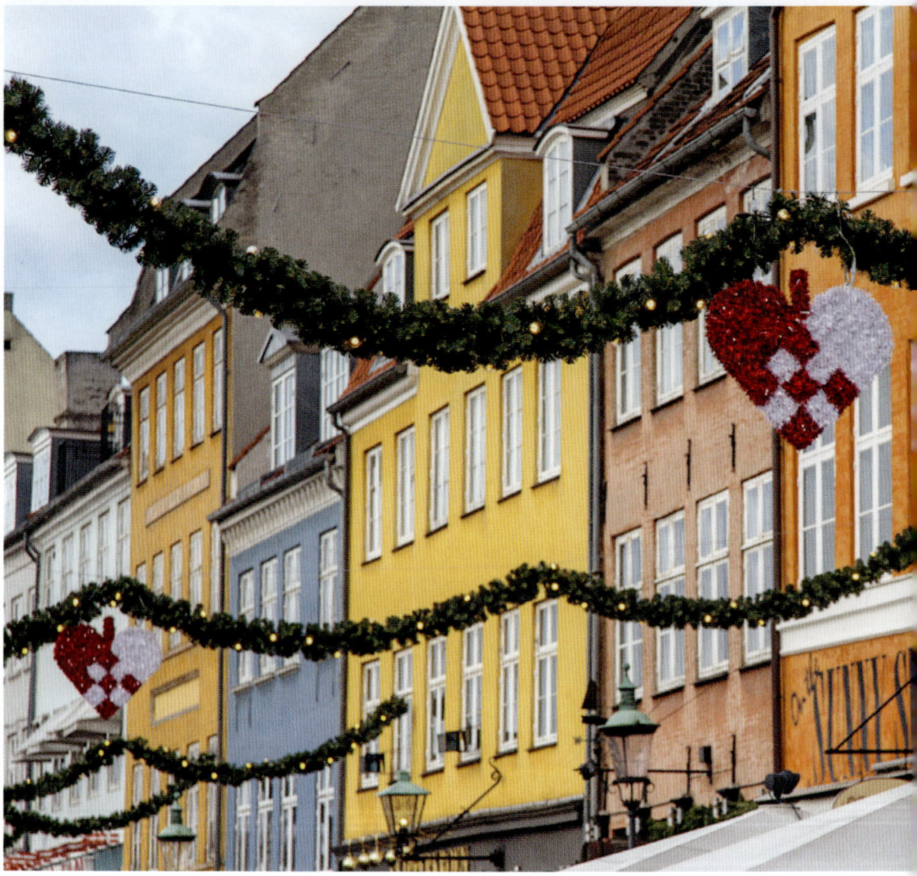

It's useful to compare cities next to each other, as we have done over the previous pages, because in doing so it quickly becomes apparent that they are all quite different, and one thing to always consider when shooting urban photography is, what makes a place unique? It could be something as simple as a street sign or a feature like the 1920s Metro entrances that scream 'this is Paris,' for example. You don't have to be original – look out for that Brooklyn Bridge shot on page 52 when you watch films or TV shows set in New York and you'll start seeing it everywhere.

If you get close enough to look at the details of a city or building, you can often get to the heart of what gives it its character. Scale back your perspective from the wider scene to the elements of the city that are different from anything else, for example the signage on the London Underground or Berlin's Ampelmännchen; in the Netherlands, bicycles are a prominent feature of the urban landscape, and can become a visual shortcut for the city of Amsterdam (as in the image opposite). You don't necessarily want to set out with a predetermined vision, however. Part of urban photography is about discovering the environment around you, so head out with your eyes and mind open.

APPROACH

For this type of photography, a versatile zoom lens with a lot of reach, so that you can home in on the details you're trying to capture, will serve you well. In terms of composition, don't just take a photo of a specific element, but try to give it some context, experimenting with your framing and the position from which you take the photograph, to find the best possible view.

Alternatively, you could use a macro lens to capture the city at an extremely small scale – whether your subject is the intricate detailing on a door, or an interesting pattern in the paving.

ABOVE
Nyhavn in Copenhagen, Denmark, is known for its colourful facades.

RIGHT
Sometimes photos just say everything they need to say about a city! However, a prominently black-and-white composition with a striking pop of colour in the graffiti offers a different view of Amsterdam from the run-of-the-mill bicycle imagery.

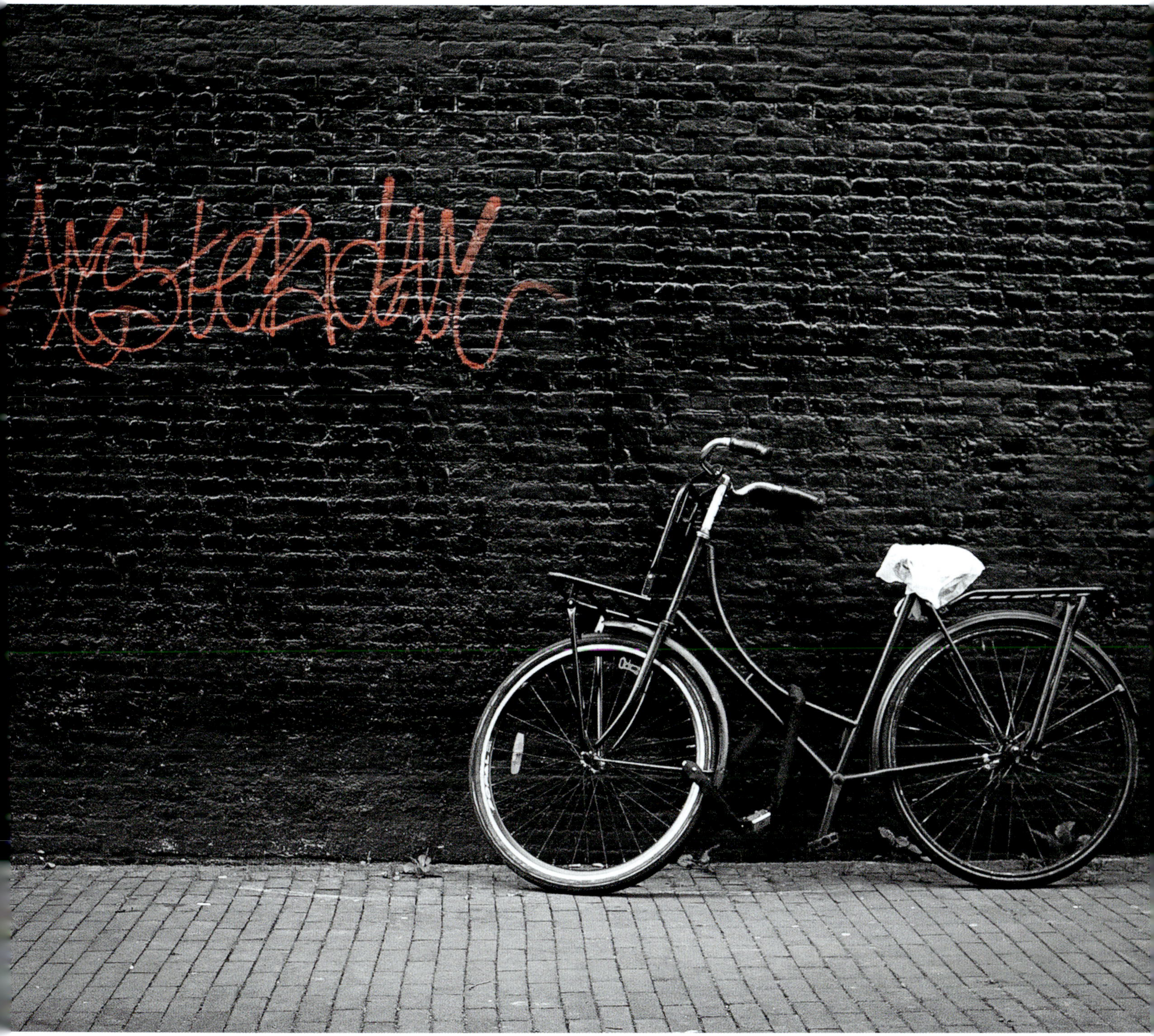

TAKE TO THE SUBURBS

When shooting urban photography it is easy to want to head straight to the city centre, but you shouldn't overlook the suburbs.

HOUSING & INDUSTRY

In the suburbs, you can pick out interesting housing developments; a good example of this is Les Espaces d'Abraxas in Noisy-le-Grand, on the outskirts of Paris. Admittedly, there aren't many suburban developments like this in the world: a huge postmodern concrete housing estate designed by Ricardo Bofill that would be better suited as a set in a dystopian movie. (In fact, it was used for a scene in *The Hunger Games* movies.) These striking concrete structures have features from classical architecture, but are produced on a scale not really seen in Renaissance architecture. The buildings have to be seen to be believed. If impressive housing developments are in short supply, an alternative may be found in the city's industrial areas, which are often home to huge, historic factories – some of which may be more elegant than contemporary housing, and more evocative of a city's past.

GREEN SPACE

This is something that is often quite lacking in city centres, with a few notable examples, such as the various large parks throughout London. In the suburbs, you're more likely to get engrossed in nature, with more wildlife and green space available to photograph. In UK suburbs, you often get foxes prowling the streets at night, while in America you might get raccoons. Animals can provide a fascinating (and testing) subject to photograph in urban environments, as the juxtaposition of nature with the quintessentially man-made environment provides an interesting narrative reference.

LOOKING BACK AT THE CITY

Another good reason to head to the suburbs is the views you can get looking back into the city. From the suburbs, you can use a telephoto lens to pick out the skyline, framing the high-rise buildings in the city centre. There is a lot to cover on capturing cityscapes, so we'll take a look at this in more detail in Chapter 6 (see from page 108).

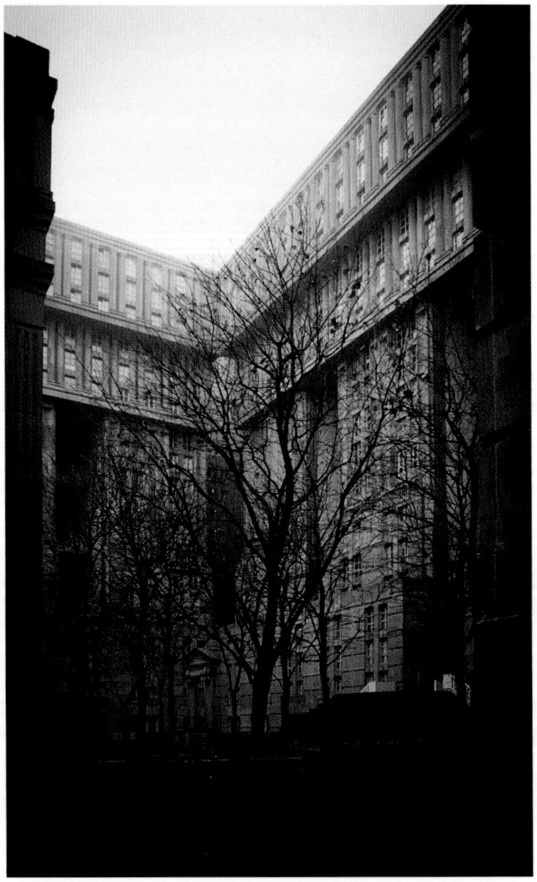

LEFT
The overbearing concrete structures of Les Espaces d'Abraxas work well in black and white.

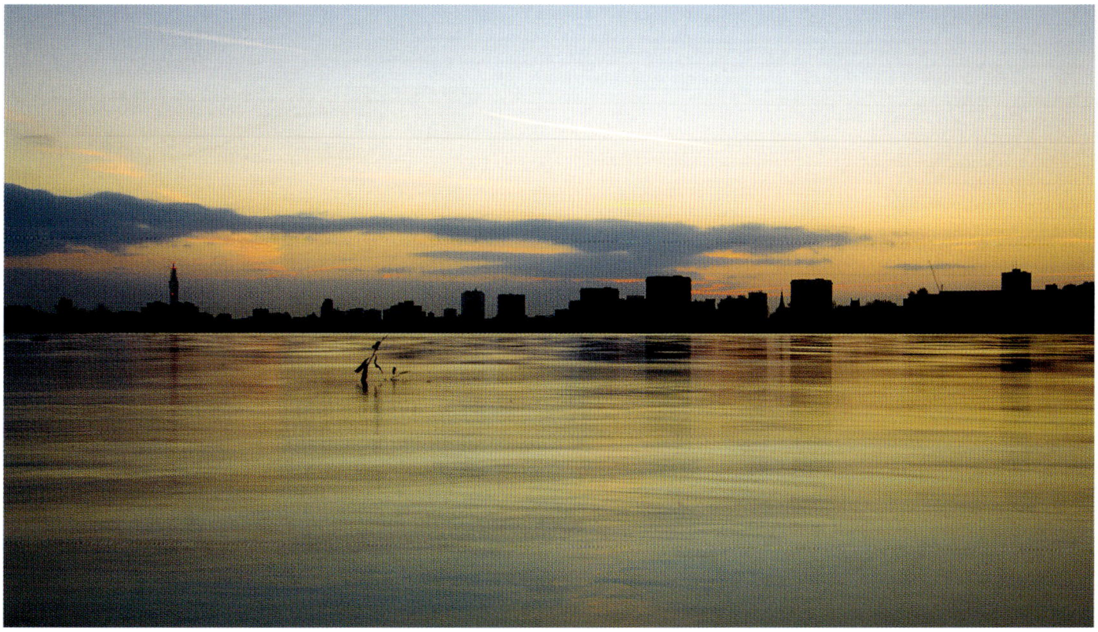

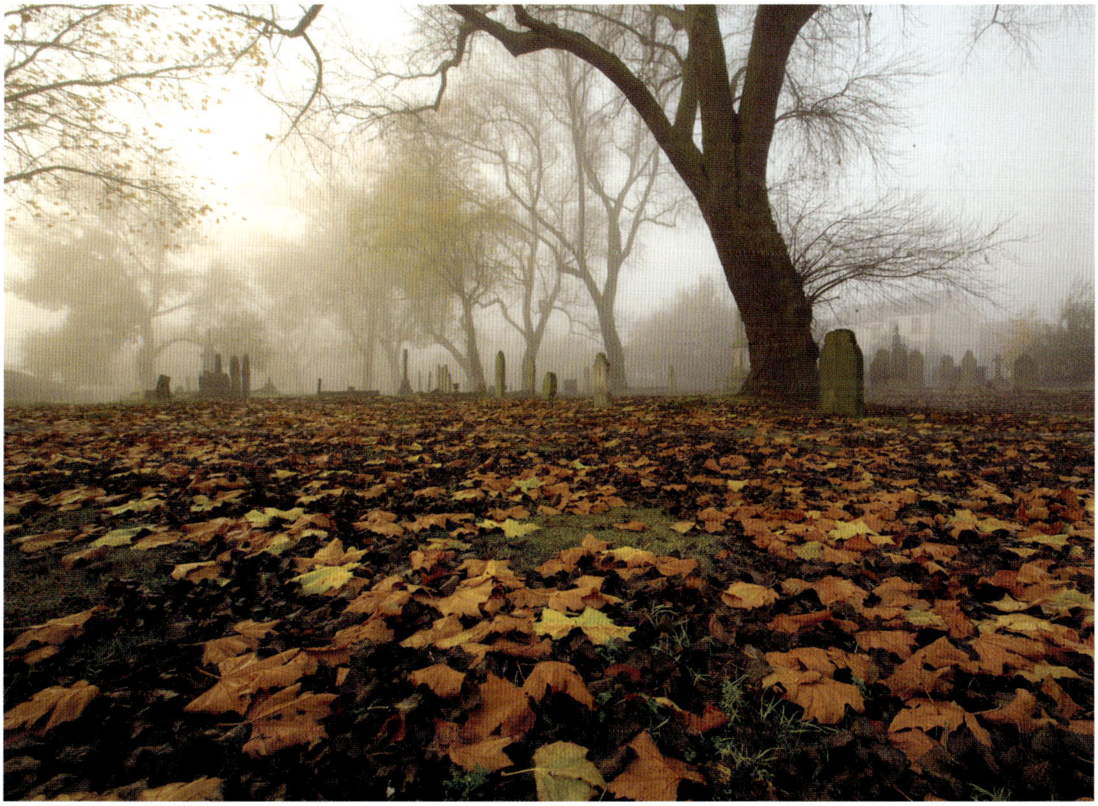

RIGHT, TOP
The city in silhouette as viewed from the suburbs.

RIGHT, BOTTOM
Parks and cemeteries give densely populated city centres and sprawling suburbs some much-needed space and greenery, and are as much a part of the urban environment as the built-up areas.

URBAN RAW

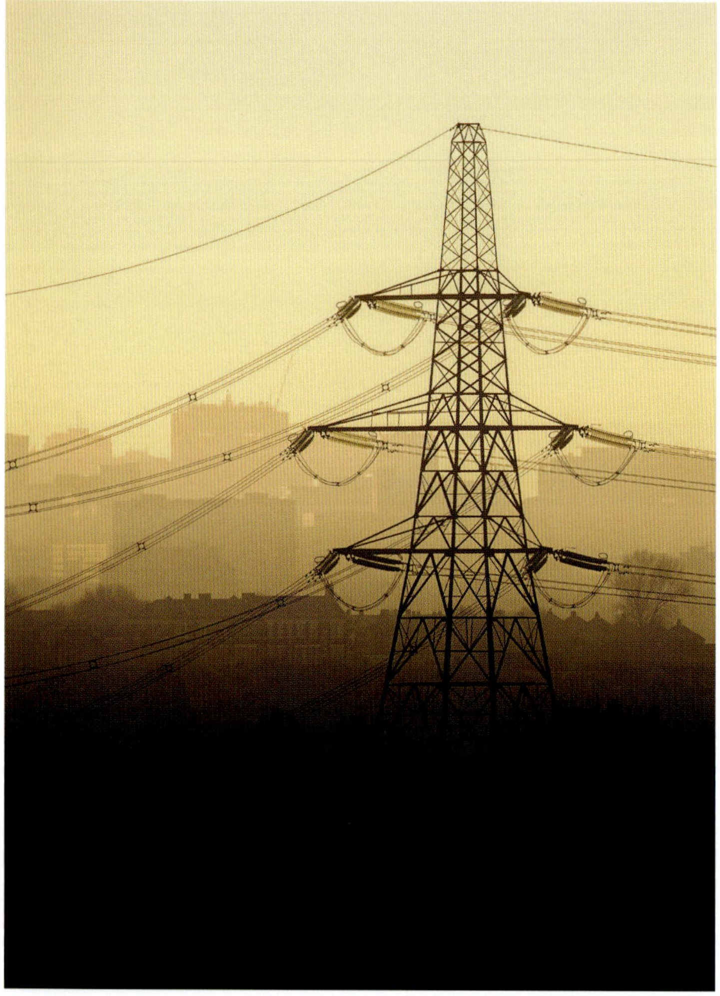

Cities, by their nature, are places undergoing endless demolition and construction, changing over time. They can also be highly polluted and are not always the most aesthetically pleasing spaces, sometimes overrun by litter, graffiti and decay. It's important that this side of the city is also captured, as it is a valid part of the urban environment, and offers some interesting subjects and spaces to shoot.

So we might ask, how can we celebrate this side of the city through photography? Think about the infrastructure that is needed to sustain a city. The roads that snake their way around, under and over city centres. The powerlines and factories in the suburbs, which feed the city and provide the industry to serve it. These places can be extremely interesting and show that unexpected viewpoints can provide the strongest photographs.

Building sites provide a good place to start if you're looking to capture the grittier side of urban life. You could capture the construction or destruction of a building as a time-lapse or photo series. Shoot the crane as it eats away at the structure day by day, which often causes a lot of smoke and dust, creating a great atmospheric scene for your shot.

In terms of photographic style, what do you want to achieve here? You might opt for a reduced colour palette to show off the industrial nature of the scene in its most murky context. You could even use black and white to exaggerate those strong contrasts you observe on a textured piece of concrete, or the silhouette of a power line leading into the city centre shot in monochrome. Or you could go the opposite way and capture a scene with extreme saturation, to suggest there is still beauty in these raw places.

ABOVE
An ordinary pylon becomes a structural play of lines and patterns when shot in silhouette.

OPPOSITE
Motorway underpasses can offer strong shapes to play with, as well as frequently being sites for graffiti artists to show off their skills.

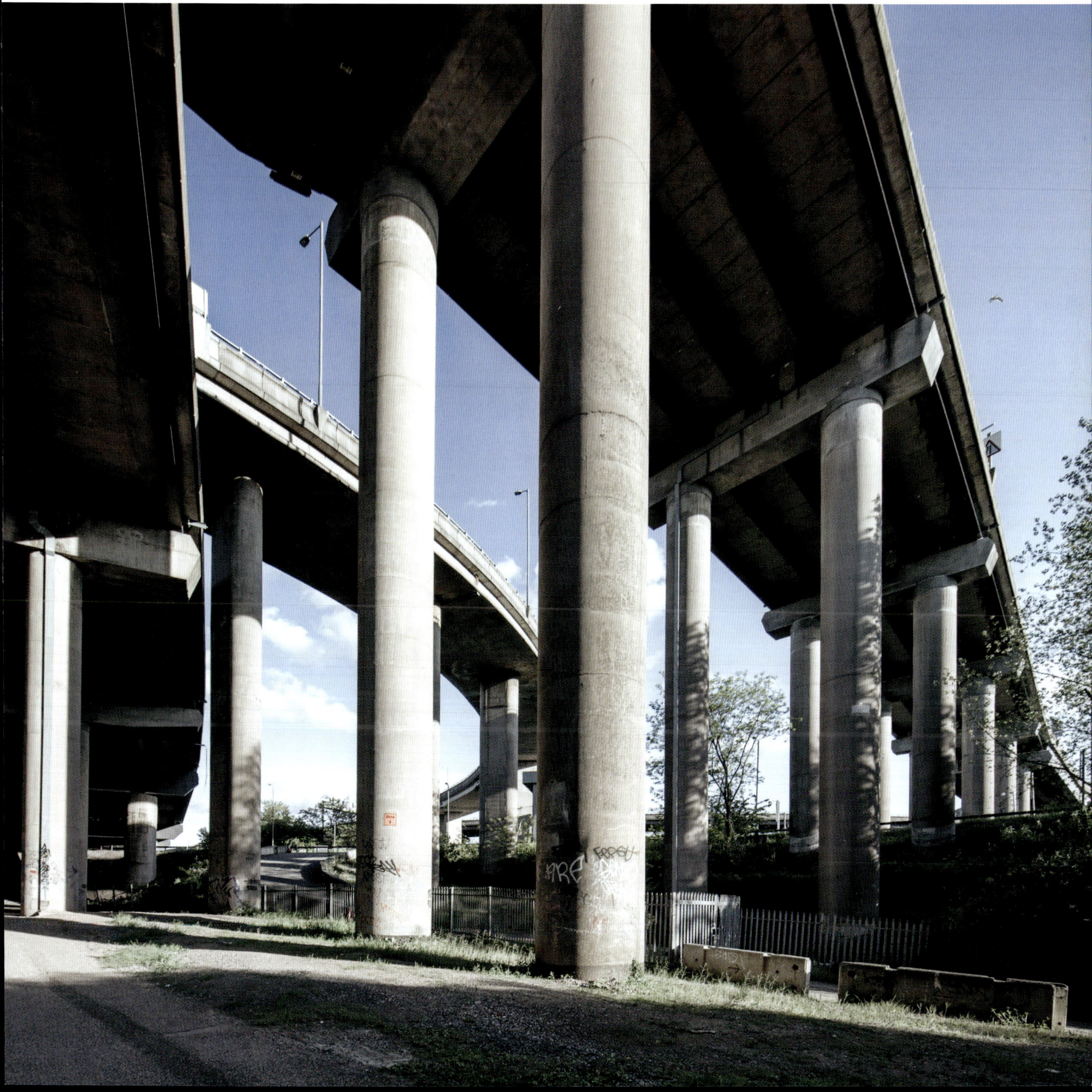

HERO
VIVIENNE GUCWA

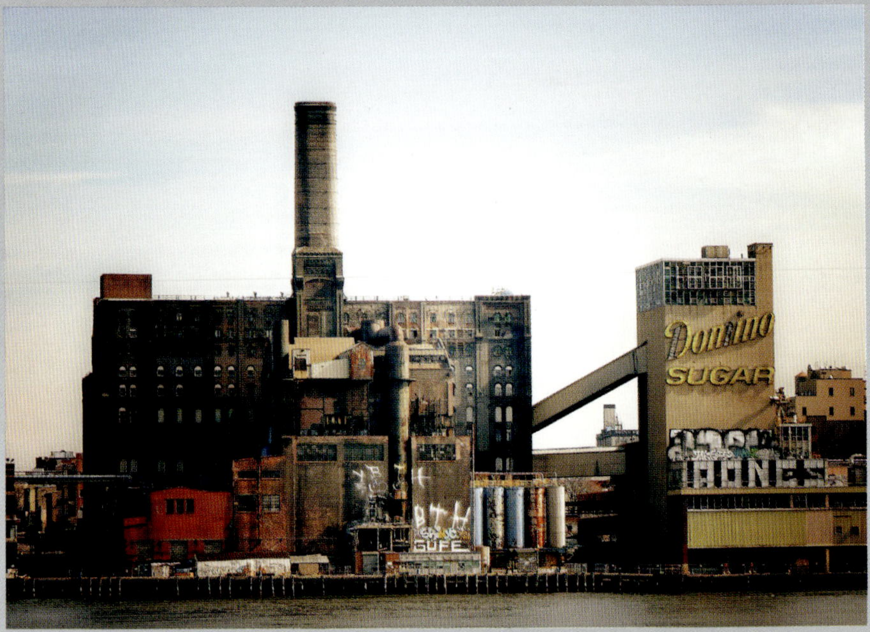

For roughly a decade, Vivienne Gucwa has been shooting and sharing her vision of New York City. Born in Queens, Gucwa started taking photos with no formal training and a cheap point-and-shoot camera. Since then, her photo blog has gained thousands of followers, she has been a Sony Artisan of Imagery, and she has published two photo books. What marks out her photography is a recognizable style, which always suggests intimacy between the photographer and this city.

Gucwa is one of those photographers who illustrates the idea that when you know your city, you take better photos. Central Park in the autumn sunlight and white in the snow; the Manhattan skyline in the morning light and at sunset; passersby lit by streetlights, or hidden behind umbrellas in the rain – Gucwa's photography proves that there really are no bad conditions for photography.

The way Gucwa has achieved this is simply by walking – and having her camera with her. The most extreme example of this is when she decided to head out on a trek through Central Park in the middle of a blizzard. This dedication and spirit of exploration has rewarded her with some of her most iconic photos – it is strange to see the city so empty, its usually busy streets take on an apocalyptic mood.

When it comes to street photography, the lesson we can learn is about patience. This is always true for street photography: you find the perfect scene, and then you wait for the extra thing to enter it, whether that's a sudden beam of light, or the right person walking through it.

ABOVE
The Domino Sugar factory in Williamsburg, Brooklyn.

RIGHT, TOP
A line of iconic yellow taxis outside Washington Square Park in Greenwich Village, Lower Manhattan, provides the perfect backdrop for a good street scene. The woman's red-patterned umbrella and bag add the perfect complement.

RIGHT, BOTTOM
Summer rain on Pell Street, Chinatown, Lower Manhattan.

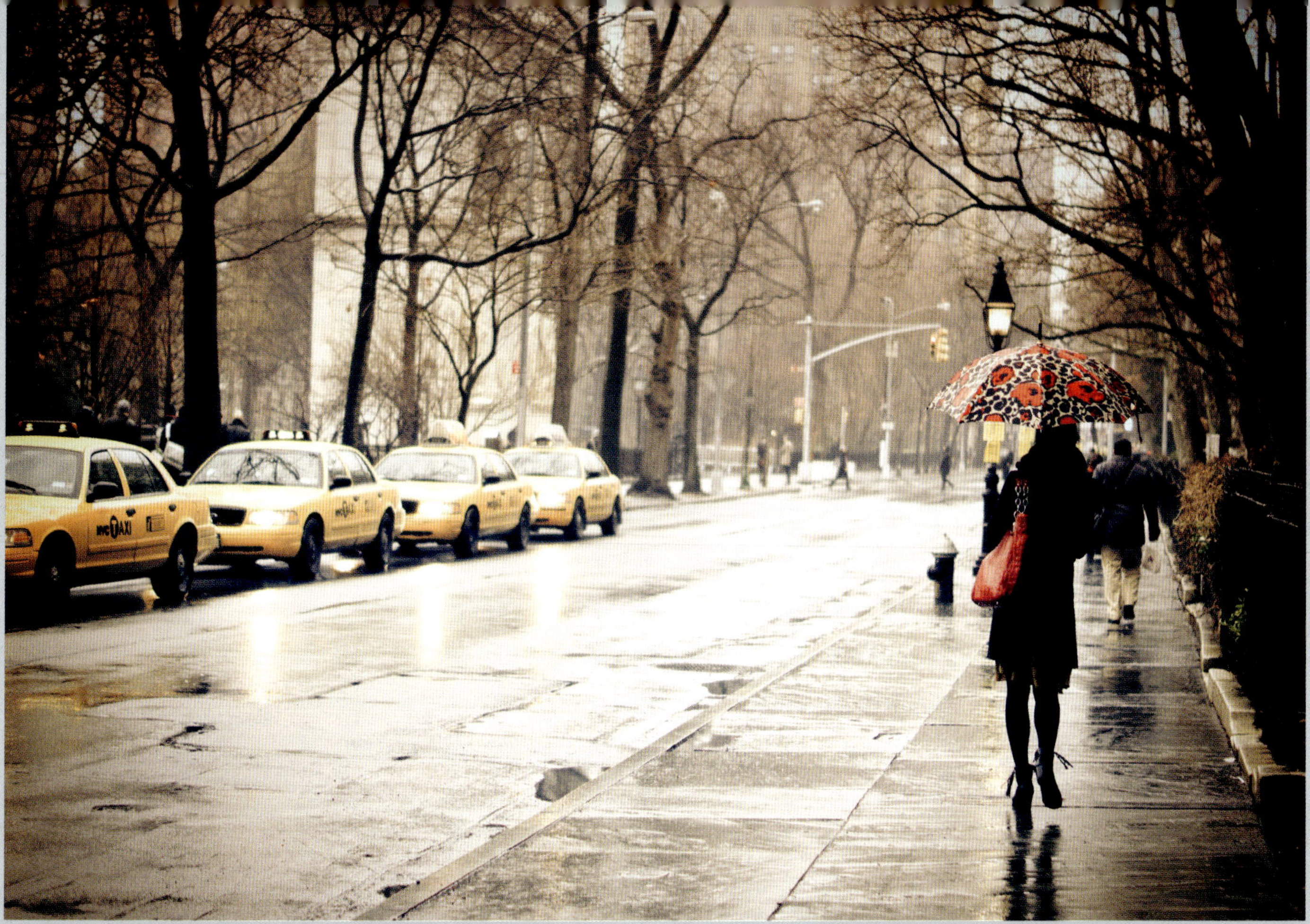

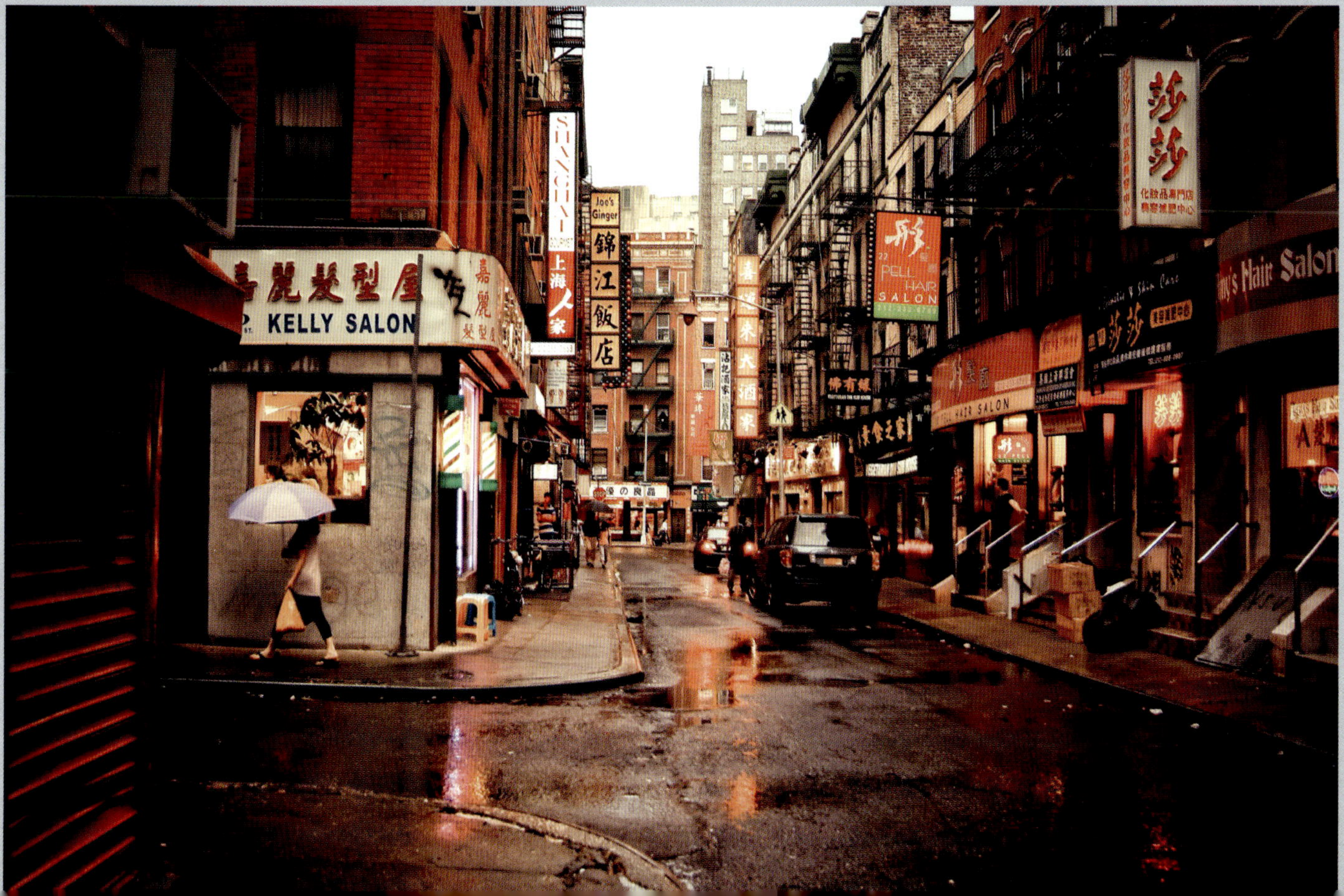

嘉麗髮型屋
KELLY SALON
SHANGHAI
上海人家
Joe's Ginger
錦江飯店
PELL HAIR SALON

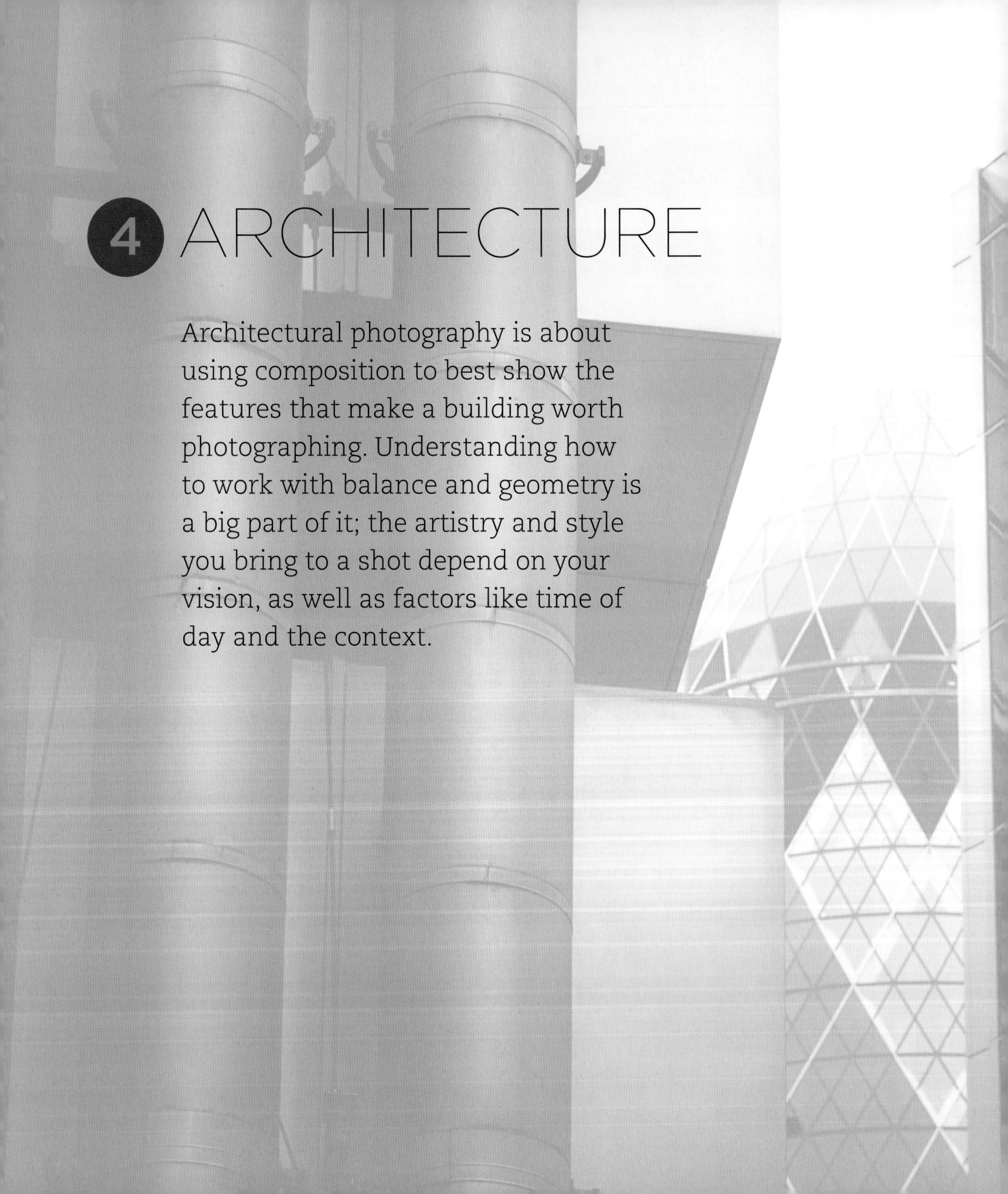

4 ARCHITECTURE

Architectural photography is about using composition to best show the features that make a building worth photographing. Understanding how to work with balance and geometry is a big part of it; the artistry and style you bring to a shot depend on your vision, as well as factors like time of day and the context.

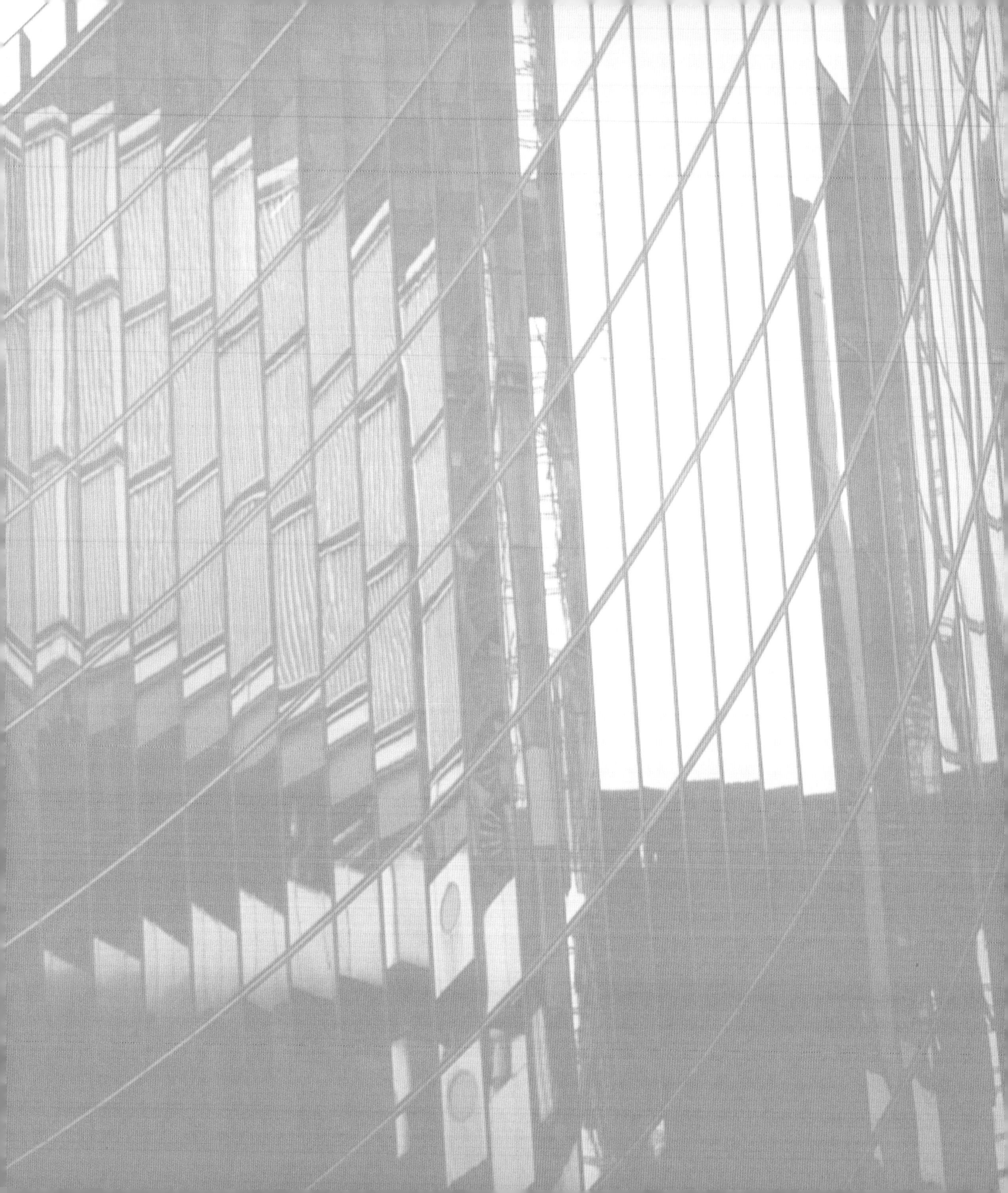

THE ARCHITECT'S VISION

Every building you stand in and every piece of public space you occupy has been designed by someone. The architect, landscape architect or town planner has spent years thinking about how you experience a space, and how spaces will work in connection with each other. Knowing this, you can begin to decode the buildings that form the urban fabric around you.

Look for clues in buildings. It's no coincidence that the walls of buildings next to each other line up, or that the paving around them is aligned with the columns on the front of a building. If you look down at the floor you can find the line in the tile that lines up exactly with the centre of the building, and this is where you place yourself in order to capture the perfect flat view of the facade or interior.

Think about how the building makes you feel and try to capture that with your photography. The best architectural photographers find interesting compositions through their experience of the space, ones that were not even imagined by the architect.

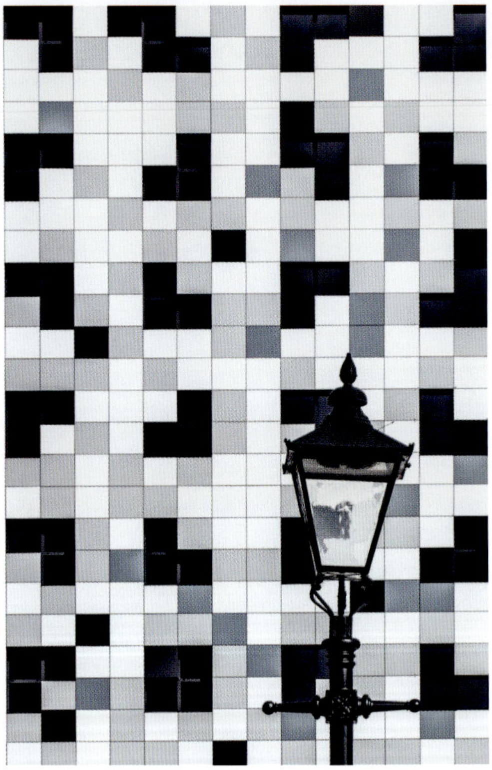

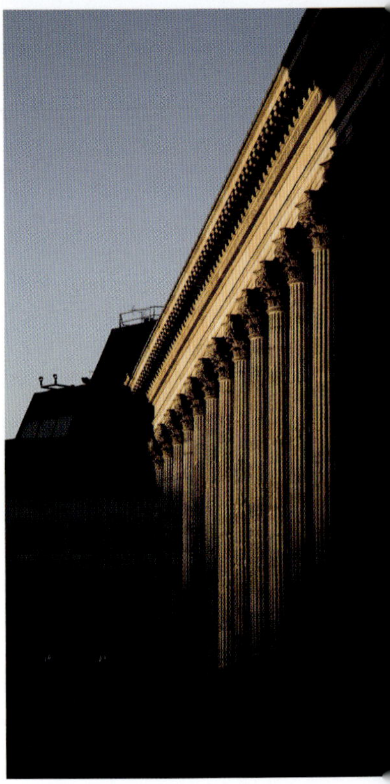

Look at the details of the building. Concentrate on the windows, for example, or a specific piece of the building's structure that you find interesting or beautiful. It was Ludwig Mies van der Rohe who famously said that 'God is in the details.' When it came to his buildings, his attention to detail was immaculate, so you know that their minimal aesthetic was the product of an elaborate process.

Remember that buildings are dynamic structures. They change depending on the light at various times of the day and different times of year. See how the light is hitting the building, and if it isn't right, store that knowledge away so that you can come back to capture when you have those ideal conditions. Buildings also rely heavily on context. If you find yourself getting too obsessed with smaller architectural features, try thinking about the building from a more human angle, and use people to complement the composition. The right person in your shot can portray the language of the building, and bring animation to its solid permanence.

ABOVE, LEFT
The patterned tile background wouldn't mean much on its own. The addition of the lamp post brings context to contemporary architecture.

ABOVE, RIGHT
Classical architecture viewed at sunrise, when the light sculpts its textures and adds drama.

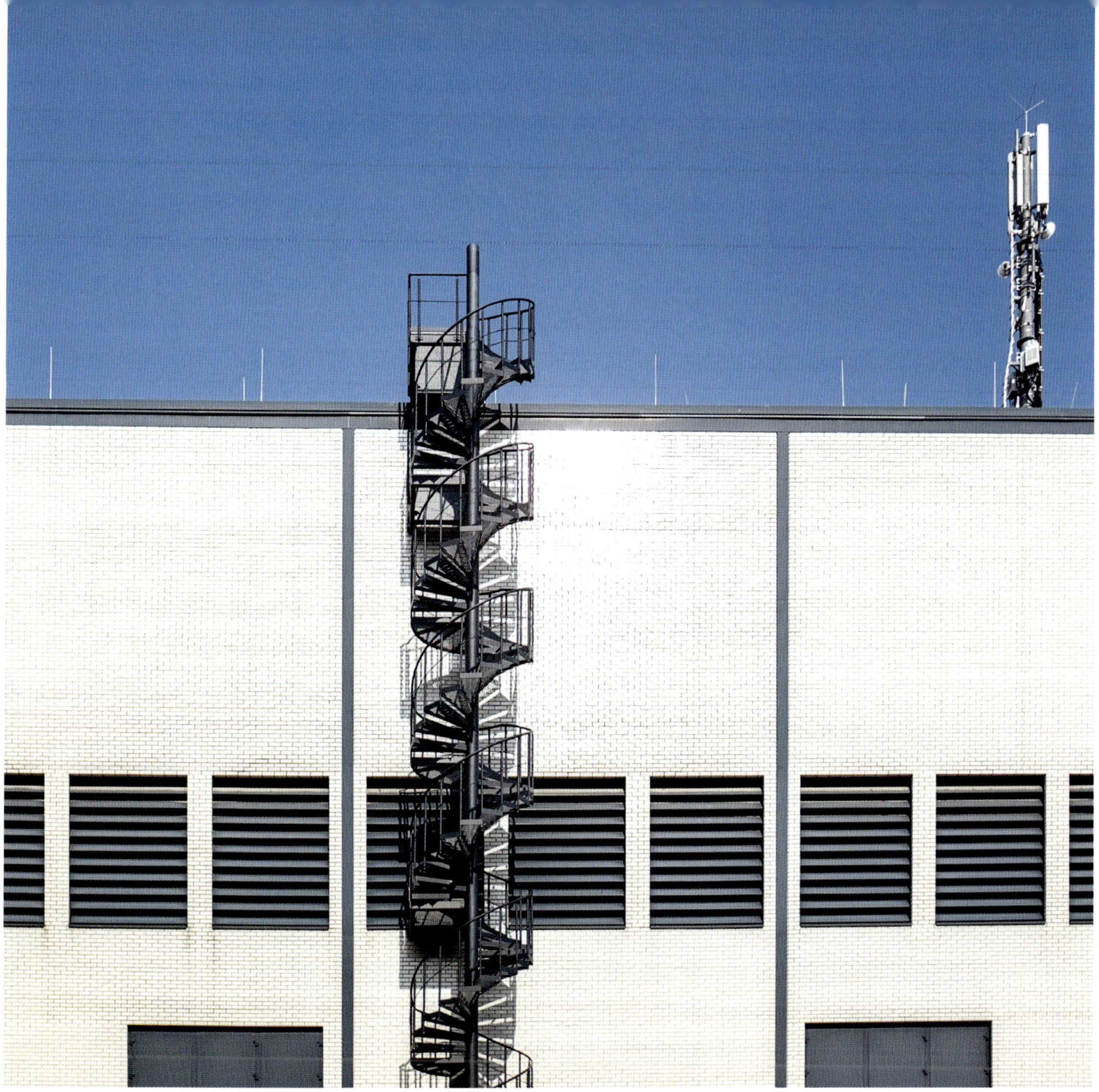

THE CLIENT'S NEEDS

When you approach architectural photography from a commercial perspective you need to understand the client's expectations. In many instances, it will be the architect or another designer of the building, and they might take you around and through the building and tell you what they want from the photographs. It is important to listen to their direction, but through your own experience, you may be able to pick out angles and details that not even the architect has appreciated.

One key question to ask prior to your visit is whether there are any important features that the client wishes you to focus on. It may be that there is a specific detail, a piece of technology or a key viewpoint that was the cornerstone of the design. It will be worth coming up with a few different ideas about how you might approach this detail before the day.

ABOVE
For some photographs, it just won't do to have clouds in the shot. A moody sky might work for certain kinds of clients, but the majority will want to show their building(s) in the best light.

COMPOSITION

The key to a successful architectural photograph is powerful composition. Here I show ten compositional tricks that are particularly relevant to architectural photography. You can, and should, take risks to push your photographs further, but these give you a guide to keep in the back of your mind when shooting.

RULE OF THIRDS

This has to be the most famous of all the photography composition rules. It is so popular that the majority of cameras and smartphones provide the option to have guidelines on their viewfinders or screens to help users compose their photos. Its application to architectural photography is particularly relevant. The origin of this rule is in the mathematical principle of the 'golden ratio', which many architects used as inspiration when designing their buildings. In fact, it is said that even Stonehenge is set out according to the golden ratio, but more recently, Le Corbusier used it for scale and proportion in his modernist designs.

The rule of thirds splits an image into three segments along the vertical and horizontal axes. Using this rule, you don't put the line of the landscape or pavement directly in the centre of the image, but instead place it along one of the imaginary horizontal lines that divide the frame. In the same vein, you would place focal points on the lines, or where the horizontal and vertical lines intersect.

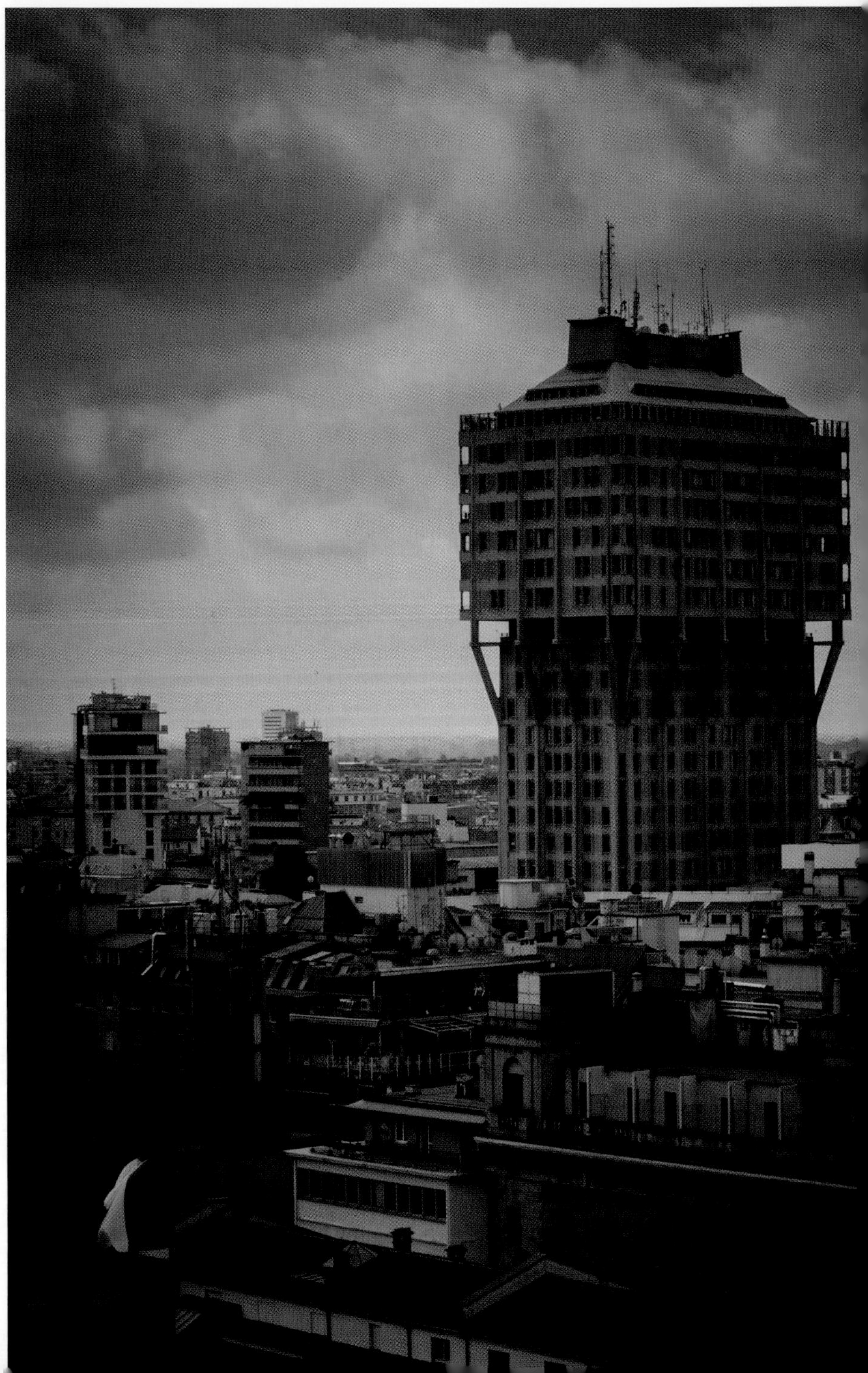

RIGHT
The structure that dominates this shot is fairly central on the vertical axis, but placed off-centre horizontally, and is arguably more interesting than had it been placed right in the middle of the frame.

SYMMETRY

Most buildings are designed with a certain degree of symmetry, but this doesn't need to be interpreted in the literal sense when approaching a photograph. Symmetry can be implied simply by having a central line down the centre of the composition, as in the example of the cathedral on page 22. It can also be created more loosely by finding two objects that are similar and positioning them equally from the centre of the frame.

LOOK UP

Looking directly up offers a unique perspective for the photographer to capture. People rarely actually look up at buildings, so this gives the photographer the opportunity to capture something the average person doesn't usually appreciate. The first thing to do before taking a shot looking up at a building is to, oddly enough, look down. As mentioned, you can look for architectural cues on the ground that will lead you to a good position to execute the photo. For instance, by walking along the line of an aisle in a cathedral, or by following the clues of a patterned floor, you can find the perfect position to capture the symmetrical composition of the vaulted ceiling.

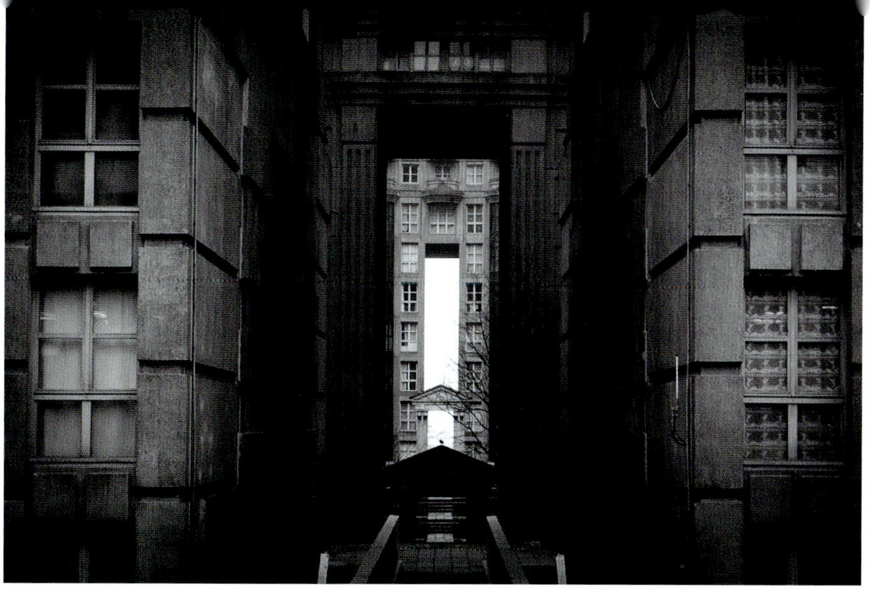

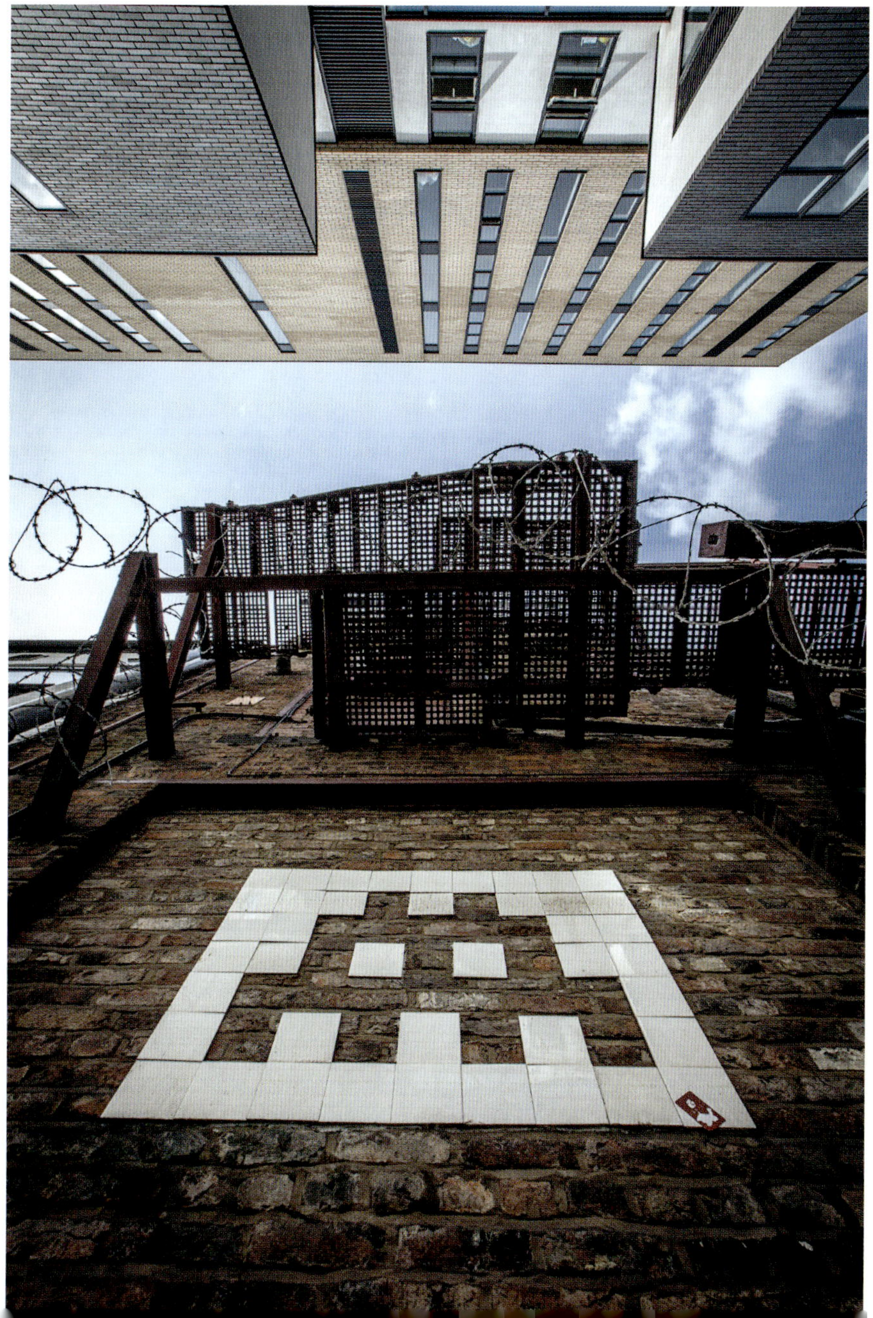

RIGHT, TOP
Symmetry can give a powerful image. Finding arches or the gap between two similar buildings, you can add an extra dimension, showing something in the distance.

RIGHT, BOTTOM
Looking up can offer an unusual view of the world, particularly when there's a powerful focal point to catch the eye and lead it upwards.

LEADING LINES

When looking at the majority of buildings you instantly notice that they are composed of a series of lines and angles. The leading-lines principle uses them to draw the viewer's eye through a photograph. It might be a line of columns receding into the distance, clearly defined floorboards leading your eye to one corner of the frame, or street markings that point towards the subject. As you frame your shot, keep your eye out for any lines that could be exploited in this way.

FLAT LINES

This is an important principle in architectural photography, and again it relates to the way in which a building is designed. When architects create drawings for a building, they produce an elevation view of the exterior facade, which is a flat perspective of the building used to give dimension to areas like windows, doors, and the external fabric. This photographic principle aims to replicate this view but in the real world, by distorting the image. When you look directly at a building at a right angle to the facade, the shape of a square building (for instance) will appear slightly trapezoidal, as its parallel lines converge towards the infinity point in the farthest distance, somewhere up in the sky. You can use a tilt-shift lens to correct this while taking the photo, but these are quite expensive pieces of kit. Alternatively you can use software to correct the perspective in post-production (see pages 164–65). Another way to produce this effect is to elevate yourself to the centre of the building in terms of the overall height, in a building directly opposite, for example and then take your shot from there.

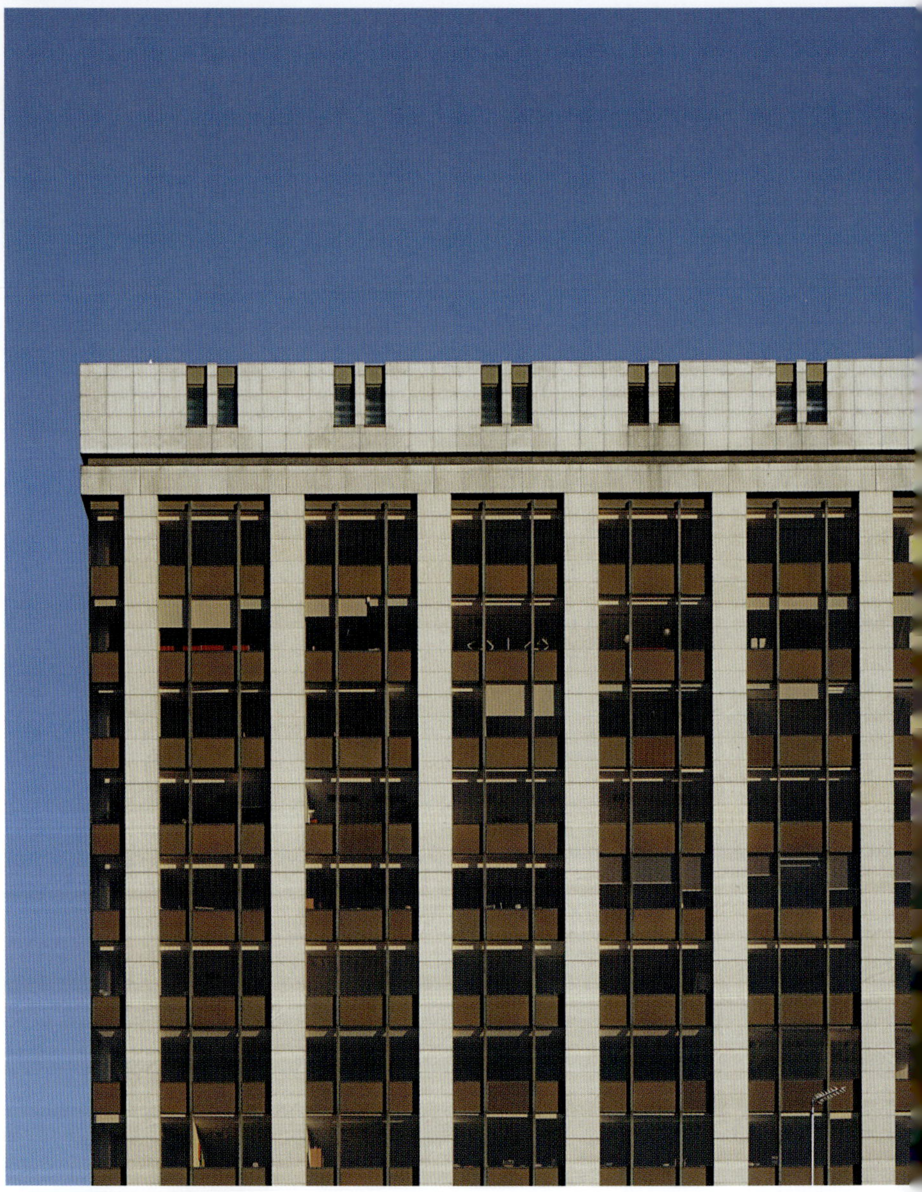

ABOVE
A perfectly square shot of a building is interesting visually, because it's not what our eyes usually see. Because it takes a bit of work to get this uniform straightness, it also elevates your photography,

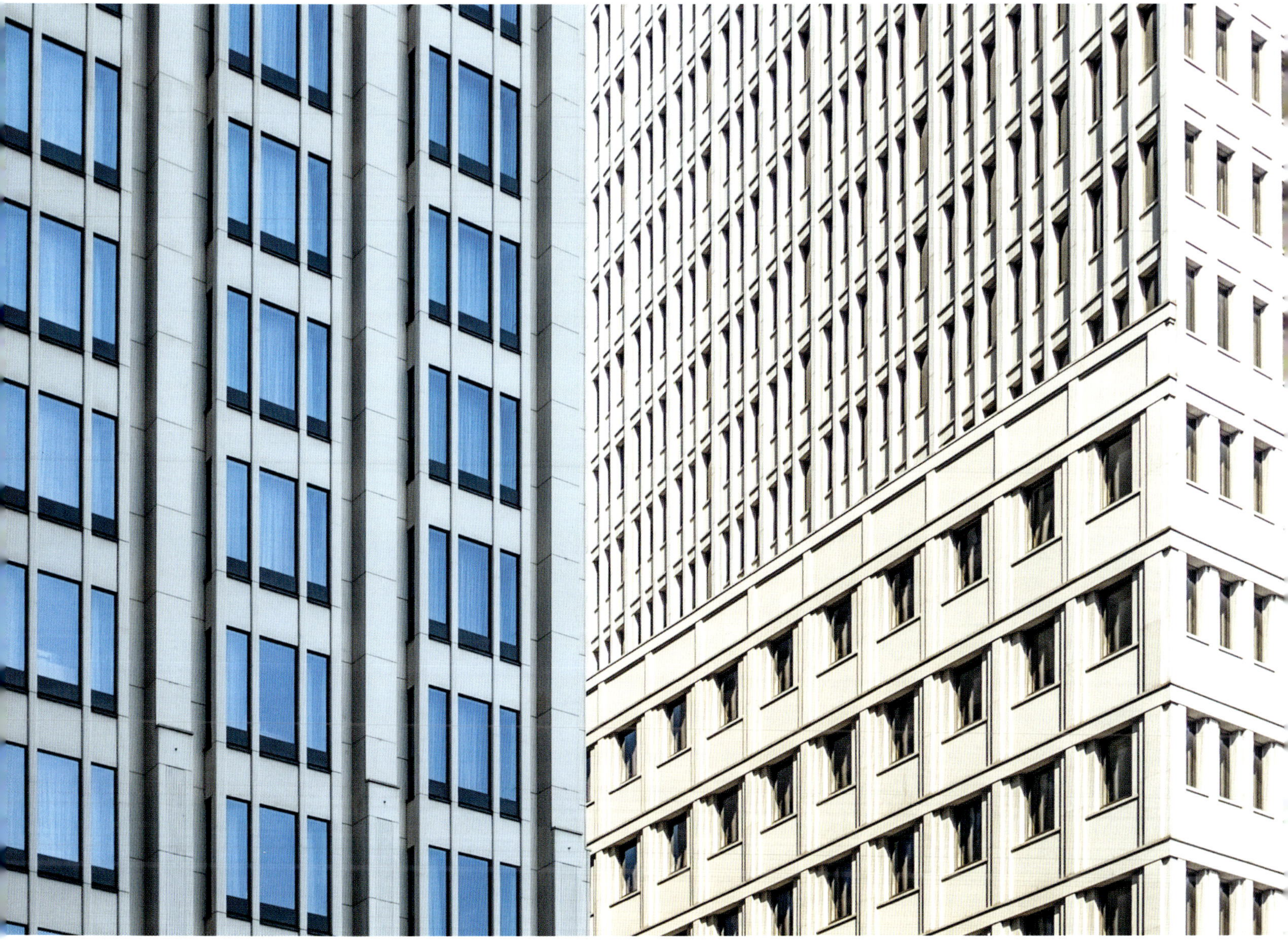

ABOVE
In a built-up city, getting in close and capturing two buildings with no space in between can give you a lot of lines to lead the viewer's eye all around the frame.

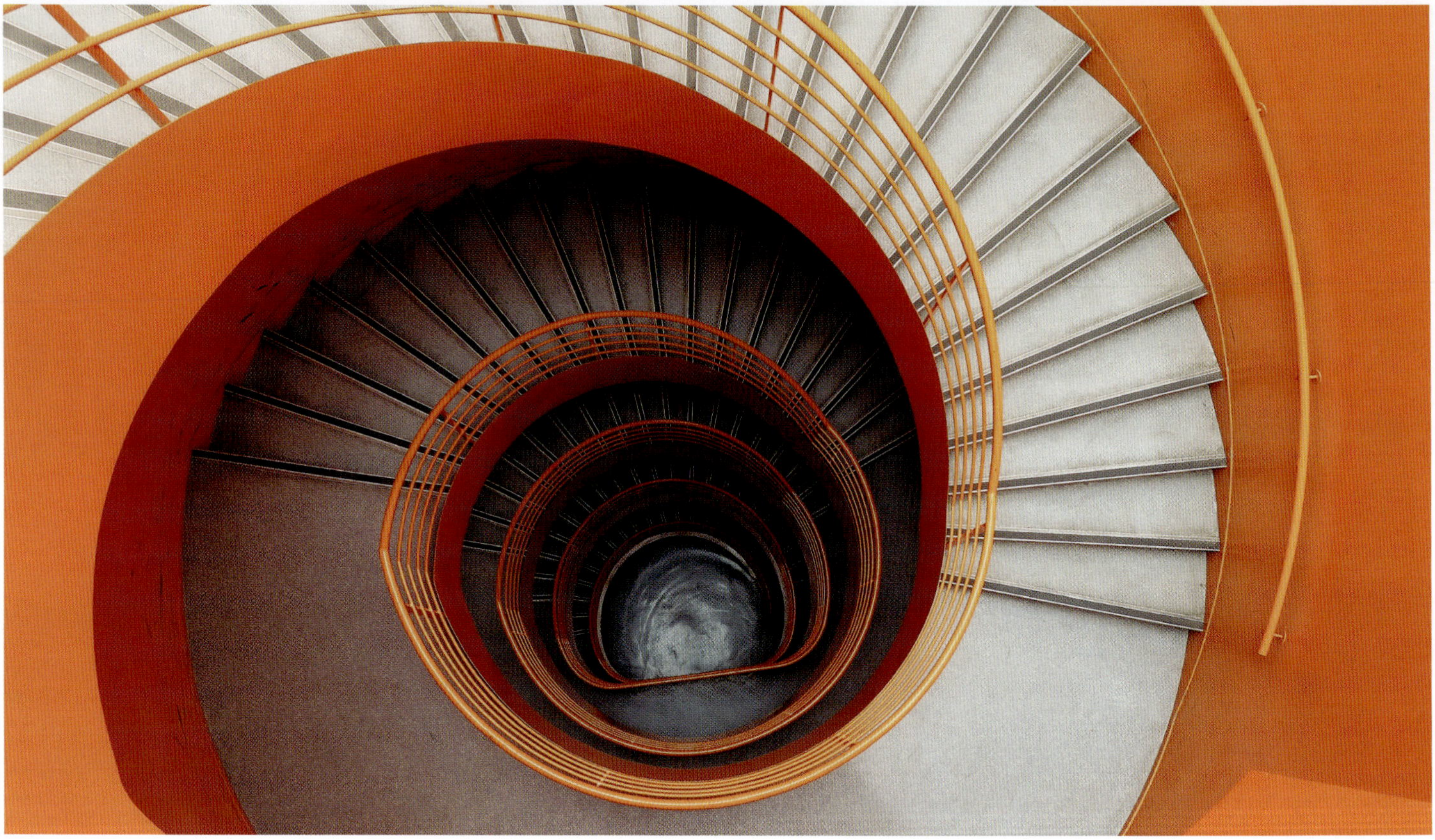

SHAPE

Geometry is a key thing to consider for composition, so look out for strong shapes in architectural elements. It could be a circle, which is a great shape to concentrate in the centre of a photograph, or a solid square. Different shapes bring different associations, as the artist Wassily Kandinsky theorized about. Kandinsky had some strong opinions about shapes (he considered the circle 'dull', for instance, although made plenty of use of the shape in his paintings) but you can come to your own conclusions, which may change according to different contexts. When you find a shape, think about what it signifies to you, and how you can express that association in your photograph.

COLOUR

Colour is not just ornamentation – it can be a compositional element in its own right. Solid blocks of colours, and a limited palette of just a few hues, can be effective in architectural photography. Like shape, colour has a symbolic element, which Kandinsky also wrote about. It tends to present stronger associations to a viewer than shape does, and it is known that different colours have different properties. Reds tend to pop out, for example, while blues recede. You may not have any control over what colours you have to work with, but by learning more about colour theory – the principles of optics and colour behaviour – you can choose how to work with those that are available.

ABOVE
A spiral is always a powerful shape, combining a continuous line for the eye to follow. Orange is a warm, dynamic colour which pops out, contrasting well with the stairwell.

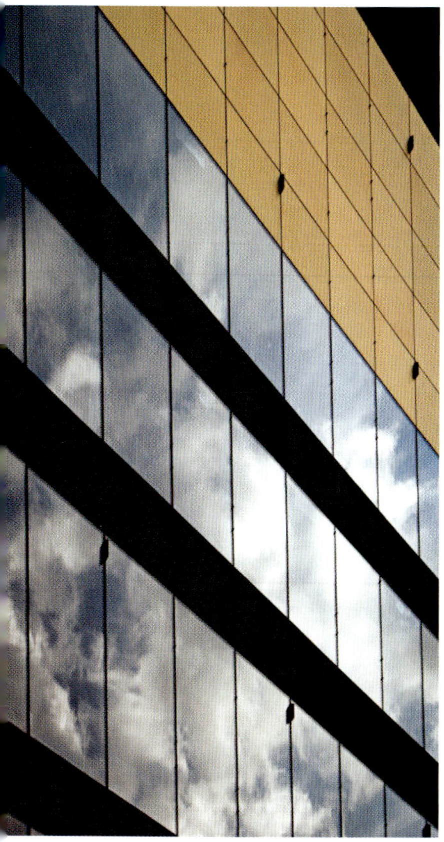

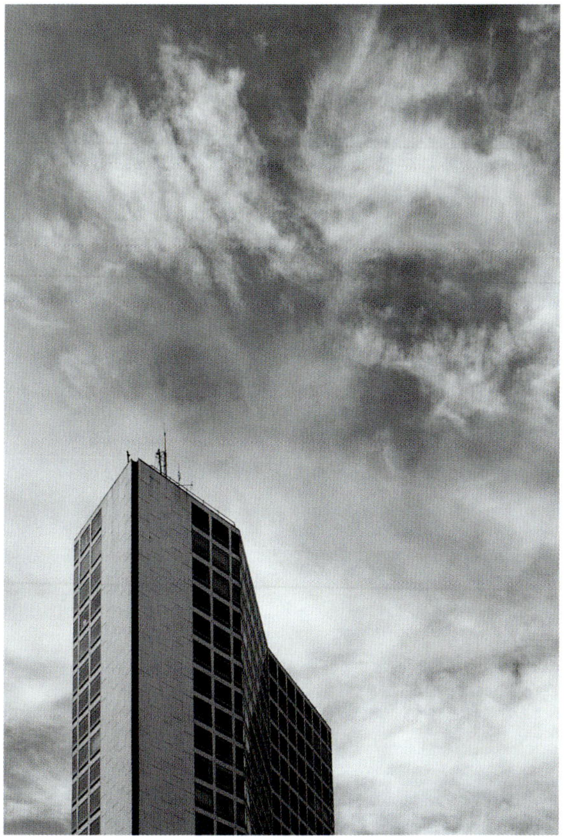

FILLING THE FRAME

This principle encourages you to get in close to your subject, filling the frame (or the majority of the frame) with it. Removed from context, this can be a good way to really focus on architectural details, or other compositional elements like lines and colours.

NEGATIVE SPACE

The empty space in an image is just as important as the subject that is the focus. In the opposite vein to the above principle, this rule makes your focal point just a small part of an otherwise empty frame. It doesn't have to be literally empty – abstract surroundings such as a cloudy sky or a blurred background work for this too. By enhancing the negative space in the composition, you define the subject as the positive space, and can make a more powerful statement about the architectural subject.

CLEAN LINES

Minimalism in photography can be achieved by creating a composition of clean lines. Try shooting the side of a blank wall or building and splitting the composition by using half of the building and half of the sky. It helps if it is a clear day so the sky appears as one block of colour, to contrast with the facade of the building.

ABOVE, LEFT
Filling the frame is a great way to capture attractive details, like clouds reflected in a glass building. You can approach this by getting close physically, or isolating the detail in a telephoto lens.

ABOVE, MIDDLE
Negative space can help you to capture a sense of scale, as well as to isolate a shape or detail of a building from distracting surrounds.

ABOVE, RIGHT
This photo is almost abstract, playing with only two colours and a smooth, clean line.

HERO
SEBASTIAN WEISS

The photographic work of Sebastian Weiss has been an inspiration to me, for his compositions which turn buildings into something more resembling abstract art. In particular, we can note his use of negative space in order to emphasize the geometric shapes and patterns of buildings. His work showcases architecture in its most sculptural form, where compositions are created by the outline of the building against the sky.

His shots of Santiago Calatravas's Ciudad de Artes y Ciencias (City of Arts and Sciences) in Valencia are exceptional to me, and worth looking up. Calatravas's work takes an organic form that verges on the sculptural. He takes cues from the natural world and reproduces them in his architecture, with some of his buildings representing the wings of a bird (see the Milwaukee Art Museum), or resembling a skeletal form (see World Trade Center Terminal in New York City). In Valencia, his bright white buildings that utilize symmetry, repetition and curving geometric shapes play brilliantly to Weiss's style of photography.

Weiss captures architectural details by picking out elements of the architecture either by getting in close enough to capture only their sculptural patterns, or by using the negative space around them to draw attention to a shape. In post-production, he also amends the colour of the sky, which features heavily in his shots, often as a consistent block of colour, increasing the saturation or the temperature to make these dramatic shapes stand out even more vividly.

RIGHT
The vivid blue sky that characteristically fills much of Weiss's frame highlights the sharp curve of the Church St Marien in Schilling, Germany (designed by Königs Architekten).

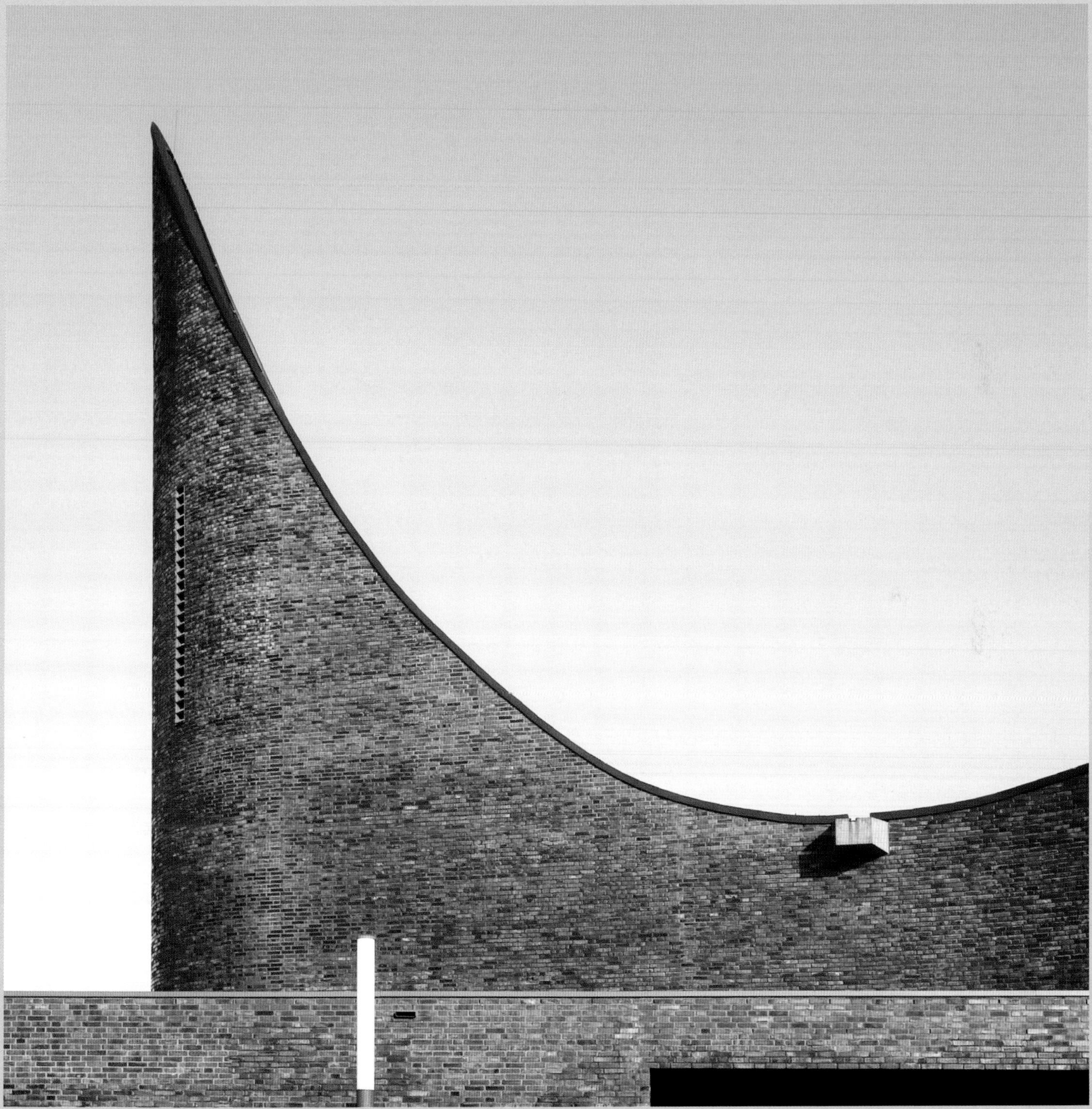

CAMERA SETUP

While telephoto and good zoom lenses are ideal for capturing details, other kinds of architectural photography require a setup that utilizes the wide-angle end of the spectrum. On a full-frame body, you may need to go wider than 24mm to achieve the shots you require, especially for interior perspectives. The wide-angle lens of a phone camera may offer a large enough field of view for most shots, but in darker situations it may not give you enough in terms of quality.

When working with complex shapes and precise geometry, a wide-angle tilt-shift lens is the best solution. With this piece of kit, the perspective in the photos can be adjusted through shifting the lenses to the right angle, which means that you'll be able to capture all those right angles and vertical lines perfectly on-site, rather than relying on post-production.

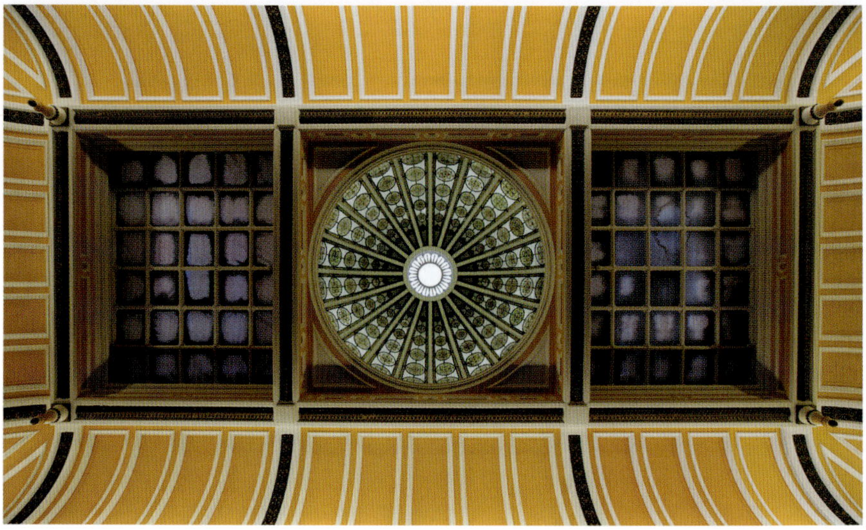

USING A TRIPOD

In order to get the crispest images, especially when shooting interiors, which are often darker than your eyes would have you believe, you will likely be forced to extend the shutter speed to the point that a tripod is required. Alternatively, you might be working with a narrow aperture, at an average value of *f*/11, for example, in order to get everything in a large space in focus, which may then also require a slow shutter speed. Using a tripod and slowing the shutter speed can also allow you to capture the effect of movement in a space; people walking around a building or cars in the street. Anything over 1/15 seconds can start to produce this effect, although it does depend on the speed of the movement, so I recommend doing a few experiments.

But in order to achieve the level at which you will get the most out of using a tripod, the best advice may be to leave your tripod at home. By doing this you free yourself from the shackles of slow photography, not to mention the burden of having to carry the tripod around with you all day. This way you can really explore a building, get to know how it feels, and seek out the best spaces for compositions that tell its story. You may end up compromising on quality, due to poor light quality, or falling short of an absolutely perfect composition, due to not spending ages composing the frame – but you will simply take more photographs without a tripod. You will also find out, when you later review them, just how many shots really don't require a tripod at all, as well as the kinds of situations when you will actually benefit from using one.

ABOVE
Capturing the full detail of this ceiling required a wide-angle setup, as well as a tripod.

RIGHT
When it comes to capturing highly ornate architectural details, a tilt-shift lens will allow you to achieve perfect perspective. As previously mentioned, these lenses are not particularly cheap, however.

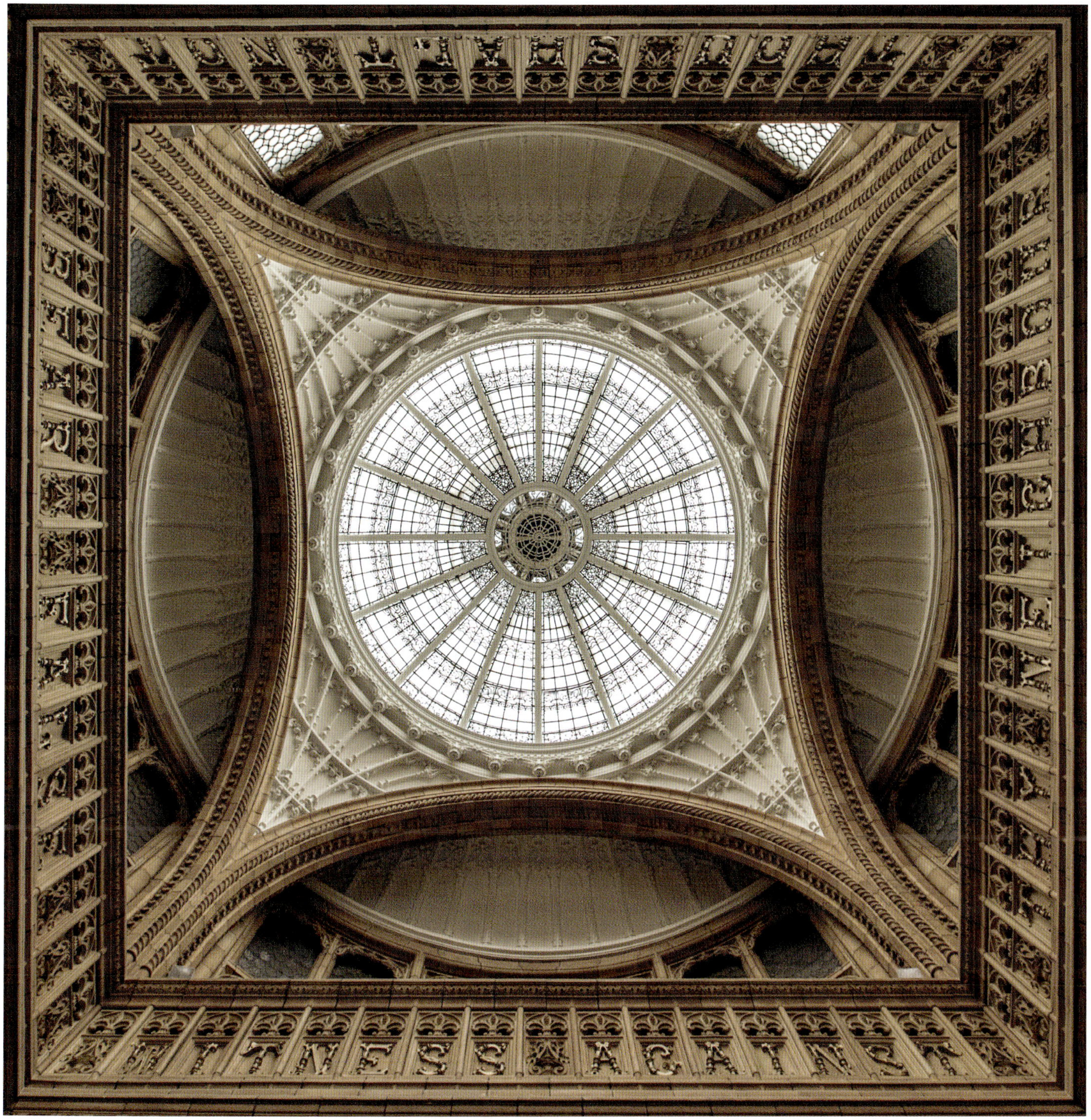

CONCRETE

I cannot write a chapter about architecture without talking about one of its most revolutionary materials: concrete. Concrete buildings have been built since the turn of the 20th century, but it is more typically associated with the Brutalist architecture that flourished in the 1950s to '70s across the globe. Brutalism is a utilitarian aesethetic that embraces a kind of ugliness, in terms at least of the way it ultilizes raw materials like exposed concrete and infrastructural elements, but it produced highly experimental works of architecture that many nevertheless consider to be beautiful, and which are a joy to photograph.

Concrete is an amazing material to photograph due to its texture, imperfections, and harsh nature. One tried-and-tested approach is to shoot it in black and white. You need to have a good reason to shoot without colour, but concrete offers this because of its consistent surfaces and solidity of form, which can be powerfully animated by shadows.

The concrete in brutalist buildings often forms the most expressive part of the design, as it is a material that can be moulded into any form imaginable. Buildings of this style often consist of harsh angles and unusual textures. Dramatic by nature, black and white is the ideal form for emphasizing the moodiness of this architecture. In more recent times, there has also been a renaissance in using concrete contemporary architecture now that the techniques for casting it have evolved from the rougher mix of large stones and cement prevalent in the 1960s. The concrete that is used in contemporary designs often has a smoother surface, and can be moulded into more complex organic forms, thanks to advances in technology.

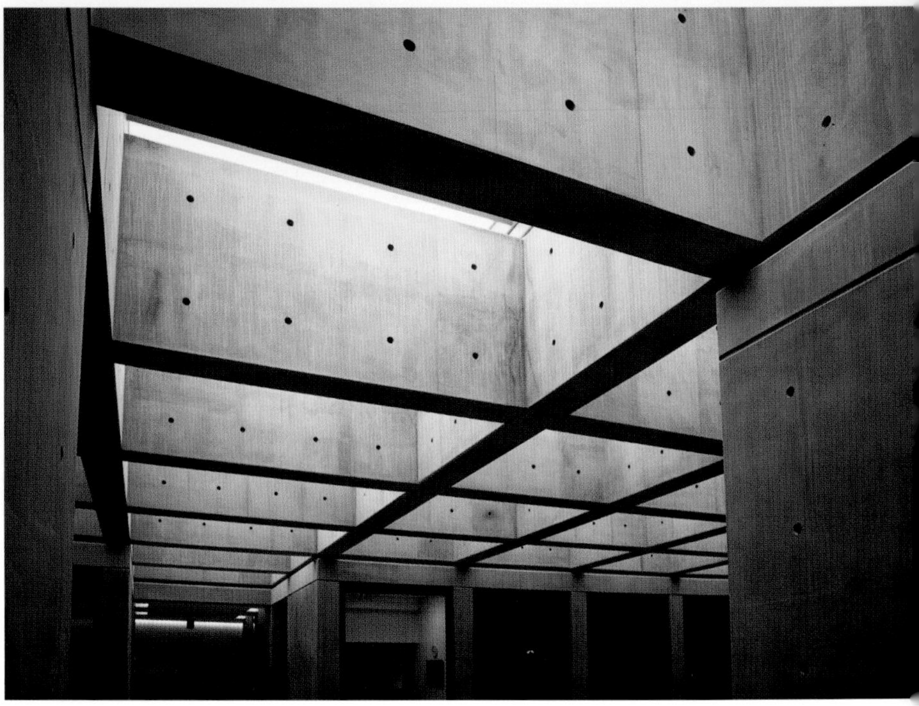

ABOVE
In this shot of the exposed concrete structure of the Angel Building in London, the play light and shadow across the concrete ceiling structure help to make the photo work in black and white.

RIGHT
The shapes textures of this 1960s tower are extenuated by the use of black and white in the photograph.

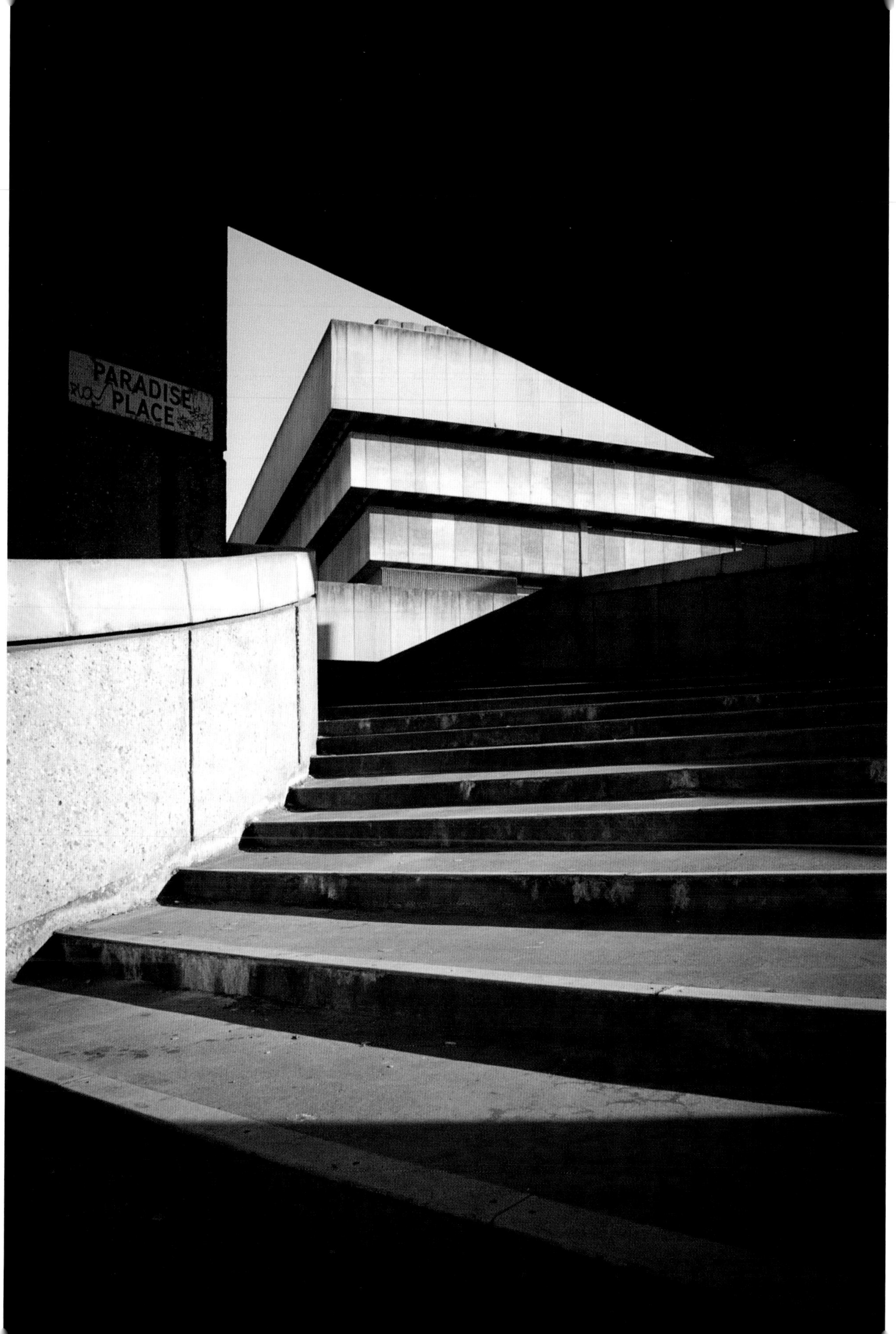
PARADISE
PLACE

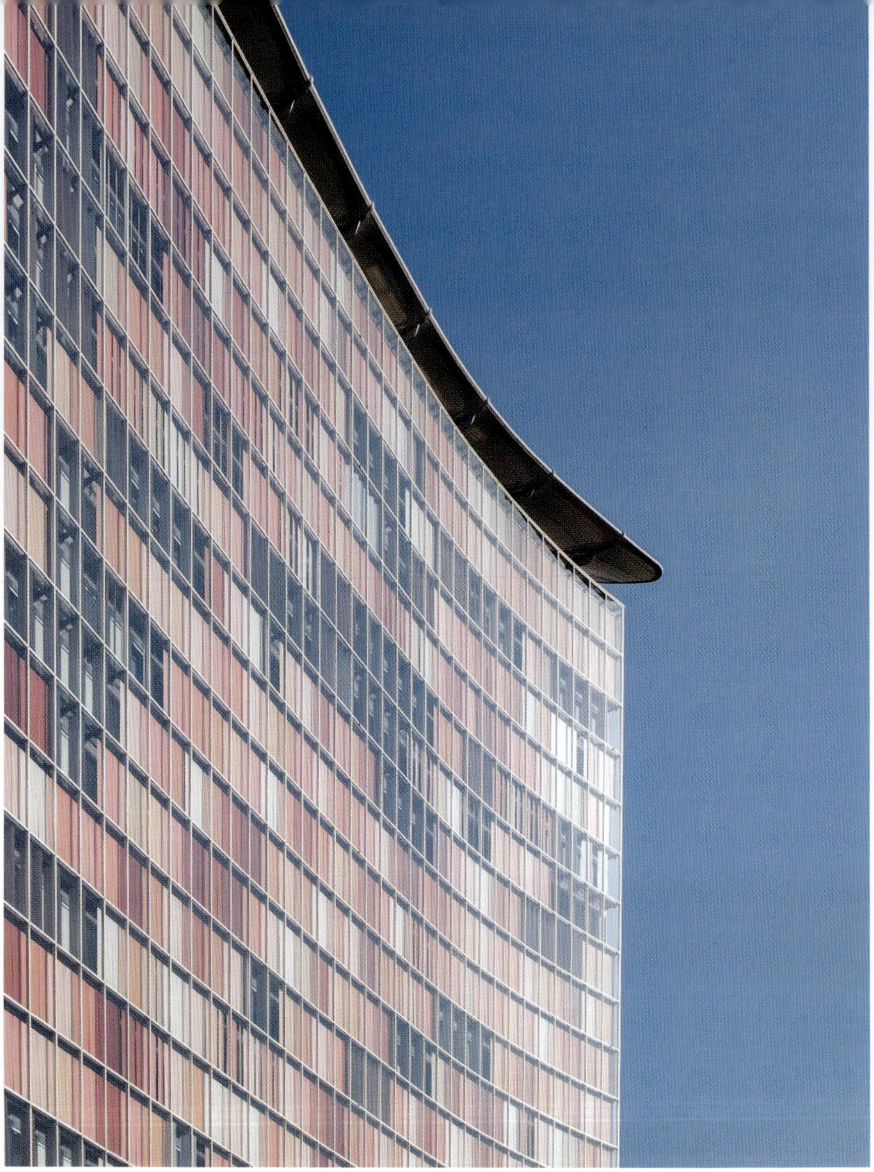

GLASS

Today, the hulking structures of concrete favoured in the 1970s have been largely replaced by enormous glass structures. Advances in technology mean that cities are now complemented by huge buildings comprised entirely of glass on the outside. Since the 1980s, tall skyscrapers have been built with facades made up of glass systems, and it is difficult to miss their prominence on the skyline. Much of the time, these glass buildings offer interesting structural shapes rather than the stark textured geometric textures of their concrete counterparts, but this material provides other qualities for a photographer to play with.

Firstly, glass is great for forming reflections of other buildings and also for reflecting sunlight into places you wouldn't expect to see it. You can use glass as a mirror and the buildings as a series of elements reflected within it, creating an effect much like a funfair hall of mirrors. Think about how the reflections create patterns on the street and appear to paint the pavements with different colours and interesting shapes. At night, you can use these reflections to even greater effect. The image opposite shows the refection of the colourful street below in the glazed facade, giving a blurred, abstract effect across the regular grid, although by looking closely you can make out some elements within the reflection.

Think also about the transparency of glazing and how that can be used to create interesting compositions. The different colours of the blinds in the building in the shot above animate the composition. The view will change throughout the day as people open and close their blinds in different parts of the building.

If the concrete architecture of the 1950s to '70s represented one vision of modernity, contemporary glass structures equally represent today's mantra of the modern. Buildings used to be built from the outside in, the shape of the external structure lending itself to concrete; now, buildings are formed from within, and the glazing forms a delicate wrapping around the building, shielding it from the outside. This is the beautiful aspect of these contemporary buildings, one which we can use to our advantage as photographers.

ABOVE
Capturing the changing shapes and patterns formed by the blinds drawn and open throughout the day would make an interesting project for a photographer with patience.

RIGHT
This shot highlights the potential of glass to create interesting reflections. All the different colours sit on the surface of this shot like oil, but some recognizable features are also visible.

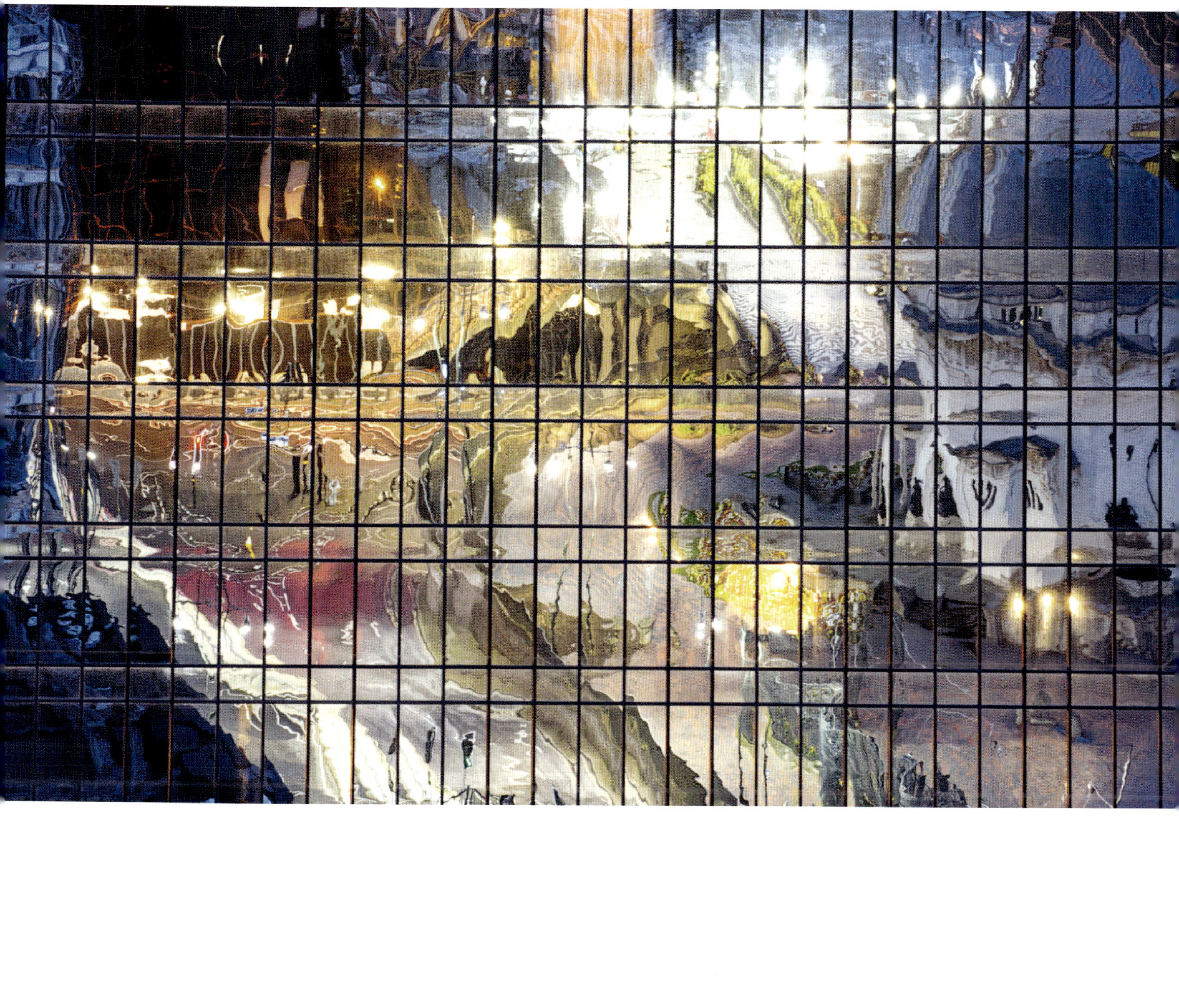

FINDING YOUR ARCHITECT

ZAHA HADID

Zaha Hadid was an Iraqi born architect whose practice created some of the world's most iconic buildings. I've picked out her work because it represents the epitome of contemporary architecture, and always offers excellent photographic opportunities. Do some research to see if there are any of her buildings close to you, or take the opportunity to travel to one of them to appreciate how spectacular they are in person.

Her work pushes the boundaries of architecture, using parametric modelling to form sculptural forms that flow to create spaces and places. The Heyday Alive Cultural Centre in Baku, Azerbaijan, has an undulating roof that appears to softly melt over the building to shelter the spaces within. The Aquatics Centre in London has a central roof that is supported in only three places, creating a cathedral-like space within for the main swimming pool. The list goes on, but every building she created is a unique piece of architecture that responds specifically to its particular context.

One such example of her work is the MAXXI Museum in Rome, Italy, shown here. This concrete structure won acclaim for the way the spaces for the galleries are woven around the central atrium space, which runs as a curve from one end of the building to the other. The space is full of flying staircases that transport you between the gallery spaces over multiple levels.

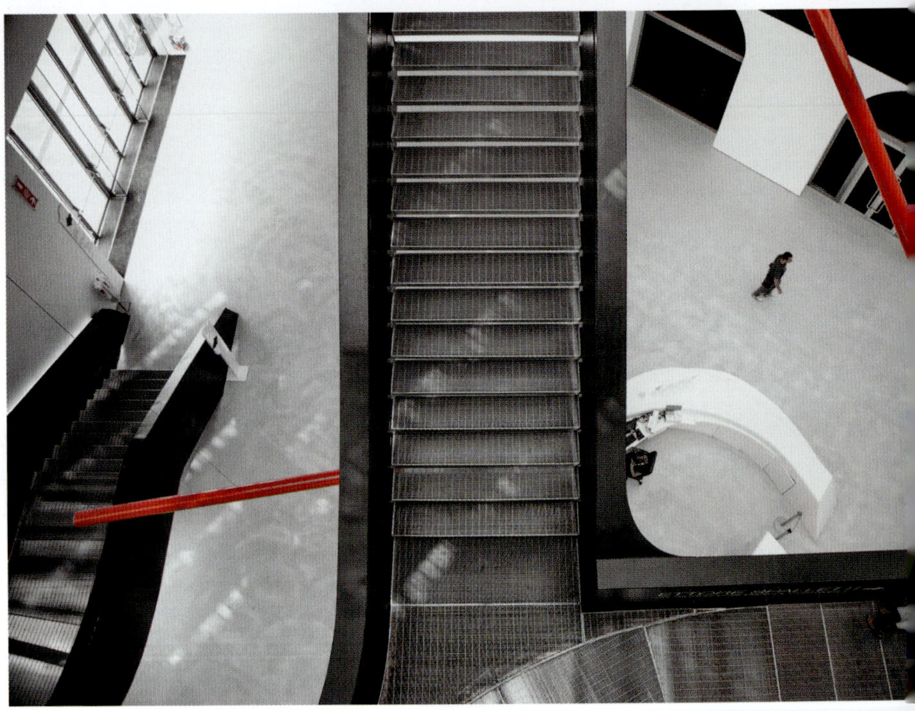

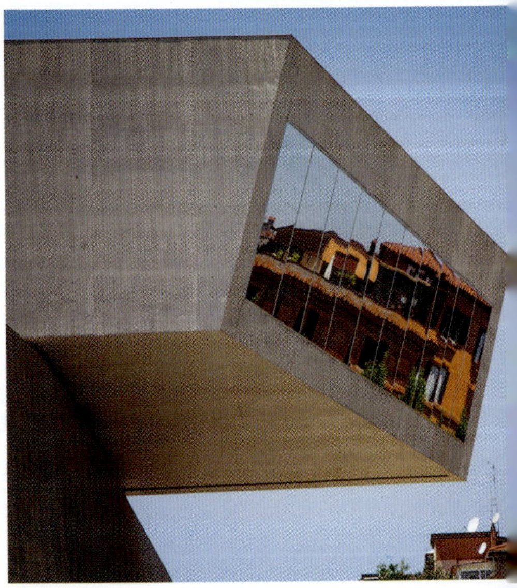

ABOVE
The staircases are one of the key features of the MAXXI Museum in Rome, so I would focus on these in a visit. The result is almost abstract, helped by the very limited colour palette.

RIGHT
Another main feature of the museum, and strong shapes and complementary colours are always good to photograph.

LUDWIG MIES VAN DER ROHE

Ludwig Mies van der Rohe was one of the most famous and influential architects of the early 20th century, pioneering modernist architecture alongside his contemporaries Le Corbusier, Walter Gropius and Frank Lloyd Wright. The modernist style was one of simplicity and extreme clarity. Van der Rohe's buildings are based around open spaces, in which minimal structure is used – moving away from the notion that walls should be load-bearing and rigidly define internal space. He used modern materials like steel and large amounts of glazing to create his modernist aesthetic.

The Barcelona Pavilion shown here was constructed for the 1929 International Exposition in Barcelona, Spain, and it is a great example of modernist architecture. It uses extravagant materials but has a simple form, with fully glazed walls and a roof that appears to float over the small walls that hold it up. The walls are carefully positioned to define the internal space, and internal courtyards are incorporated as places of tranquility within. The famous Barcelona chair, which was also designed for the exhibition, is the only piece of furniture used, and a sculpture is the only other object of note to break the fluidity of the space.

The building is great to photograph due to its clean lines and rigorous attention to detail. If you are able to visit, think about symmetry and how you can use the strong 90-degree angles of the building to create bold and graphic compositions.

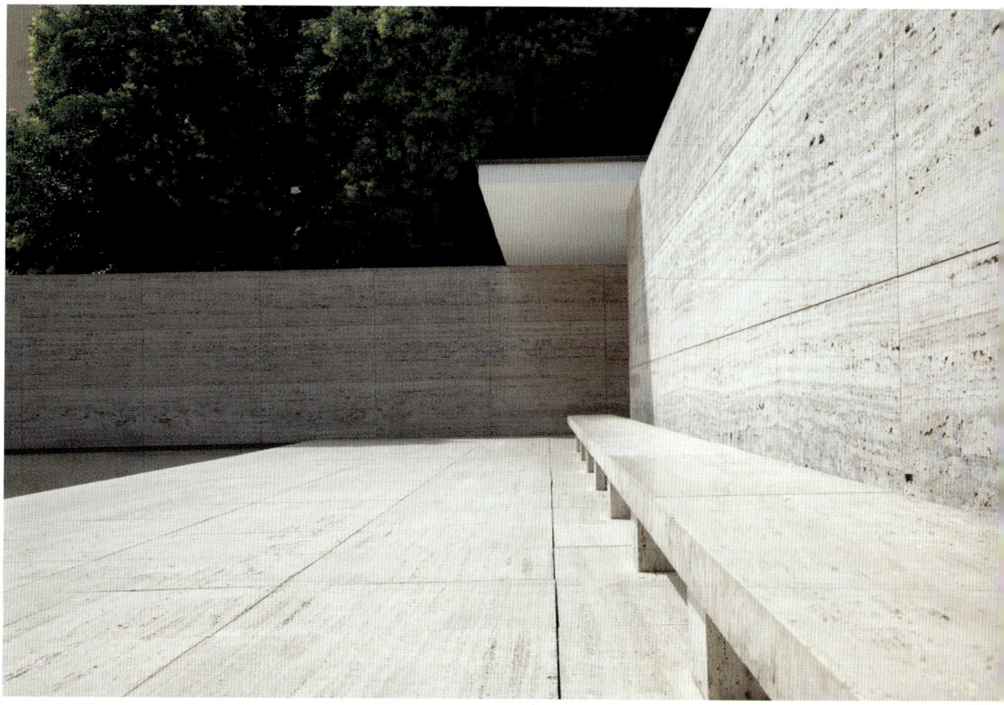

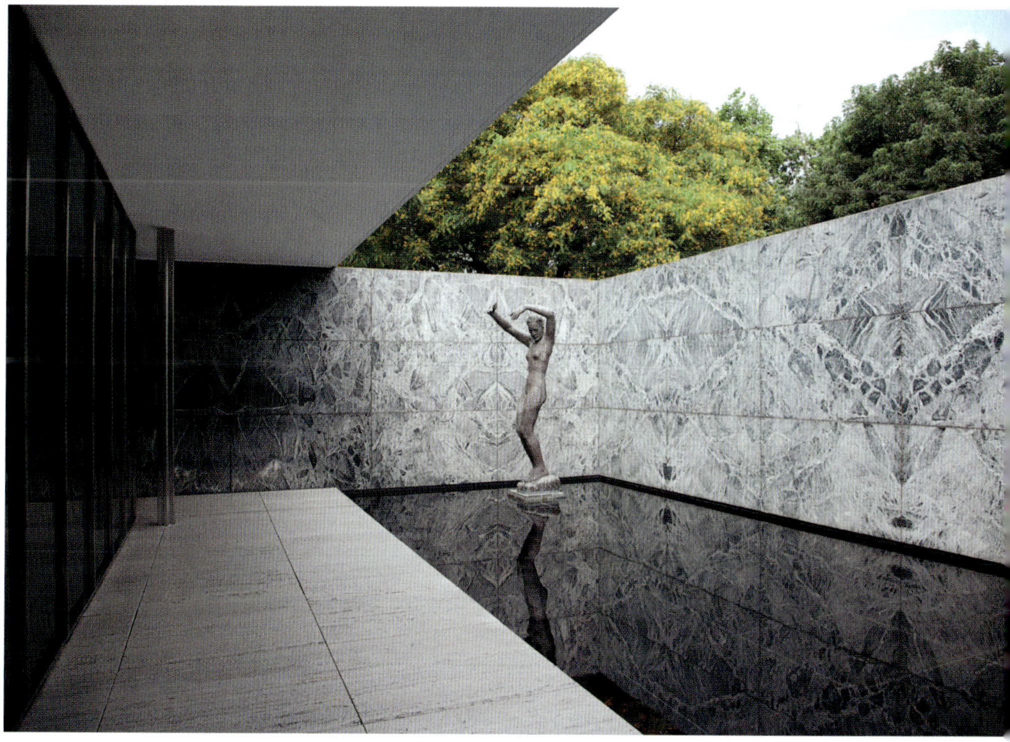

RIGHT, TOP
Clean lines convey the light in this tranquil, airy space.

RIGHT, BOTTOM
Look for lines and shapes to divide the frame and draw the eye towards a focal point.

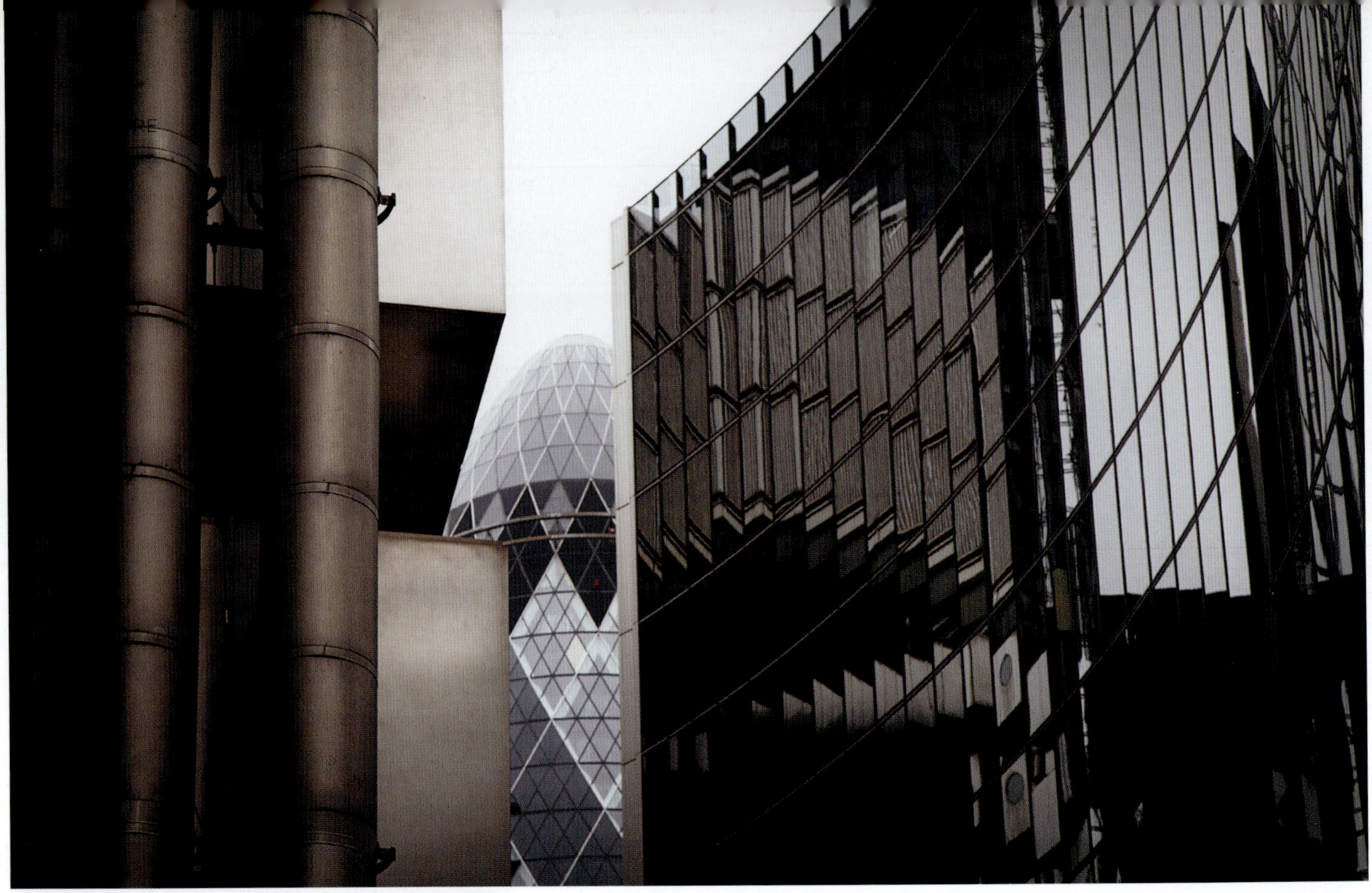

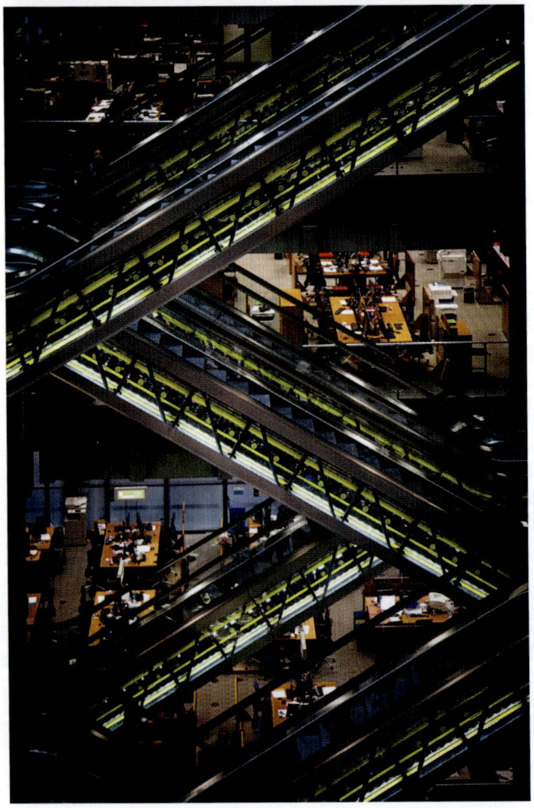

RICHARD ROGERS

Rogers is a British architect famous for his so-called high-tech architecture. One of his most notable works is the Pompidou Centre, an expressive steel frame structure quite unlike its surroundings in Paris. His highly engineered approach led to a long list of buildings with intricate detailing to the structure, often sculptural in form. The structural trusses that hold up the roof at the Barajas Airport in Madrid are painted a striking colour that draws attention and is the most significant part of the building.

The landmark Lloyds building in London, shown here, is a fine example of Rogers's architectural approach. The ductwork, lifts and pipework, which would normally be hidden away, are exposed on the facade of the building. The concept was first used on the Pompidou Centre, and the approach gives interior spaces that are completely free from services, creating large open-plan areas that can be modified over time.

ABOVE
The Lloyds building, on the left here, in the context of the other fantastic, modern architecture that London is known for.

LEFT
The zig-zag of the escalators brings an appropriately dynamic sense to a busy workspace.

RIGHT
As previously mentioned, looking directly up is a great way to offer a new perspective, and it works brilliantly here to capture the impressive structure of this space.

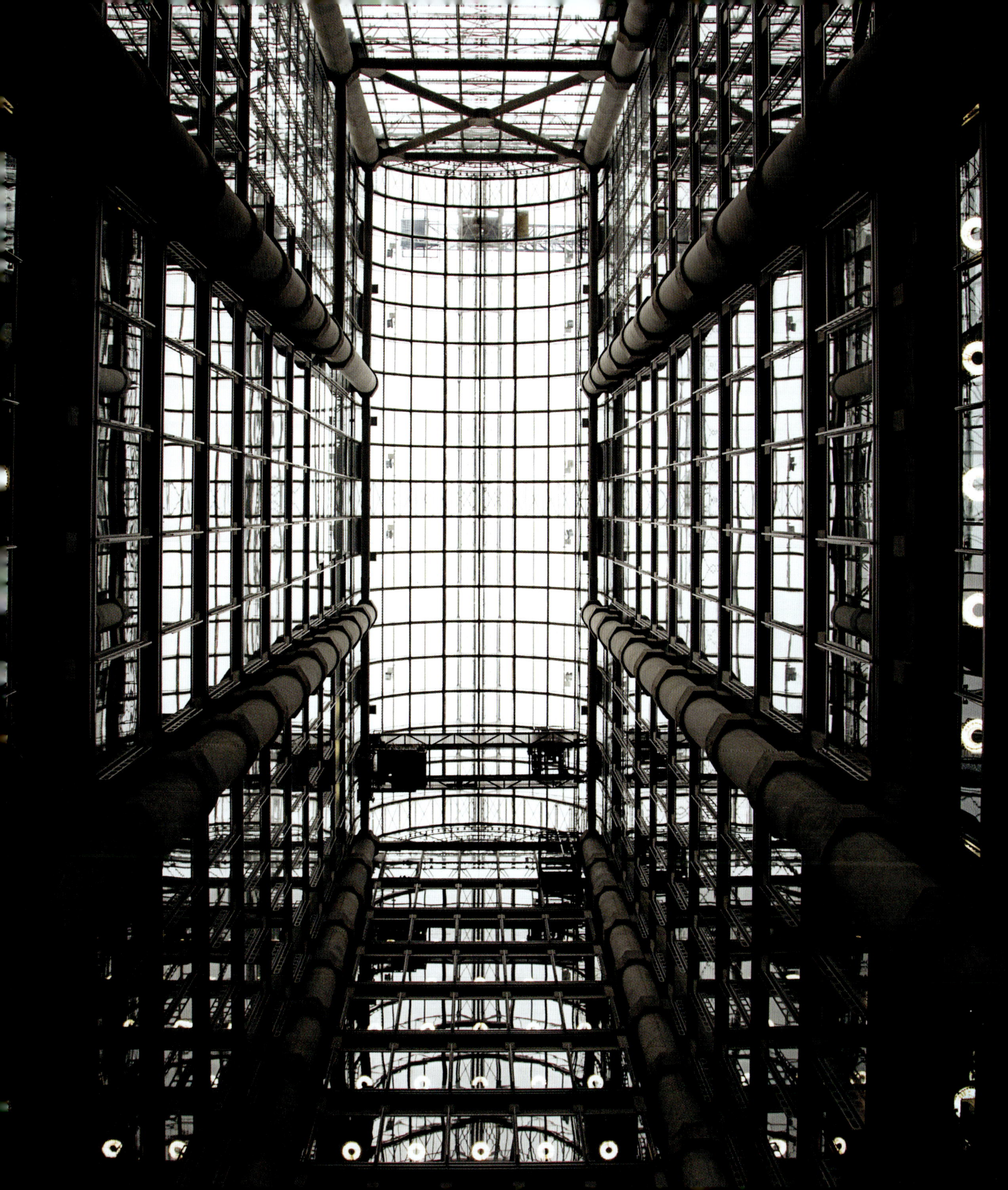

5 CITIZENS OF THE CITY

Street photography may be the single most challenging genre of urban photography. It's about the chance encounter, so a huge part of it is out of your control. Photographing strangers can be daunting – to catch the candid moment, you're not generally asking people's permission before you press the shutter. But the citizens of the city are an important aspect of urban photography, and you'll be missing out if you don't give it a go.

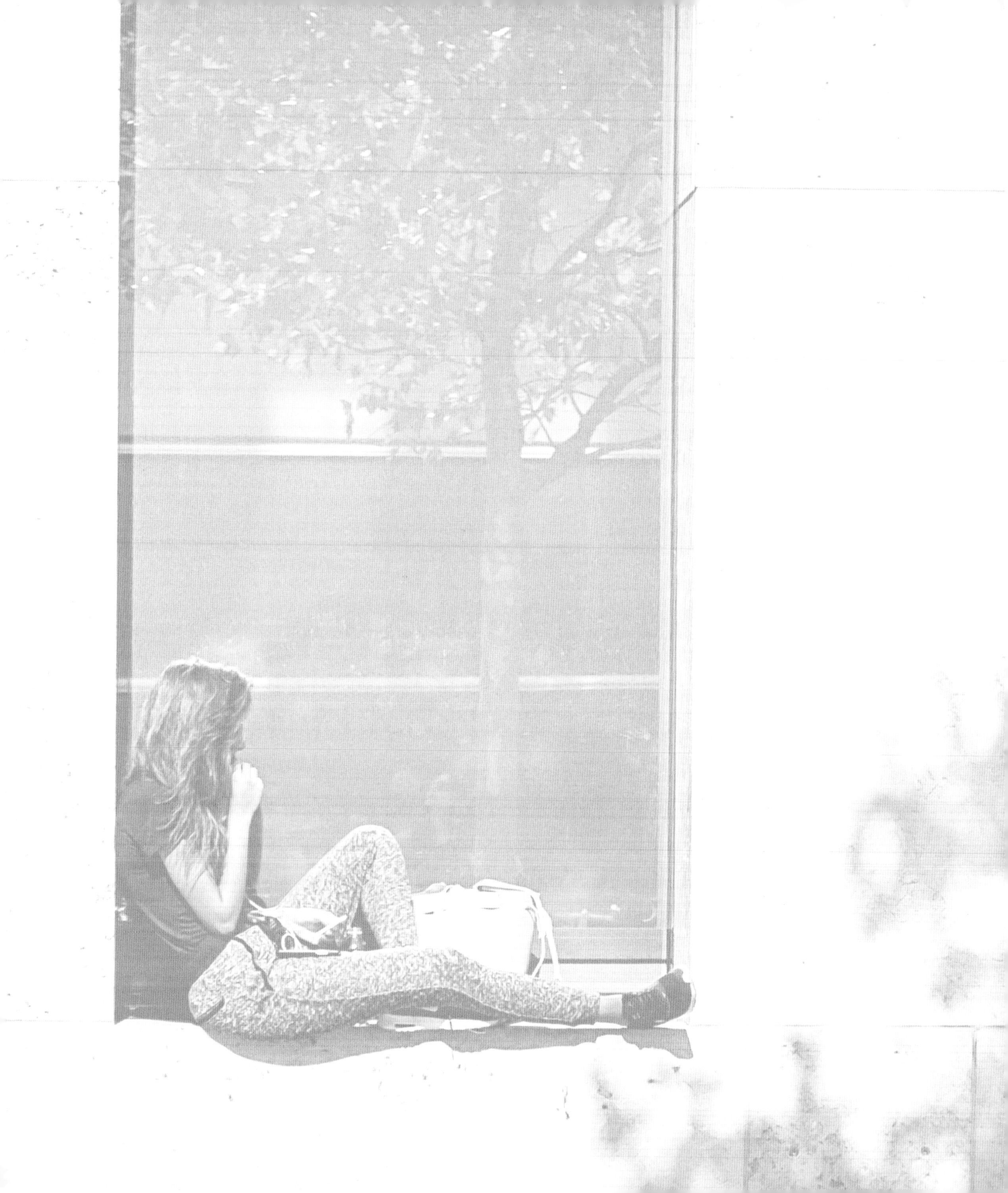

STREET PHOTOGRAPHY

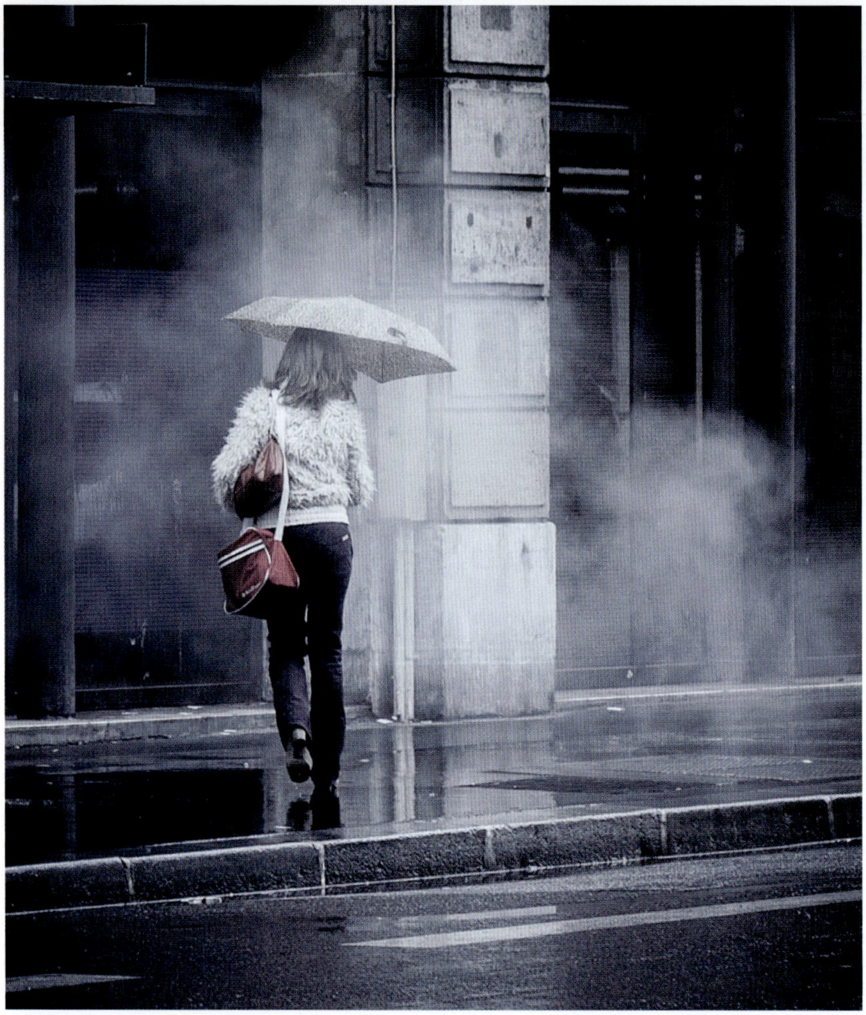

Street photography has many definitions. It was born out of a desire to capture the everyday life of people and places, while providing a narrative that invokes a reaction from the viewer. It's the man reading the newspaper in a café, the dog with sunglasses on or the lady dressed in bright colours, walking down the street. The results are moments in time that can tell a story that may be a provocative comment on society, a humorous moment or simply something that's visually stimulating.

Street photography is about capturing humanity. When you take to the streets, you want to be in tune with what is happening around you, always looking out for that perfect moment. Switch your phone off or turn it on silent, take your headphones out, and dial into your surroundings. Concentrate on observing, and see the photographic opportunities around you. It may be someone who stands out from the crowd, or a piece of street art that you'd like to use as a backdrop – and then you stop and wait for the right person to walk past it.

Street photography makes a good contrast and complement to more traditional urban photography styles, which are centred around the solid built environment. With street photography, you're looking for the fleeting things, so it gets you to think on your feet on a completely different level, and being constantly on the lookout for 'the shot' certainly sharpens your photographic eye.

ABOVE
Moody weather like this gives a perfect backdrop for street photography. You line up your shot, and wait for the right person to walk into it.

OPPOSITE
Children run through the Botanical Gardens in Paris. This was a chance capture, when they ran across the frame, demonstrating the incidental nature of street photography.

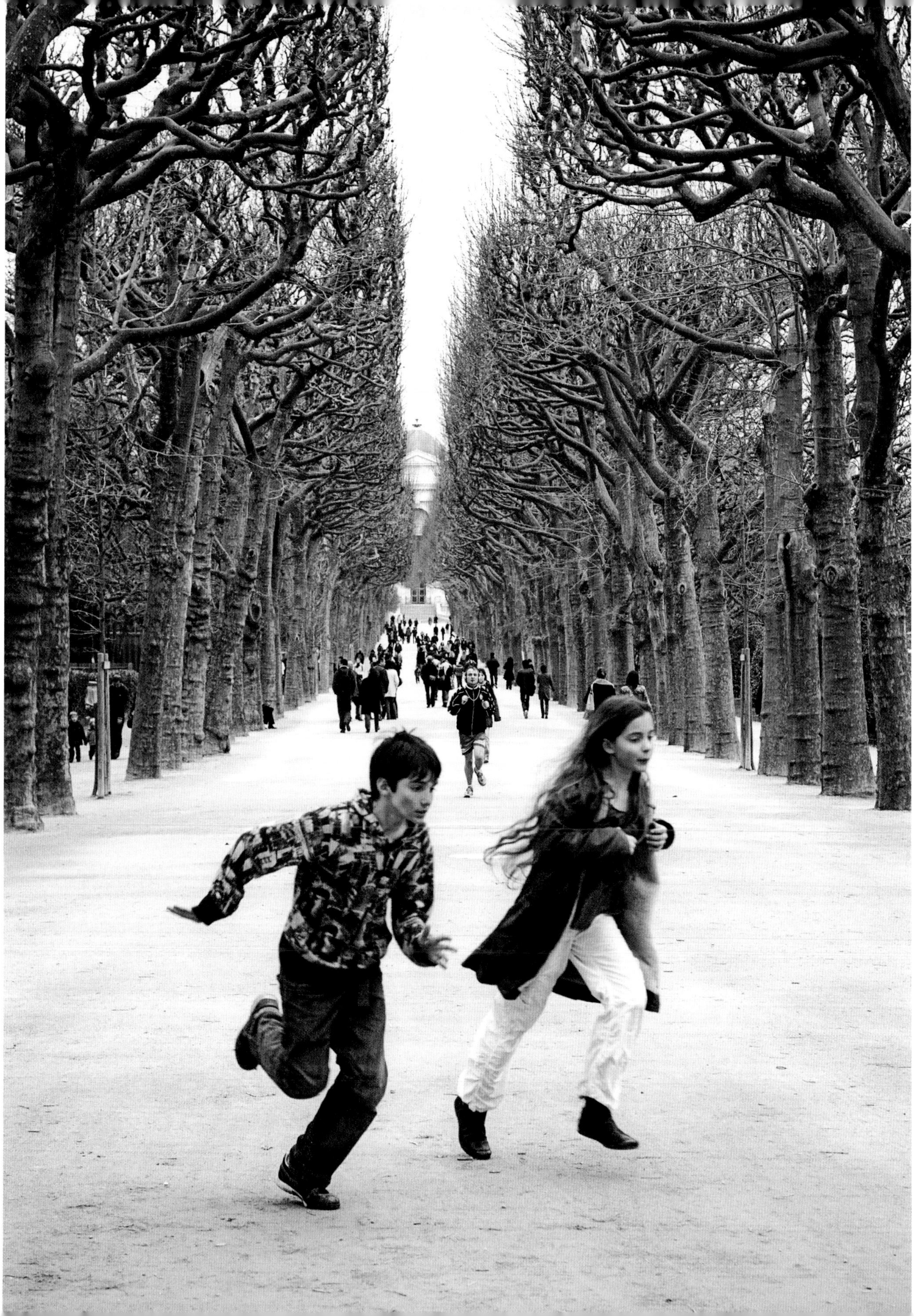

HERO
HENRI CARTIER-BRESSON

Henri Cartier-Bresson is famous for his photographs of Paris, and he is thought of as one of the pioneers of street photography. He was driven by what he called the 'decisive moment', meaning not only the moment in which a photograph is taken, but also much more than that. The meaning is demonstrated in many of his most famous works, the standout being a shot of a man leaping off a ladder into a puddle (right). The man is caught mid-flight, a millisecond before he hits the water.

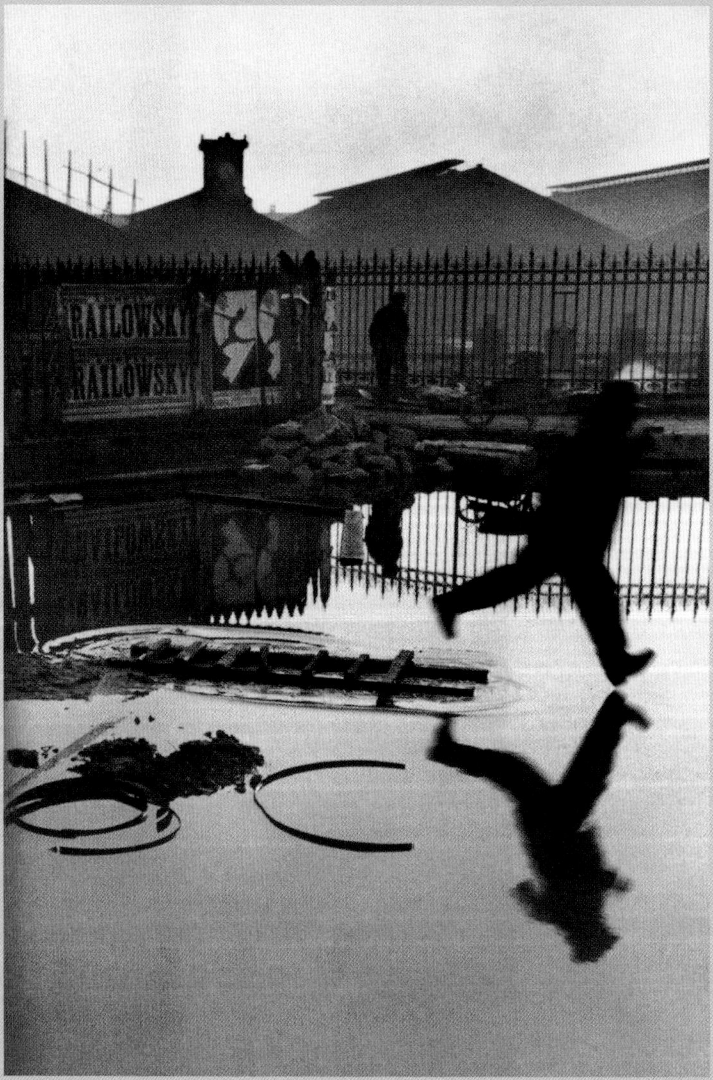

If you're looking to try and emulate the style of Cartier-Bresson, make the 'decisive moment' a kind of photographic philosophy. This is about the anticipatory aspect of street photography: if you spot a scene where something might happen, then you can simply stand and wait for whatever it may be to unfold in front of your lens. Think as well about composition. The cyclist in Cartier-Bresson's photograph opposite completes to composition. The stair and curving street just wouldn't work as well without the cyclist moving through it.

His photographs are so powerful in the way they are executed that it becomes unimportant whether or not they are perfectly in focus, or the lines perfectly straight. This is the beautiful thing about street photography: The most important thing is always the what and why of the photo.

LEFT, BELOW
Gare Saint Lazare, 1932.

BELOW
Hyères, France, 1932.

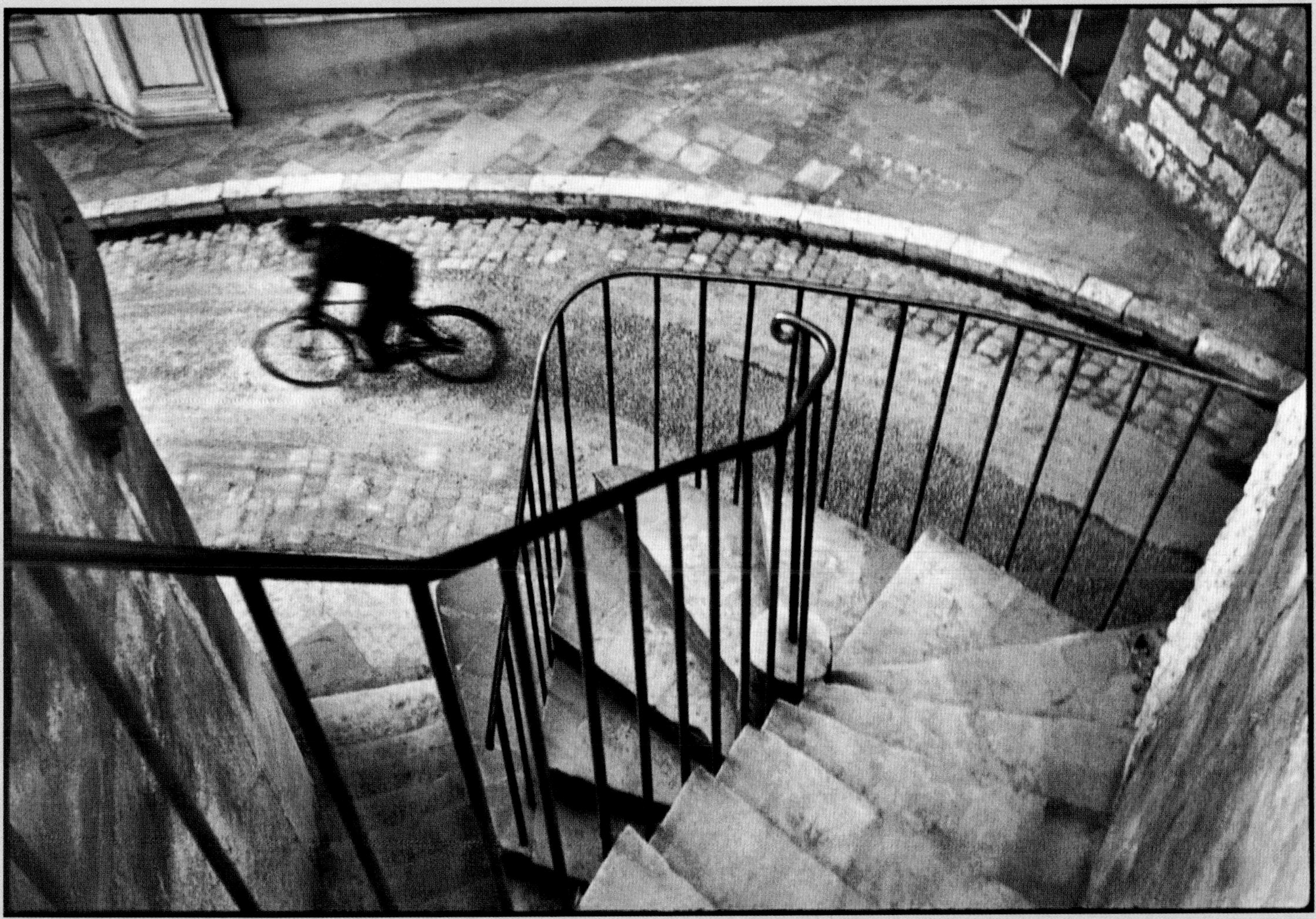

STREET KIT

When approaching street photography, the first thing on your kit list is a good pair of shoes, because you're going to be doing a lot of walking!

Next, think about which camera is best for the type of shots you are after. Generally, the smaller, the better. You want to be as inconspicuous as possible, so your smartphone might be the best choice, or even a small point-and-shoot. With street photography, you don't always have much time to set up your shot, so something that is intelligent with its automatic settings will come in handy.

If you are using a larger DSLR or mirrorless camera, you might want to use a prime lens. The first reason for this is that it will usually be relatively small on your camera body and therefore shouldn't draw too much attention. The second reason is that prime lenses usually have wider maximum apertures, which can make all the difference in low-light situations. These lenses are often referred to as 'fast lenses', because the wider aperture allows a faster shutter speed, and you can find lenses that offer apertures as wide as *f*/2.8 or *f*/1.4.

The choice of focal length is one that defines many street photographers' work. Many photographers swear that the shorter the focal length, the better equipped it is for street photography. You want to be able to get close to your subject in order to provide plenty of depth – a wide angle gives this dimensionality, immersing your viewer in the scene. 35mm (50mm on a full-frame sensor) is generally seen as the sweet spot for street photography – supposedly imitating most closely what the human eye sees.

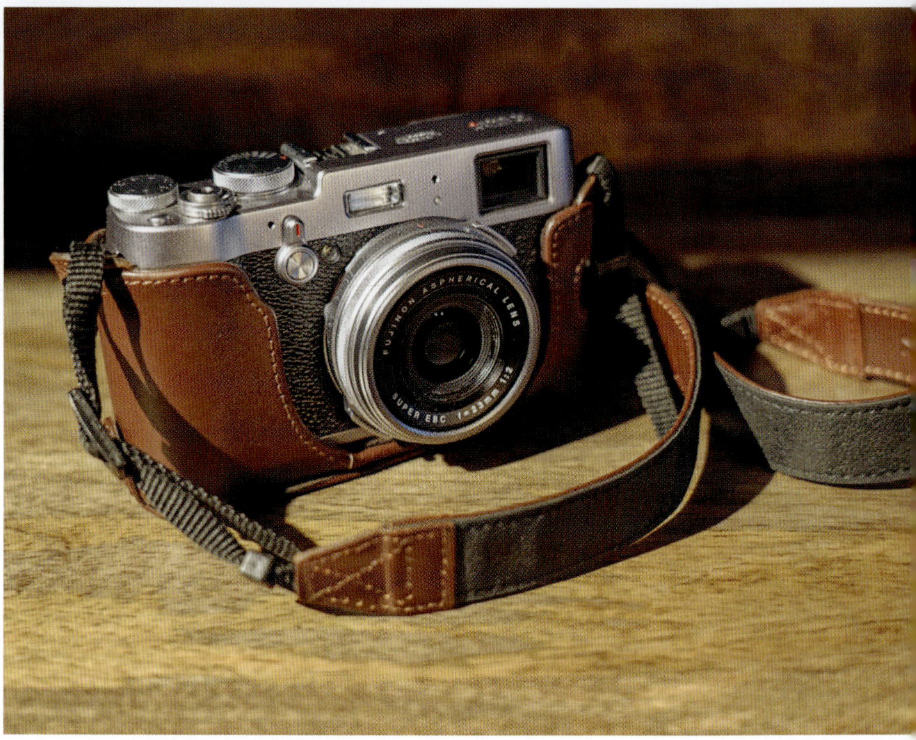

Aside from shoes, you may want to think more widely about the way you dress. Your bright new orange jacket might not be the best thing to wear if you want to stay covert! Some street photographers rather ingeniously disguise themselves as tourists. After all, who is going to question a person taking photographs in Times Square with an 'I Love NYC' t-shirt on? If you want to try this, it's a good idea to take a friend with you – not only will the company boost your confidence, but it will also help give the impression of a pair of tourists wandering the city.

ABOVE
A small camera with a fast prime lens is ideal for street photography.

RIGHT
A short focal length gives the kind of depth and dimensionality that draws a viewer into a photograph, as opposed to a telephoto lens, which will tend to flatten the view.

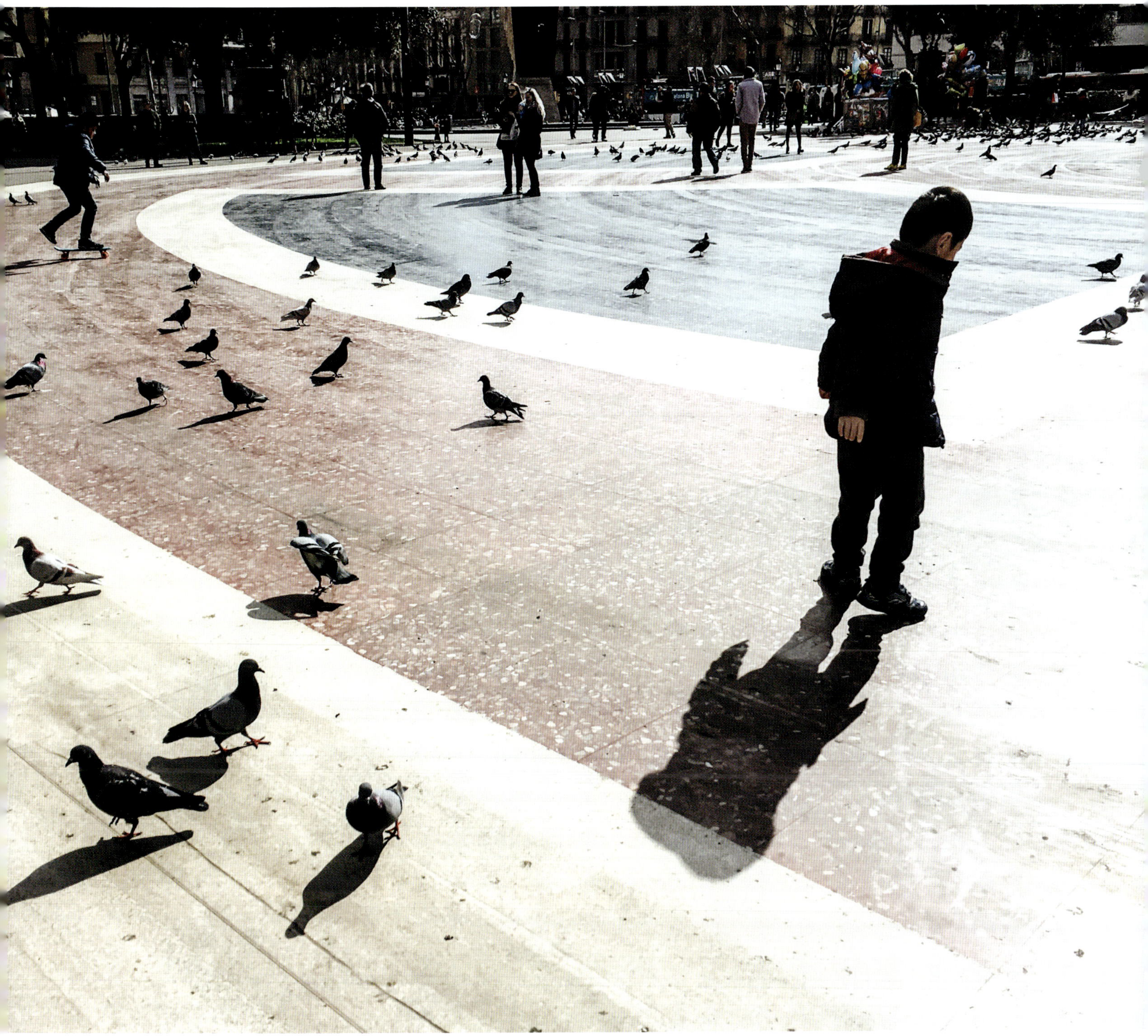

TECHNICAL ASPECTS

As architectural photography is an ideal genre for learning and practising the rules of composition, there are certain techniques and considerations for street photography that will help you get the best shots.

PRE-FOCUSING

This is a relatively simple technique in which you focus for the spot your subject will appear in before they actually arrive on the scene. This means that when you do get that perfect person, you won't lose those crucial seconds while the camera finds its focus on a moving subject when you use autofocus, or while you set it yourself. Here again, a friend can help, and using a narrower aperture (when possible) will allow more leeway for focus. Be mindful that if you are thrashing your camera around, the focus may slip, dependent on how well-weighted the focus ring is in the lens.

COMPOSITION

Composition is always important in photography, but it can be tough to think about it when you are trying to move quickly. In the chaotic urban environment, it can be difficult to set the scene prior to the shot, but by practising the rules we talked about on pages 66–71, they will become second nature. Another thing to think about is the edges of the frame. Certain objects or elements falling off the frame can be a distraction, so when you frame your shot, try to look beyond the main subject. You can of course fix a lot of compositional issues with a clever crop, as we look at on the next page.

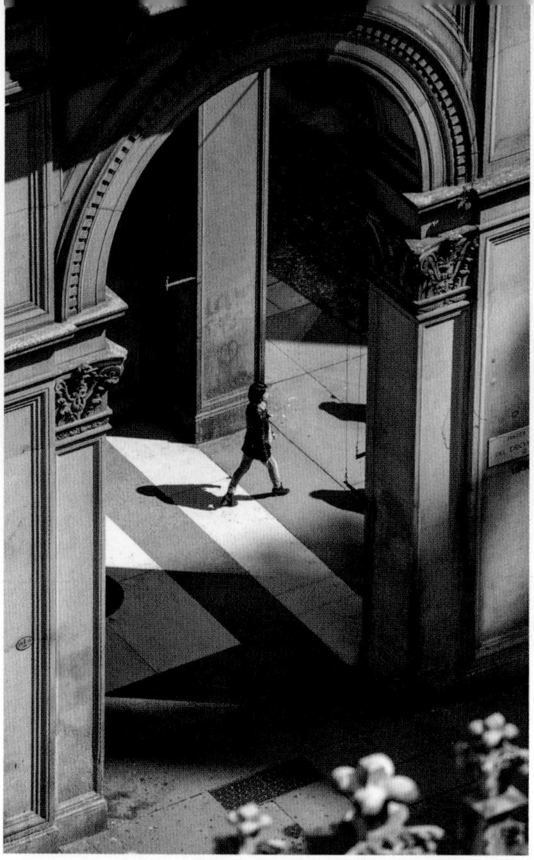

LEFT
The arch of this colonnade in Milan is used to frame the subject.

BELOW
This shot was pre-focused, while I waited for the people to come into view.

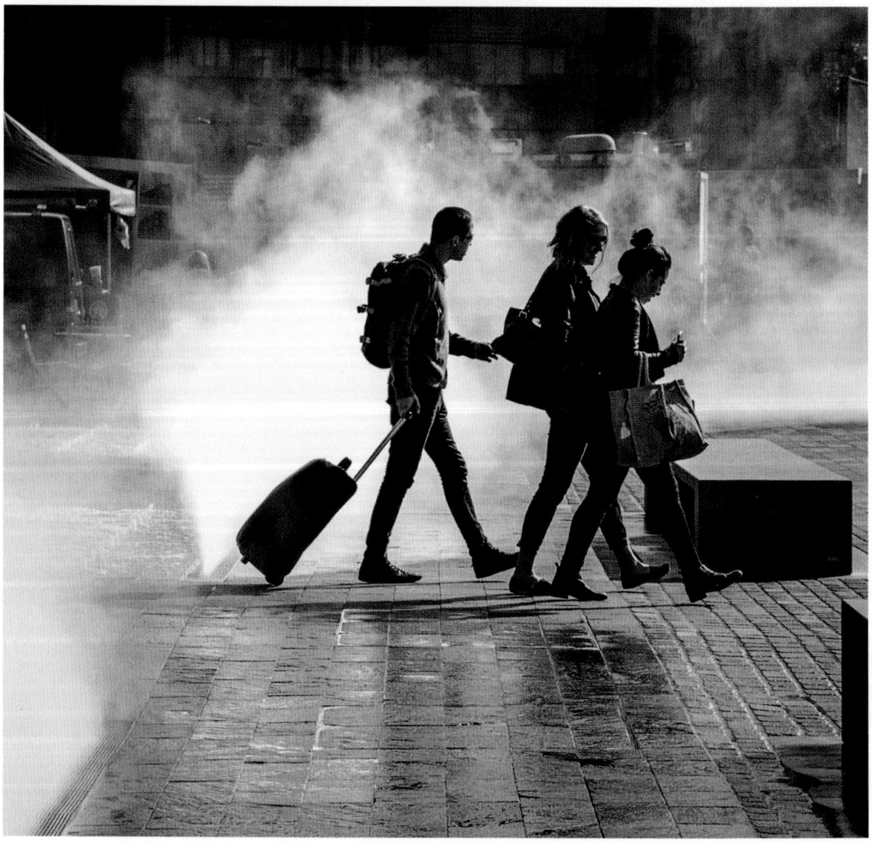

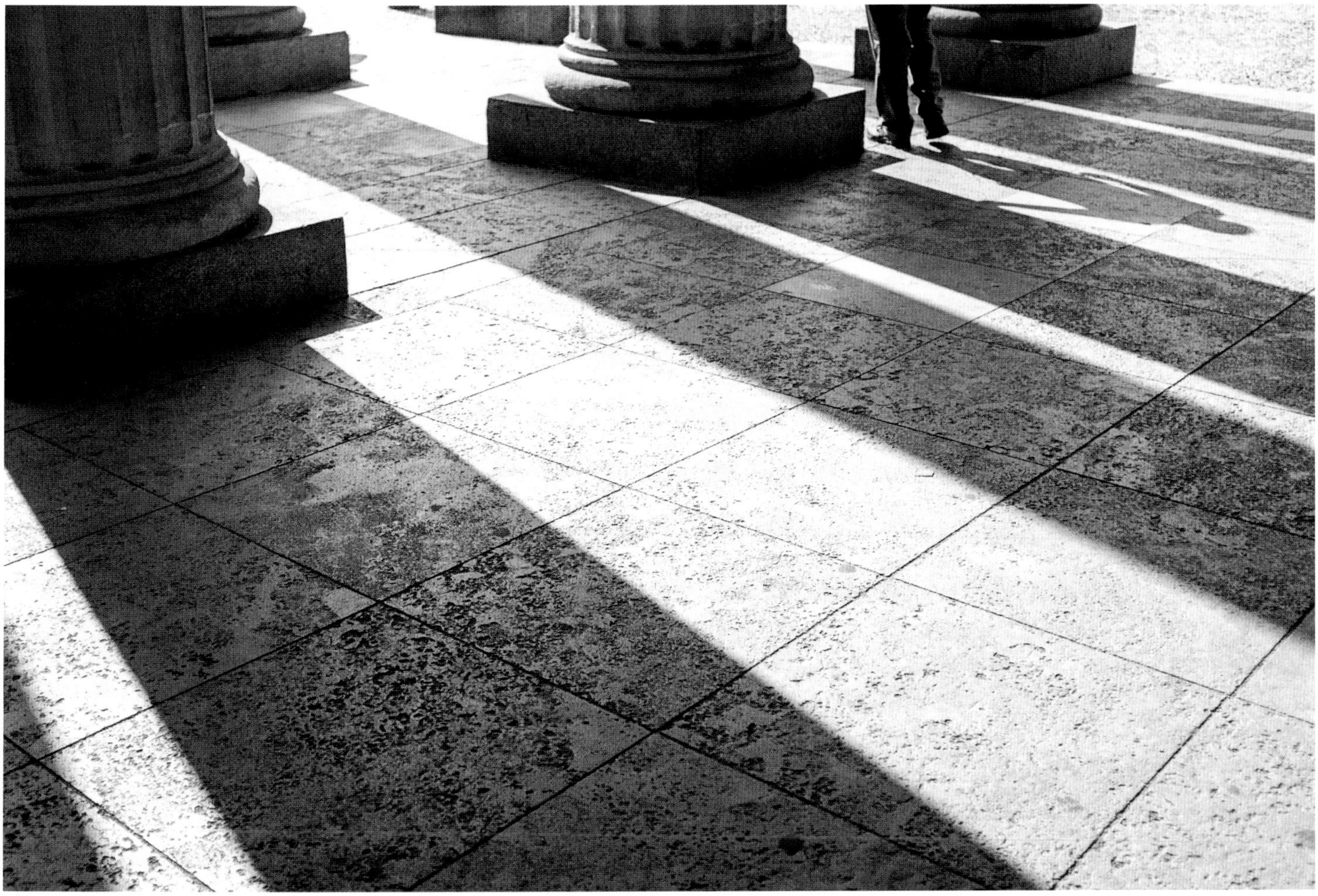

BLACK AND WHITE

Photographing in black and white is a long-held tradition of street photography, predominantly due to the fact that many of the first famous street photographers shot on black-and-white film. The format lends itself to the street because there can be a lot of unnecessary detail in the colour of the backgrounds in the urban environment, and it can also produce a grittier, more documentary feel.

CROPPING

Many street photographers argue that if you need to crop your photos in post-production, then you are probably not getting close enough to your subject. It is worth challenging yourself to get the full frame when you are on the hunt, rather than relying on post-production, because this will ultimately make you a better photographer; however, if it makes the difference between an unsuccessful photograph and a brilliant one, you shouldn't get too hung up on the idea that you can't do any editing.

ABOVE
Showing only a part of a person can make for an intriguing composition. The strong, graphic shadows of the columns, the use of black and white and the fact that the entire shadow is in the frame all help to make this shot successful.

APPROACHING THE STREET

There is no such thing as bad weather for street photography; in rain, snow and conditions that we would normally avoid, you often see more interesting behaviour – and that's exactly what we want when shooting the street.

A good way to approach street photography is to think about places and timing when something of interest may be happening. This might mean an early start to capture commuters on their way to work, people opening up shops, or taking deliveries, for example. As with other styles of urban photography, doing prior research can help a lot.

If you're nervous about shooting people you don't know, try it out on people who you know would like to be photographed, for example street performers – but do be polite and pay them! Aim to get a more interesting shot than the tourists around you may be taking, from an interesting angle, for instance. And then perhaps you can move around to capture people throwing money into the hat, or their reaction to the performance. People will assume that you are shooting the street photographer, but you're really practising for the street by capturing their genuine reactions and interactions.

PHOTOGRAPHING STRANGERS

How do you step it up? How do you take photos of strangers, and what are the best techniques? Start by thinking about permissions, and whether these are required or not. In the UK, you don't really need someone's permission to take their photo, although the normal rules regarding private land as discussed previously are in play. Across the world this is not always the case, however. Again – do your research before you start shooting.

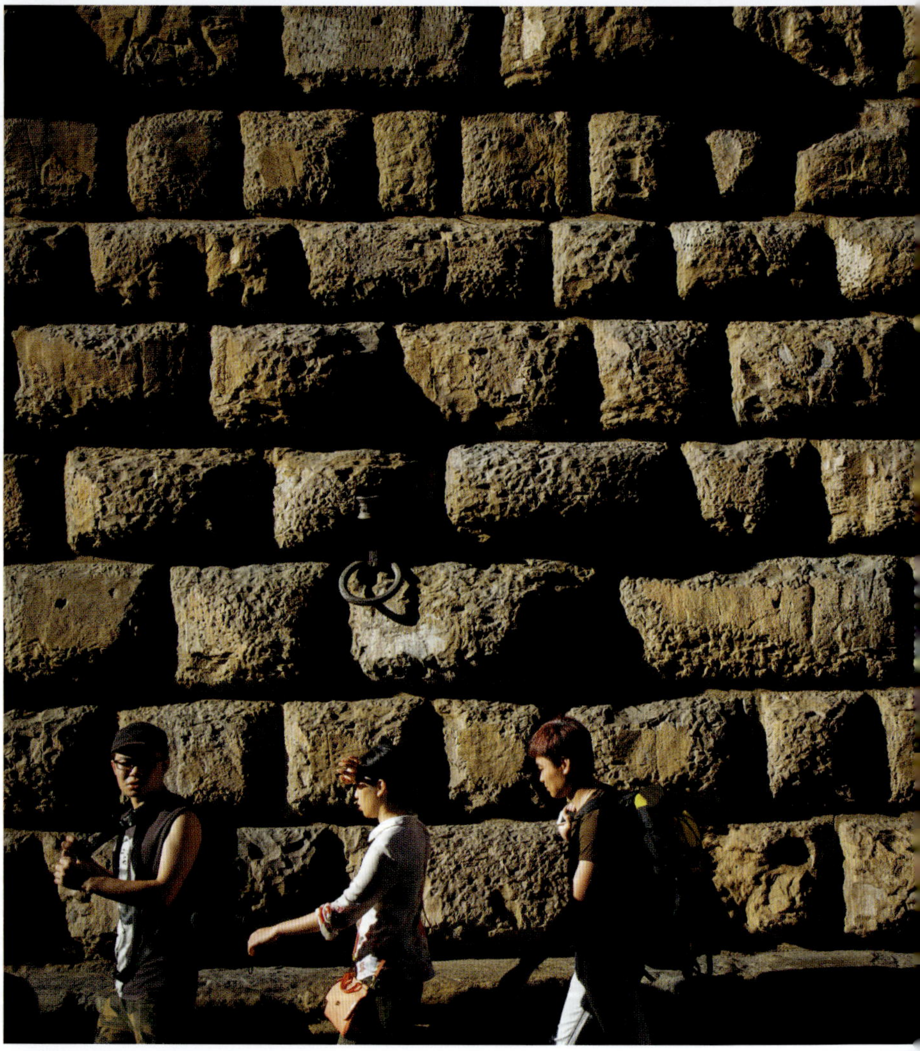

ABOVE
Shooting a wall in Florence, waiting for something interesting to happen, and the one man turns at the right second for the shot.

Depending on how you want to approach street photography, you always have the option of asking people whether they would mind having their photo taken. You will miss out on some of the things that make street photography what it is – the candid expressions, gestures, actions, etc. – since the subject is then staged and the scene is artificial. This is about building up confidence to shoot on the streets, however, and when you ask permission, you will find that the majority of people are willing to let you take their photo. It might help to pay them a compliment first so that they know that your intentions are not to show them in a bad light, and it can help to break the ice on your impromptu photoshoot. Don't feel that you have to really mean what you say – they say that the best street photographers are the best liars – but do be aware of how you are coming across, and be honest about what you want to use the photo for if you're asked.

Another method to build your confidence in shooting the streets is to think about what the worst that could happen would be if someone was unhappy with having their photo taken. If anything does become an issue, your response is an offer to delete the photo you have taken, or even show them the shot and explain what you do. Try not to get high and mighty about your right to take photos, because this will only escalate matters. You have to be prepared to meet the odd person who will take issue with it. Some people are simply more protective of their privacy, and you should respect that.

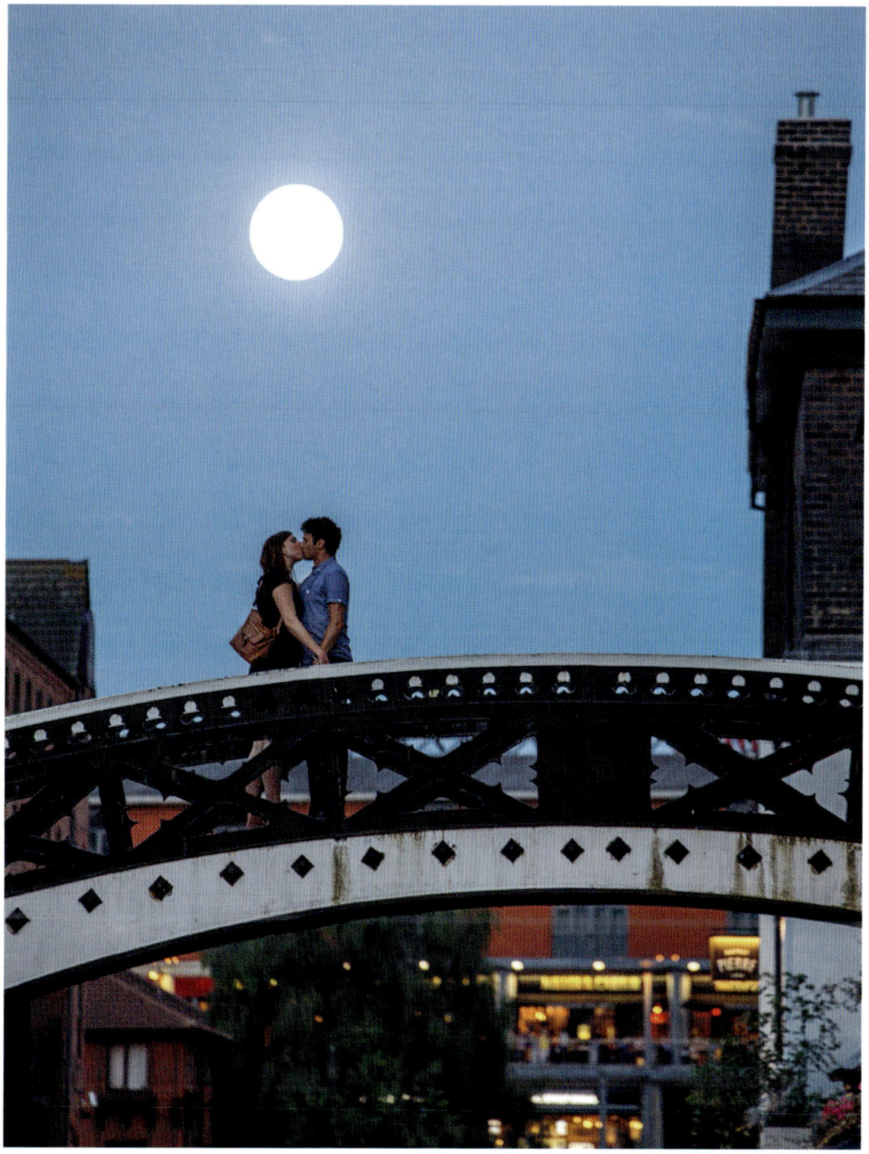

ABOVE
This couple was unaware they were being photographed in front of the full moon on a telephoto lens.

YOUR INVISIBILITY CLOAK

Some people have no trouble with this, but for many it can be a real challenge to build the confidence to approach this type of photography. You might get a moment where you see something out of the corner of your eye, but you are not really that comfortable with getting the shot. In this instance, you could try one of the following tips regarding technique that can help you to become an invisible photographer on the streets. When people don't know you're shooting them, you also stand a better chance of getting the genuine moment, so this advice is really for everyone.

Don't Shoot Them: Pretend you are shooting something behind the person in the frame. When they move out of the shot, keep shooting (or pretending to shoot) the background to convince the person that they weren't part of the original photo.

Disguise: Much like the last technique, you can disguise the fact you have taken a photo by holding the camera up to your eye for a bit longer. Someone may have clocked the fact that you had just got a photo of them, but when they look back and see you still standing there, they will assume that you are shooting something farther away.

Eye Contact: An important thing to remember is not to make eye contact with your subject, because they will immediately know that you are up to something. If you do make eye contact it is easy to look aggressive and people are more likely to be intimidated. You also lose the sense of spontaneity with the scene because they are aware of you.

Get Closer: You might think you are close to your subject, but chances are, you are not close enough. Try taking a photo and then taking a step closer, take another shot, then step closer again, and repeat. Doing this, you can walk all the way past the subject and they will have no idea that they were the subject of your photo.

Videographer: Pretend you are shooting a video. Think about the number of times you have walked in front of a camera that is shooting a video in the city – for some reason it doesn't feel as invasive as someone taking a camera up to their eye and shooting a single frame. You can try this either by setting the camera to live view or by keeping the camera to your eye and moving around. By having the camera to your eye, you will also see people's reactions much better, and this gives you a better chance of spotting something interesting.

Although these methods give you a major advantage if you want to create candid photos, it is also worth noting that on the flip side, your best shot may turn out to be of the one person who does notice you and looks directly into your camera!

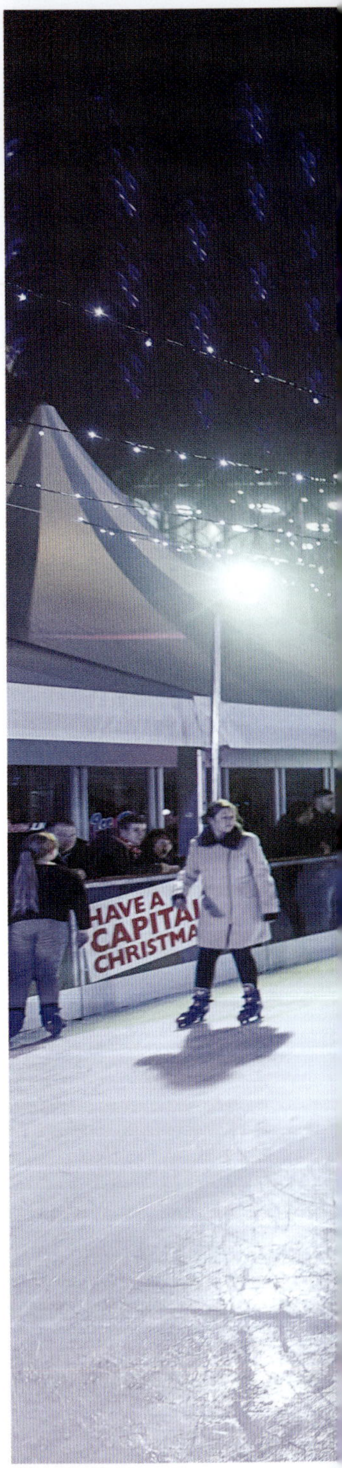

RIGHT
When people are engaged in an activity, they're not going to be looking at you. Public spaces and events like marathons, festivals and demonstrations are all good places to build your confidence.

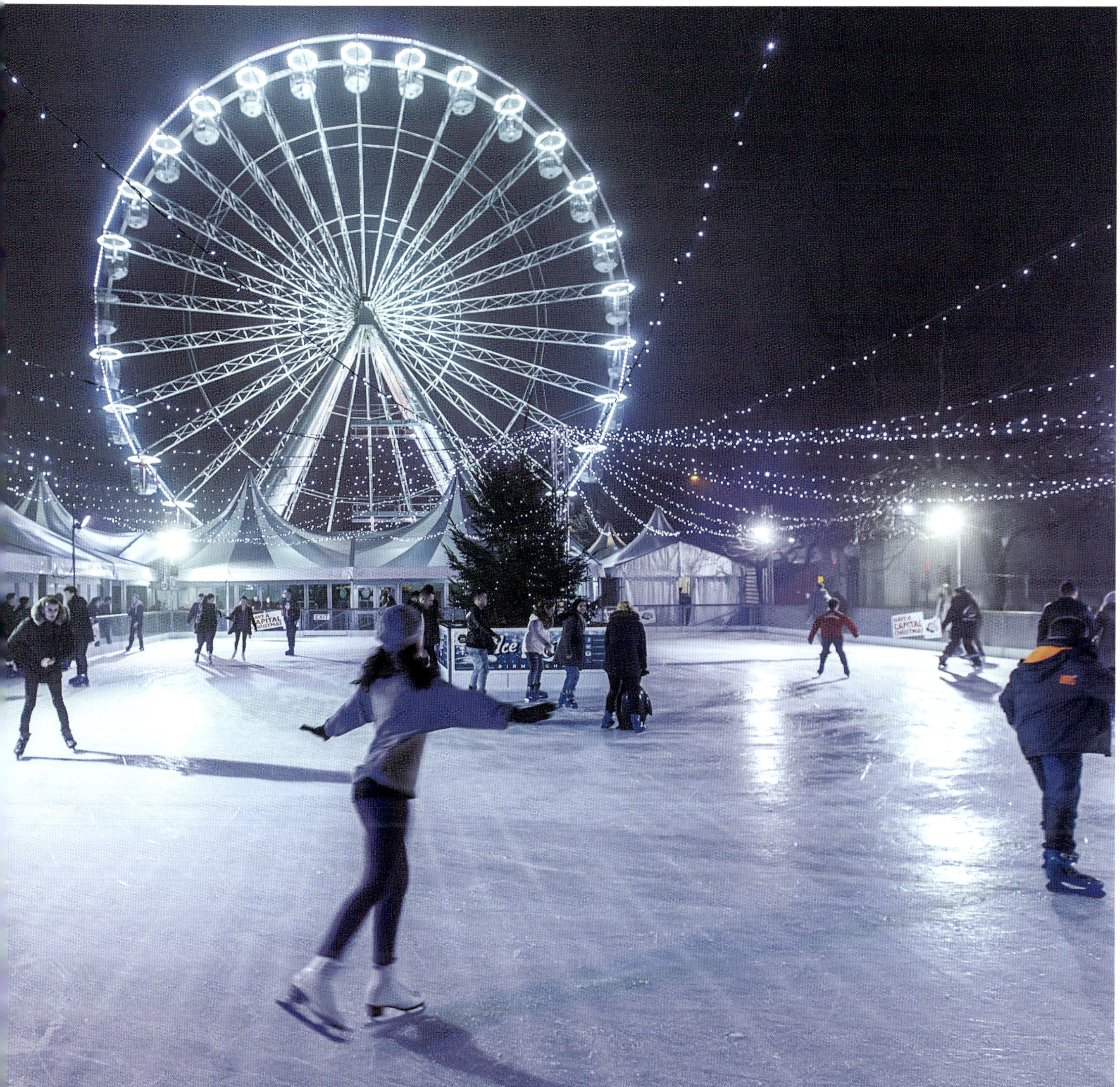

GETTING THE SHOT

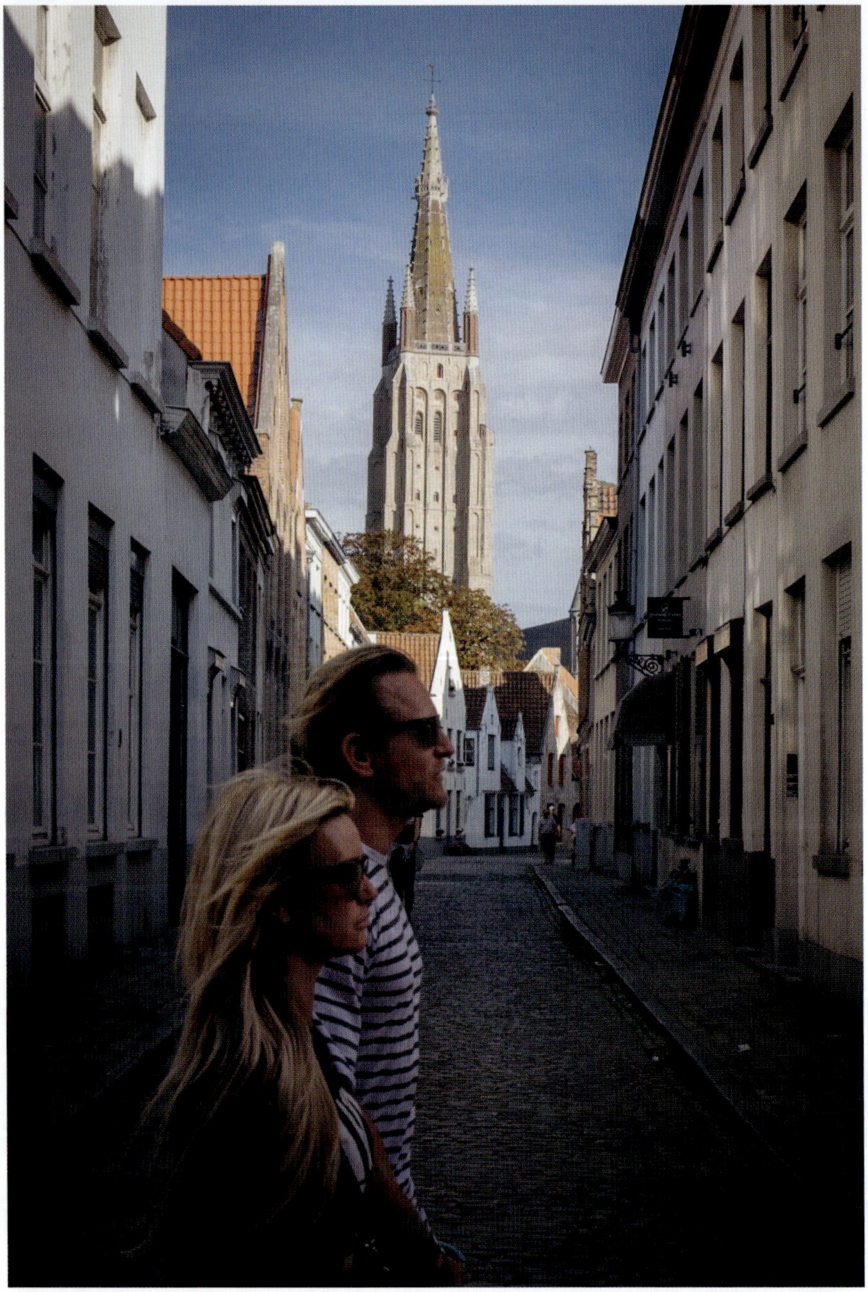

Once you've mastered how to disguise your shooting and are more comfortable shooting people on the streets, you can think more about the composition and where to stand to get the right photo. You can shoot some classic street scenes in order to get more courage and increase your confidence in capturing this style of photography.

Context: Try using something of interest to give the shot a background or a narrative. It could be a large billboard with a pertinent word on it, or some street art depicting a hand pointing in one direction. Using these is an easy way to create meaning in the photo, contrasting or complementing the subject.

Fishing: Not literally going fishing. But, like a fisherman who waits in one spot for the best catch, you wait in a good place for the shot you are after. Find an interesting setting and simply wait for something to enter the frame. You can use this method to get a stride-by style shot, capturing people walking across the frame. Try to time your shutter release with the moment someone has their legs farthest apart, because this best shows their movement, rather than giving the appearance that they are just standing.

Reflections: A way of adding an interesting extra dimension to your street shots is to seek out reflections in the city. Café windows, with the people inside layered with the people walking by outside, puddles and those nice glass buildings all work well. Alternatively, use symmetry in the photo to reflect the subject – a person on one half of the shot and a tree on the other, for instance.

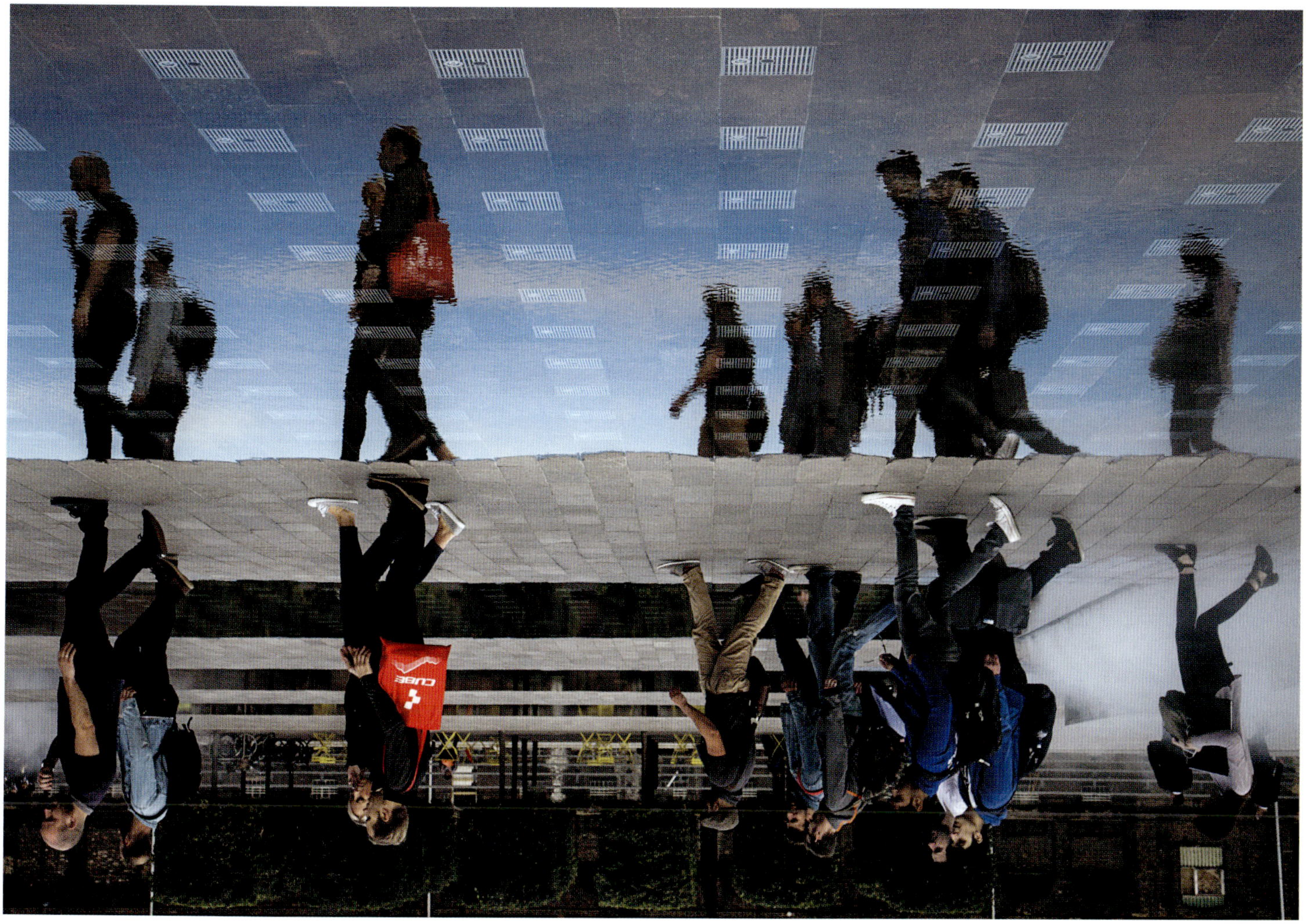

OPPOSITE
I've lined up the shot of the street, with the church lit in perfect sunlight in the background, and then I just wait for my subject to walk across my frame.

ABOVE
Not only does pointing the camera at the puddle give you a great reflection, but it also means that people won't notice you are shooting them!

Ambiguity: Find a scene that tells a story, but challenge the viewer to work out what that meaning is, or try to suggest the opposite of what is really going on. For example, you can capture someone's angry expression when they are actually laughing or being happy. You can get this in the moment between the smiles and laughter, when their face is stretched. Their gestures may contradict the apparent mood, intriguing and puzzling the viewer.

HERO
MARTIN PARR

Martin Parr is a British photographer who made his name capturing the everyday lives of people in the UK and around the world. His work shows us these things through his unique perspective. It is amazing because it challenges the way we look at the world, causes us to question how we present ourselves to others, and also what we value. Because of this, his photos are often humorous but also very accessible and entertaining.

For his *Small World* series, he documents people at popular tourist destinations. His image of people trying to capture the classic photo of holding up the Leaning Tower of Pisa is one of his more well-known shots. It is a great example of shifting the parameters to offer something that is both strange and very funny.

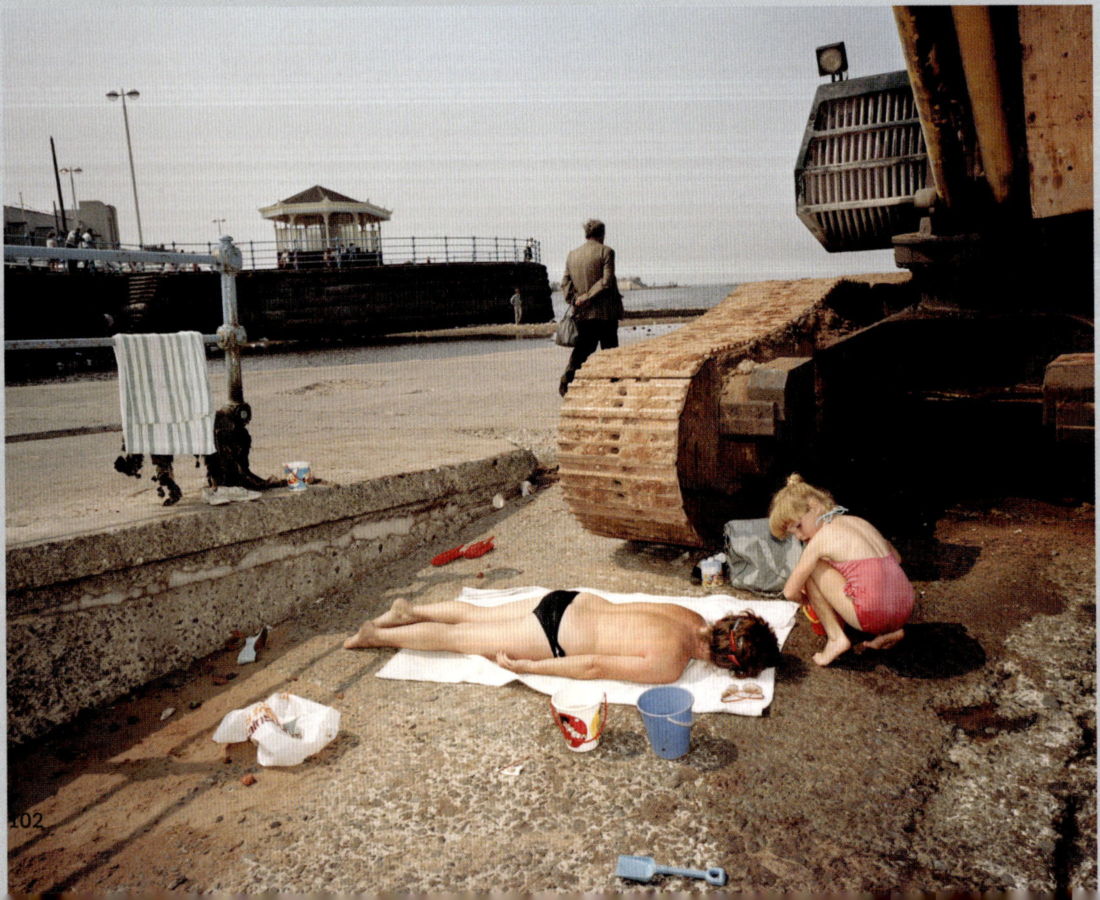

LEFT
The Last Resort 40, 1983–6, printed 2002.

RIGHT
The Leaning Tower of Pisa, from *Small World*, 1990.

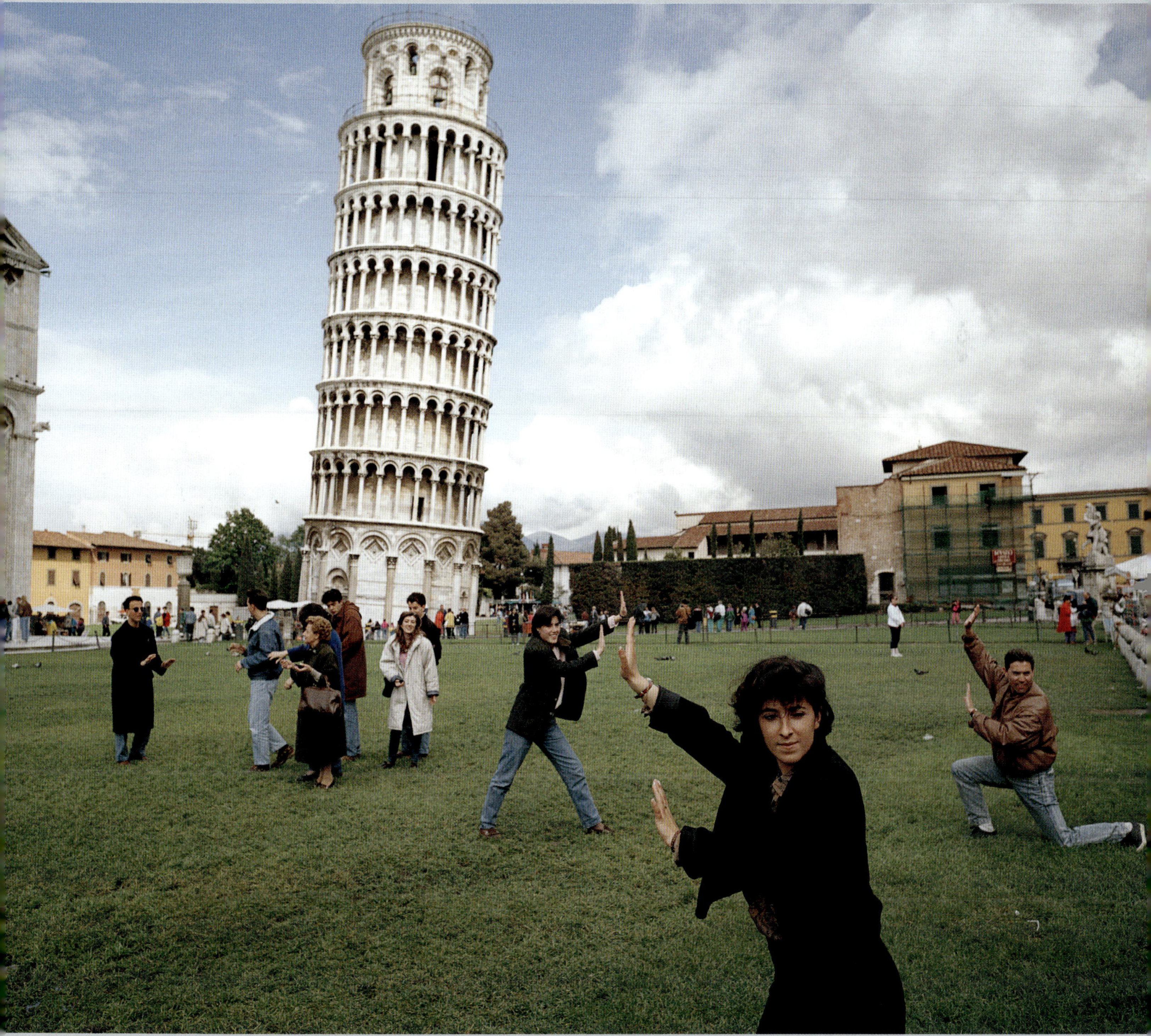

NIGHT LIFE

Street photography at night is a real technical challenge, but it can be incredibly rewarding. The lack of light means you are either reliant on switching to a higher sensitivity on the ISO or film, using expensive prime lenses with a wide maximum aperture or, usually, a combination of the two. In these situations you would usually reach for your tripod, so you can stabilize your camera and extend your exposure times, but that doesn't always lend itself to the genre of street photography.

If you're going to use your tripod, set yourself up somewhere and keep your exposure relatively short. Anything over a second will often result in blurry images, unless the subject is stood stock still, and if they are moving fast enough, you might not pick them up at all. The example on the right is a two-second exposure of a couple on a balcony, forming a silhouette with an almost blank white background. I was lucky that, on this occasion, the couple didn't move around too much, so the figures can be seen distinctly in the foreground. It may be best to set yourself up somewhere that people are hanging around, not somewhere where people are moving around at a fast pace.

If you leave your tripod at home, you'll want to look out for something to illuminate your scene. This could be a powerful street lamp or an LED advertising screen. Brassaï was the master of finding lighting, which he often exploited to great atmospheric effect. We look at his work in Chapter 7.

The last thing to remember is to make sure you stay safe at night. Be wary when you are setting up your tripod: pick a spot where you won't draw too much attention to yourself, but, on the other hand, don't set up in a dark alleyway where you can't be seen by anyone.

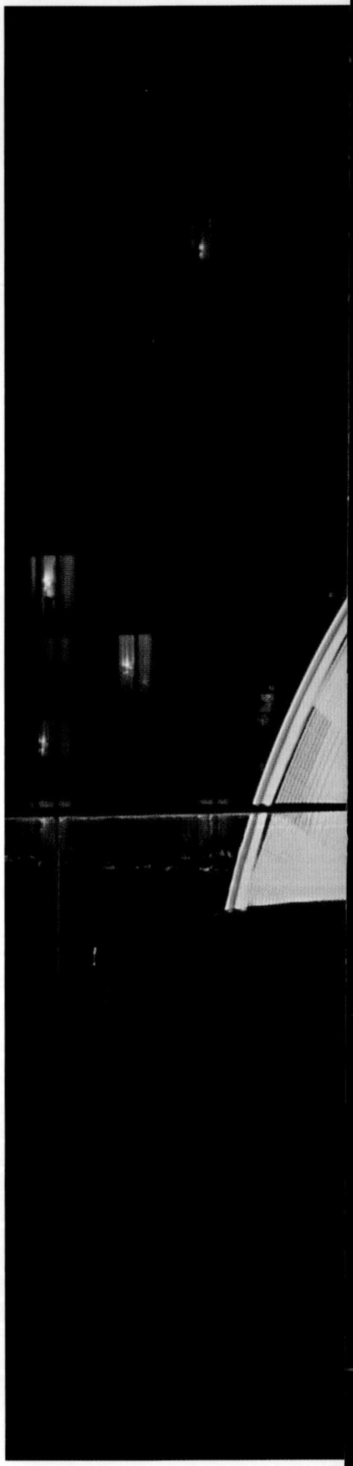

RIGHT
A couple are silhouetted before an illuminated ferris wheel. Usually you can't get away with such a long exposure, but as previously mentioned, there is a little leeway in street photography when it comes to typical no-nos like imperfect focus.

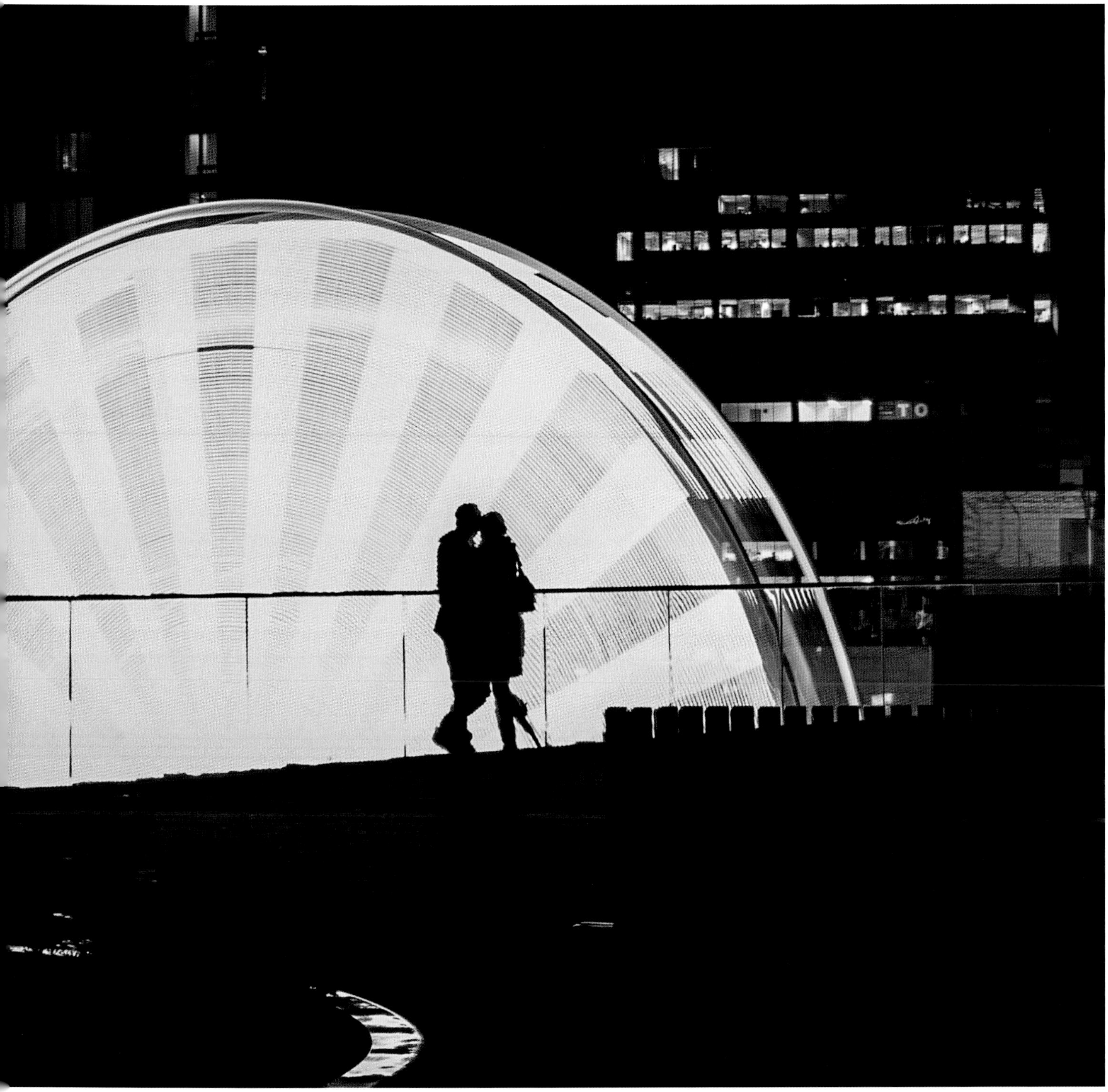

HERO
MACIEJ DAKOWICZ

When it comes to street photography at night, Polish photographer Maciej Dakowicz has made a messy art form of it. His *Cardiff After Dark* project demonstrates that the most interesting subjects for street photography often come out at night. This is another good instance of getting to know your city – in this case the Welsh capital city. Find out where the good spots are, the messy bars and hubs of nighttime activity, and you will be spoiled for choice of subject.

What you find in Dakowicz's photography is a lot of drunk people doing some very funny and bizarre things. The populous streets where they often gather provide all the lighting he needs, and he is a master of finding that perfect moment, when his subjects are at their most dynamic, or have the most intense expressions on their faces.

There are some particular considerations when it comes to shooting drunk people at night, however. The first is about safety. Drunk people can be more aggressive in general, and they may be more likely to take issue with you shooting their behaviour, so approach with caution.

The second concern is ethical. Is it right to photograph people when they're perhaps not in their right minds? And especially if you then publish these photographs in a book, a blog, or whatever form. If you are hoping to become famous for your photography, then these photographs may be widely shared. Aside from legal matters, each photographer must decide their own ethical boundaries. At the very least you should ask permission. But even then, is it really consent if they are intoxicated?

RIGHT
A lone figure in a Superman costume striding down an empty alley is suitably evocative.

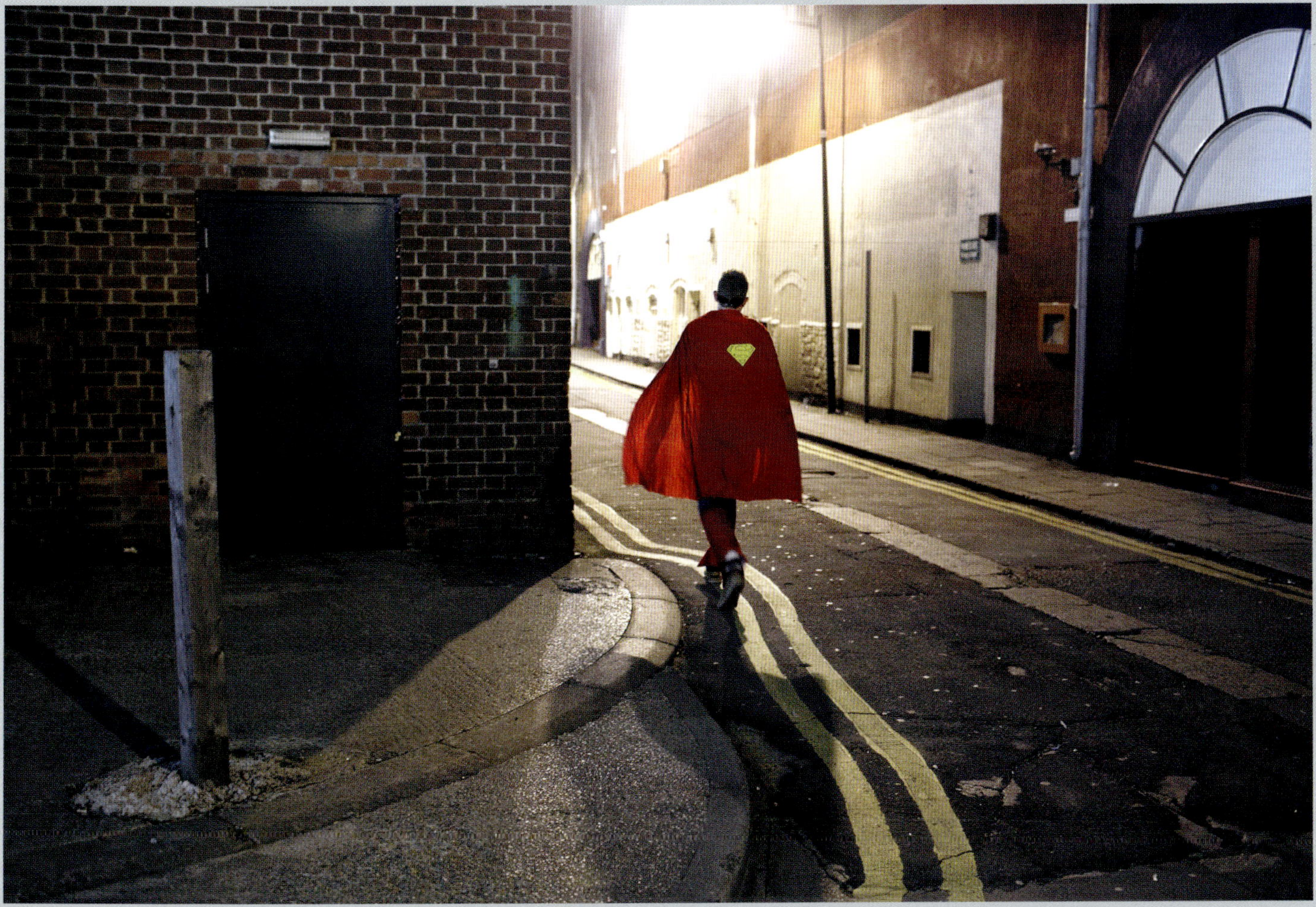

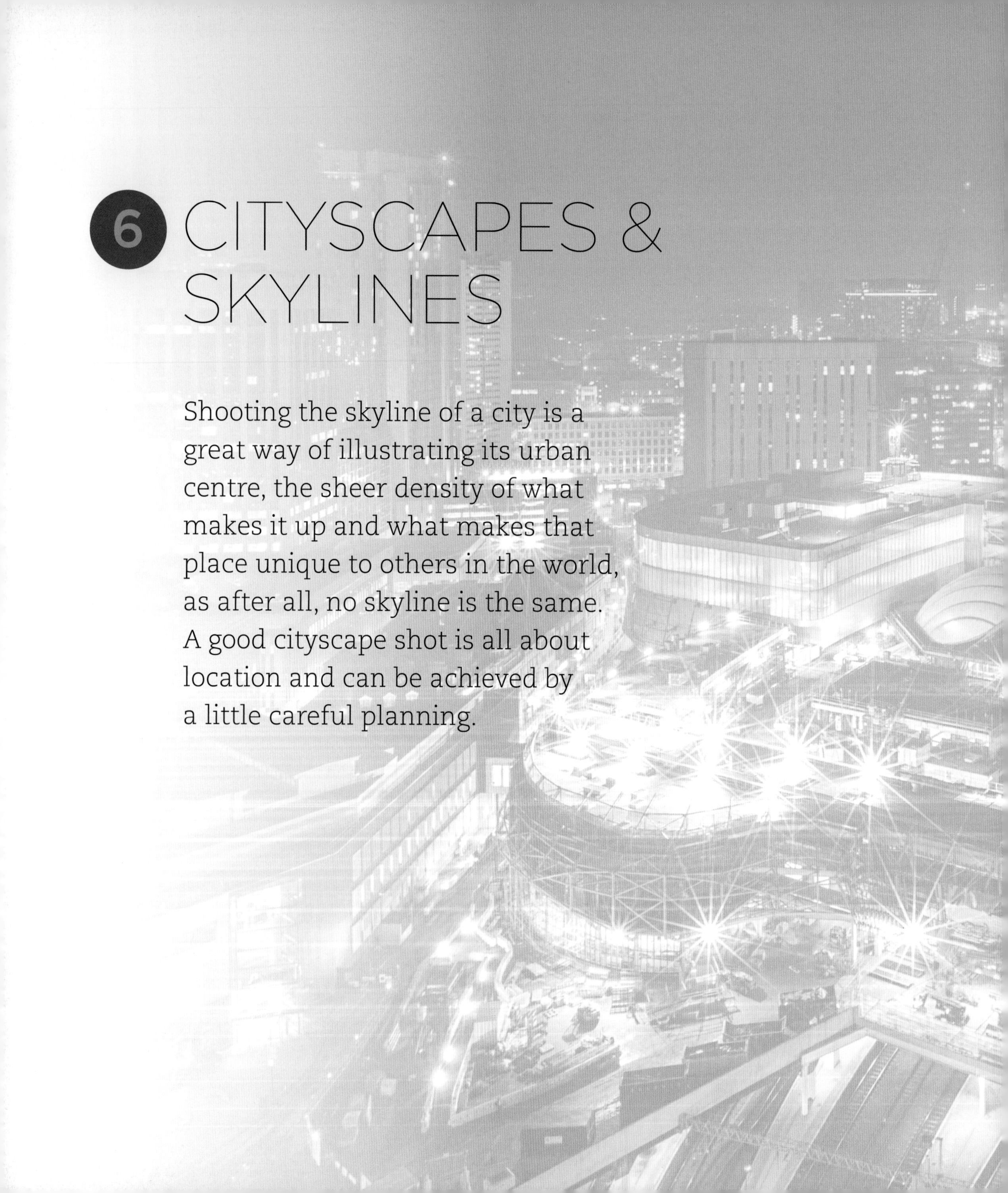

6 CITYSCAPES & SKYLINES

Shooting the skyline of a city is a great way of illustrating its urban centre, the sheer density of what makes it up and what makes that place unique to others in the world, as after all, no skyline is the same. A good cityscape shot is all about location and can be achieved by a little careful planning.

AIM HIGH

One of the best locations for shooting a cityscape is from the rooftops themselves. It doesn't necessarily have to be a particularly tall building, but it does need to be one that gives a sufficiently different perspective from being at street level. Research can help you find accessible rooftops – there may be rooftop bars you can visit, or even viewing platforms in certain buildings.

So what do you want to achieve by shooting a cityscape? I'd say cityscapes are about showing off the skyline in a way that represents what is unique about that city. This could be showing off all the impressive, high-rise buildings in the centre or a certain location, or it could be based on a particular well-known landmark, like the Shard in London, or the Empire State Building in New York City.

One approach is to shoot a high-resolution, crisp panorama, comprised of a series of shots taken with the same settings, which can be stitched together in post-production. Another option is to capture the changing face of the city over the course of a day or a few hours (the shorter days of winter are better for a full day's shoot!). Or you may just want a glorious image of the city at sunset. If it's the latter you're after, you will need to adjust your white balance settings, as these will be key in order to capture the colours of the sunset accurately. If you're shooting on a DSLR, your camera will attempt to balance the tones it considers 'too warm', and in doing so it will eradicate all the lovely reds and oranges you were hoping to capture. We'll address this issue specifically a little later, on page 114.

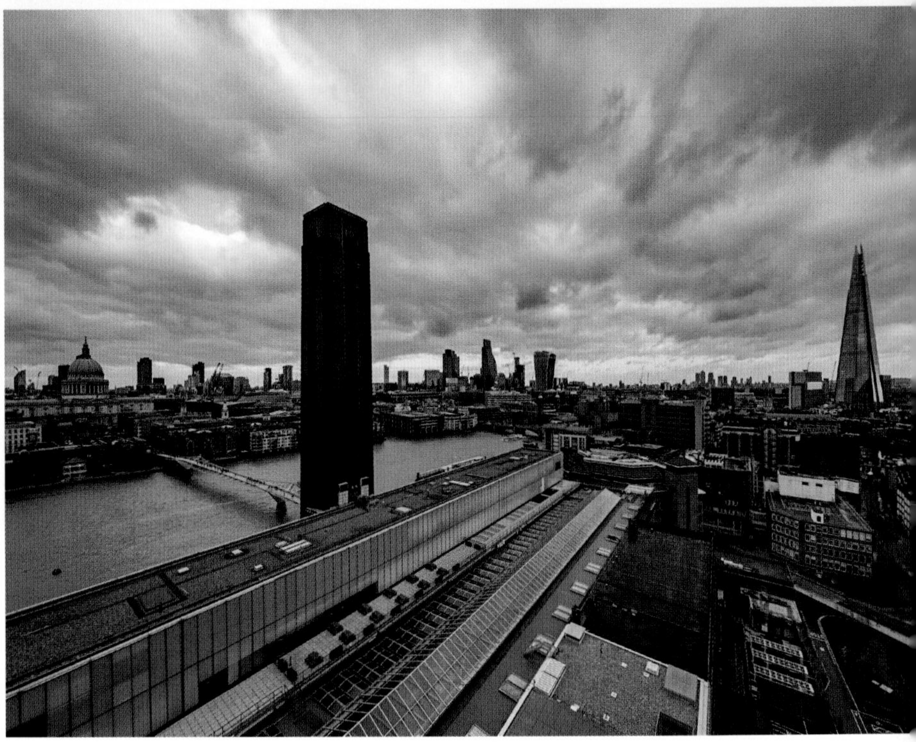

You will be best equipped to shoot a skyline using a tripod and a long lens. Often, you'll need to head some way out of the city in order to get the best profile of the buildings, and this could be quite far, so consider a lens with a focal length of at least 300mm. When working at such great focal lengths, tripods become a necessity, because at that level of magnification, the slightest shake will be amplified. Most modern telephoto lenses provide reasonable image stablization, but you may also want to use a timed shutter release (it doesn't need to be a long one – two seconds or so), to eradicate any shake.

ABOVE
A lot of publicly accessible spaces offer high vantage points in the major cities. This is shot from the public gallery at the Tate Modern extension in London.

RIGHT
A night shot from the top of the tallest building in the world (at present) – the Burj Khalifa in Dubai. This was taken behind glass, so the camera needed to be placed right up against it to reduce the reflections.

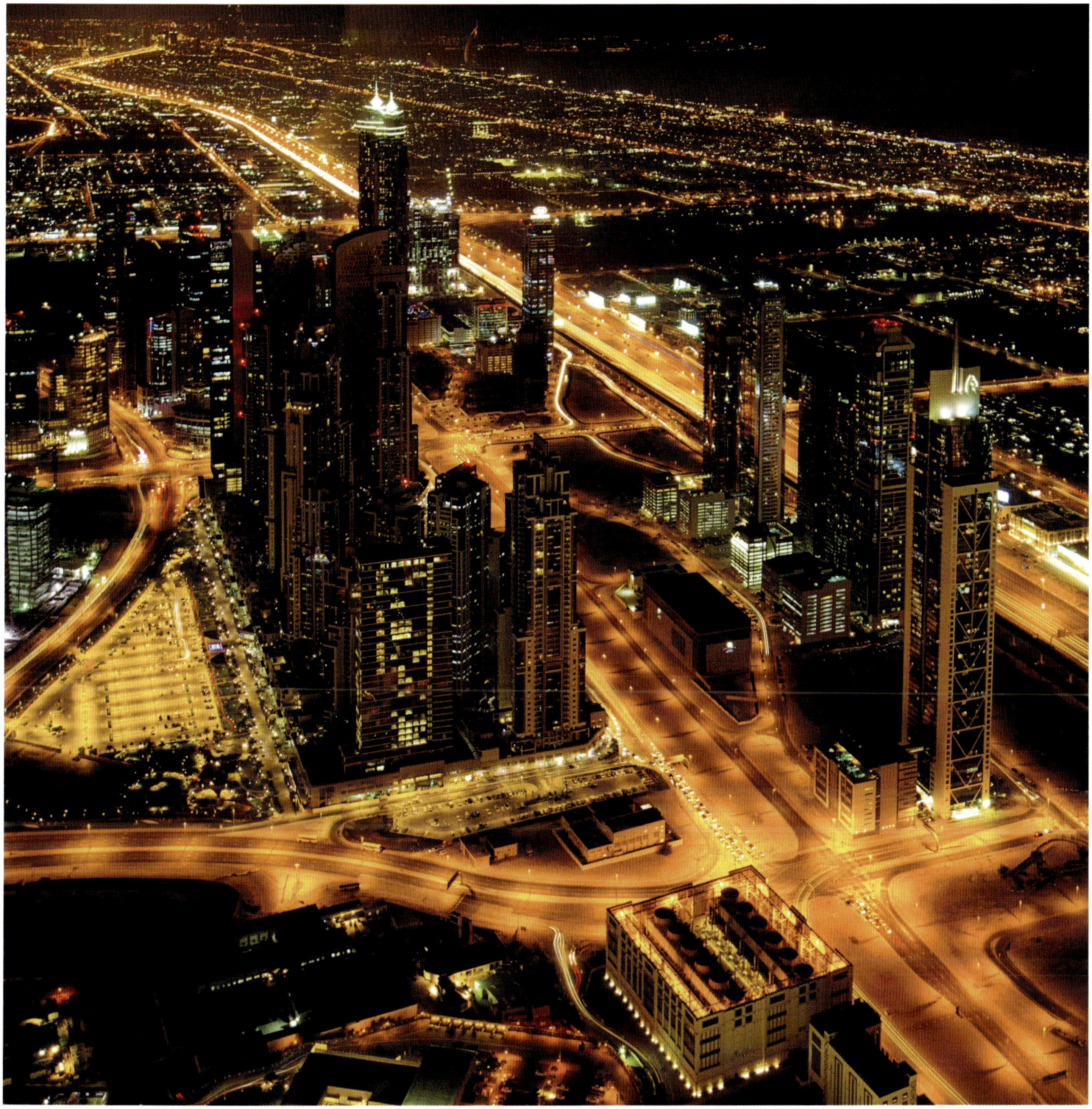

So where are the best places to shoot the skyline, and what are the main things you need to consider with these locations?

TOWERS

Look for the tallest buildings on the skyline, and then do some research, on the internet or on the phone, to find out whether there are any spaces in them that are accessible. If there aren't, then make some enquiries with the building managers and explain what you'd like to do, and they may be happy to let you up to get your shots. Think about what time you'd ideally like to be there, and how long you would like to spend there, before you get in touch, particularly if you're doing it over the phone, because you'll sound more professional and help your chances if you can be precise in your request.

It is likely that when you do gain access, it will only be to an enclosed space, either a balcony with a limited view, or a room with a better 360-degree perspective, but behind glass. Few rooftops are accessible unless you know the right people. When you shoot through glass in a room, you may get reflections, and also the glass may be slightly dirty. Press your camera solidly up against the window in order to reduce reflections, making sure you don't damage the lens glass. Then wrap your coat or another dense piece of fabric around the camera to ensure that no reflections are picked up. This method is fairly successful in the day, but it will be trickier at night, unless you are able to have the lights turned off in the space you're shooting in.

CAR PARKS

Another location that might not be the most obvious is a multi-level car park. City centres are full of these, and they can sometimes be six or seven storeys high, often with completely open and accessible roof spaces. Thinking back to our discussion regarding permissions, it is likely that the car park will be under private ownership or even owned by the local council, so it is always worth checking whether permission is required to access and shoot in it.

FROM THE STREET

Although being up high is the preferred location for cityscape shots, you can also get some interesting photos just from street level. If there are any large open spaces in the centre of the city – say a park or a large town square, a beachfront or a riverbank – then you're likely to be far enough away from the buildings to get a good cityscape. Aim to get all the tops of the buildings in, so that you can see the outline of the skyline.

FROM A DISTANCE

If you travel outside the city, you'll find many locations to get a view where it appears right on the horizon. This means that you'll be able to capture the outline of the tall buildings with just sky behind them. Ideally, this will be a perfectly clear sky, or perhaps with some attractive cirrus clouds for a bit of texture. Early mornings and late evenings can also be good for this, when the sky is graded with subtle hues from warm oranges to pale green-blues, out to a deeper blue or even violet.

RIGHT, TOP
You don't necessarily have to show the tops of buildings. This shot conveys the scale and density of London's built-up city centre by filling the frame.

RIGHT, BOTTOM
Elevating yourself gives fantastic new views of the city. Here, the warm tones of the lights coming on in the evening are echoed in the sunset on the horizon.

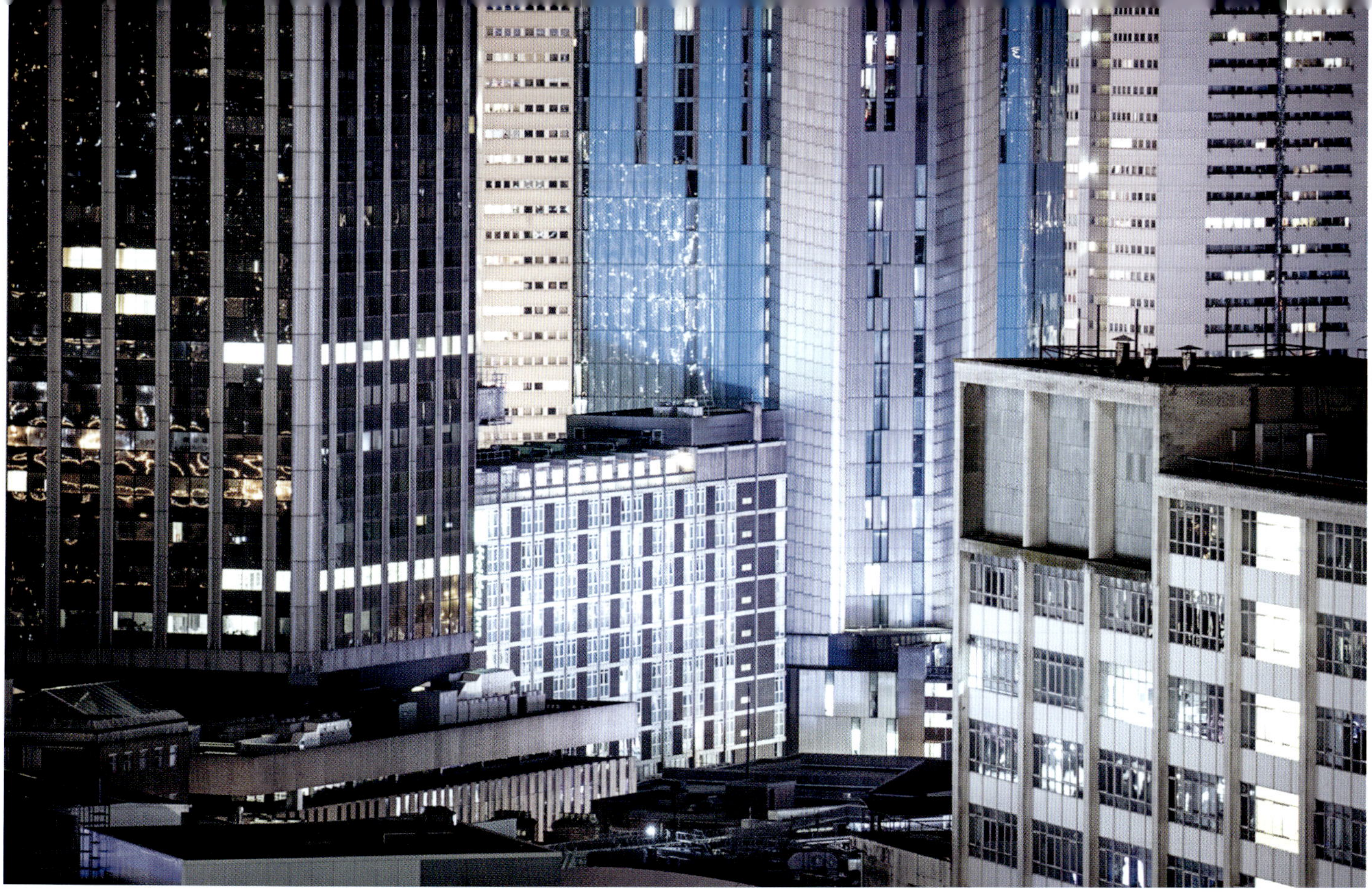

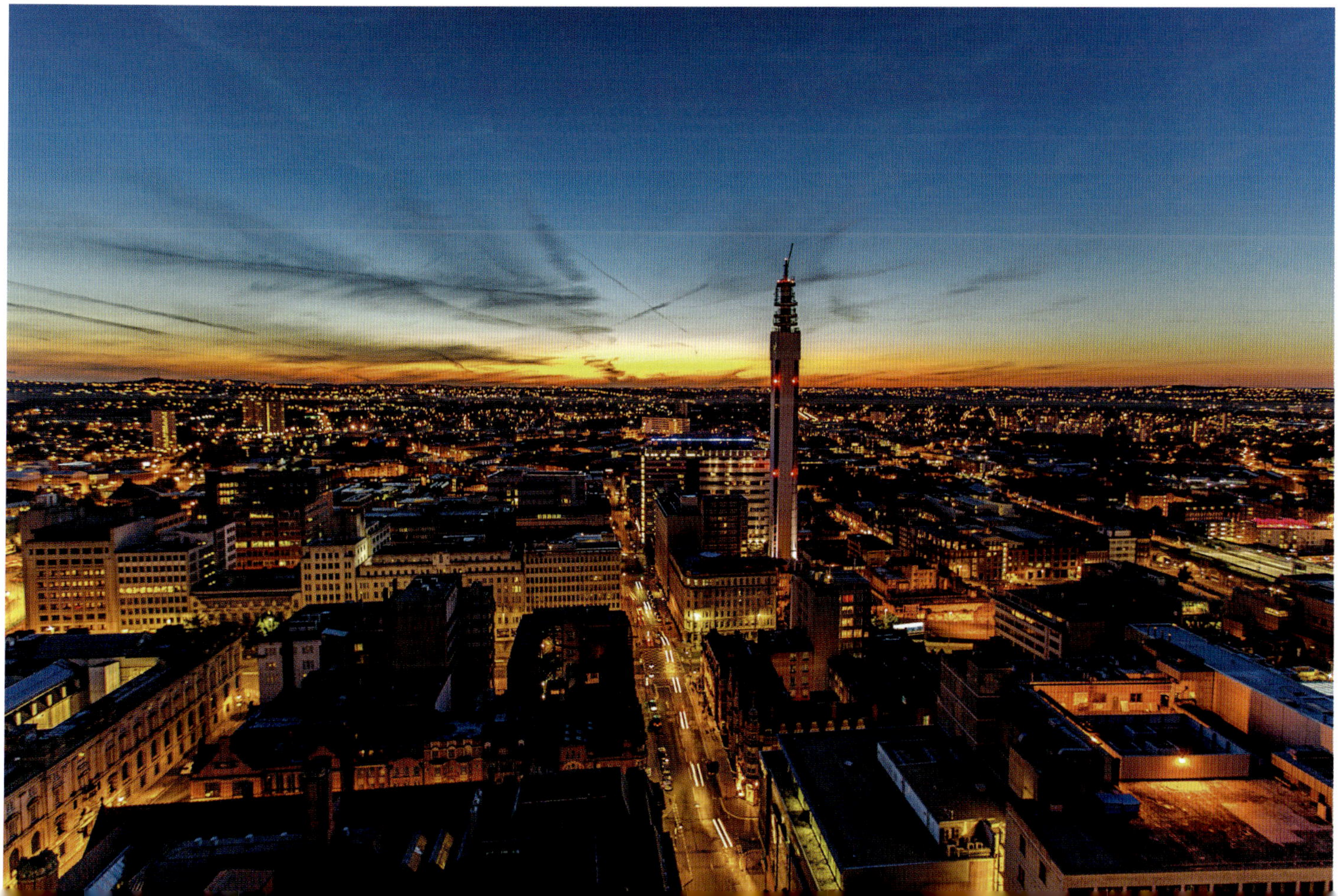

DRAMATIC SKYLINES

The success of a skyline shot is heavily dependent on the weather, and the more interesting views for this particular style of photography can usually be obtained during the sunrise and sunset hours. One thing that's important to mention when it comes to photographing the sun is that you must not look at it directly, including through your viewfinder. When it comes to composing, you can use the display on the back of your camera.

CAPTURING SUNSETS

As mentioned, your DSLR will probably try to 'fix' the overly warm tones of the sunset sky, thereby ruining the shot. It can be fixed later in post-production, if you shoot in Raw, but you may as well get it right in camera. For this, you essentially trick your camera into thinking the scene is comprised of cooler colours than it is. You can do this either by selecting the Shade profile from the white balance settings, which will overcompensate the warmth and retain a lot of saturated red hues, or, if you're a bit of a perfectionist, you can manually adjust the colour temperature, starting at around 7,000 Kelvin, taking the shot, reviewing it and adjusting as needed.

SILHOUETTE

Facing towards the sunset, you should be able to get a good silhouette shot of the distant skyscrapers about 15 minutes after the sun sets. It should be early enough that the towers don't have their lights on, and by exposing for the sky rather than the buildings, they will naturally appear darker. Also look out for some of the cloud formations we discussed on pages 42–3. Cirrus clouds occur at a high level in the atmosphere, and they are sometimes not visible until the sun gets below the horizon at the right angle to illuminate them.

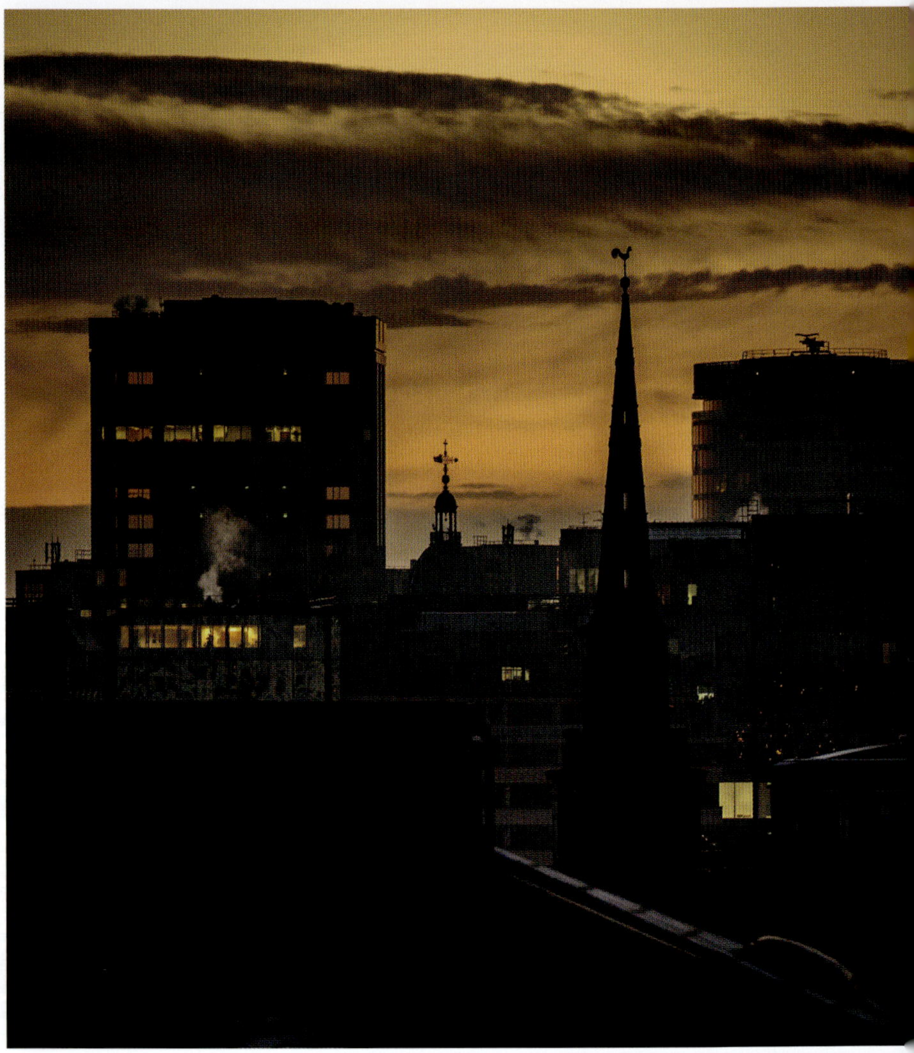

ABOVE
The shapes of the buildings are used to tell a story in this shot. Look out for buildings with distinctive shapes that are easily recognizable in silhouette.

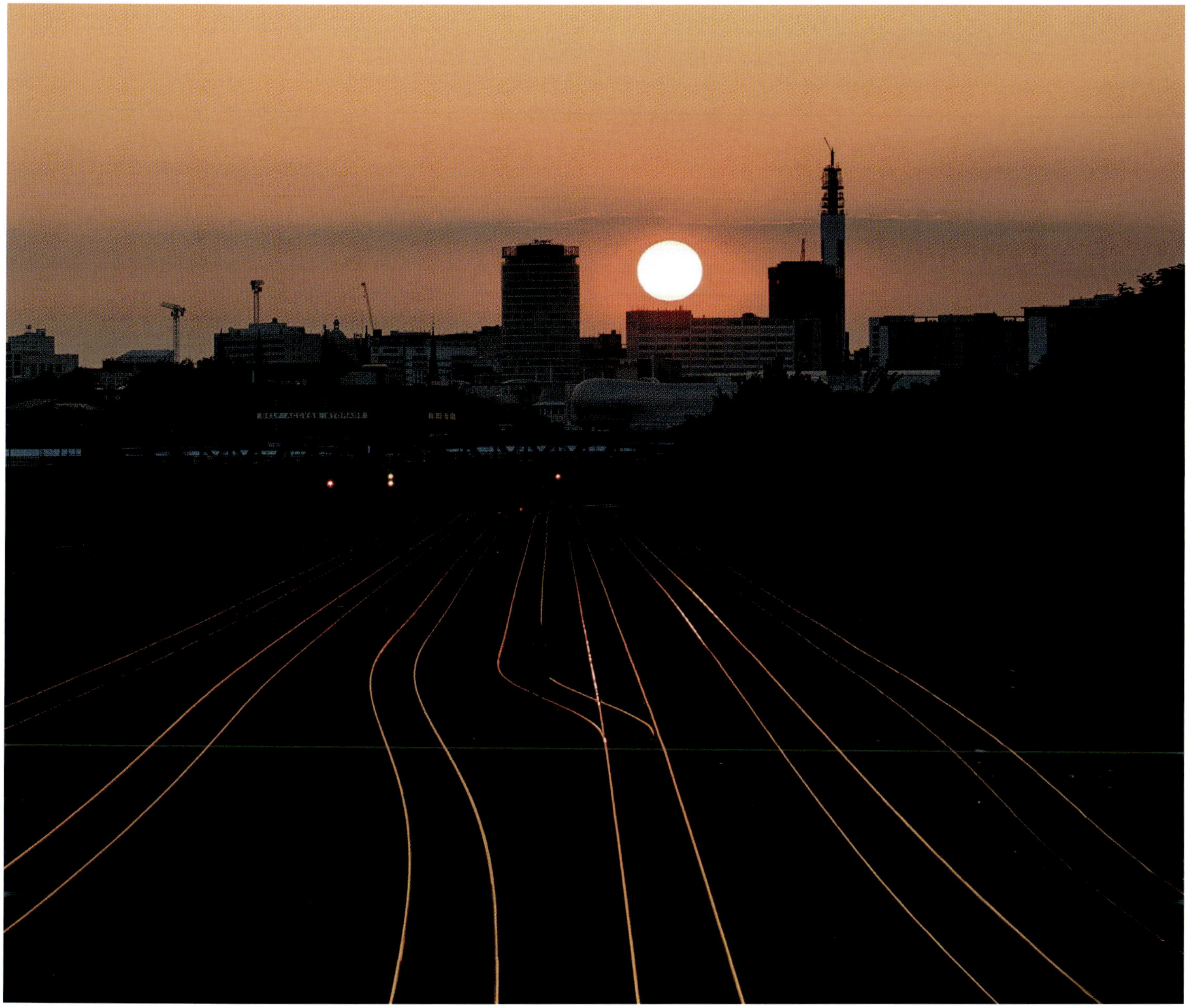

PREPARATION IS EVERYTHING

We've mentioned preparation a lot in this book, but it really is everything to a good skyline shot. This kind of photography relies on knowing where the sun is going to be at a certain time of day at a certain time of year. Sure, you can always get lucky, but if you're going to the trouble of gaining access to a high building, or heading some way out of the city, you want to get it right. Besides which, the shots you wait and plan for are always the most satisfying.

ABOVE
This photo was composed to capture the railway lines being lit by the low-level sun. Use an app to predict where the sun will be setting.

GO LONG

When taking photographs of a skyline from a distance, you can use a telephoto lens to flatten and distort the perspective, creating surreal and dramatic compositions. By using a small aperture, *f*/11 or above, you stretch the depth of field and ensure that objects that are really far apart appear to be right next to each other. The bigger the focal length of the telephoto lens, the more you can push the depth of field, so you'll see this effect when you use a focal length of 300mm or above.

Thanks to the magnifying effect of a telephoto lens, you can also produce extraordinary distortions in which a huge sun or moon appear over the horizon. First, you need to pinpoint the exact location in which it will be rising or setting, which you can do with a smartphone app, such as The Photographer's Ephemeris. The closer the sun is to the horizon, the redder it appears, but trying to achieve a perfect red sun can be an exercise of frustration in the city due to all the buildings getting in the way. Once you've pinpointed the shot, all you need is a bit of luck with the weather. Even on seemingly clear days, there can be haze and clouds on the horizon, depending on the distance you are away from the city.

COMPLEMENTING THE FRAME

When you shoot the city from a distance, so that the outline of the buildings appear on the horizon, think about what you're capturing in the space around that main focal point. Fireworks are excellent to capture from this position because the magnifying effect works on them too, so they look even more impressive than when you see them from close up. Alternatively, you could go storm-chasing and wait for a passing thunderstorm to move across the city, getting a classic shot of a lightning bolt hitting one of the tall towers – from a safe distance away, of course!

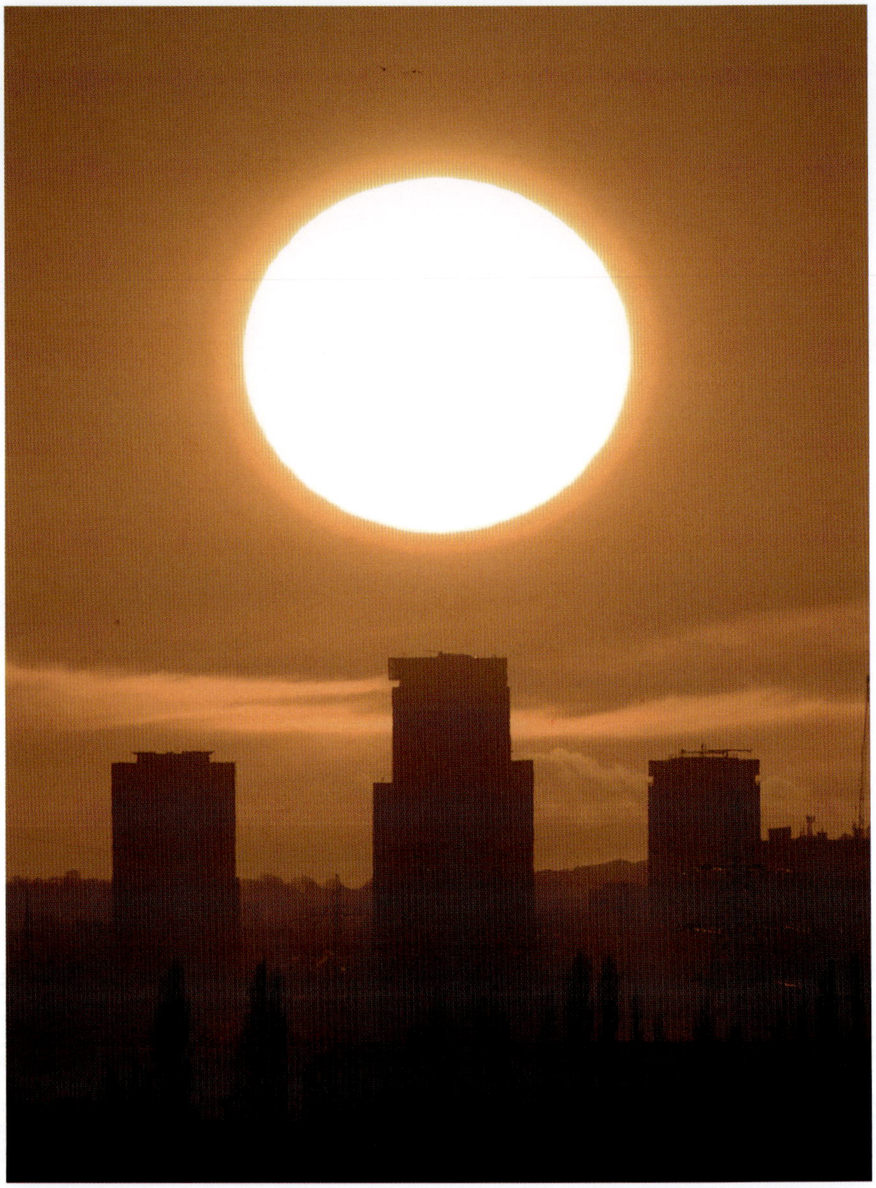

ABOVE
A huge sun, perfectly positioned above the central, and tallest tower. This perspective illusion can be stretched even further by some clever cropping in post-production, which can also be used to capitalize on a good composition.

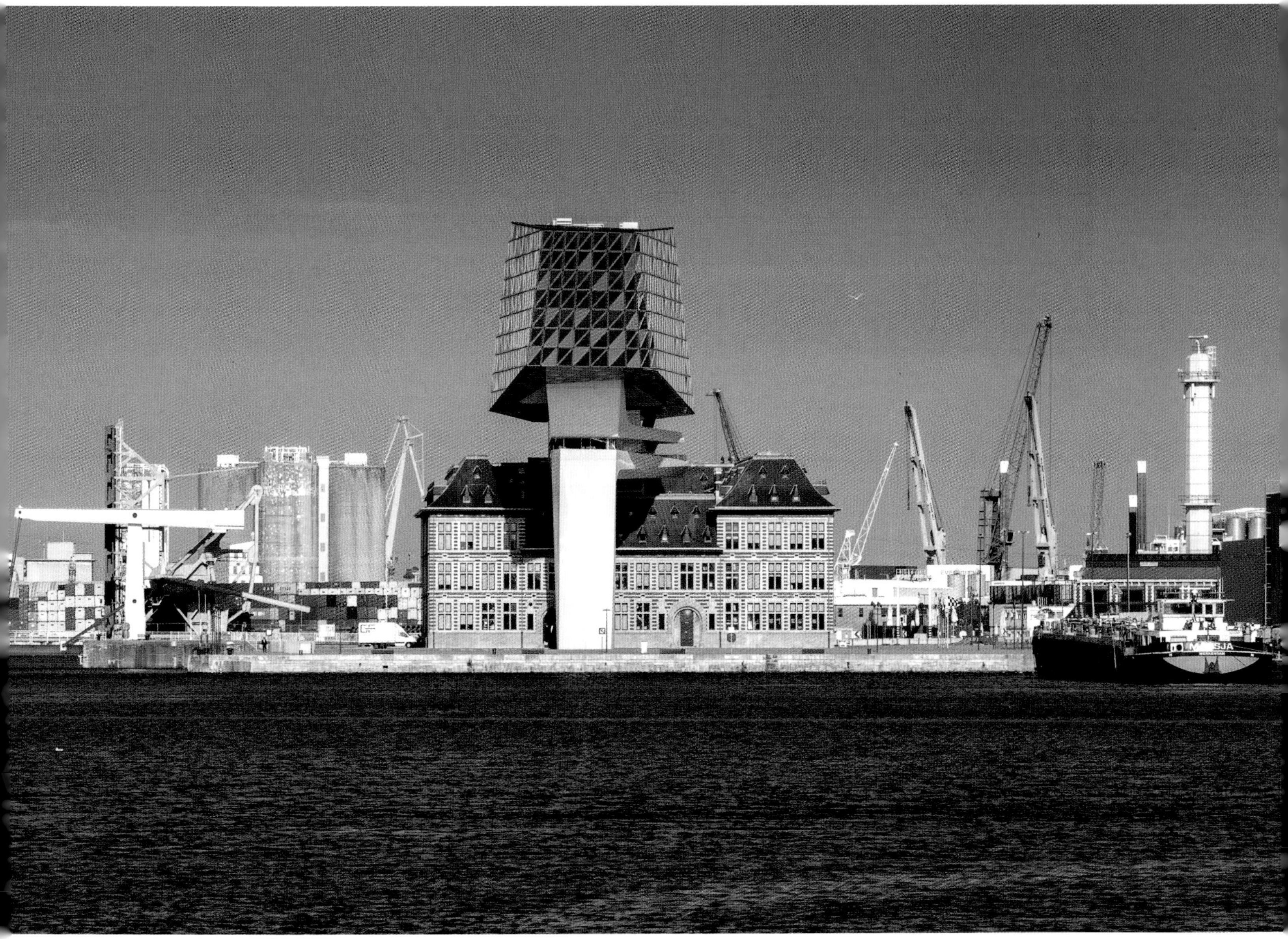

ABOVE
Complementing the frame doesn't have to be as impressive (and hard to capture) as fireworks or lightning bolts! The lone seagull in the empty sky helps reinforce the waterside setting of this scene.

THE MOON

Shooting the moon is a great challenge in itself; finding the perfect view of it in the urban environment is even trickier. Remember that it doesn't just appear night, and it appears floating near the horizon in the daytime more often than you think. As with the sun, you can use moon-tracking apps to predict where it will be, in what phase, at what time of day and year.

When shooting the moon at night, you need to use a fast shutter speed in order that it does not overexpose. Compositional issues aside, the technical challenge is in balancing the exposure of the moon and that of the city in one frame. Your camera's automatic settings are very unlikely to be able to cope with the contrast between the bright moon and the dark sky, so you need to set to manual, with settings starting around *f*/11, ISO 100, exposing for 1/250 second. Review your shots and adjust the settings as necessary; also use bracketing to produce a sequence of photos at different exposure values in one hit, so that you'll hopefully get at least one reasonably exposed shot without having to fiddle with the settings each time. If in doubt, underexpose the foreground rather than overexposing the moon. It's a lot easier to bring details out of a dark area in post-production, whereas it's often impossible to pull back any details in an overexposed area.

Finally, if you want to capture the details of the moon's surface, a long telephoto lens is a must. Again, 300mm is really the minimum for this.

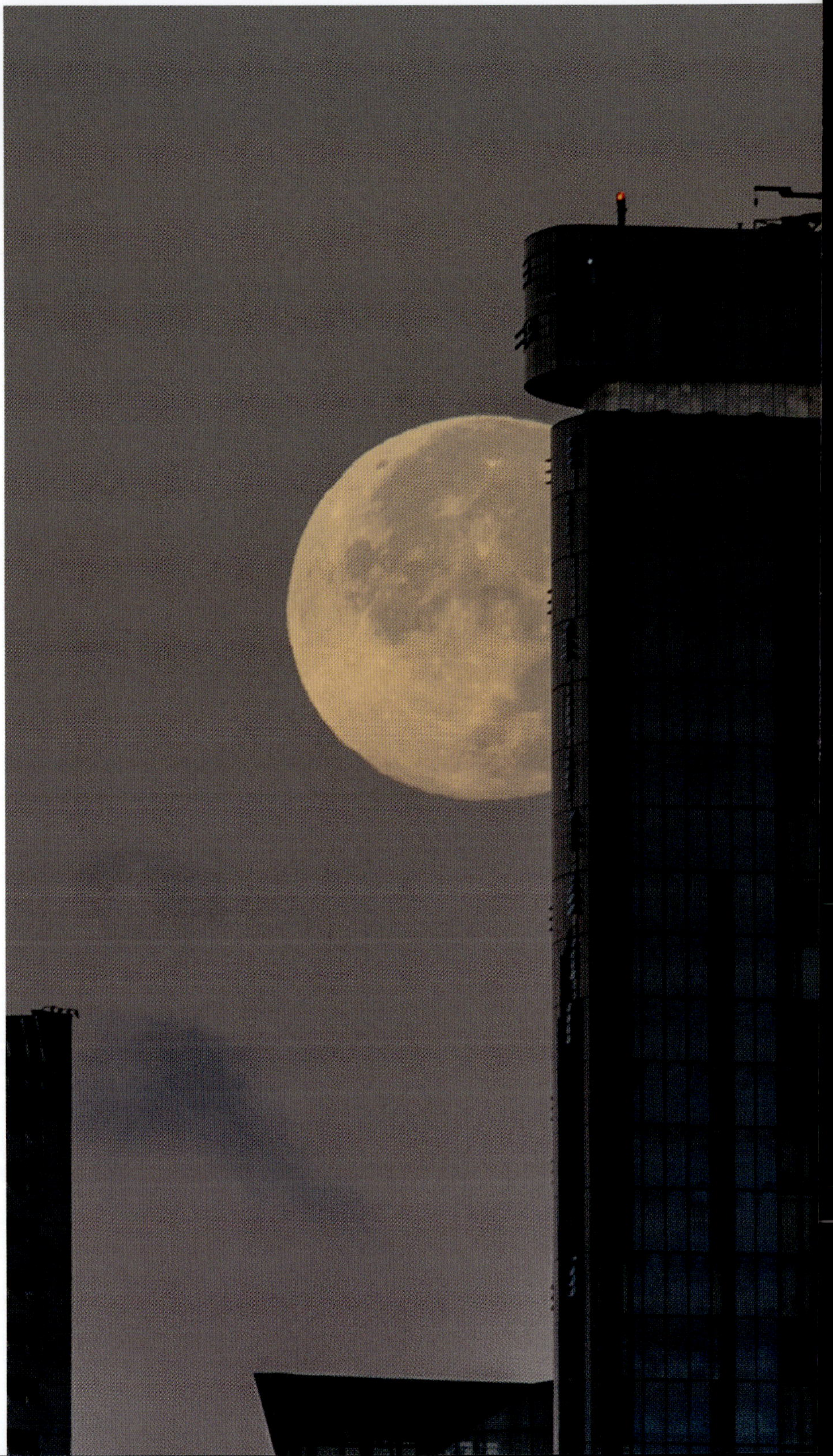

RIGHT
You wouldn't know it from a glance, but this shot was taken in the daytime, which gives you a lot more wiggle room in terms of exposure.

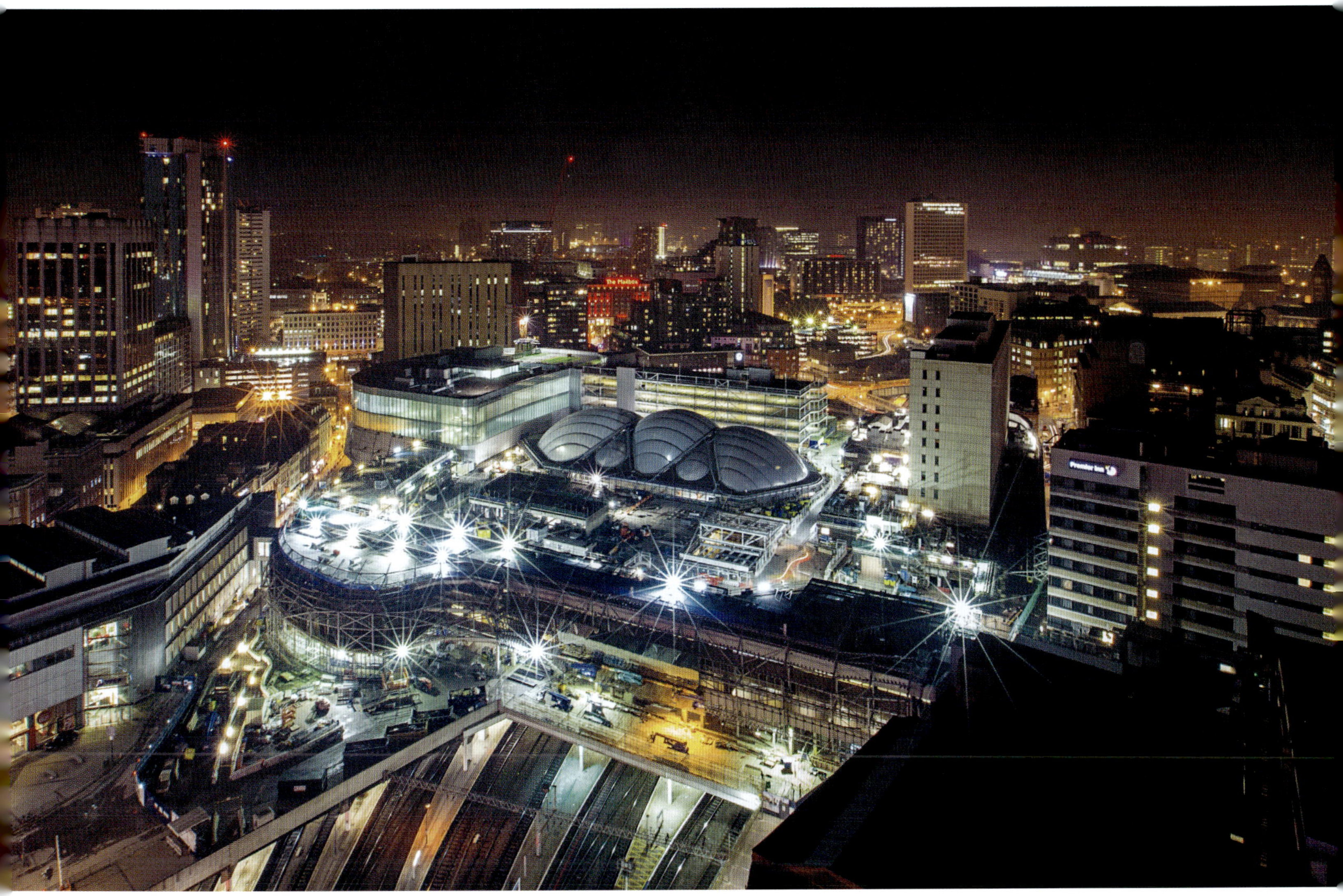

THE ILLUMINATED CITY

After sunset, the sky darkens and eventually reaches the point where the exposure required for the sky will match that of the foreground, so that you're able to capture buildings illuminated by their internal lights. There will be some light in the sky still, giving you a subtle hint of that sunset gradient, with beautiful lit-up buildings in the foreground. The best time of year to do this is during the winter months, since night falls earlier; therefore many of the towers will still be occupied at the optimum time. As a bonus, at the right time of year you might also get the moon following the sun down to the horizon at this time, so look out for that to complement your shot of the city.

ABOVE
After dark, the city is a different beast to capture. This shot was taken well after the sun had set, using f/22 and a long exposure time to create the stars from the city's lights. We'll look more at starbursts and other creative effects very shortly, in Chapter 7.

HERO MICHAEL TOMAS

Michael Tomas is a London-based photographer who specializes in shots of the city's iconic skyline. Seeking out the best views in the capital, he often takes his shots from a distance using a prime telephoto lens, which allows him to take advantage of the sun or the moon setting or rising behind the skyscrapers of the city centre. The magnifying effect of the long telephoto lens distorts these cosmic bodies into swollen versions of themselves, dominating the skyline.

Tomas is a perfect example of someone who carefully plans his photographs, seeking out the best locations in the suburbs or best viewing platforms in the city. One of his shots, capturing the sun setting in the centre of the London Eye, was taken from Greenwich Park – far away from central London where the Eye stands. The shot was precisely timed so that the circle of the sun would fit perfectly within the Eye. Shots like that, and the one shown here, simply wouldn't be possible without this level of care. When it comes to finding unique shots, Tomas really shows how far a small amount of planning can take you – even in the face of the notoriously unreliable British weather!

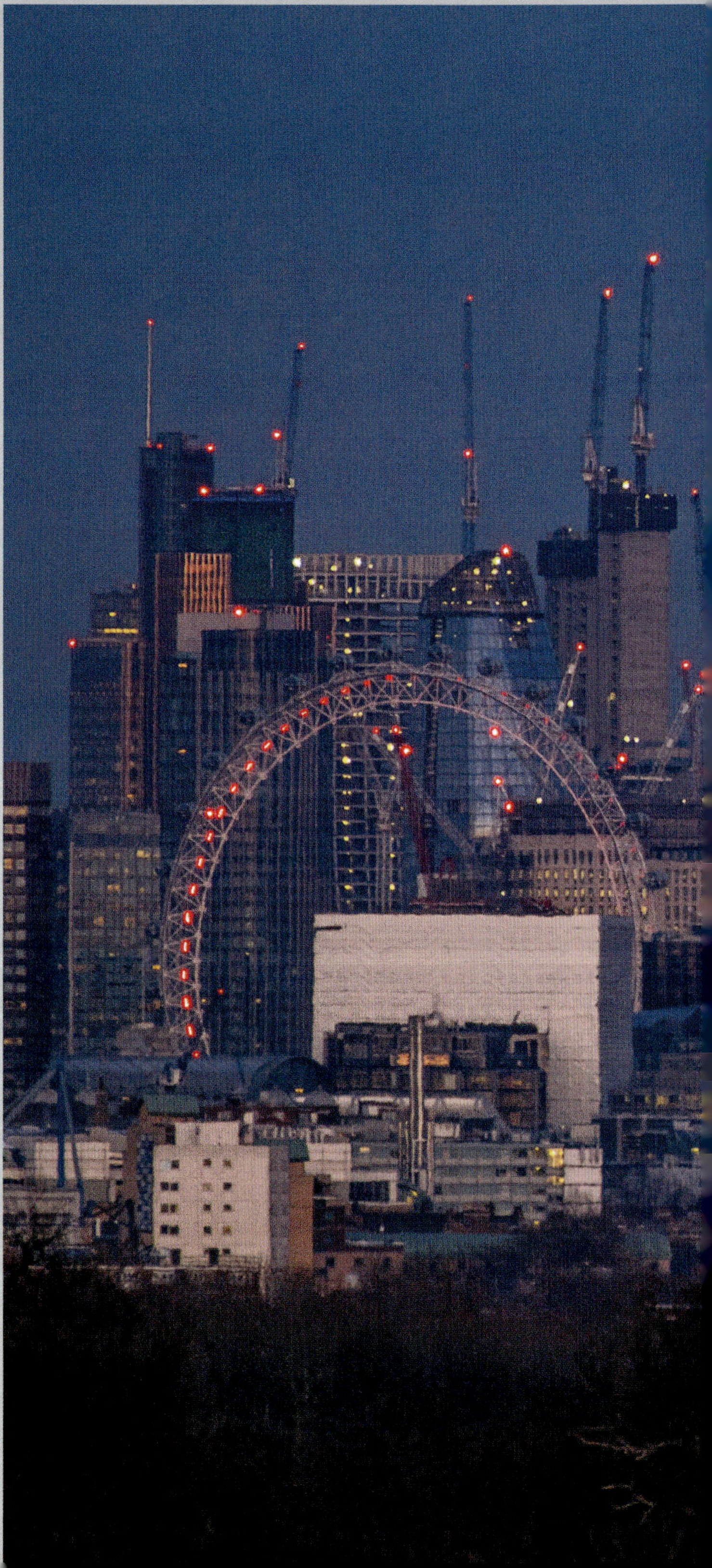

RIGHT
2016's Super Blood Blue Moon rising over the London skyline, shot from about 10 miles (16km) away, with an equivalent 1000mm telephoto lens.

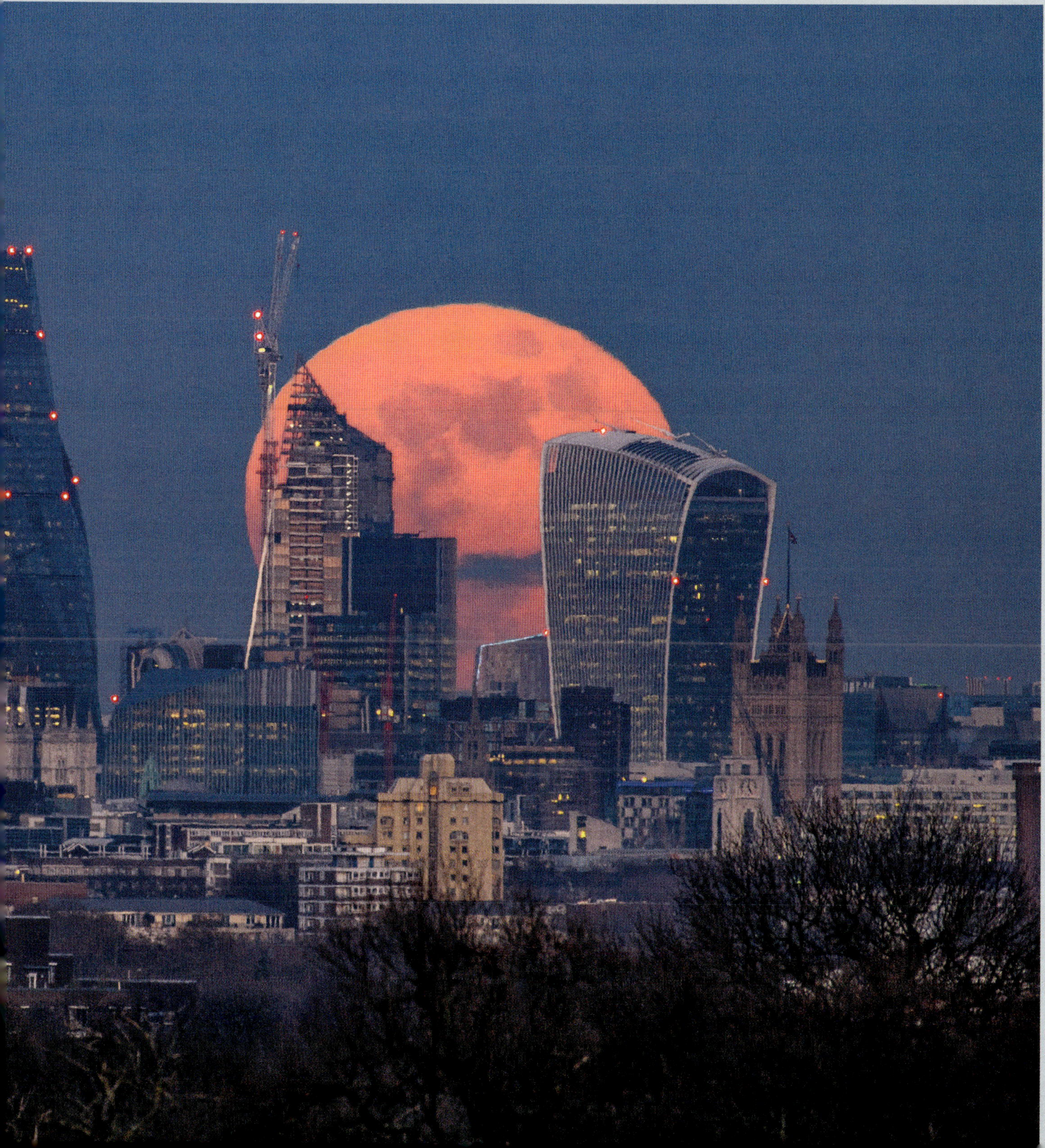

CITYSCAPE BUCKET LIST

DUBAI

The rapid rise of the skyline of the now largest city in the United Arab Emirates is nothing short of remarkable. Over the past 20 to 30 years, the landscape of the area has changed completely, the constant construction giving rise to an eclectic skyline of glass skyscrapers in two areas of the city, south of the historic centre around Dubai Creek.

The first area is concentrated on the current tallest building in the world, the Burj Khalifa. The interesting thing about this building in terms of photography is that it can be seen for miles due to the sheer scale of the structure. If you take a trip up the building you will find that you are looking down on the city from a great distance, but the perspective is unique. A few of the viewing galleries are fully glazed so you will have an issue shooting through them due to the reflections of the interior, especially at night. Luckily, the windows are at least regularly cleaned, so you don't get smears from any dirt on the outside of the glazing.

Taking photos from above is not limited to the area around the Burj Khalifa, since there is also a cluster of high-rise developments around Dubai Marina. If you go there you might stay in a hotel around this area, so it is always worth cheekily asking whether you can get a room higher up in the building to get 24-hour access to spectacular views across the city. On the balconies at Grosvenor house, you look out towards the Palm, as well as other tall buildings. If you wander around the marina itself, there are some great views of the structures, with a chance to get reflections on the water.

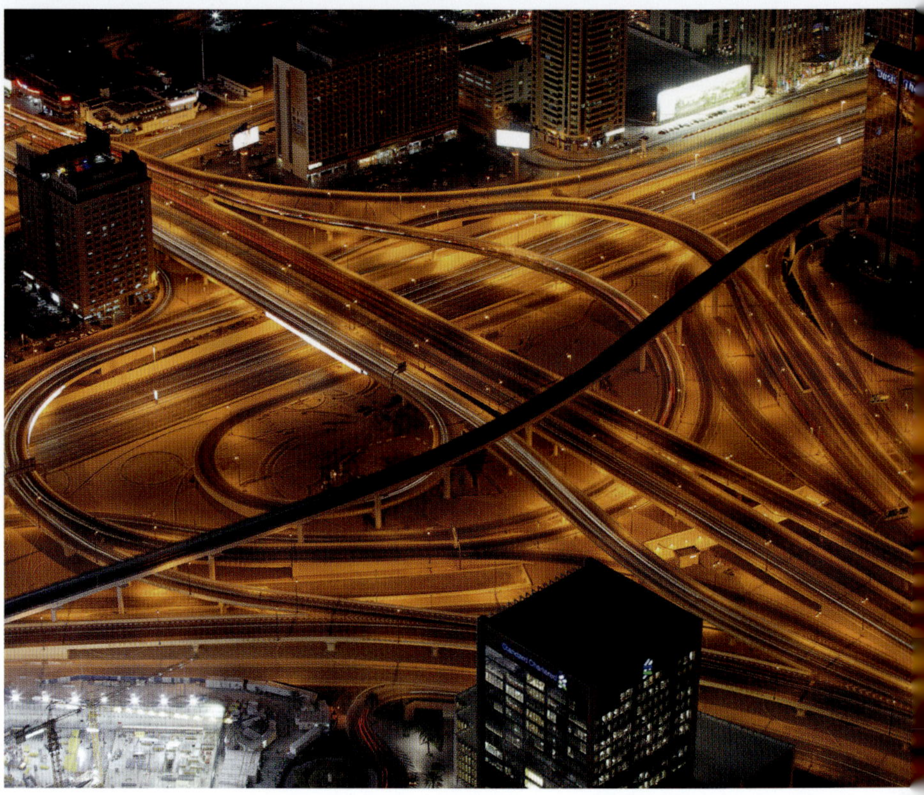

For a view of the complete set of skyscrapers around Dubai Marina, you can go out onto the Palm, which is an artificial island created in the shape of a palm tree. On the far west side of the island, you can view all of the buildings from the side of the road.

One thing about the United Arab Emirates, and other countries close to the equator, is that the sun rises and sets very swiftly, making those sunrise and sunset shots rather trickier to capture.

ABOVE
This unique view, taken from the Burj Khalifa, looks like it could be shot from a drone.

RIGHT
The buildings around the Dubai Marina, with the perfect clear skies you might expect, show why this would be a dream destination for any urban photographer.

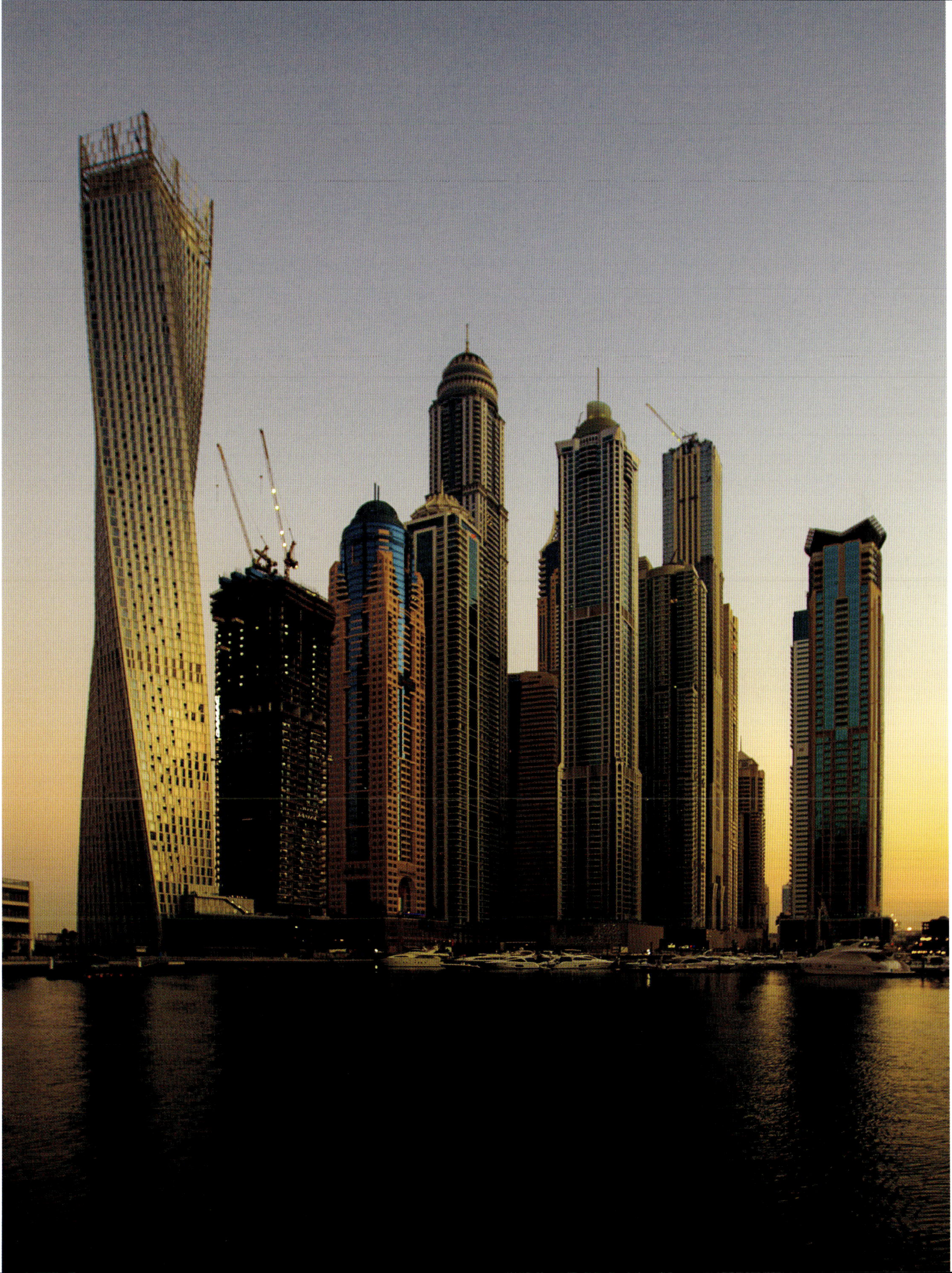

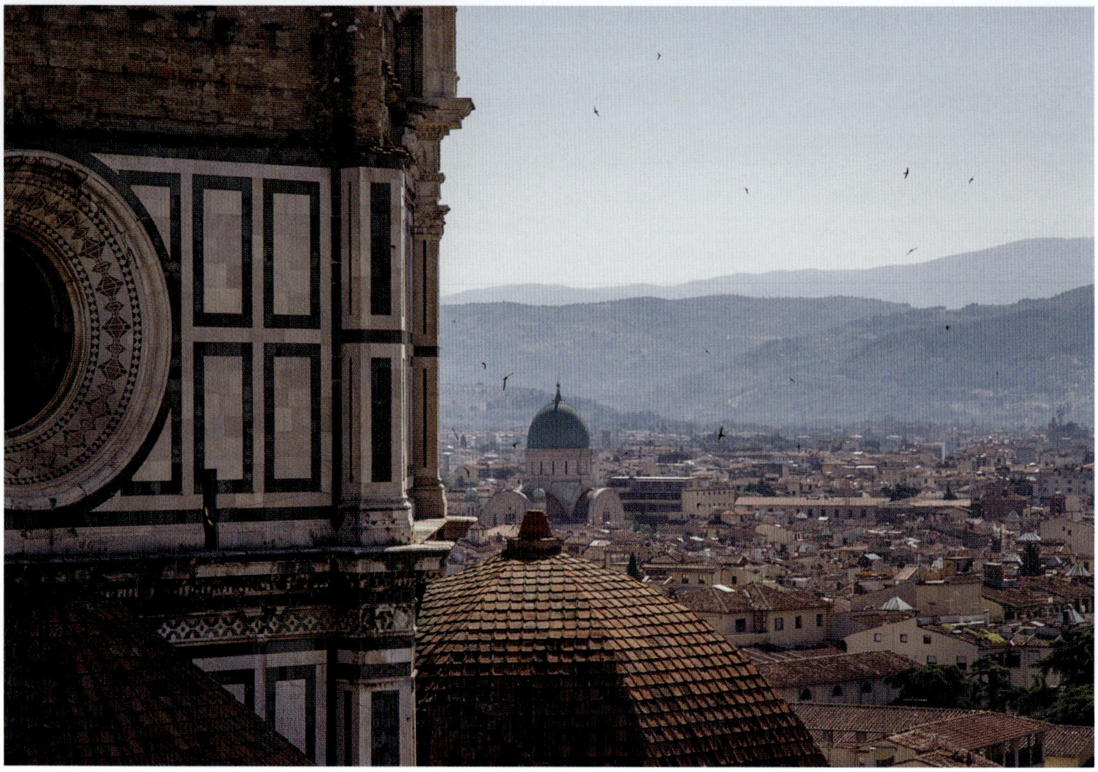

FLORENCE

When we think of city skylines, we typically think of huge glass skyscrapers, but Florence has nothing of the sort. This city is in stark contrast to Dubai, with its rich historical significance and classical Renaissance architecture. This gives a different focus for your photography.

The most famous structure in Florence is Filippo Brunelleschi's Cattedrale di Santa Maria del Fiore, which rises above the city. The majority of buildings in the city are at a standard height thanks to strict planning laws that prevent anything above a certain height, adding further emphasis to this building. The best location for viewing the cathedral in its urban context is up at the Piazzale Michelangelo, which is perched on the side of a hill overlooking the city. If you go up there for sunset in the summer, the sun will set just to the left of the central area of the city, creating an amazing backdrop to the classical architecture, silhouetting the cathedral in front of the hills beyond, and highlighting the Rialto Bridge as it reflects off the river.

The contrast between day and night is an interesting aspect to consider when shooting in Florence. At night, the main buildings are the centre of attention, illuminated on the skyline, but in the day, looking down at the city, you see the amazing terracotta colours of the rooftops. This can be used to complement the features on the Cathedral, as the example above shows.

LEFT, ABOVE
The cathedral in the foreground creates a dramatic sense of scale, showing it properly in its context.

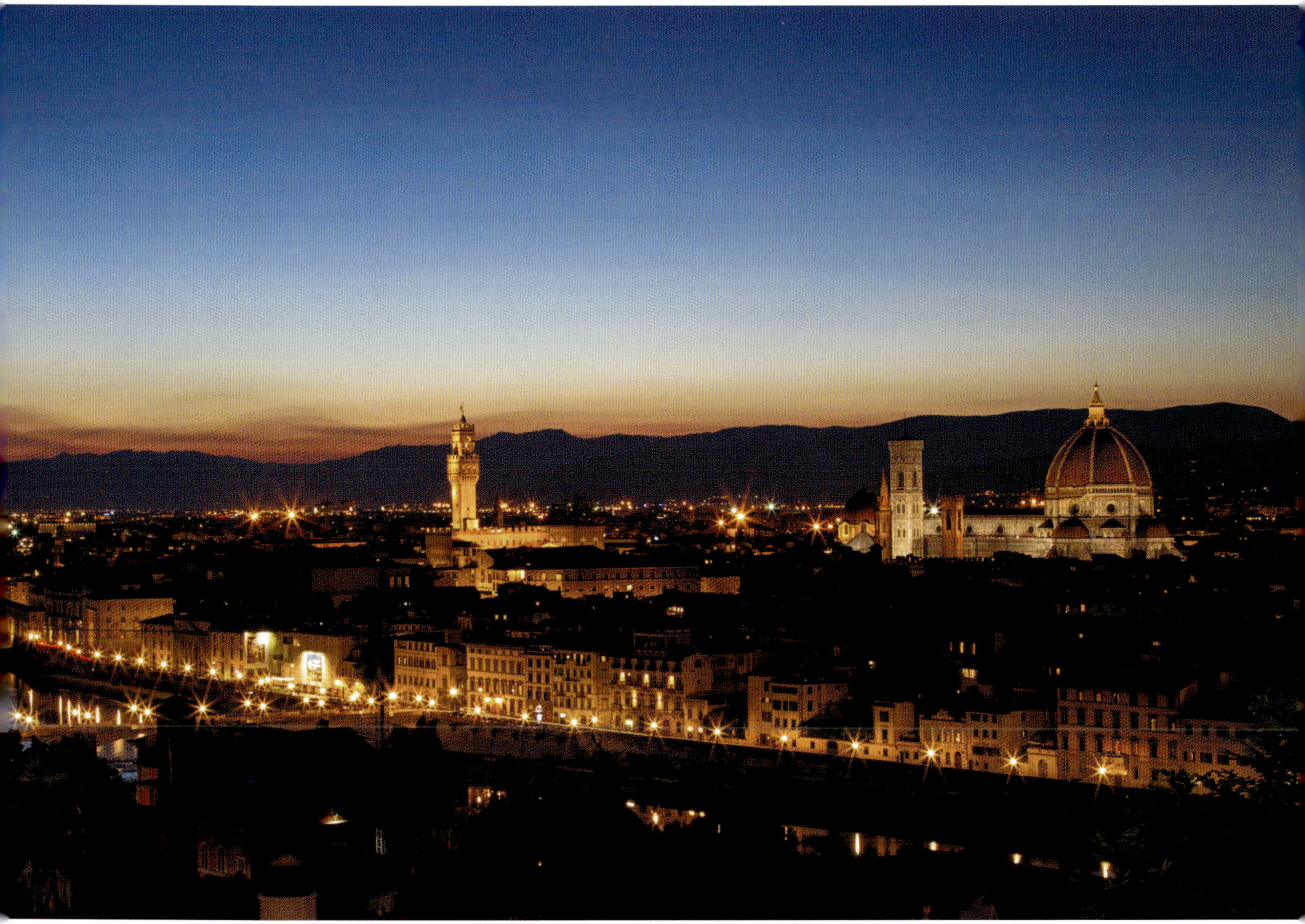

ABOVE
The view from Piazzale Michelangelo after a summer sunset, with the lovely graded colours of the sky complementing the layers of light and dark in the city.

PARIS

Paris has a unique skyline and, like Florence, there are restrictions on the height of buildings, so anything tall – like the Eiffel Tower – really stands out. It's always tempting to think that the best views of Paris will be from the Tower itself, but that means not including it in your shot. In order to get a shot of the skyline with the Eiffel Tower in the frame, check out the viewing platform at the Tour Montparnasse, because this sits on the axis directly opposite the Tower. From here you get an interesting view of the large skyscrapers in the La Defense area of the city, contrasting with the silhouette of the Eiffel Tower. Another amazing view of the tower is from the Esplanade du Trocadéro, where you can capture the silhouettes of people standing in front of it.

While photos of the skyline are usually limited to shots of the Eiffel Tower, another interesting aspect to capture is the street (beginning at the Avenue des Champs-Élysées) that runs all the way from the Place de la Concorde, right in the city centre near the Louvre, out to La Defense on the outskirts. From each end, you can see the Arc de Triomphe in the centre on a clear day.

You see a lot of photos of Paris shot in black and white, and I think this is for many reasons. This goes all the way back to the photography of Henri Cartier-Bresson, and a sense of capturing the atmosphere of a vibrant city which is rich in cultural heritage as well as architecture. Another slightly less exciting but equally relevant point is that converting a photo to black and white on a gloomy day can enhance the atmosphere of the shot, and with Paris situated where it is in northern Europe, the weather is not always bright sunshine!

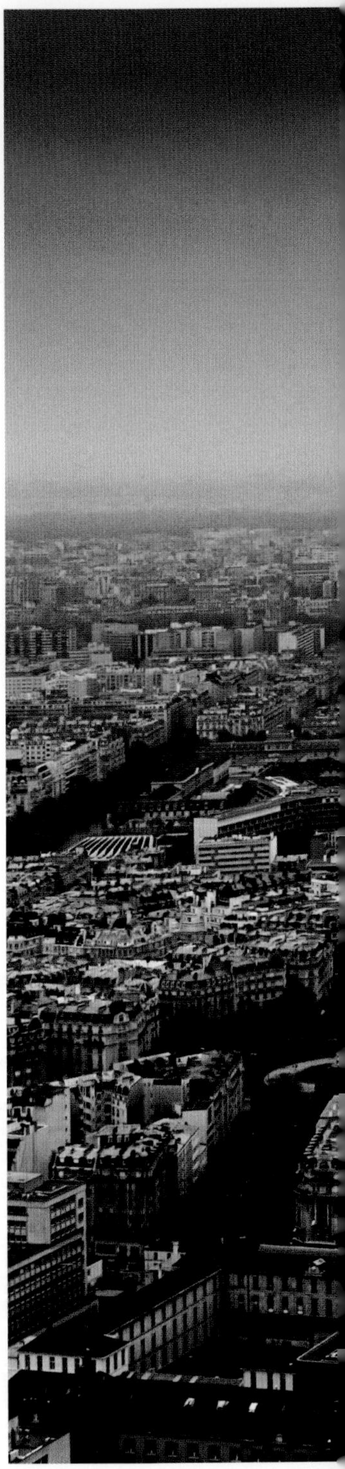

RIGHT
The Paris skyline, as viewed from the Tour Montparnasse.

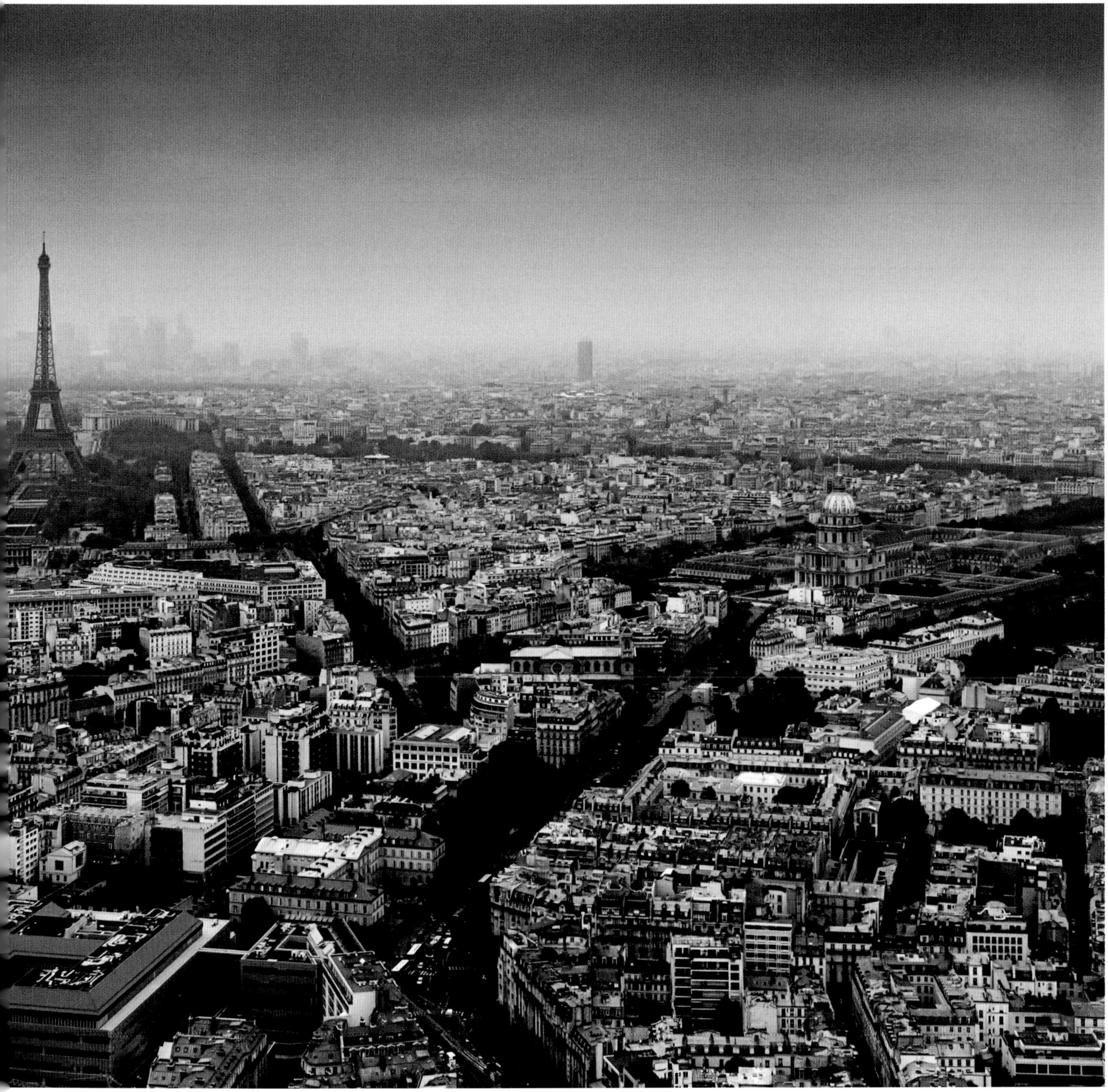

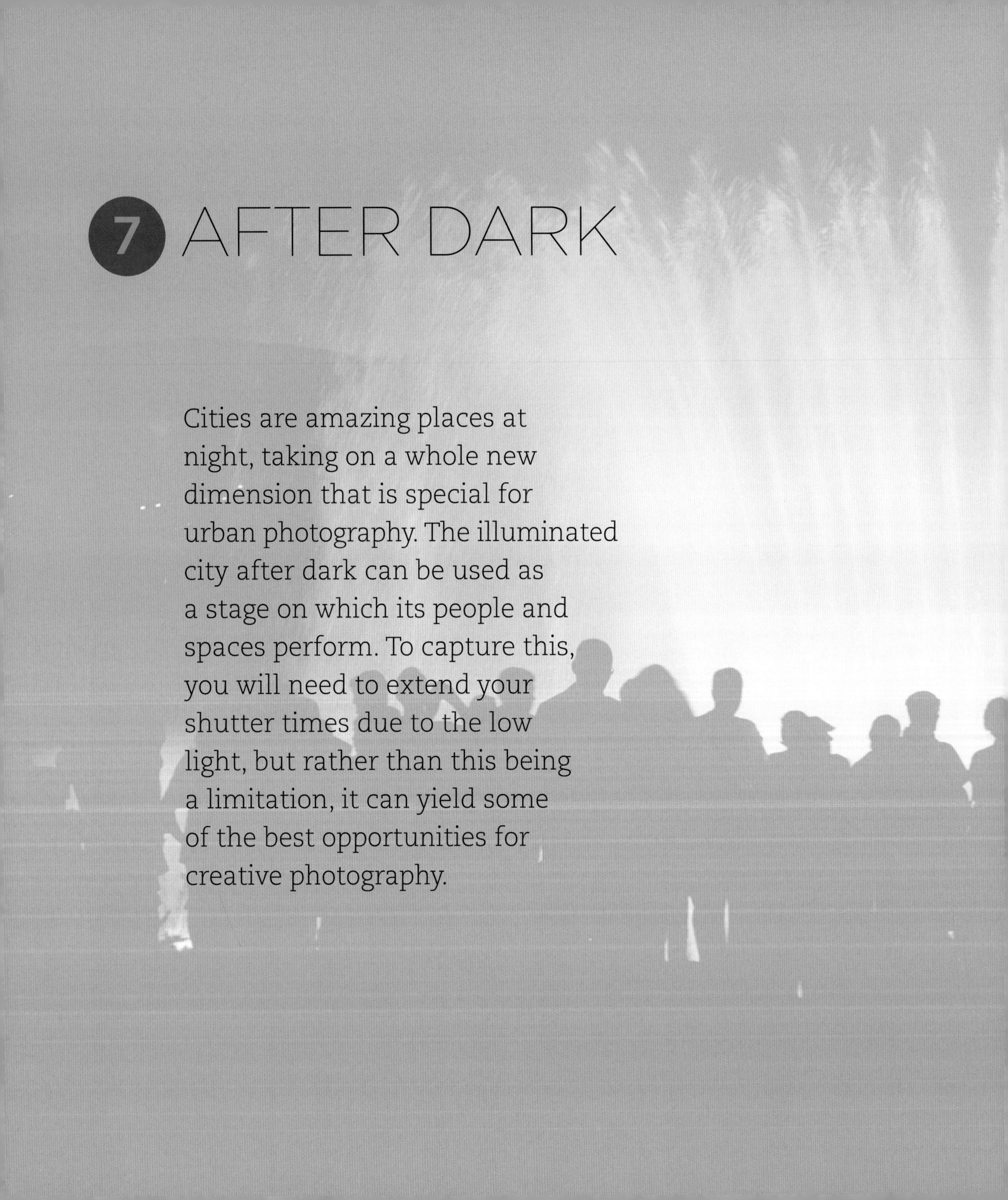

7 AFTER DARK

Cities are amazing places at night, taking on a whole new dimension that is special for urban photography. The illuminated city after dark can be used as a stage on which its people and spaces perform. To capture this, you will need to extend your shutter times due to the low light, but rather than this being a limitation, it can yield some of the best opportunities for creative photography.

Allianz

CITIES COME ALIVE AT NIGHT

After the sun sets, cities become completely different places, and all the settings you've been concentrating on for your photography in the daylight take a back seat. Locations that were not particularly photogenic in the stark light of day start to become beautiful under artificial illumination. These are places like the roads and tramlines that snake their way through the city, the lit backstreets and the multicoloured lighting from signage that can be used as backdrops to your urban shots.

There are a few places in the world that are famous for being hotspots for night photographers. Tokyo is a great example, exemplified by its fully lit tall skyscrapers and its hundreds of thousands of neon signs that line the stores and restaurants at street level. The signs really make the city stand out from anything else in the world, and when you see an image from Tokyo, you recognize instantly where it was taken. Your own urban space may be a far cry from the neon of Tokyo, but you can still think about areas of the city with similar characteristics and approach them as if they were Tokyo itself.

There are a few things you'll need in order to shoot the city at night. The first on the list is, of course, a tripod, which is an essential tool for dealing with longer exposures. You might also want a camera that has a high ISO capability, and a fast lens for handheld shots. A torch would be useful to check settings on camera (use a red torch if you are doing astrophotography) and could be used for light painting. Last of all, make sure you've got a warm jacket, as temperatures can plummet in the evening.

It's worth taking a moment to consider the time of year and how this might be best suited for photography after dark. In the UK, we have an annual 'bonfire night', where fires are lit and fireworks are set off. Christmas and Diwali involve a lot of decoration and use of lights for each celebration, and there are plenty of other local festivals, holidays and customs that involve bright, decorative lights.

Walking the streets at night can seem like a daunting task, but it doesn't need to be as it is one of the best times to capture life in the city. Use your common sense and don't go anywhere too off the beaten track, and if you are anxious, you can always take a friend out with you. You could also visit the place in the day so that you are more familiar with it when you visit again in the dark.

RIGHT
Looking down on the streets below, at a city illuminated by the streetlights.

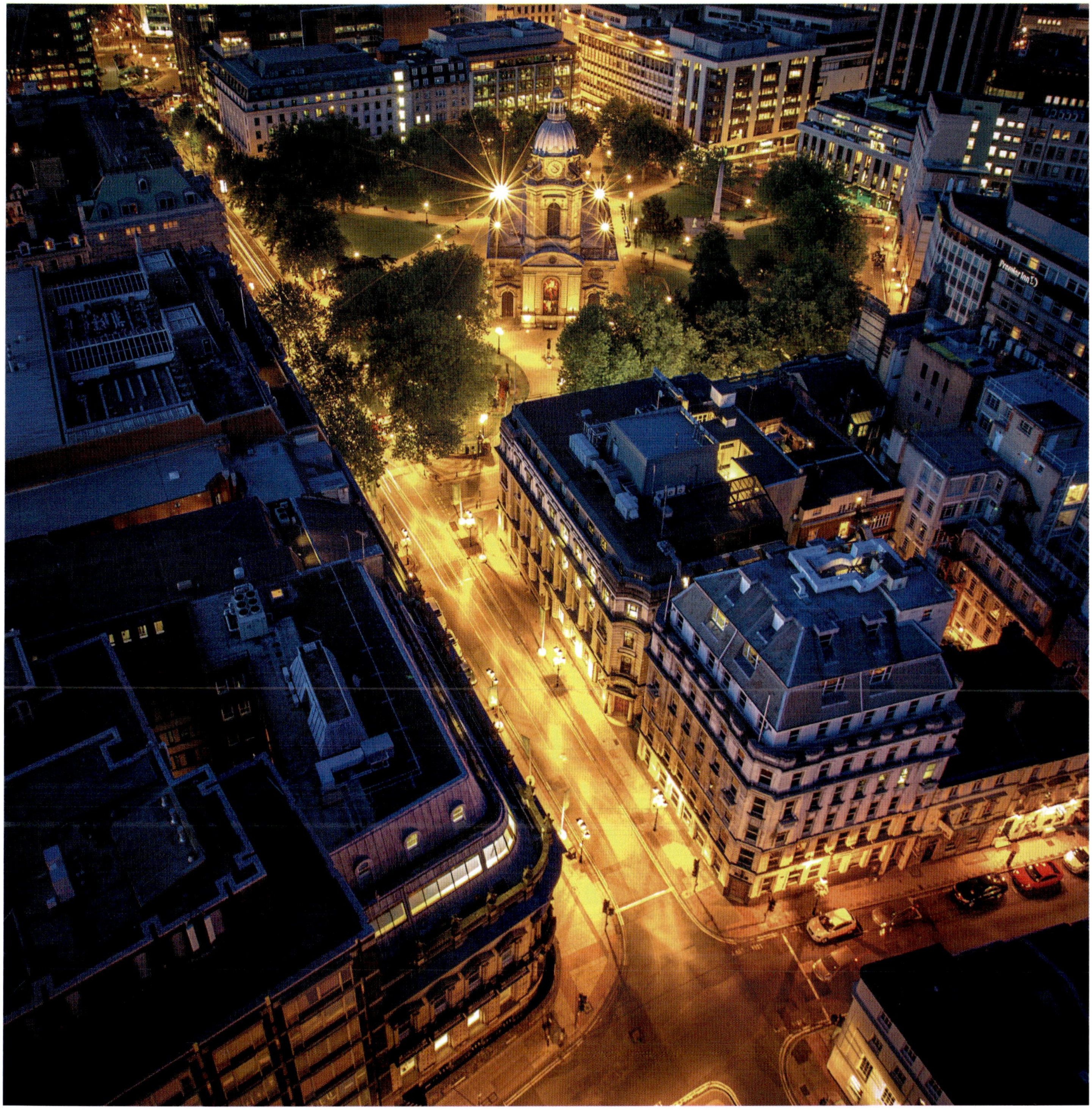
Premier Inn

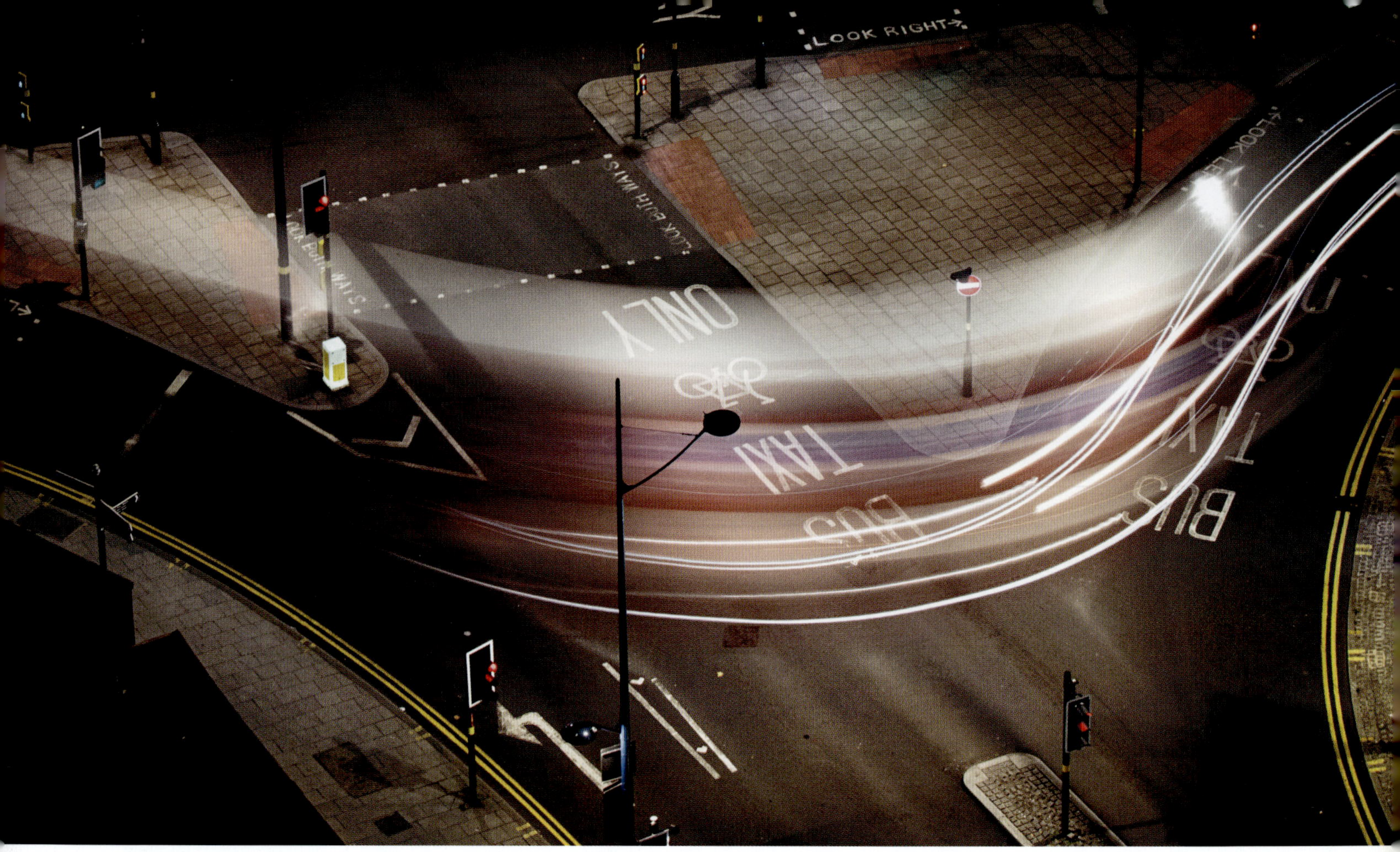

GETTING CREATIVE

At night, due to the absence of natural light, your camera naturally struggles to take sharp photographs. It compensates for the lack of light either by extending the time the shutter opens in order to gather enough light on the sensor, or by setting your sensitivity to a higher ISO (or using a higher-sensitivity film). Doing the latter can result in a grainy image if you push it too far – but many modern cameras can cope incredibly well with a high ISO (years ago, an ISO beyond 3200 would have been considered 'too high', but this is no longer the case). Extending your shutter speed, however, allows you to produce some fantastically creative photographs, so it's time to embrace your tripod.

TRIPOD

A tripod stabilizes the camera in low light, so that the extended shutter times do not become an issue. In addition to the tripod, and especially if you are using a traditional DSLR, you may need to use a shutter release cable or timer, to avoid any shake from you hitting the shutter and also from the mirror moving before the shutter opens. Wind can also cause your camera to wobble, so you need a tripod that's light enough for you to carry easily, but also sturdy enough to counter the wind. You may also need to find a well-sheltered area to set up in. With all these factors in place, you can open the shutter for several seconds and have a crisp image.

ABOVE
A stable camera taking a long exposure should produce a crisp background, while movement is captured over the top.

RIGHT
Setting up your tripod in the middle of a road isn't always a good idea, but at night the roads are much quieter and you can take advantage of the viewpoints offered.

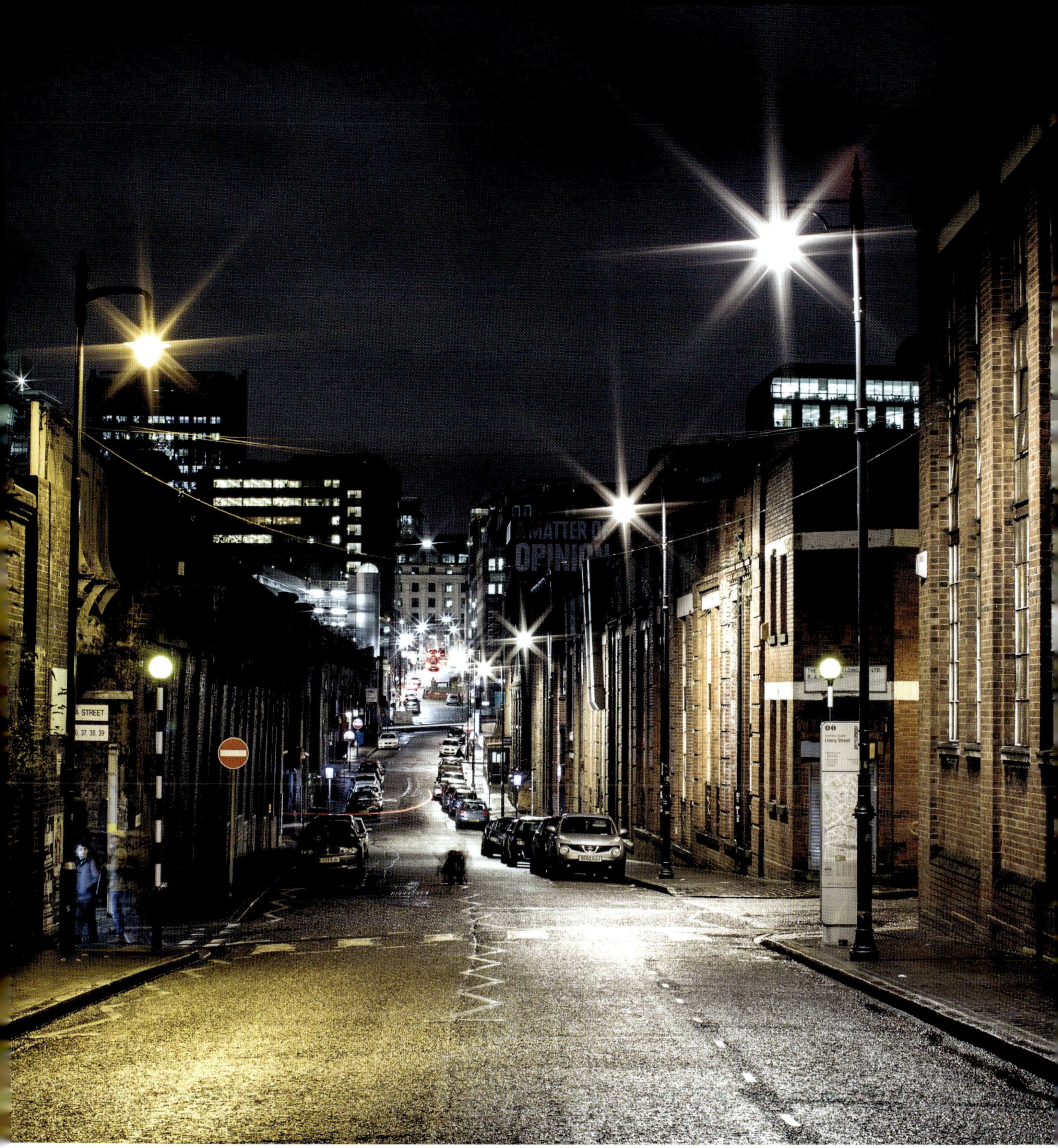
STREET
Livery Street

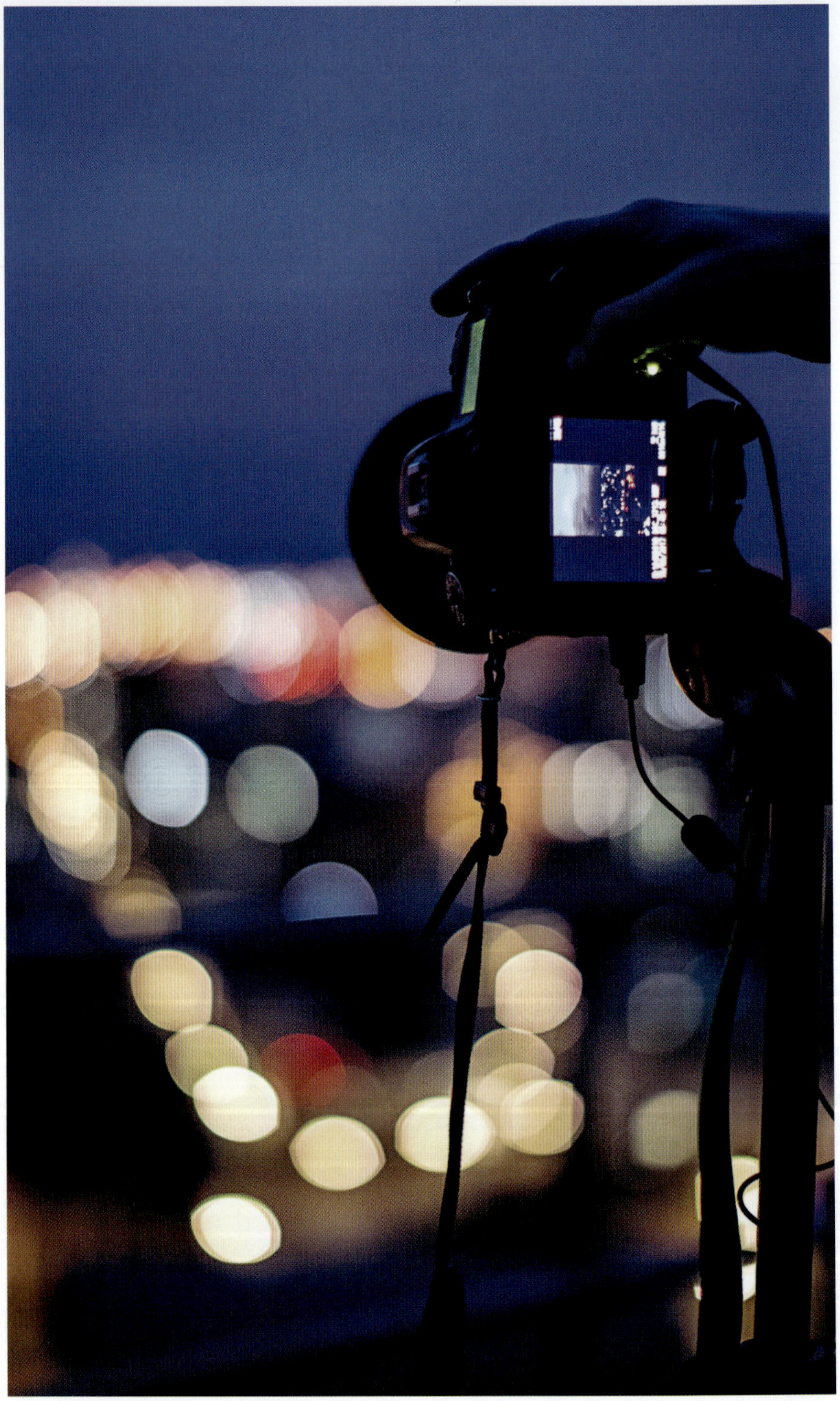

SMARTPHONES AT NIGHT

No matter how good your phone's camera is, smartphones have small sensors in comparison to DSLRs, so they are not naturally very good at taking photographs in low-light conditions. However, much that you can do on a DSLR can also be done on a phone: again, you'll need a tripod, and there are many on the market specifically for smartphones; chances are that you'll also need to download an app that lets you manually set the shutter time. After that, you should be able to enjoy most of the techniques we look at here.

BOKEH

'Bokeh' describes the effect when a shallow depth of field produces an (intentional) extreme out-of-focus background, with any light in the background picked up as a series of abstract circles. It is particularly relevant when photographing at night because city lights are often coloured, and under the distortion of bokeh they can become as decorative as fairy lights. This can make a good background for a sharp foreground subject, or work as an abstract image on its own. Look out for clusters of lights you can use to create this effect, such as a row of streetlights or festoons. The trick to producing a good bokeh effect is using a wide aperture; the size of the light circles increases with the lower the f-number. If your lens doesn't open beyond, say *f*/3.5, you can still produce the effect by increasing the distance between the foreground subject and the lit background.

RIGHT
Lights in the far distance are pleasingly distorted, while the camera in the foreground is sharp.

OPPOSITE
At night you can produce attractive, fully abstract images using bokeh.

LIGHT TRAILS

When you open your shutter for 15 seconds, 30 seconds, or even several minutes, movement is captured in an interesting way. In the image on page 133, you can see how the people on the left-hand side have become blurred, even ghostly. The longer the shutter is open (or the faster they moved), the more pronounced this fading would be, until the figures disappeared altogether because they themselves produce no light to capture, and the ambient light of the scene fills in the space left by their absence. Objects that produce light, such as car headlights, however, will be picked up more definitely, so that if you take a long exposure of a busy road, the vehicles disappear, but their light trails remain. Following the same principle, you can capture fireworks fully exploding and even the lights from an airplane taking off, as you're capturing a moment that happened over an extended period of time in just one frame. To capture light trails, you'll need to experiment with the shutter speed, but ten seconds is a good speed to start at.

RIGHT
Here, the light trails add dynamism to the solid structure at the centre of the image. This was taken with a shutter speed of 15 seconds.

BELOW
A long exposure from above shows off your city's networks in a beautiful new, ahem, light.

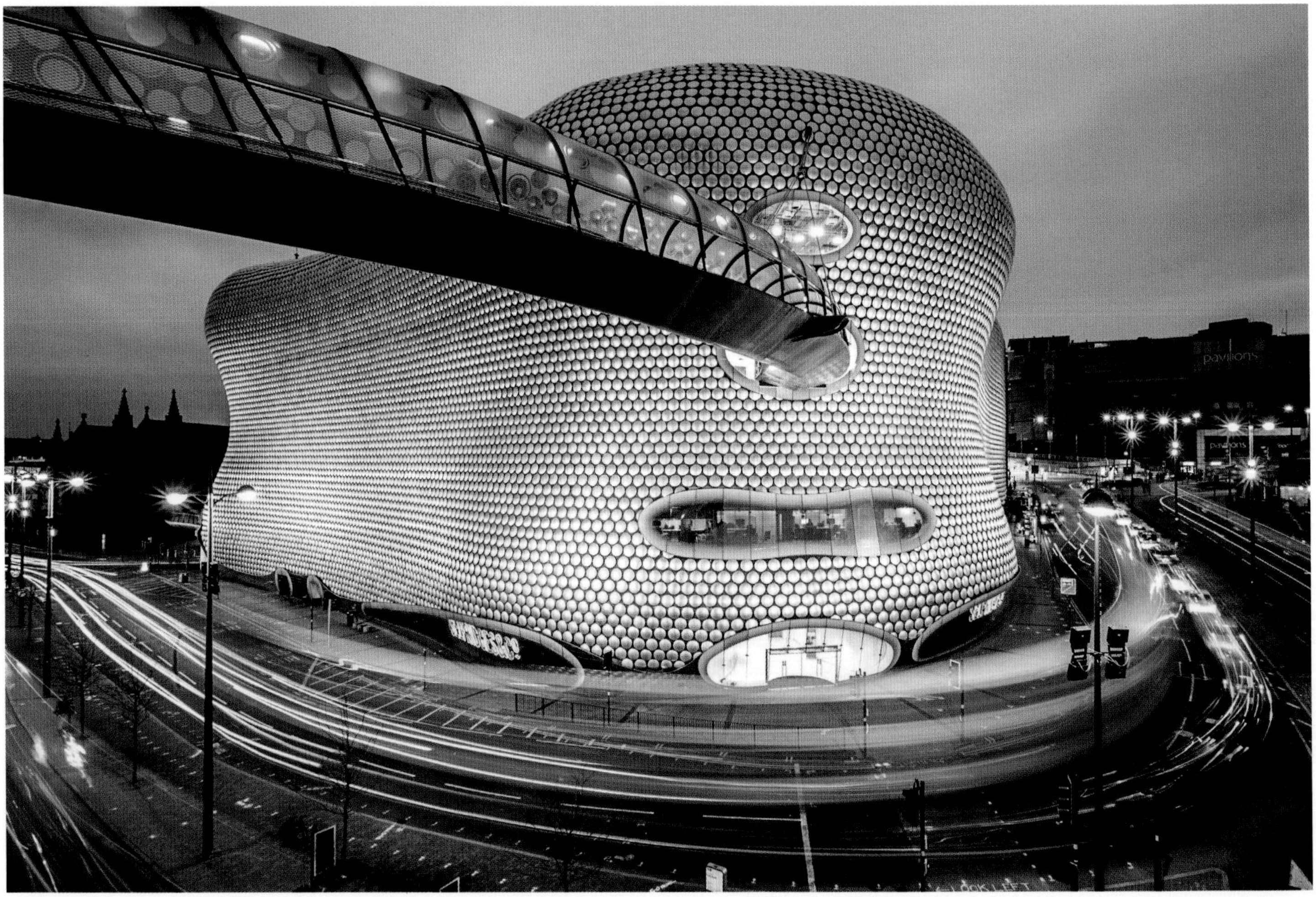

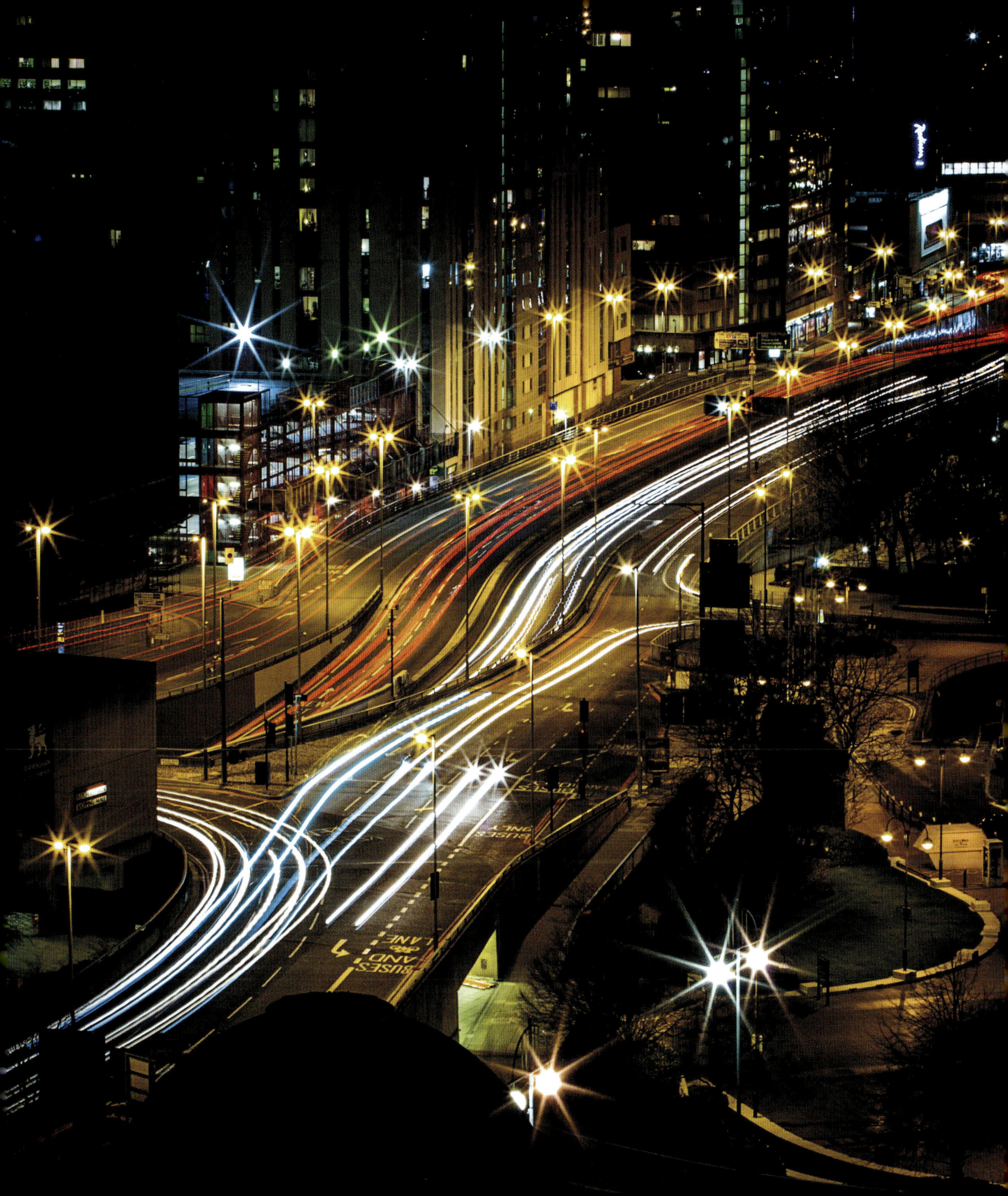

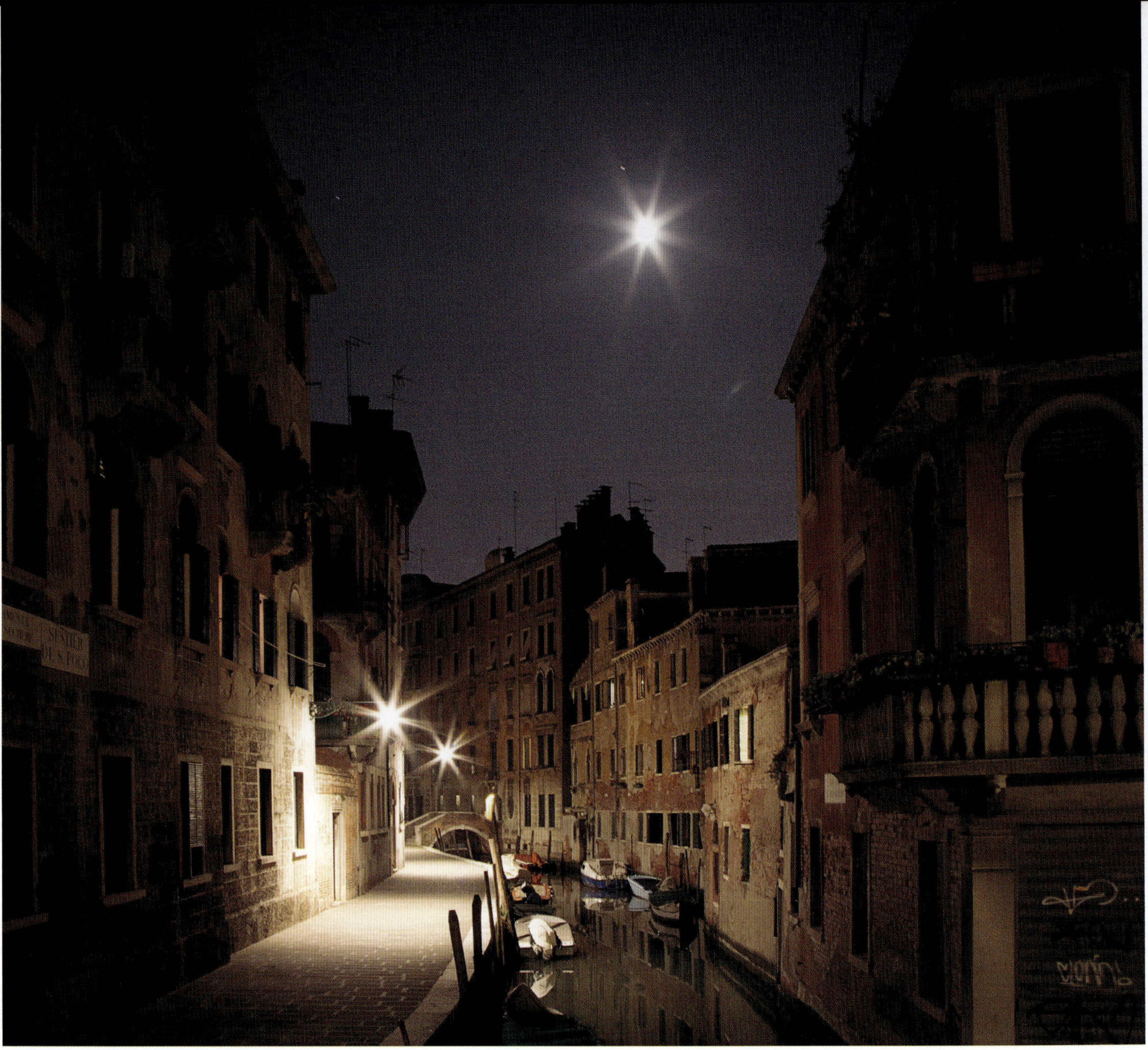

SEEING STARS

Another trick of night photography is turning any static lights in the scene into stars. When you look at a light and squint your eyes, you'll find that the light flares out from the edges, as it diffracts into your retina. The same principle applies to cameras, so if you stop down your aperture to its narrowest opening, for instance *ƒ*/22, compensated with a long exposure time, your camera is effectively squinting. Try this by pointing your camera directly at a light source and shooting the same shot at *ƒ*/2.8 and again at *ƒ*/22, and then compare how the light behaves differently.

ABOVE
Attractive stars complement the romantic canals of Venice.

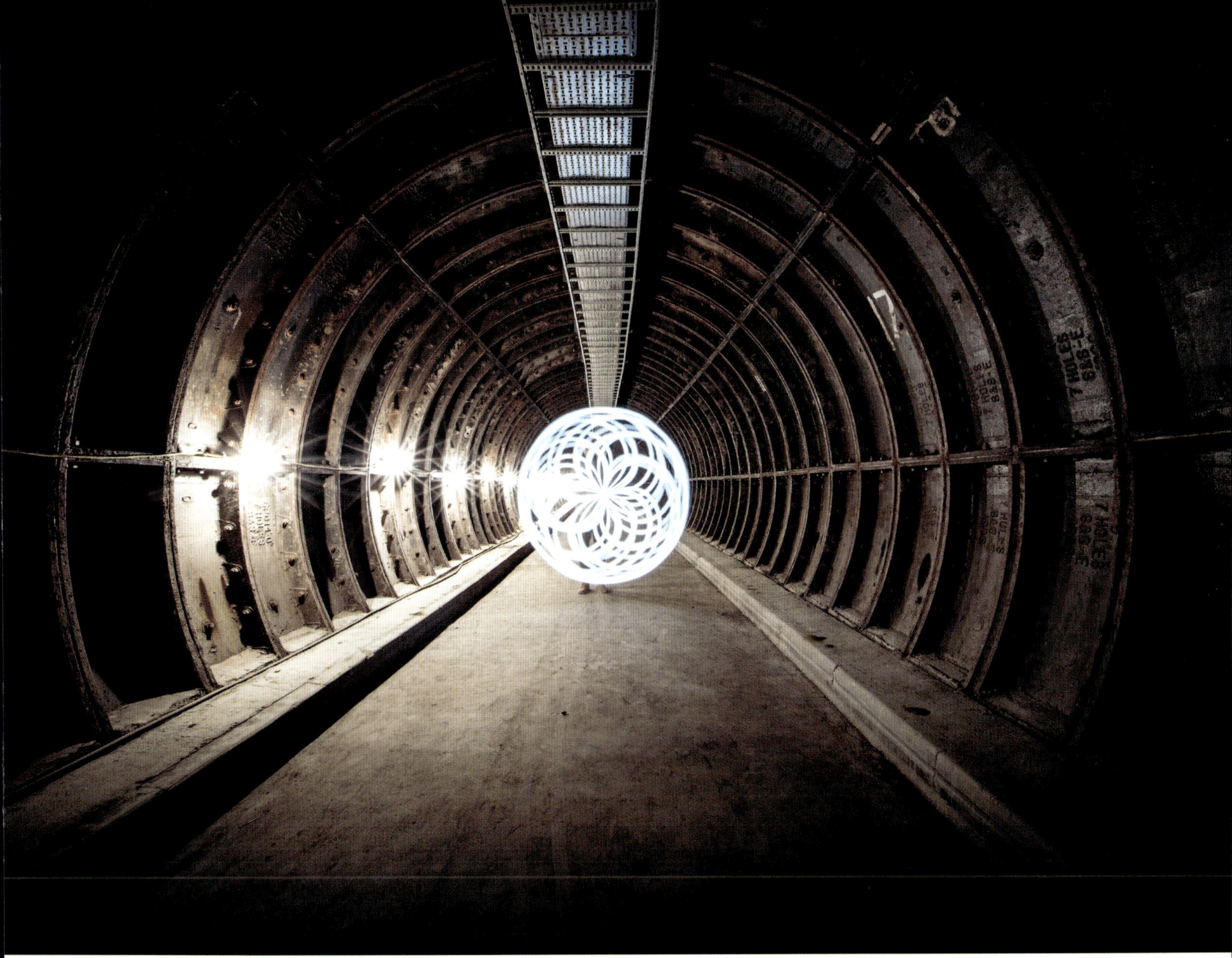

ABOVE
This atmospheric tunnel setting is the perfect place to play with light painting, spinning a Pixelstick to create a circular pattern.

LIGHT PAINTING

By exactly the same principles as shooting light trails, you also can manipulate light in order to create patterns to photograph. You can do this with a simple household torch or even the torch on your phone. Set your camera up for a long exposure and move the lit torch around for the duration of the exposure. Try writing your name. Stepping it up a notch, you can buy light sticks specifically designed for long exposures, such as a Pixelstick, which will paint a pre-selected pattern for you. By spinning the stick in a circular motion, you can also create attractive spirograph-type patterns. Another popular technique is using lit wire wool, which produces a sparkler-like effect. As some wires come free from the main ball of wool while you spin, this can produce beautiful shards of light. Because the wool is on fire, this is not the safest technique to use in the city, or in general, so if you do want to give it a shot, make sure you watch a few tutorials, and don't do it in a busy public place!

NIGHT CLOUDS

When shooting the city at night, you need to extend your exposure time to get the subject of the photo to show, even if your aperture is open wide. When you do this, you will notice that in the background, the clouds have moved. This can be frustrating when it leads to an image looking out of focus, but when it works, it can give a powerfully atmospheric look to your shot.

The best clouds to look out for in this instance are the fast-moving, low-level ones. Even with short exposures of say five seconds, you get an interesting effect, with lines in the sky that appear to strike out into the corners of the frame. Try not to extend your exposures too far because you will end up with a flat white sky in the background. As ever, it is worth experimenting with different exposure times depending on conditions.

BELOW
Long exposure on a wide-angle lens captures the clouds moving and appearing to come from the same point in the sky.

RIGHT
Cloud movement can be used to highlight the foreground subject.

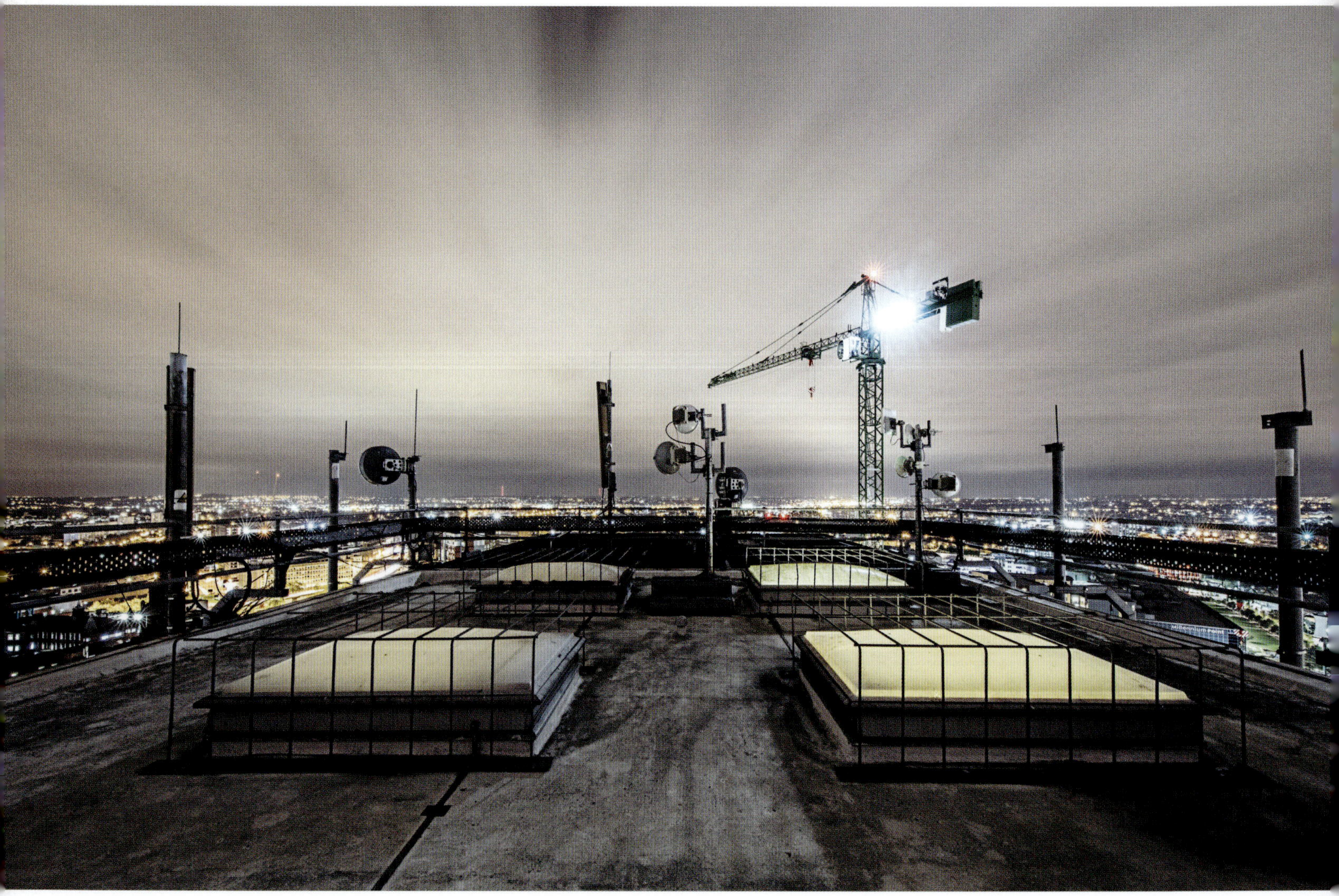

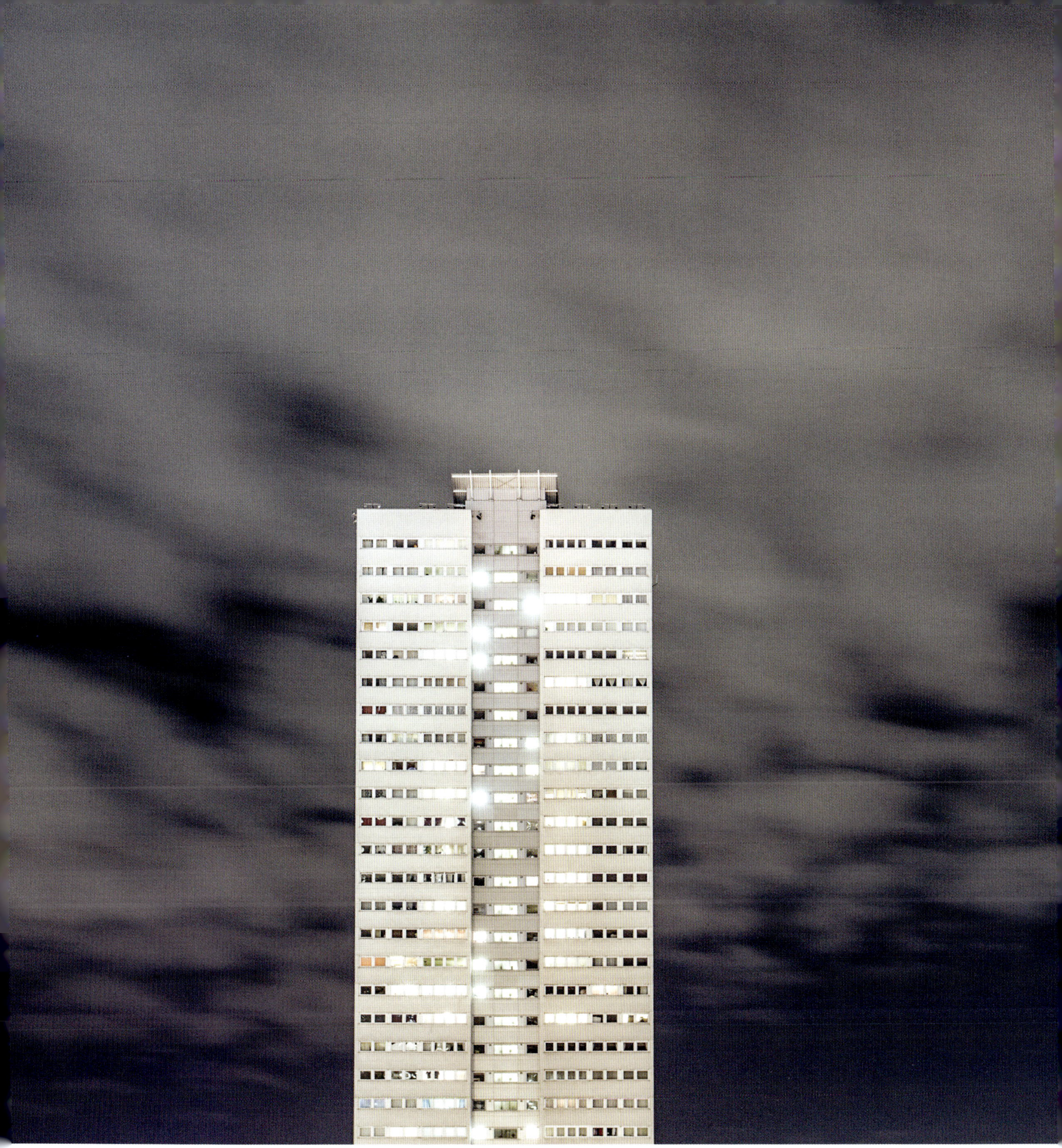

HERO
BRASSAÏ

I've talked about the way the colours of the city take on an extra dimension at night, due to the eclectic mix of lighting, but one of the most inspirational urban night photographers didn't use colour in his photos at all. The Hungarian-French photographer Brassaï took the majority of his photographs at night or in low light, all in black and white. His work centred on the streets of Paris, where he lived from 1924 through to the end of his life. Frequently, he captured the café culture and the people of this bohemian world, but many of his photographs are unpopulated or sparsely populated atmospheric street scenes, in which the artificial lights of the city or the light they cast becomes the most important element. In many of his photographs, a mist or haze hangs in the air, helping to enhance any lighting effects as it highlights the streams of light from the high-level street lamps. His use of artificial light at night and the shadows that they cause are unparalleled, and were revolutionary for photography.

To capture photos in a similar style, you first need to seek out interesting light sources in your city. Many of Brassaï's images show a long line of lights receding into the distance, which is a highly effective way of showing perspective. Look for a long avenue with equally spaced lights on either side to create the sense of a colonnade shrinking to the vanishing point in the distance. These same lights can produce beautiful, sculptural shadows and contrasts, quite different from anything you see in the daytime, and highly sympathetic to shooting in black and white.

The right type of conditions also help add to the atmosphere. The kinds of conditions you normally avoid in urban photography play to Brassaï's style of photography – here, mist and fog really come into their own. This serves to demonstrate again how there are no universally 'perfect' conditions in urban photography. As with each of the different approaches, genres and styles in urban photography, attempting to emulate something of Brassaï's style gives you a new challenge, a different set of rules and conditions to consider in your photography, and new aspects of your environment to appreciate, perhaps for the first time.

RIGHT
Pont des Arts, c.1932.

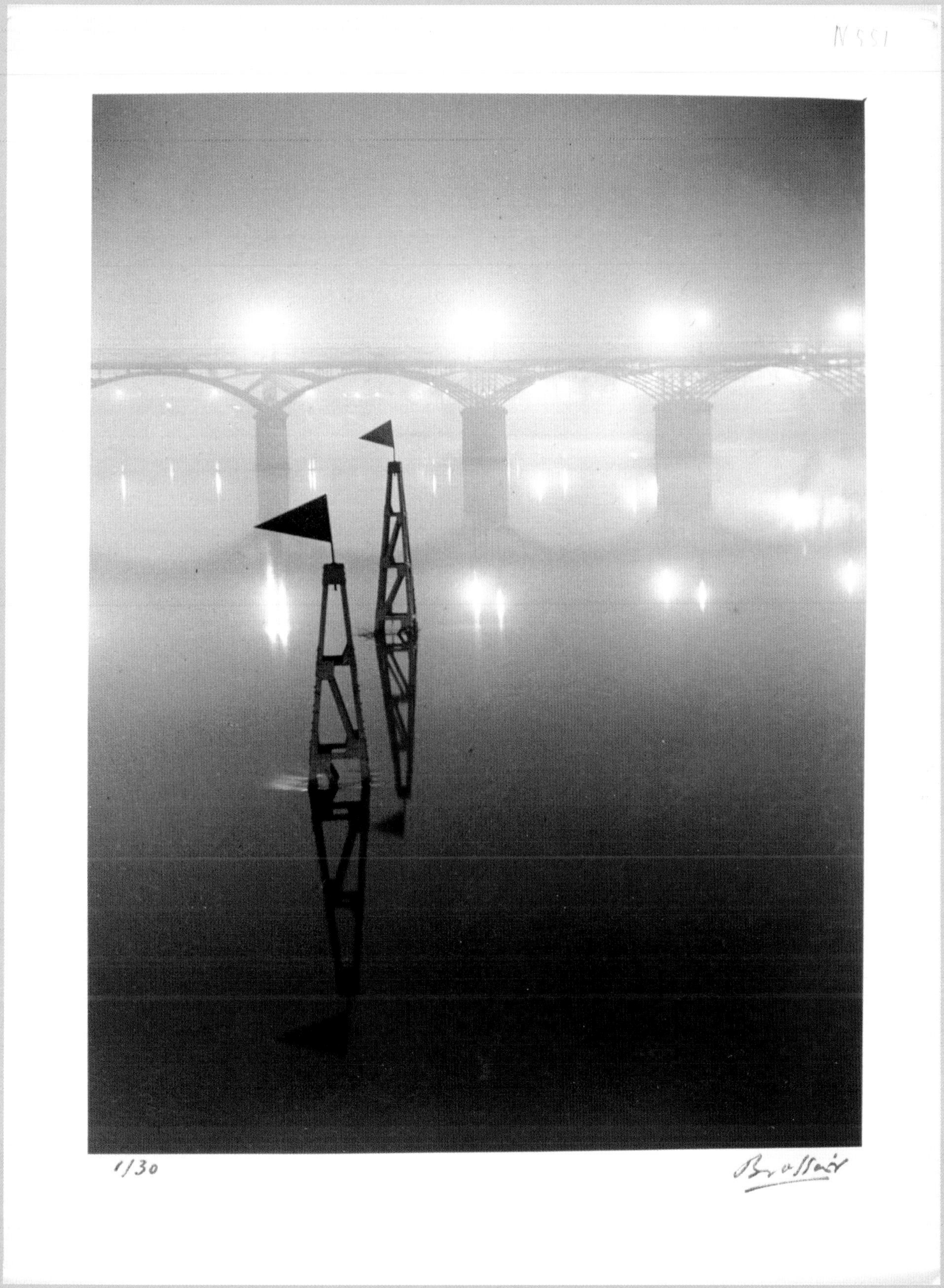
1/30
Brassaï

ASTROPHOTOGRAPHY

Shooting astrophotography in the city is a challenging but rewarding venture. You would be forgiven for thinking that attempting to photograph anything astronomy-related in the city is a non-starter due to light pollution, but if you can find the right position, there is great potential for it.

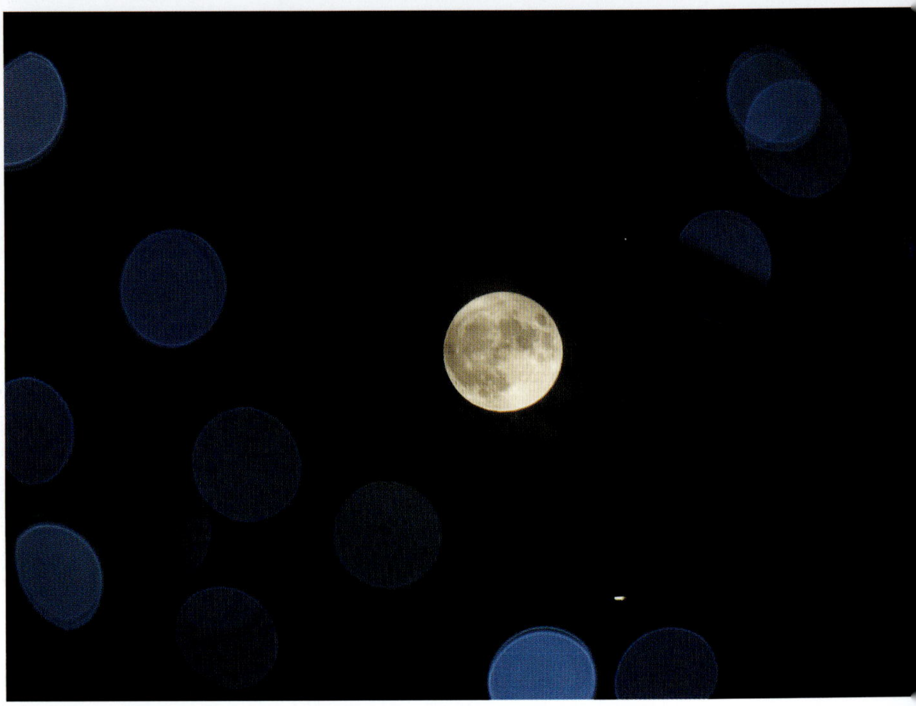

MOON

The first step into astrophotography in the city is looking out for the moon. In the last chapter, we looked at the challenge of shooting the skyline of a city with the moon in the background. The moon is also a good subject in itself; alternatively it can be used to complement a subject, as in the image opposite. The moon's cycle has two phases worth focusing on: the crescent moon and the full moon. When the crescent appears around the time of sunset, low on the horizon, it is easier to expose for than the full moon high in the sky. The times of year when the moon is in this phase and position will of course vary depending on where in the world you are, so you can use an app like The Photographers Epheremis to see when this conjunction will occur. Because the moon is low on the horizon, it's also the ideal time to use it as a complement to the main focus of your composition.

The full moon is much more difficult to expose correctly. One option is to overexpose the shot and create a star-like effect with your camera set around *f*/22 as I have noted (see page 138 for an example of where this works well), but this is not always what you want. The best time to shoot the full moon is when it appears on the horizon just after sunset, when the light reflected by the moon is comparatively muted so it's easier to correctly expose for both the moon and its surroundings.

ABOVE
The full moon shot through the lights of a Christmas tree. Here, the distant object is in focus, while the foreground lights are thrown into that attractive bokeh blur.

RIGHT
Shooting the moon in the daytime makes it easier to expose correctly. You can see a tell-tale beam of sunlight shining on the building, but converting into black and white makes it easier to focus on the moon.

STARS

Light pollution in cities is a big problem for stargazing, but some cities are better than others for both viewing and photographing the night sky. Shooting the stars in Hong Kong is out of the question due to all the lights on the buildings, but there are cities without as many lights. If you seek out a space with a small amount lighting, you will find that your eyes quickly adjust to seeing the night sky. It takes about 20 minutes for your eyes to adjust to see all the visible stars, and remember not to look into any lights or even look at your phone because this will temporarily ruin your star vision. Use a red torch, because this has no effect on the way your eye adjusts to seeing in the dark.

Once you can see the stars, you can set up your camera to capture a star trail, which is a series of long exposures that can be stacked together using software in post-production. Don't extend your exposure time too much because you can lose definition in the stars. A 30-second exposure is a good place to start; then work with what exposure is best for the conditions. Pick an urban location that has interest in the foreground, or, as in the example to the right, pick out the base of a building looking directly up so that the stars appear to trail around the top. Star trails work as a unique background to a scene, so think about the best dark urban location you can find and give it a try.

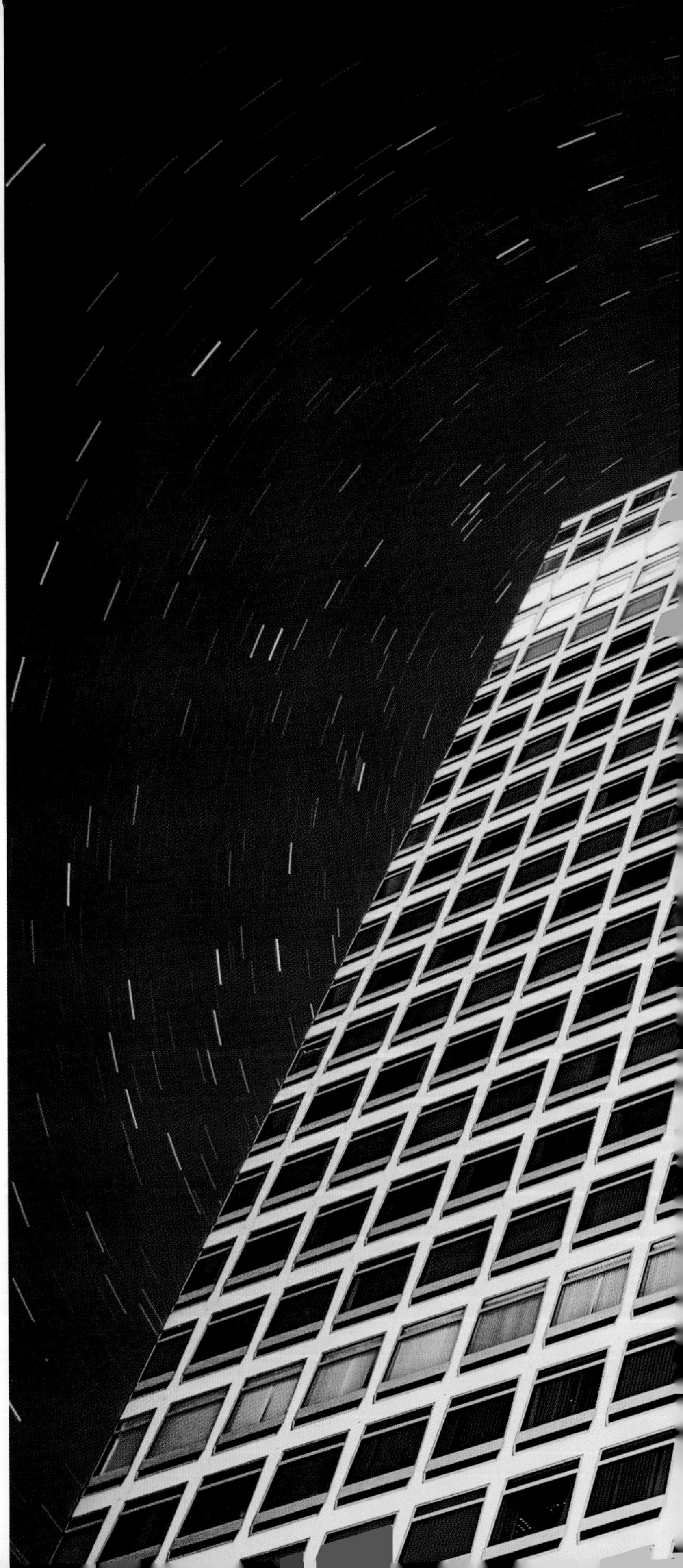

RIGHT
Shooting a star trail up from the base of a building gives an effect where the stars seem to halo it.

8 POST-PRODUCTION

The advent of the digital age of photography has meant that post-production has become one of the key elements of a photographer's workflow. It offers the opportunity to enhance, reduce and further develop their work.

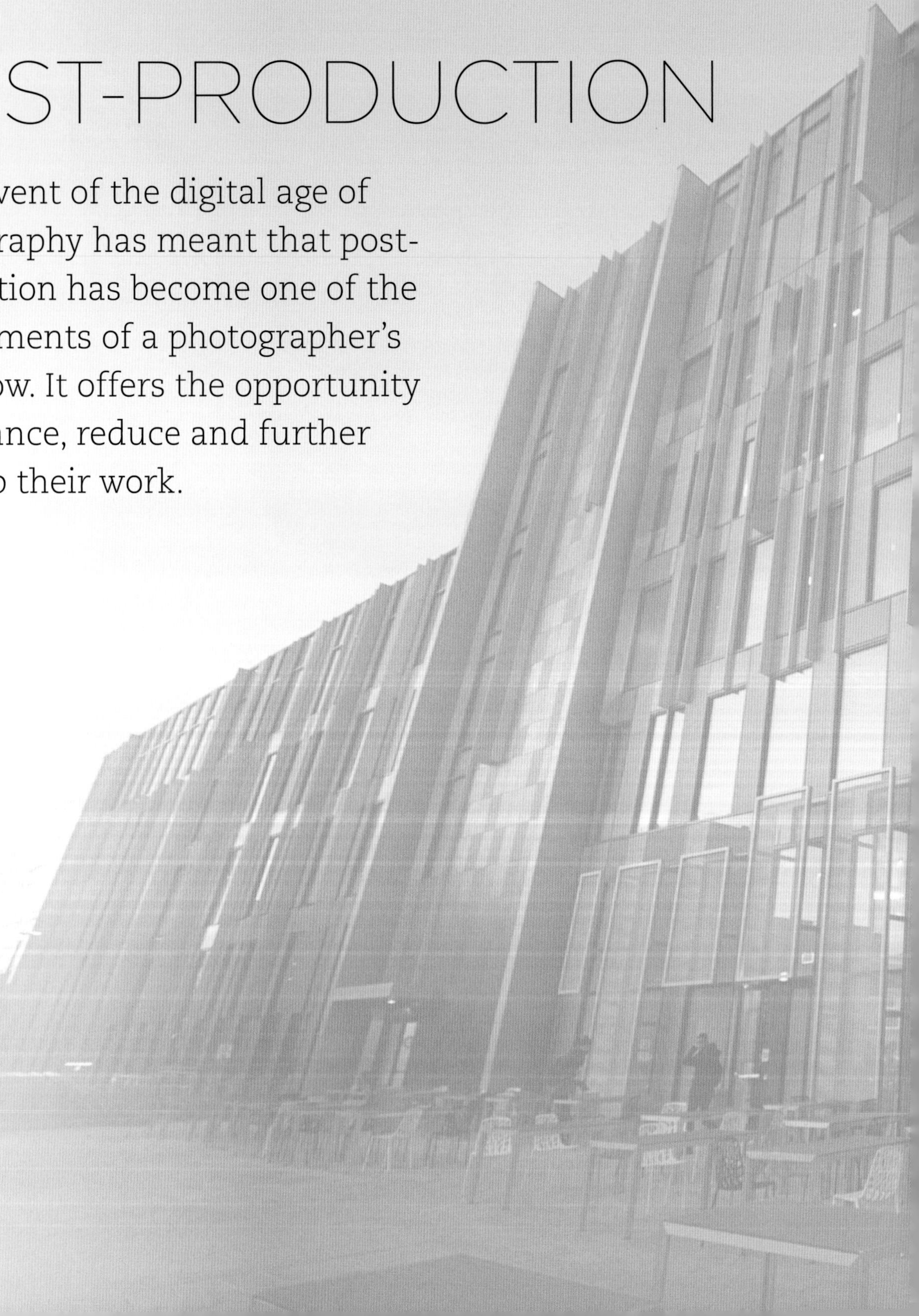

WHY SHOOT RAW?

In digital photography, it's easy to get confused by the different terminology used for file formats and what each type of file format does. We will look at the standard formats used by the popular global camera manufacturers and compare the advantages and disadvantages of each.

JPEG

This is the most common image format for the majority of cameras, so when you buy a new camera the default file type will be JPEG. The big advantage of this format is the small file size, meaning you'll be able to fit a huge amount of photos on your memory card. Another advantage is that it is the most common file type used on the internet, so most websites and apps will accept JPEG files if you want to upload them to print, or even take them to print in a shop. The only disadvantage of the format is that to get the small file size requires a degree of compression. This means that you don't get the full quality your camera is capable of,and every time you edit a JPEG and resave it, the quality will be even further reduced.

RAW

A more complex alternative to JPEG is the Raw file, which is available to use on the majority of cameras at the professional end of the market. In contrast to a JPEG, Raw files contain all the uncompressed data that the sensor has captured, allowing not only for a better-quality image, but also for much more freedom when it comes to editing the file. The biggest disadvantage of this type of file, then, is the size, which is usually three or four times the size of a JPEG, meaning that your memory card gets filled up much faster. The format also isn't generally used on the internet or at photo kiosks, so you'll have to convert to JPEG before sending them to print. One possible compromise is to set your camera to shoot both a Raw and JPEG simultaneously, so that you have a JPEG on hand should you need to send a file out quickly or get it printed right away.

The greatest advantage of shooting Raw is the editing capabilities it opens up. With a Raw file, the data from the file is unchanged – although you will need specialist software to be able to make the most of it. However, it is a huge advantage. When you shoot a JPEG, the camera is making a best guess about the settings required, and it throws away the information that isn't associated with these settings. In contrast, when you shoot Raw, all the information is saved, meaning you can edit the colour balance, exposure and other details much more easily and without a loss of quality. In addition, editing a Raw file is 'non-destructive', which means that whatever edit you make won't overwrite or throw away any of that data. All the software is doing is saving the commands you have given to amend that image. The most surprising thing you'll find when shooting Raw and then running through the editing process is the detail that is saved. The subject may be underexposed in the original photo, but you can often bring back a lot of the lost detail when you edit the Raw file.

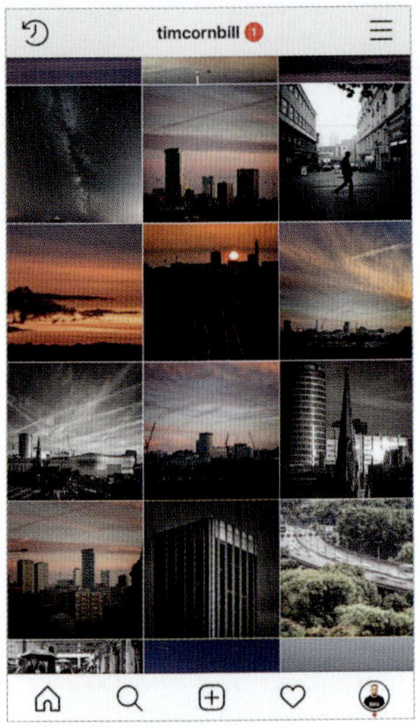

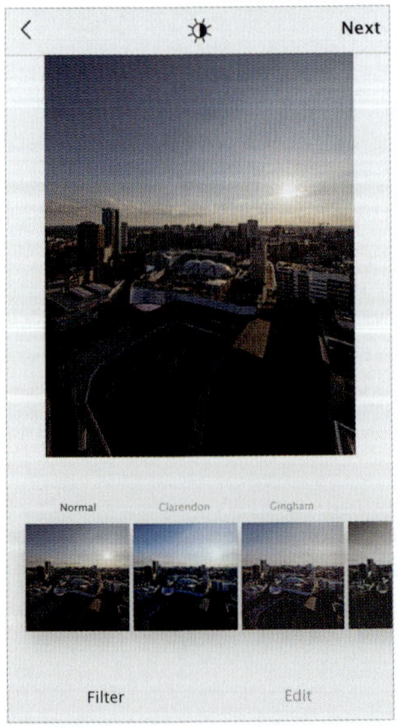

ABOVE
Not only is Instagram a great way to get public exposure for your photography, but it also has some powerful editing tools, as well as the ability to apply filters.

SOFTWARE

For anyone looking to get into editing their photographs there is a great range of software available, ranging from free apps to more expensive licensed software.

MOBILE APPLICATIONS

A huge number of smartphone apps have excellent editing capabilities, making them a great go-to tool for editing photos on the move. The most versatile of these is Snapseed, which visibly supports Raw files. It really provides all the functionality you'll ever require to edit your shots. You can change the levels and curves, and crop and rotation, as well as access a number of filters and editing presets, like HDR Scape, Drama and Vintage, to give your photo an unique aesthetic. Another good smartphone app is Instagram, which features some powerful editing tools, much like Snapseed. While the scope of features it provides is limited in comparison to Snapseed, it makes up for that by providing an extremely popular platform on which to get your photos noticed.

DESKTOP APPLICATIONS

As with smartphone apps, there are many to choose from, but a few editing programs dominate the photography industry. The first is Adobe Photoshop and the second is Adobe Photoshop Lightroom.

Adobe Photoshop: First released in 1988, Photoshop has become so popular with photographers and other digital artists that 'to Photoshop' as a verb has made it into common parlance. When you hear about a photograph that has been Photoshopped, it may not have been edited in this particular software, but capability of the editing functionality within it is so powerful that it has influenced the whole industry. As well the standard framing, lighting and colour editing functions (and so on), Photoshop also allows you to work with layers and masks, and lets you perform some very minute and delicate operations to a professional level. There are two major downsides to Photoshop: The first is the pricetag, which is fairly steep if you're not intending to use it professionally. The second is that it is not the most intuitive software to use, and there can be a steep learning curve. Photoshop Elements is a cheaper and more basic version of the same software, and other developers also provide similar editing functionality at a lower cost.

Adobe Lightroom: Lightroom is another stripped-down version of Photoshop, but it is specifically targeted at the editing of Raw files, along with having the capability of acting as an indexing tool. It is also relatively inexpensive and because of this, it is the perfect tool for any photographer who wants to edit Raw photos and also keep their photo collection well organized. For this reason, over the following pages we focus on this program.

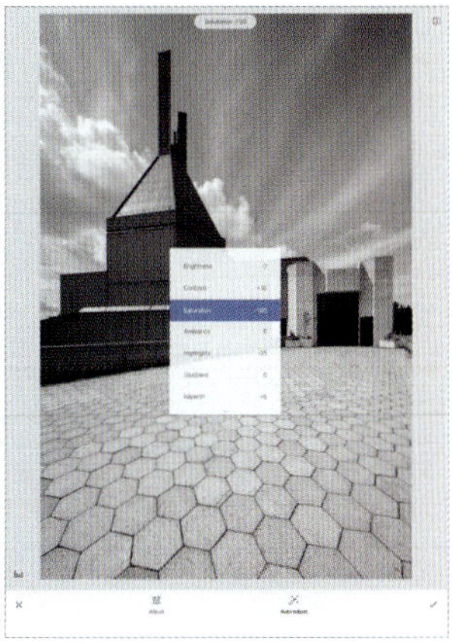

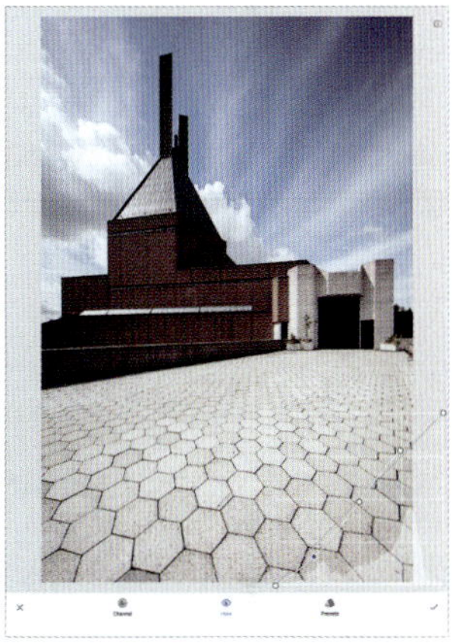

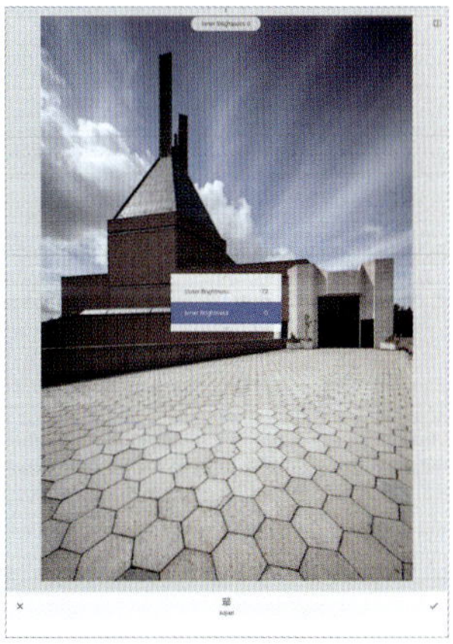

ABOVE
Snapseed is an excellent mobile editing app, with a huge number of different features and functions.

LIGHTROOM

Before running through a few tutorials around editing your photos, it's worth taking a moment to look at a few basic principles of how to set up Lightroom so you can get the best out of it. In order to show your photos in Lightroom and import them into your library, use the following advice to ensure an efficient workflow.

FILING SYSTEMS

Different people have their own way of filing photos, so this needn't be followed to the letter, but it does provide a sensible starting point.

Firstly, you need to organize your photos in folders on your computer so that when you import them into Lightroom, they will be ordered into a logical structure that makes it easy to find them. One tip is to order folders by date, so all your photos from one year are within the folder for that year, probably further broken down into sensibly labelled folders within that. The subfolders might be ordered by month, by genre, by place, etc. You might label each of these folders by the year, month and day, with a description at the end, for example, '2019_06_17 London Architecture'. Starting from the date is a good idea, because it ensures your folders will be easy to locate.

IMPORTING INTO LIGHTROOM

Once you've got your photos into some sort of order on your computer, you can then import them into Lightroom. You will find that they import in the same order on the left-hand side of the screen as the system you applied on your desktop. Lightroom then has a series of extra functions that will let you further organize your photos. The best thing about this that is does it without moving them on your hard drive, so you can create a personalized and perhaps highly specified ordering system for a particular project, while leaving the photos in an easy-to-locate order on your computer. These specialized folders are called Collections, and can be found if you scroll down on the left-hand side of the screen. You can create Collections to order your photos into subcategories, such as a certain genre or project title. You might want to create a portfolio collection, where you store all your strongest photographs. You can even create 'smart' collections, in which you set a rule by which photos will automatically be filed in that folder as you import them. This could be filtered by something in the metadata, for instance photos taken on a certain camera or even a certain lens, or by adding keywords to certain photos.

DEVELOPING

You'll note that next to the 'Library' tab on the top bar is the 'Develop' tab. Clicking this will open up a new window, within which you can process your images using the functions on the right-hand side of the screen. Over the next few pages we run through some examples of useful edits you can do in Lightroom that are relevant to urban photography. These will give you a taste of what's possible, but there is a whole world of image manipulation in Photoshop and Lightroom, which I certainly recommend exploring.

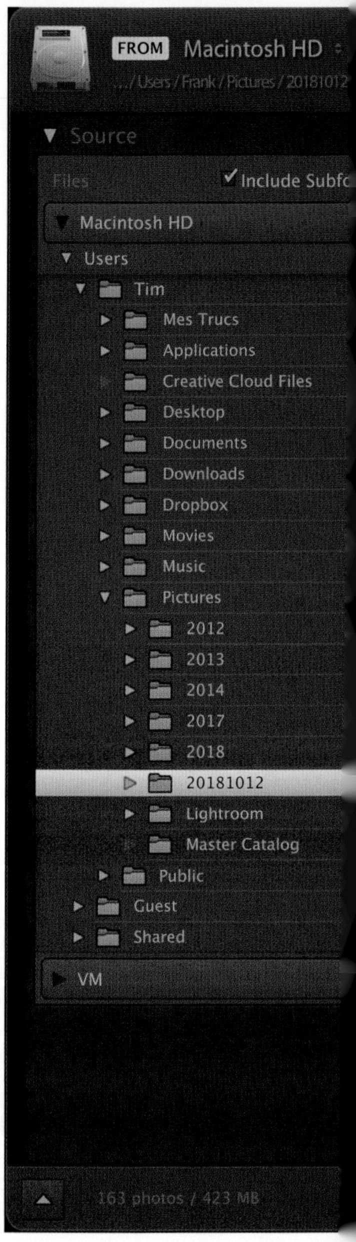

RIGHT
The import screen in Lightroom. On the right-hand side, you can set the programme to rename your files and even add metadata.

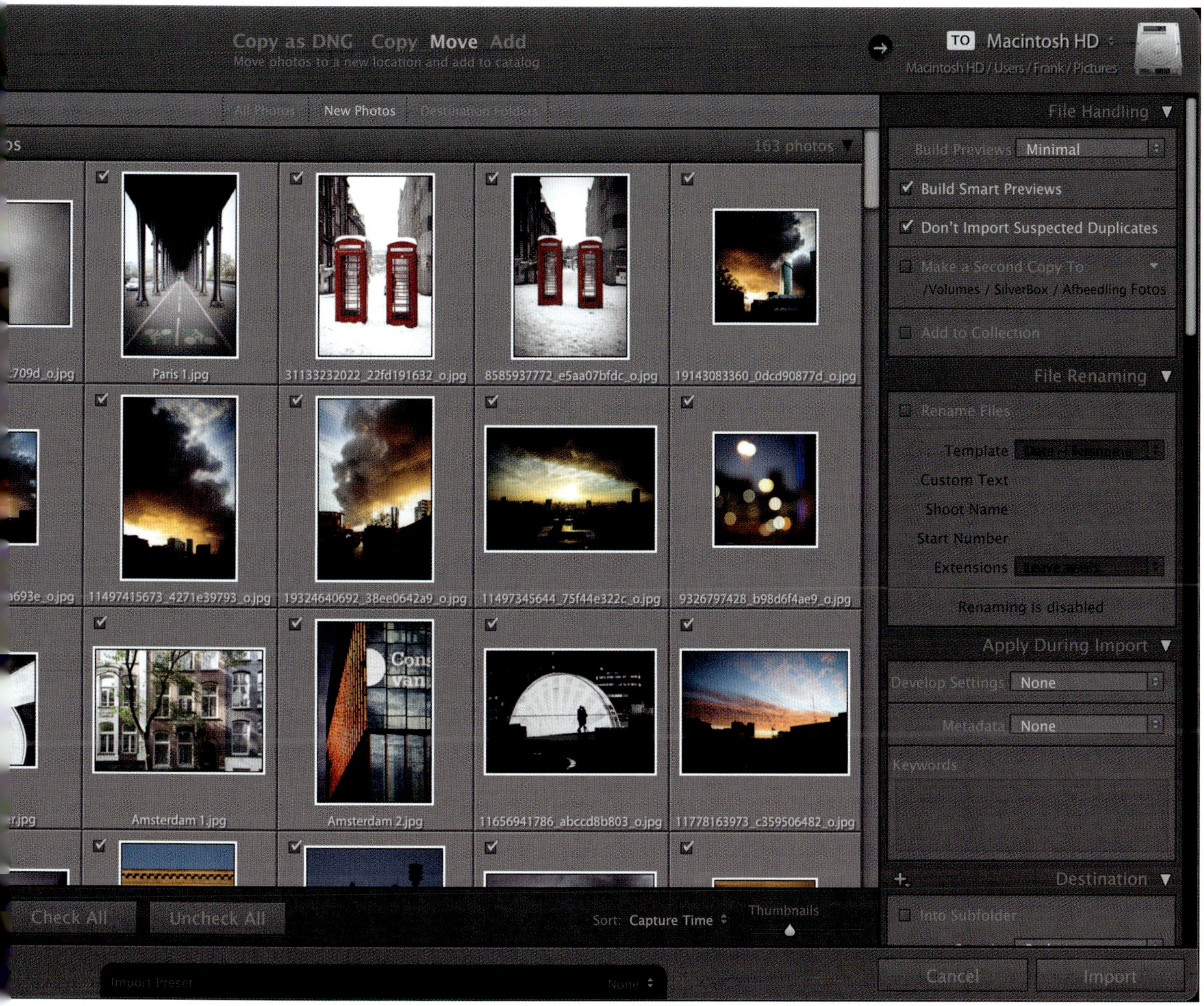
Copy as DNG Copy Move Add
Move photos to a new location and add to catalog
TO Macintosh HD
Macintosh HD / Users / Frank / Pictures
All Photos
New Photos
Destination Folders
163 photos
File Handling
Build Previews
Minimal
Build Smart Previews
Don't Import Suspected Duplicates
Make a Second Copy To:
/Volumes / SilverBox / Afbeedling Fotos
Add to Collection
File Renaming
Rename Files
Template
Custom Text
Shoot Name
Start Number
Extensions
Renaming is disabled
Apply During Import
Develop Settings
None
Metadata
None
Keywords
Destination
Into Subfolder
Paris 1.jpg
31133232022_22fd191632_o.jpg
8585937772_e5aa07bfdc_o.jpg
19143083360_0dcd90877d_o.jpg
11497415673_4271e39793_o.jpg
19324640692_38ee0642a9_o.jpg
11497345644_75f44e322c_o.jpg
9326797428_b98d6f4ae9_o.jpg
Amsterdam 1.jpg
Amsterdam 2.jpg
11656941786_abccd8b803_o.jpg
11778163973_c359506482_o.jpg
Check All
Uncheck All
Sort: Capture Time
Thumbnails
Import Preset
None
Cancel
Import

TUTORIAL
ONE

SUBTLE CHANGES

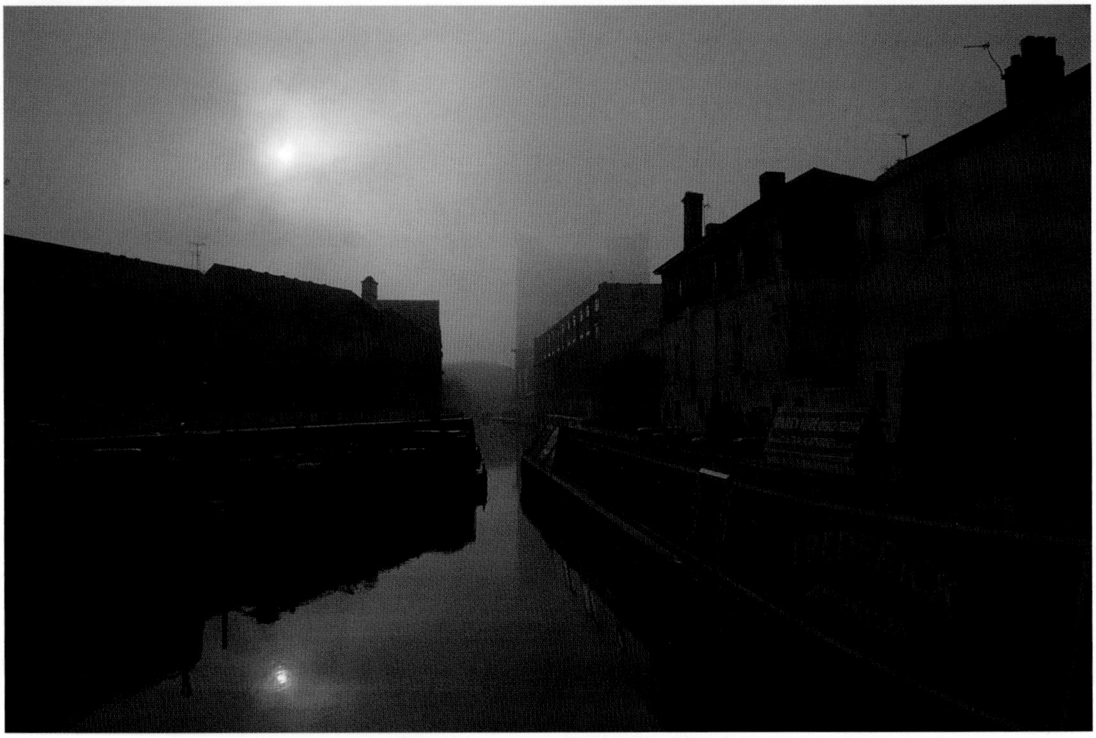

Our first tutorial features a photograph taken in Gas Street Basin on a misty winter's morning. Reflecting the weather, it's pretty dark and gloomy, with a lot of detail lost in shadow. It was saved as a Raw file, however, so this tutorial will demonstrate how much information you can pull back, and turn a pretty bad photo into a pretty good one.

COMPOSITION

Look at the composition of the photo. As previously discussed, it is always good to clean up the edges of your photo so that the viewer can concentrate on the main subject. A couple of elements are distracting on the right-hand side, such as the edge of the signage on the narrowboat at the base of the frame, and the chimney at the top. By cropping tighter around these, you can easily get rid of them. You do this by selecting the rectangular box with a dashed outline on the top right-hand console.

LEFT, ABOVE
The original photo. There's plenty of potential, but it certainly needs some work.

THIS PAGE
At the near right, we see the Crop tool. With this you can straighten the photo, as well as crop. Far right shows the crop in action; gridlines dividing the frame into nine sections help you think about the rule of thirds. Below we see the final composition.

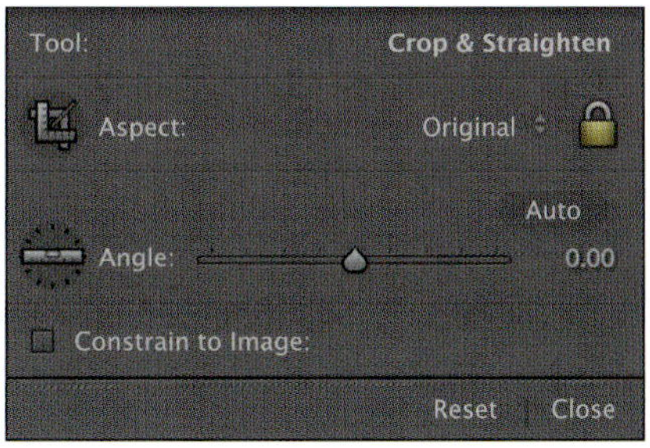

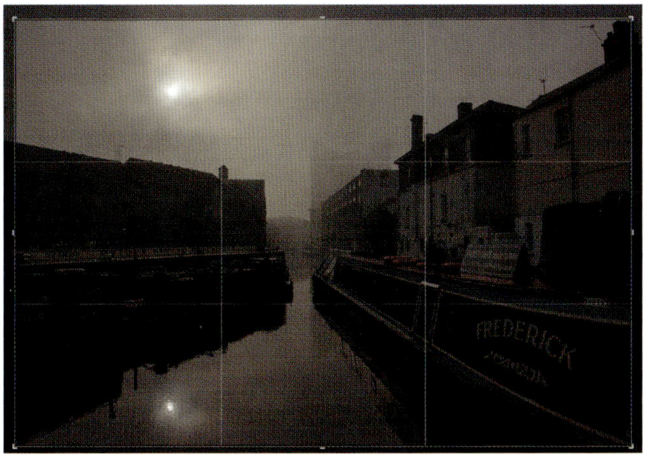

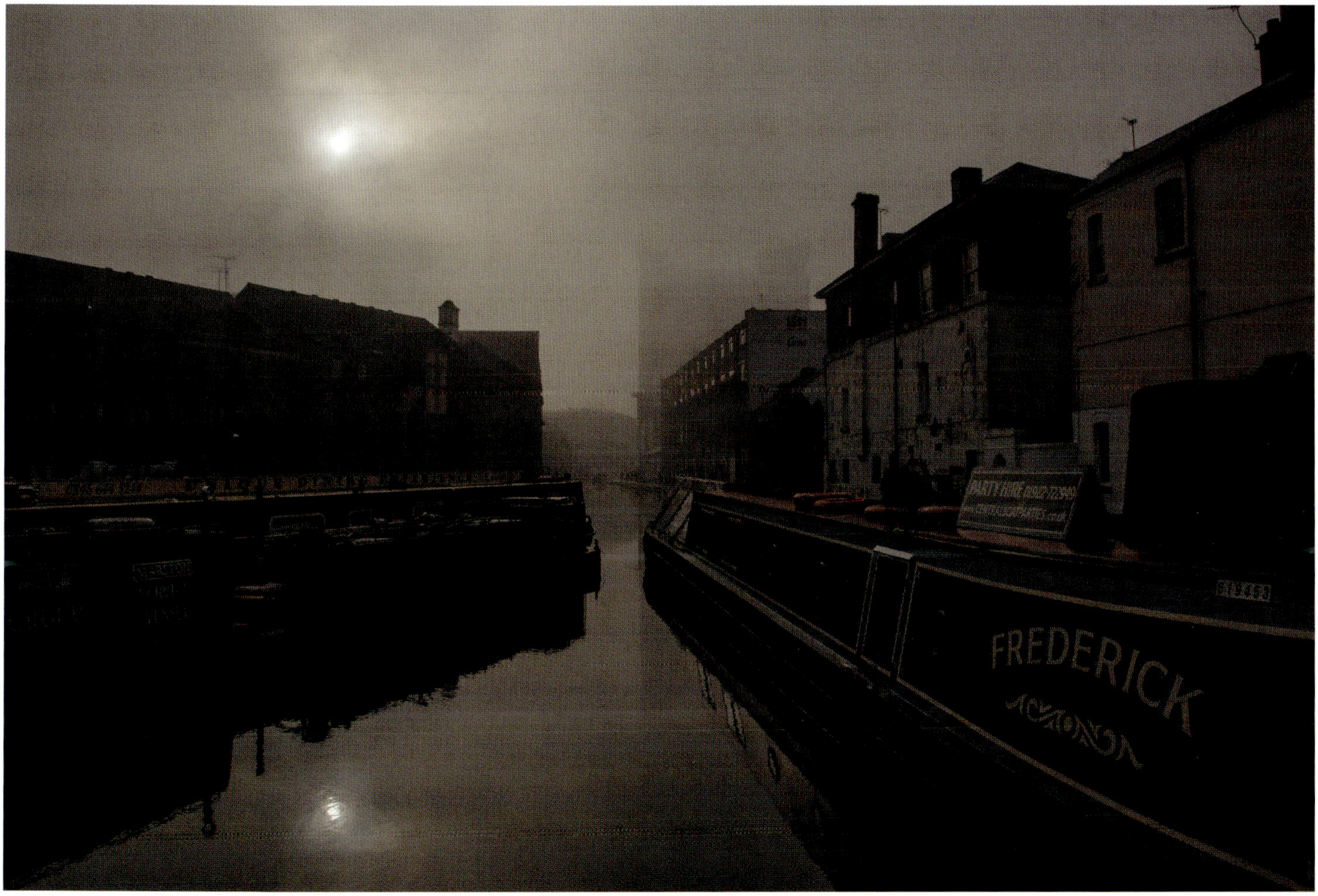

SPOT REMOVAL & SPOT HEAL

A useful function, found next to the Crop tool, allows you to remove any small blemishes you have in the frame. These may be have been caused by a spot of dust on your sensor or lens, or it might be a small amount of lens flare in the corner of the image. In the top left-hand corner of the photo are three small spots, which we are now going to remove. First, I highlight the area around the patch I want to clean up. Lightroom then asks you to select another area of the photo, which it pastes over this spot. It is more intuitive than you would think, but obviously the area you're pasting over needs to be similar in content to the area to be cleaned. If you're working with a larger blemish, keep moving the selection around to make it look as natural as it can be.

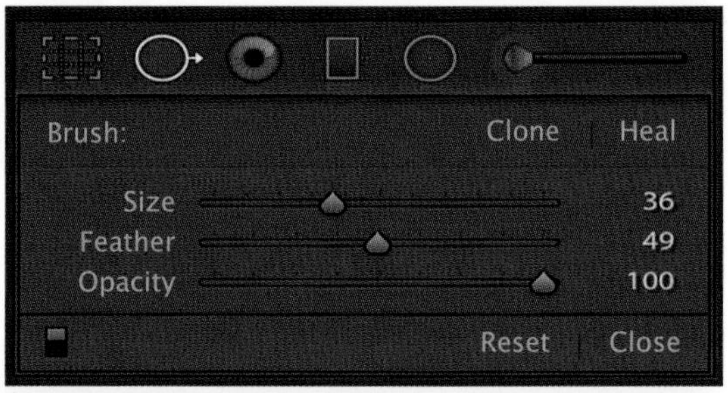

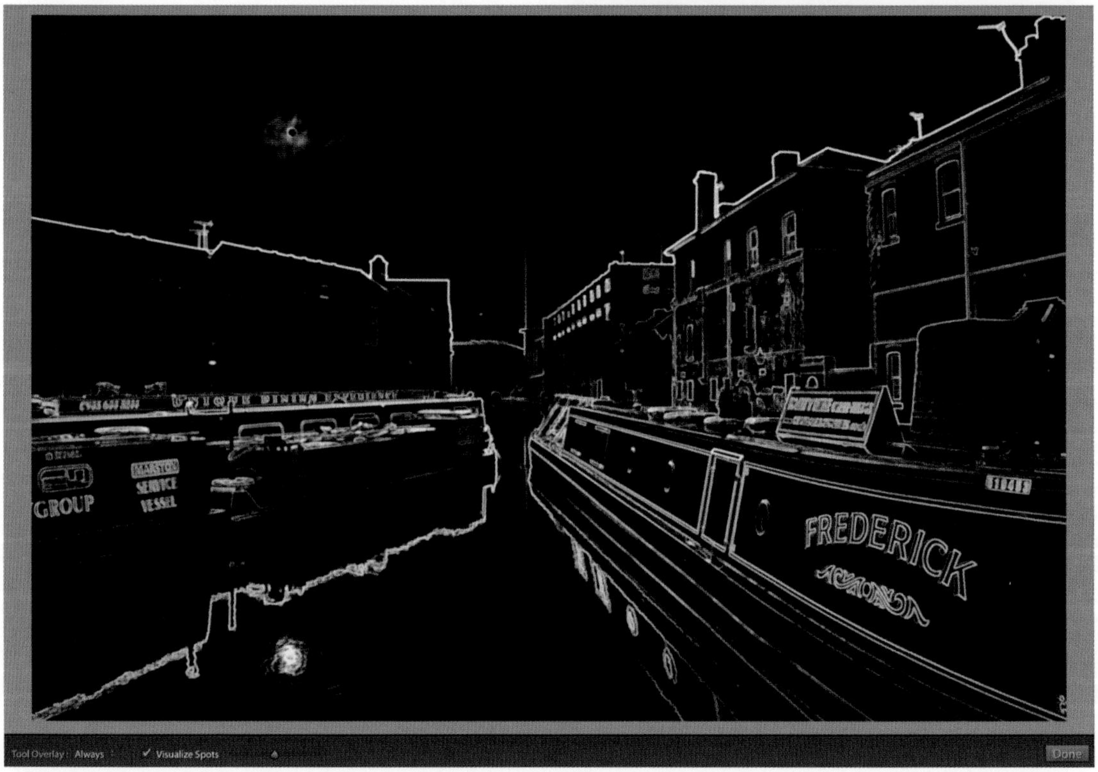

LEFT, TOP
The spot-removal tool, also known as cloning. You can adjust the size, shape and behaviour of the brush used to apply the treatment.

LEFT, BOTTOM
Turning on mask overlay makes it easy to see spots in an otherwise clean sky (or other background).

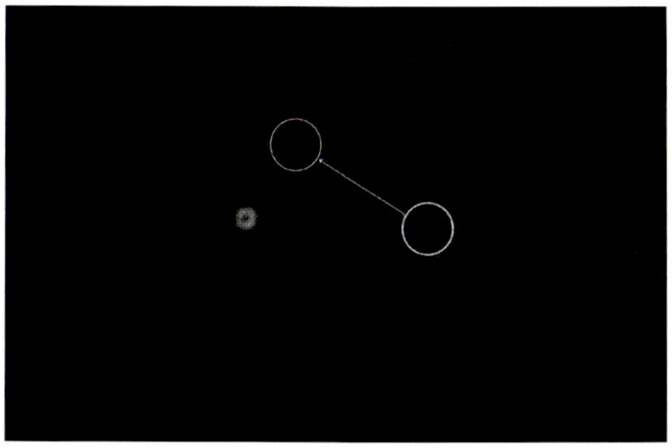

LEFT
Zooming in on the mask overlay view, you can more easily see these spots we want to eradicate.

BELOW
It's incredibly easy to edit out the unwanted parts of a photo using this tool. The only thing to be aware of is that the larger the patch you're replacing, and the more complex the background, the harder it is to keep it looking natural. For this reason, try not to overuse this tool.

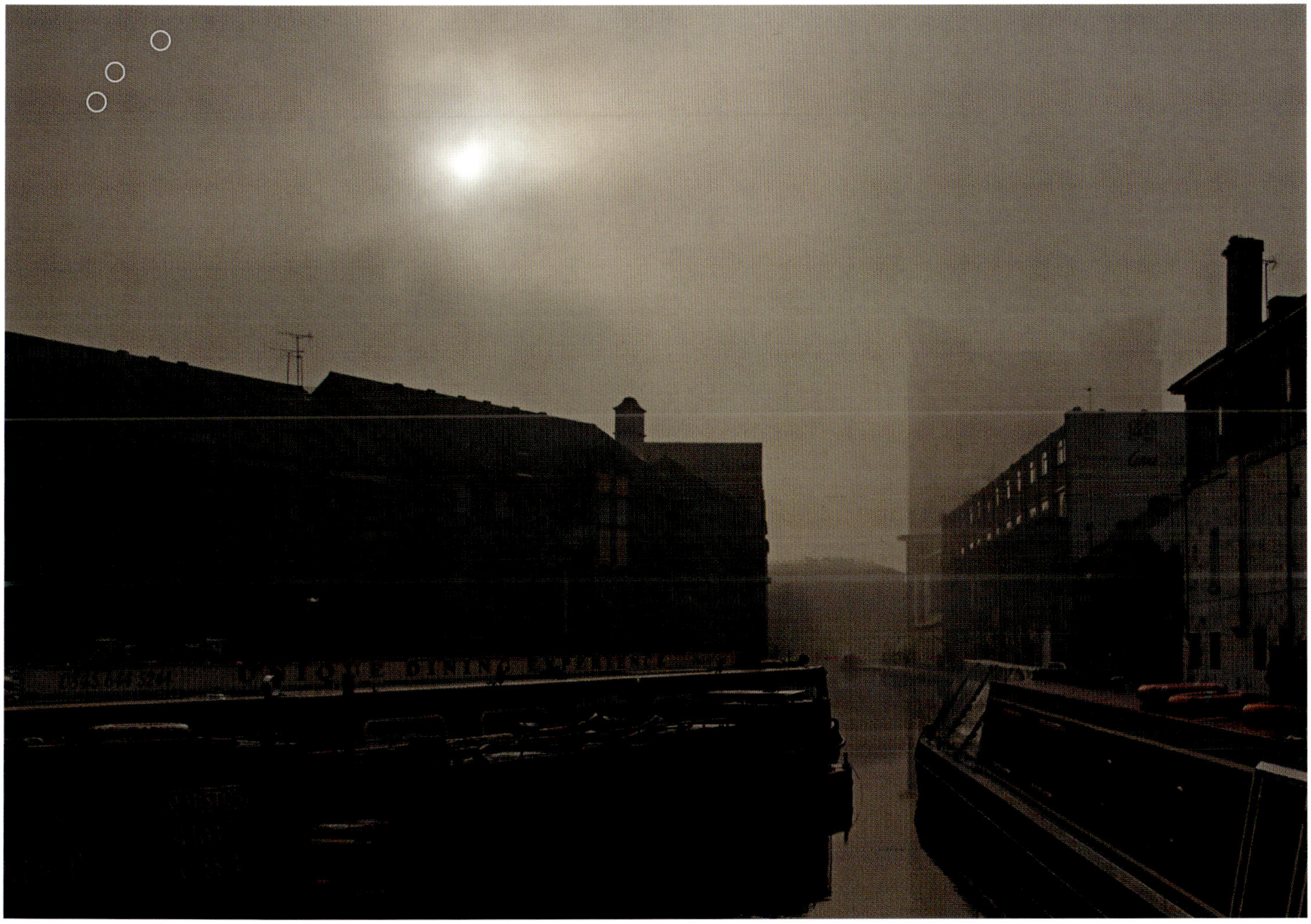

HIGHLIGHTS & SHADOWS

The original photo was slightly underexposed due to metering for the sun, just about to break through the fog lifting in the canal basin. Because this is a Raw file, there was a lot of hidden information in the photo that could be brought back to enhance it. In the Basic tab, below the bar for cropping, you'll see a slider bar for adjusting the highlights and the shadows in the image. These control the brightest and the darkest elements in the photo, so that you can tone down anything that's too bright and lift areas that are too shadowed. Open a photo and slide the bar from left to right, and you'll get an idea of all the hidden elements. With this particular shot, I reduced the highlights so that more detail of the disc of the sun can be seen, and increased the shadows to bring out some detail in the darkest areas of the image.

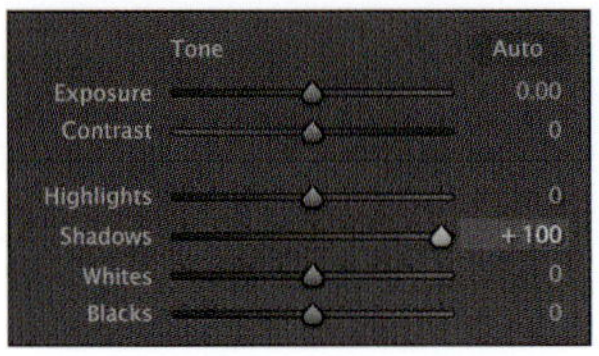

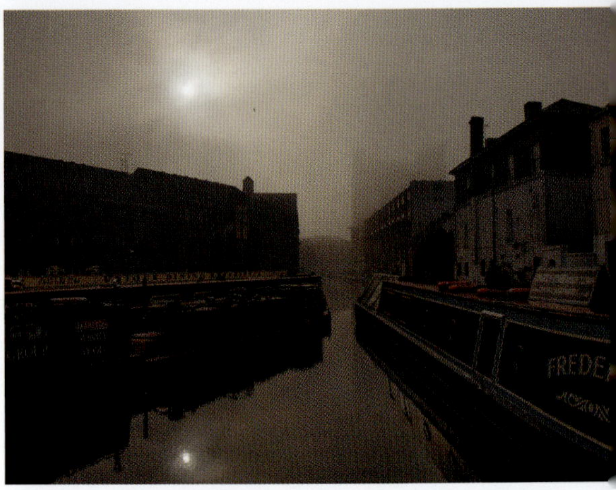

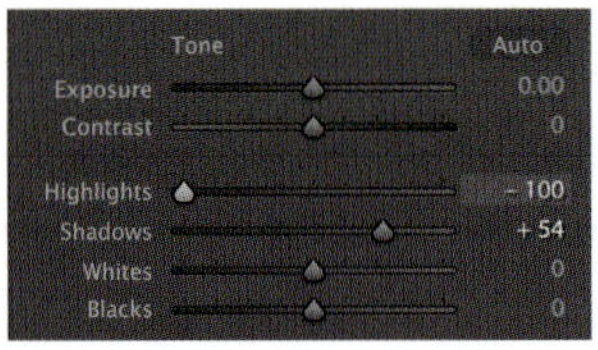

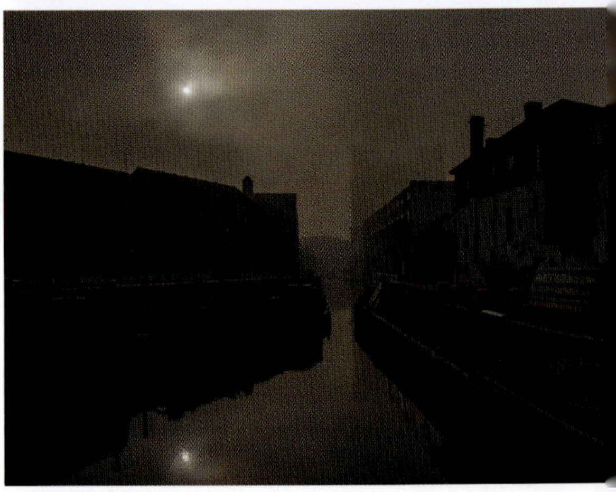

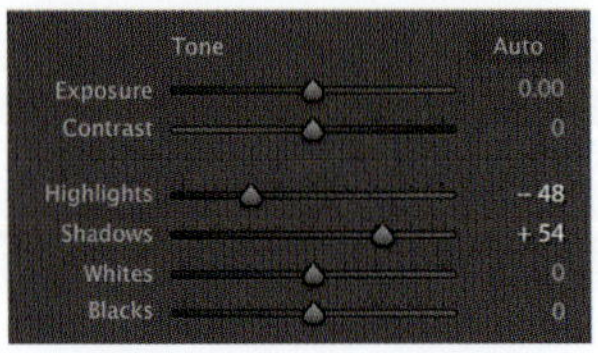

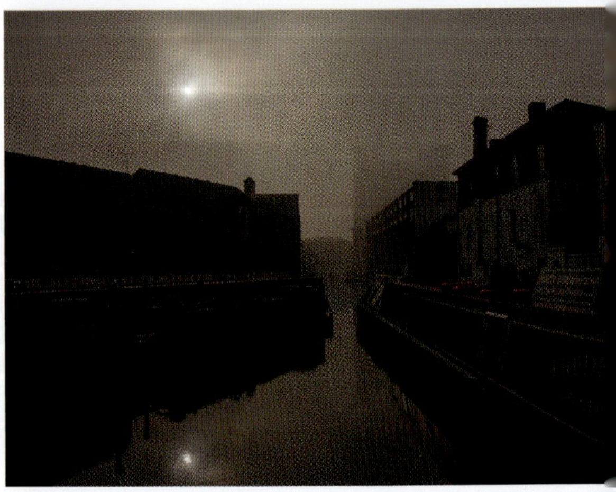

THIS PAGE
These examples show the effects of pushing up the shadows as far as you can, which lightens the sky considerably, as well as the details on the boats (top); pulling back the shadows all the way, which gives more details in the clouds but loses detail in other foreground elements (middle); and (bottom) the final adjustment, which offers a good balance.

COLOUR TEMPERATURE

The final change I want to make to this photo is to adjust the colour temperature. When this shot was taken, the camera was set to Auto White Balance (AWB), where the camera makes a judgement on the lighting conditions and uses these to set the temperature of the colours in the scene. AWB generally aims for a neutral tone, which is why it ruins your sunrise/sunset shots. Here, it took out a lot of the colour that was evident to the eye when the shot was taken, so the Temperature slider has been adjusted to the right to return some of warmth to the colours, bringing back the slight red hue that the camera assumed must be an error.

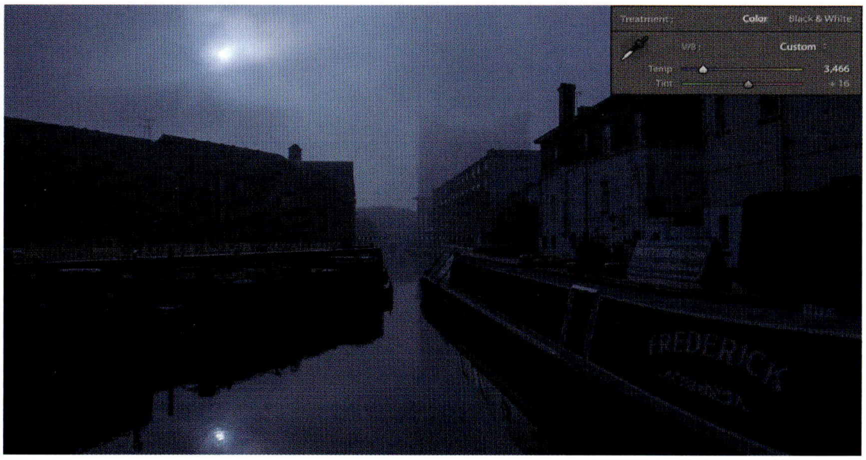

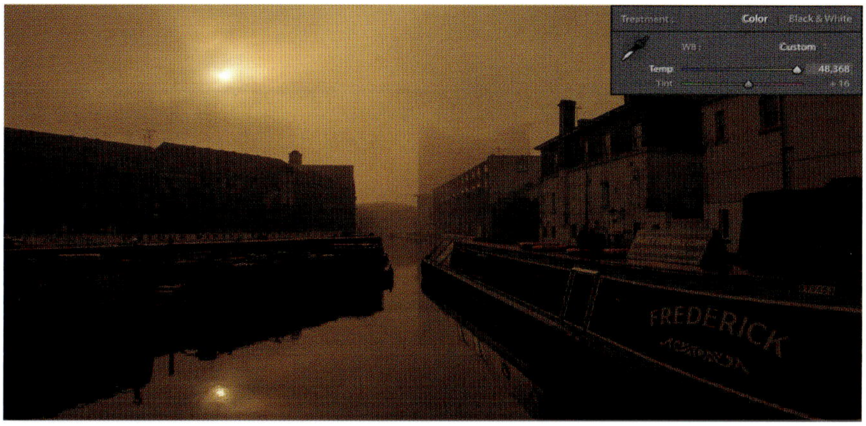

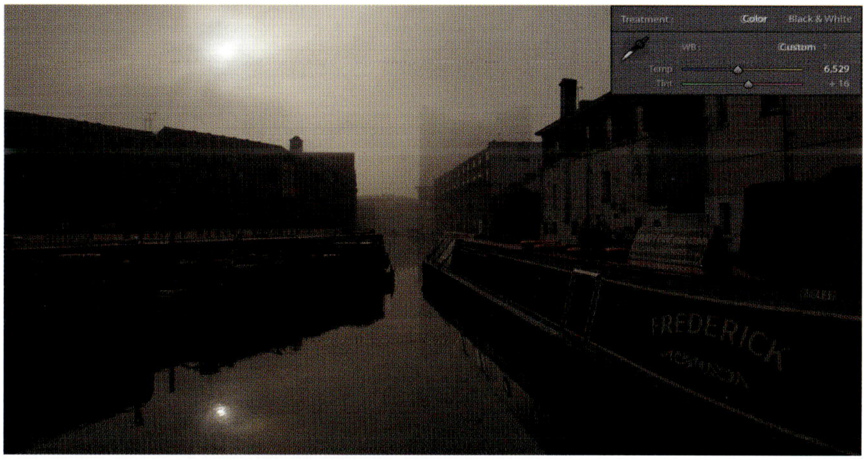

THIS PAGE
Here we see the effects of sliding the temperature all the way down to the coolest hue, so it adds a blue colour cast to the image (top); all the way to the warmest hue, turning the image unnaturally orange (middle); and finally the right balance, which is subtly warmer than the original photo saved by the camera, closer to original scene.

TUTORIAL
TWO

IT'S WHAT YOU LEAVE OUT

What you leave out is important when considering the composition of a photograph, and the on shown is an extreme example of that. This shows that there may be an amazing photograph hidden within even the most mundane of shots. This might not be down to any lack of skill – you could be out one day and see something out of the corner of your eye, and realize that you've only got a wide-angle lens on you when the shot calls for a close view, for example. This was the case in this instance, where a 50mm prime lens was used, with a view to cropping out to get the detail desired. Thankfully, with most modern cameras, cropping on this scale is not a significant issue with regards to the image quality, due to the high pixel count on digital sensors.

It also goes to show that you should never give up on an image until you've had a chance to properly assess it on a bigger screen than the back of your camera or your phone screen. When you do consider your photos, crop is one of the first things you can look to in order to make an easy improvement, or even to save a shot.

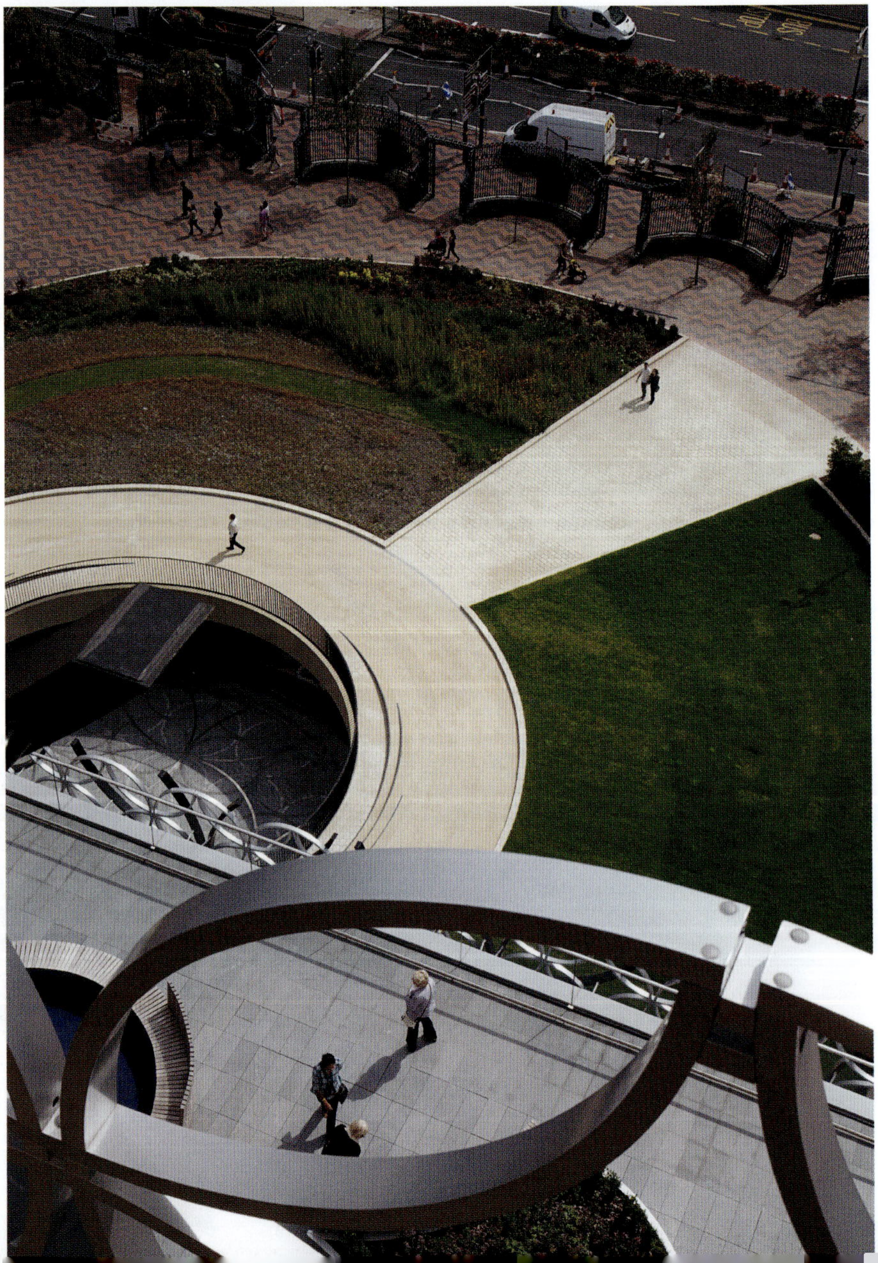

RIGHT
The original image is hardly an inspiring shot, and not what I had in mind when I took it.

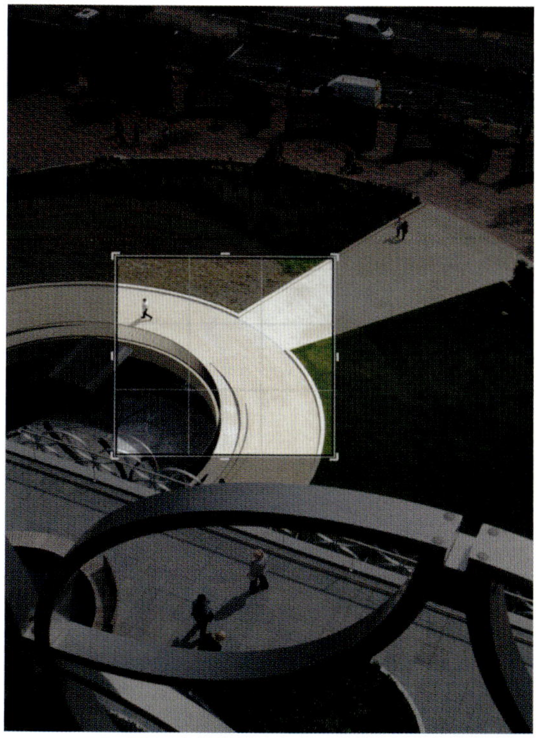

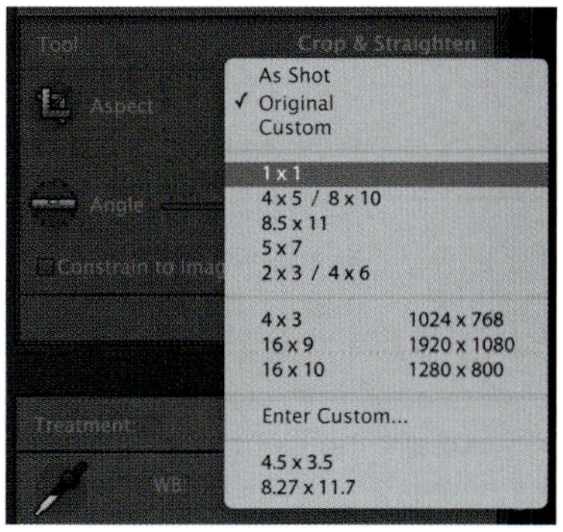

THIS PAGE
As well as adjusting crop freely, you can also select a fixed-ratio crop. There are a number of standard presets, such as 1 x 1 for square, as used here, or you can choose a custom ratio, which you can also set to pixels, or mm, cm or inches, if the image needs to fit a particular size for screen or print.

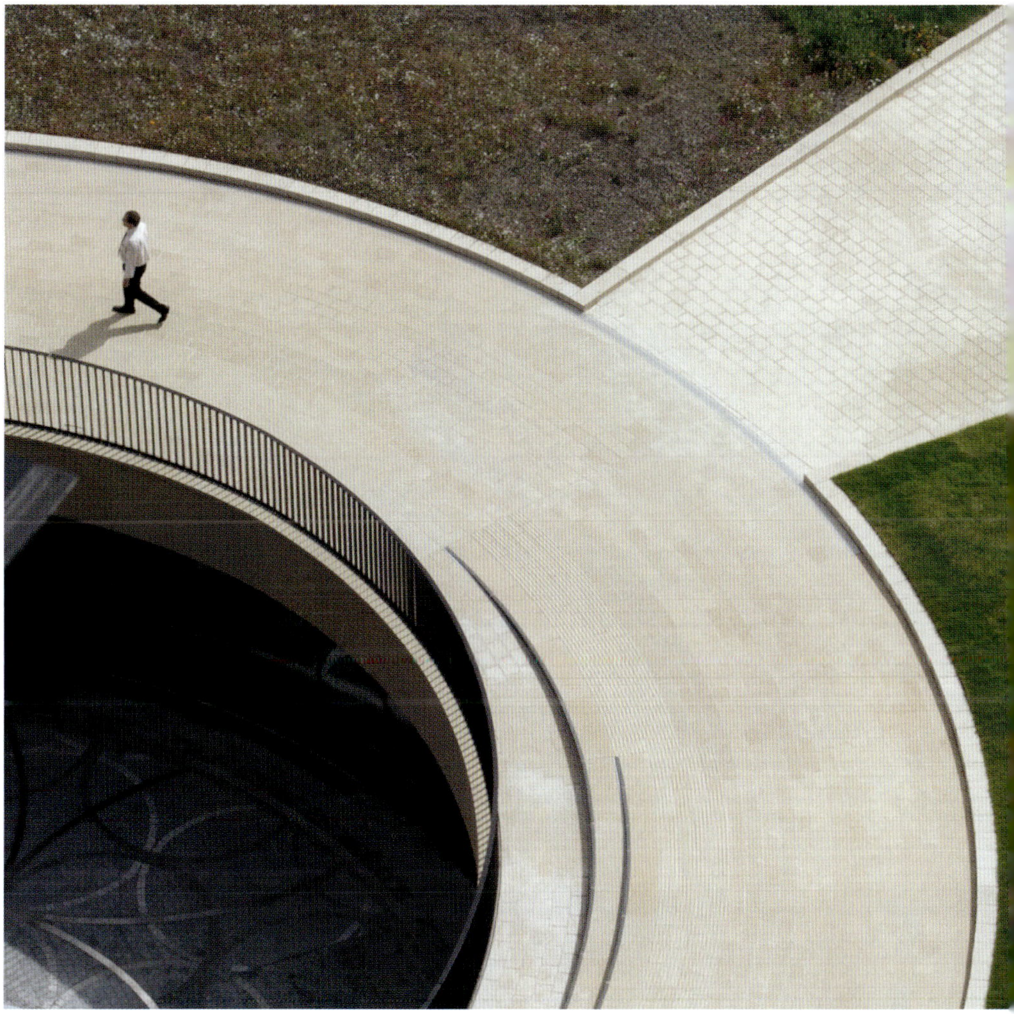

PHOTO WITHIN A PHOTO

As with the previous tutorial, the first thing to do is to decide on the crop of the image to obtain the desired composition. The aim for this was to create a composition that filled the frame, so the crop was taken in to the edges of the paving in the centre of the original image. This removes all the distractions of the fencing and other people walking around, allowing the viewer to focus on the main subject: the man walking around the amphitheatre. A square crop was used because it balances the image well, making the leading lines of the paving pattern terminate in the corners of the image. Look back through your own shots of the city. See if there is anywhere you can spot any small but important details that could be cropped in on to create a more refined composition, without worrying too much about the aspect ratio of the image.

BLACK & WHITE

I've mentioned previously that you should have a good reason to switch a photo to black and white. In most instances, the more successful black-and-white photos are the ones where the photographer was already thinking in black and white when they hit the shutter. This wasn't the case with this photo, but once I'd cropped it, it occurred to me that black and white would work well, since the grass around the paving at the top of the image was rather sparse, which can be disguised by removing the colour. A graphic composition also often lends itself to monochrome, so it was at least worth trying.

The Black & White button next the Colour tab on the right-hand side of Lightroom's Develop screen will convert the photo. You can then adjust the Whites and Blacks sliders individually, in order to play around with the contrast of the image. This particular photo works best with a sharper, harder contrast; therefore the Whites were increased to pop the white colours in the photo, while the Blacks were brought down to darken the areas of grass, creating a nice frame to the composition.

If you want to really get to grips with editing in black and white you can use the Black & White Mix tab farther down the right-hand side of the screen, which separates the colour channels in the spectrum. Playing with these can adjust the tones quite considerably, producing very different effects, so it's worth experimenting with this tool.

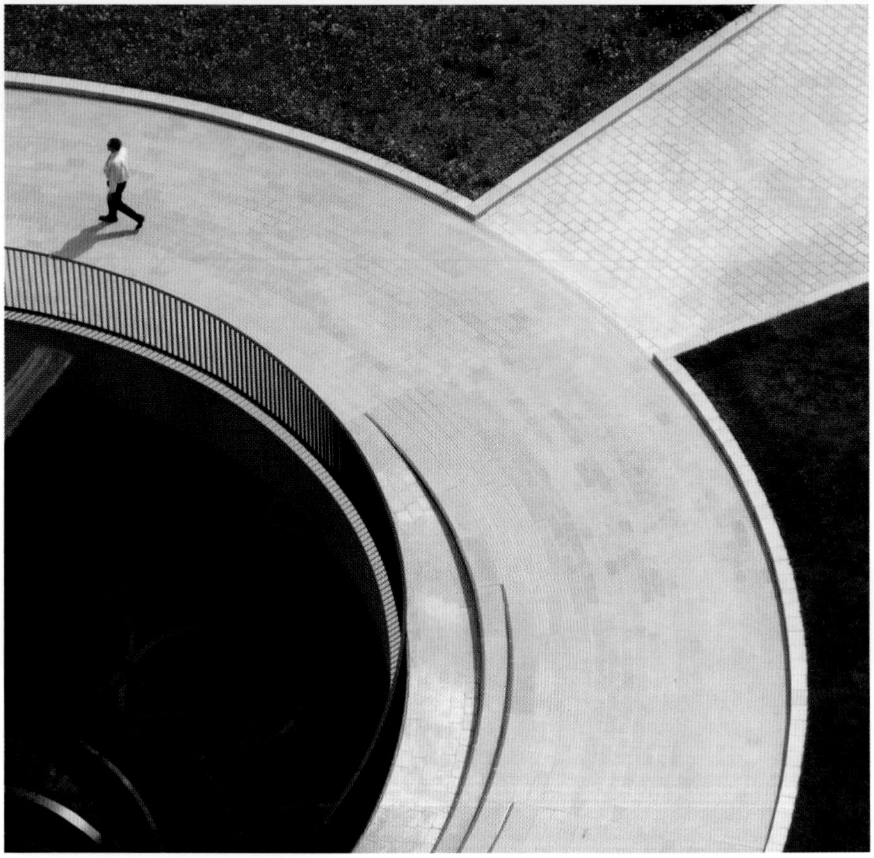

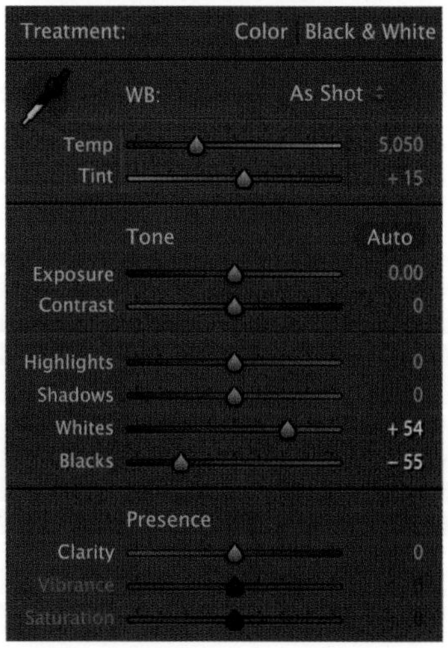

LEFT & ABOVE
Clicking onto the Black & White button converts the cropped image into black and white. You can then adjust the exposure in this photo to increase or decrease the highlights, shadows and contrast.

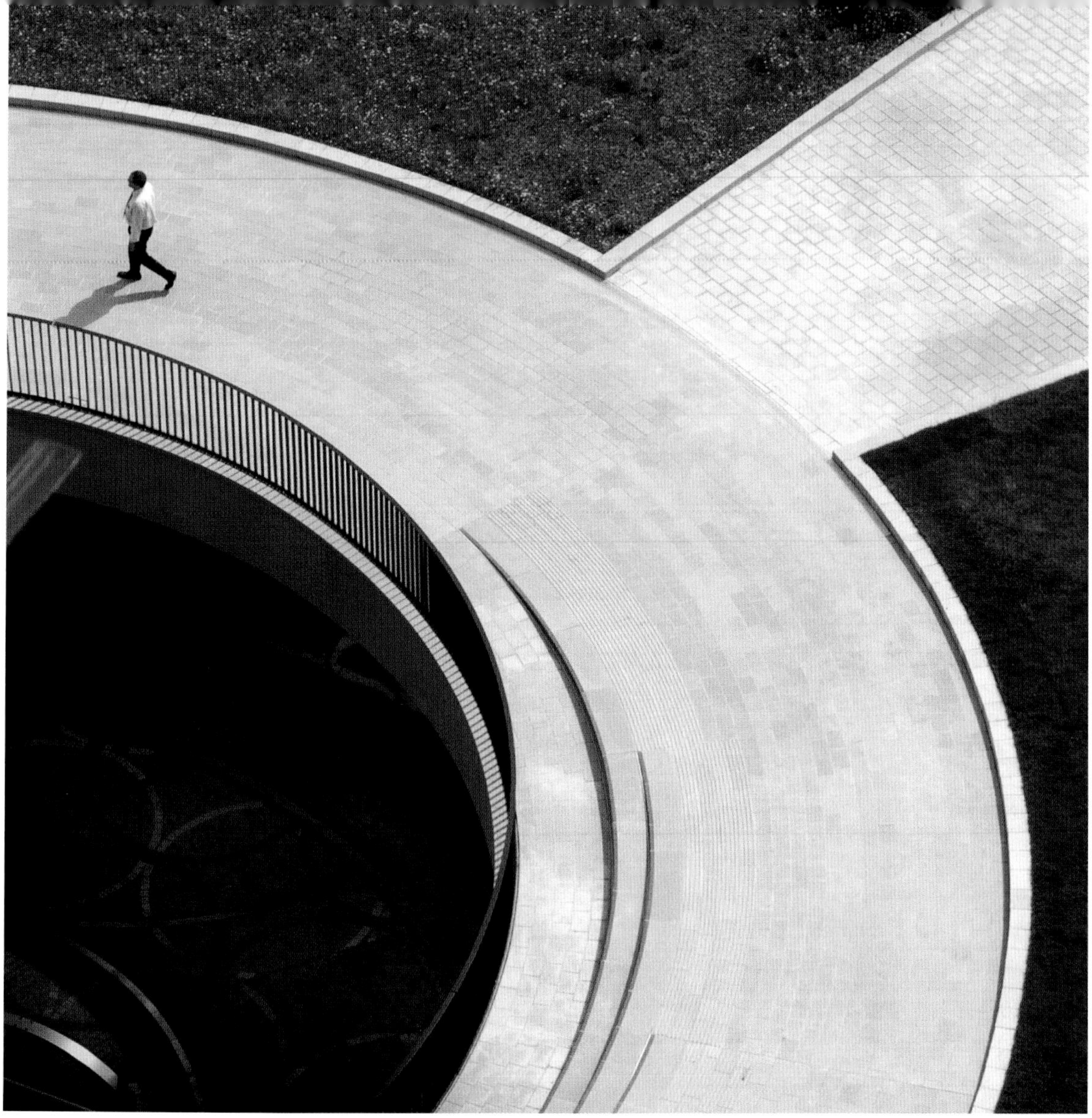

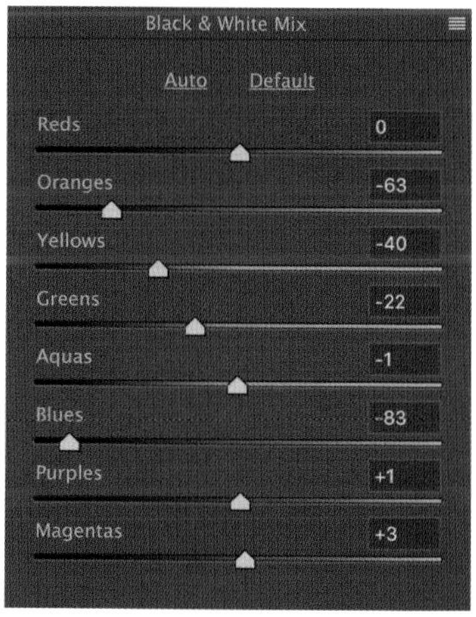

LEFT & ABOVE
Adjusting the colour mix in your black-and-white photo is a further function, which allows even more control over the tone of the photo. Above, we see the final image; a far cry from the rather dull photo we saw on page 160.

TUTORIAL **THREE**

PERSPECTIVE CORRECTION

Our third look into editing in Lightroom is an example of how to correct perspective in a photograph. The shot is of the University of Birmingham New Library, and it was taken on a wide-angle lens to get the whole building into the frame. The idea was to get a perspective that would make all the vertical elements of the façade parallel, but this was not possible on-site as I simply couldn't get any further back to take the shot. The shot was taken as far back as possible, looking up from the corner of the building. You can see the classic keystone effect in the image directly to right on this page, in which the parallel lines of the building appear to converge towards the sky. This is a typical problem in architectural photography, and one that can easily be corrected in Lightroom.

TRANSFORM

You can correct the perspective of any photograph using the Transform tool in Lightroom. You'll find this by scrolling down the various function on the right hand side of the Develop screen. It has an 'Auto' function, which is generally very good at correcting lines with minimal effort on your part. As this is an extreme example of correction, the Auto function was only the first step in correcting the lines.

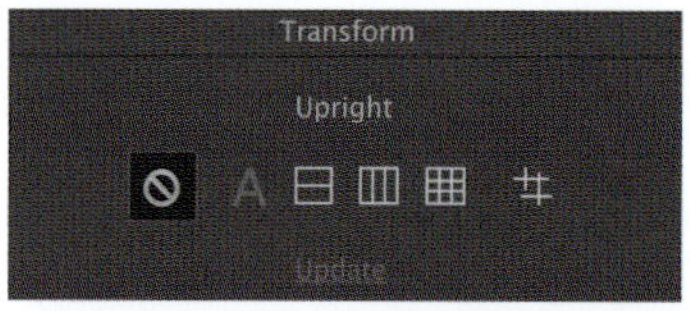

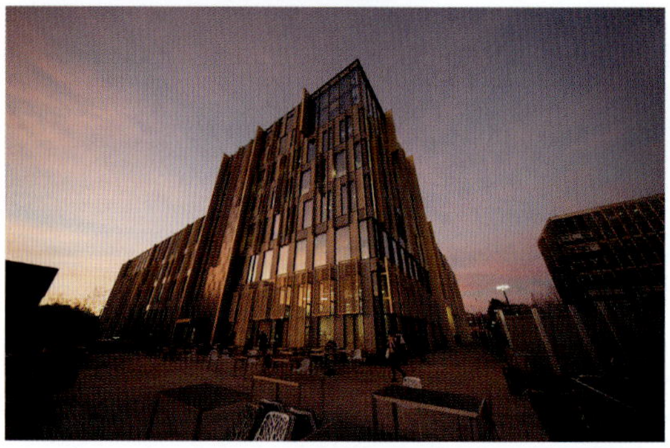

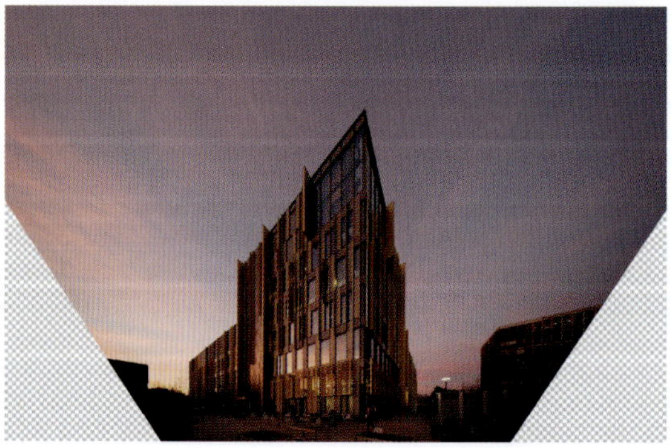

TOP
The Transform tool in Lightroom: the 'A' character second from the left indicates the Auto function, which will try to correct the horizontal and vertical lines in your image.

MIDDLE
The original image, clearly showing the classic keystone effect.

BOTTOM
The image as it appears after you've applied the transformation. As you can see, correcting the perspective results in empty areas of canvas that need to be cropped out of the shot.

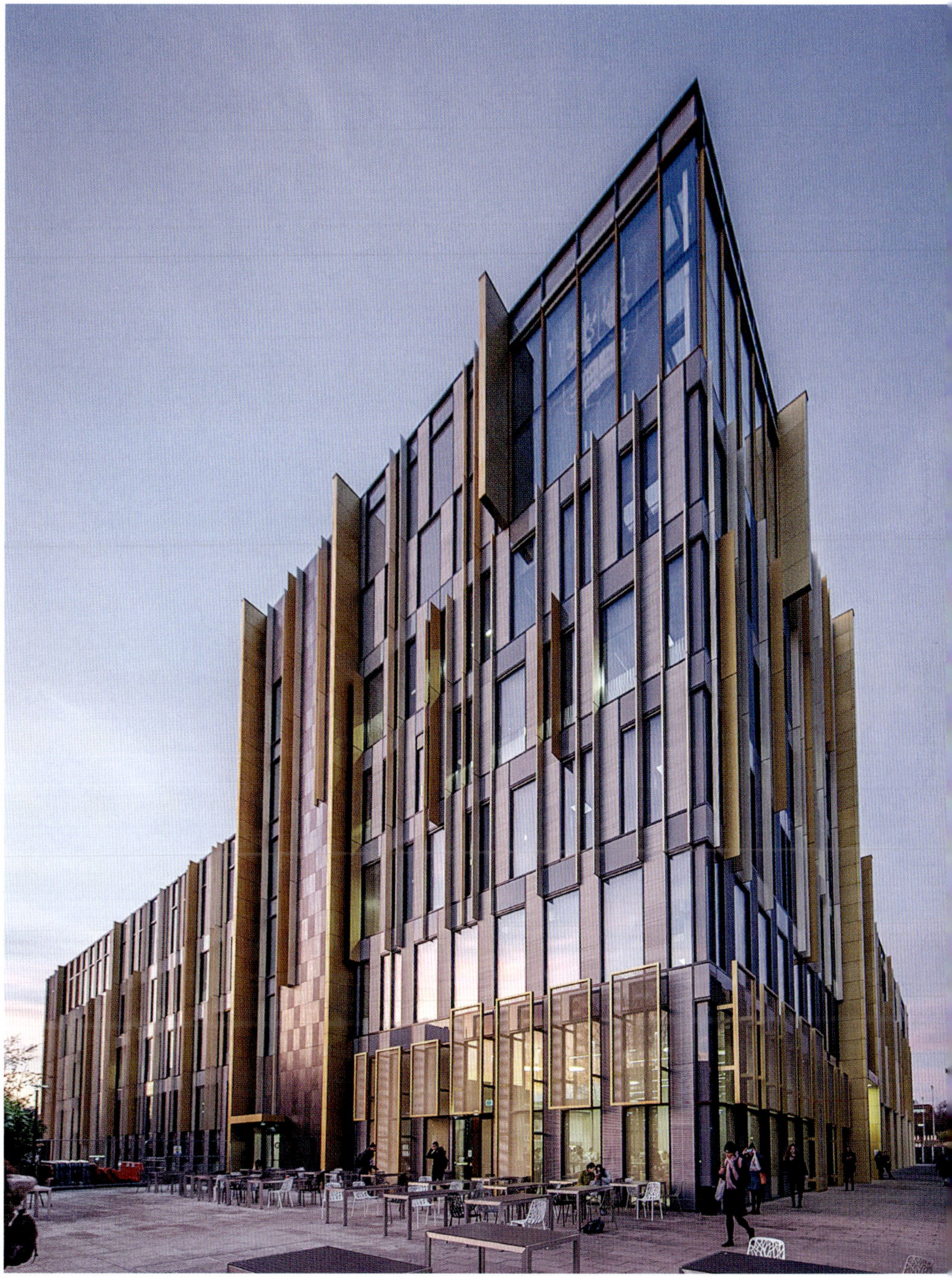

Once this was done, I then manually tweaked the vertical slider in the Transform tool panel (sometimes you may need to adjust the horizontal one too). Move the vertical slider until all the verticals are parallel. You may then also have to adjust the rotation of the shot (under Crop & Straighten panel shown on page 155) to get the perfect perspective; the building may also appear slightly squashed. You can then use the 'Aspect' function on the same Crop panel to stretch the photo in the desired direction.

It is worth noting that making corrections to this extreme, there will be some loss of photo quality detectable at the top of the building. The pixels in that area appear softer because they have been stretched. It's for this reason that professionals will use a tilt-shift lens, when the sharpness needs to be perfect throughout the image. You can check this using the Zoom tool on the left-hand side of the screen, zooming in on different areas and comparing the sharpness. It's not worth getting too hung up on this, though, because it will often only be detectable when your image is displayed at a large scale.

RIGHT
The finished image, with correct parallel lines. You can see even at this scale how the top of the image suffers from being stretched.

TECHNIQUE

Over the previous few pages, we have covered some of the most useful edits you can make in Lightroom. Most editing software provides similar functionality, just appearing slightly differently. But there are a few other general approaches that you can adopt while editing, not necessarily specific to Lightroom, that will help you to create better photographs.

Thumbnail: When you are editing your photos, keep clicking back to viewing the photograph as a thumbnail, or very small on your screen. This helps you to see if there are any glaring issues with the overall composition, which you often don't spot when you are concentrating on one area. They say that the best images always work as thumbnails, so it is something to think about if you are spending a lot of time on one single image.

Upside Down: Another tip for editing is to look at your images upside down and see if anything doesn't look right. It might be a distracting plant pot in the corner of the photo, which you didn't notice when it was the right way up.

Experiment: Just as I advise taking as many photos as possible, the same applies for editing. Try editing the same photo in different ways, and see what works best. In Lightroom, you can create a virtual copy of your photos. As you edit the Raw file, you can create multiple versions that all link back to the same file on your hard drive. All you need to do is to right-click the image and select 'Create Virtual Copy'. You'll then have a fresh version of the file that you can edit independently from the last one.

Presets: If you find yourself applying the same edits over and over again, or you want to edit multiple photos in the same style, you can save a series of edits, or a particular setting in a tool panel, as a preset for future use.

Once you are happy with the edit, you can save its settings by clicking onto Presets on the left-hand side of the Develop screen. You can then check all the boxes relating to the elements you have changed that you wish to save, such as highlights, shadows, colour temperature, and so on.

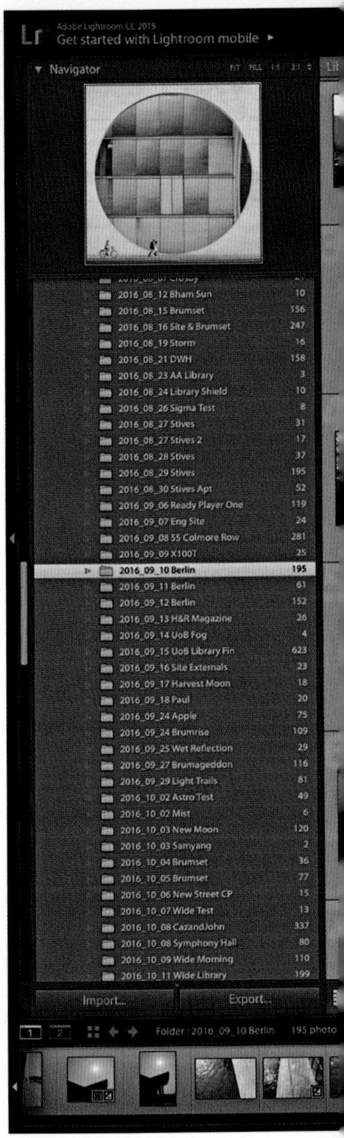

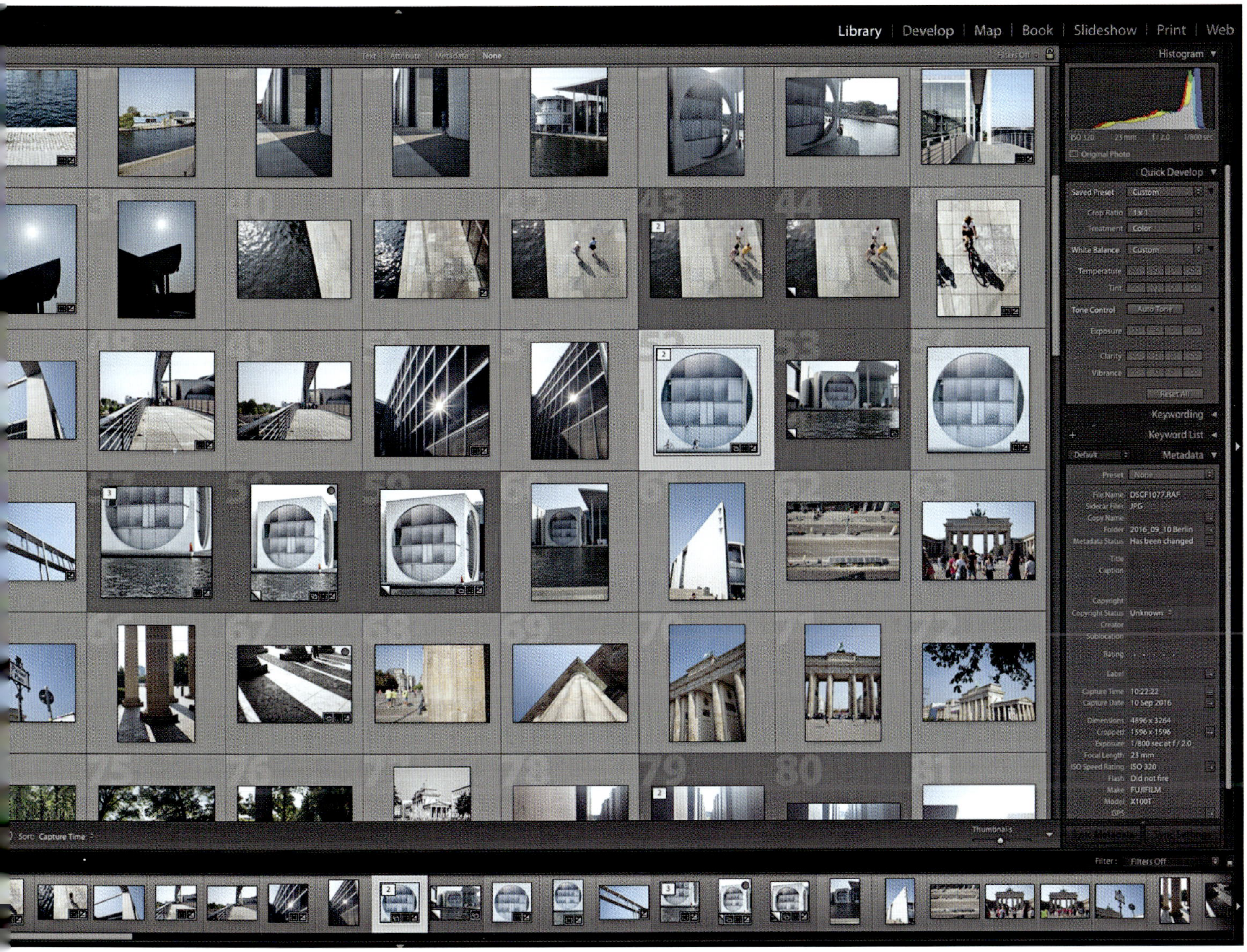

ABOVE
Click onto your Library screen, or even the folder on your desktop, to view how the image looks in its thumbnail form.

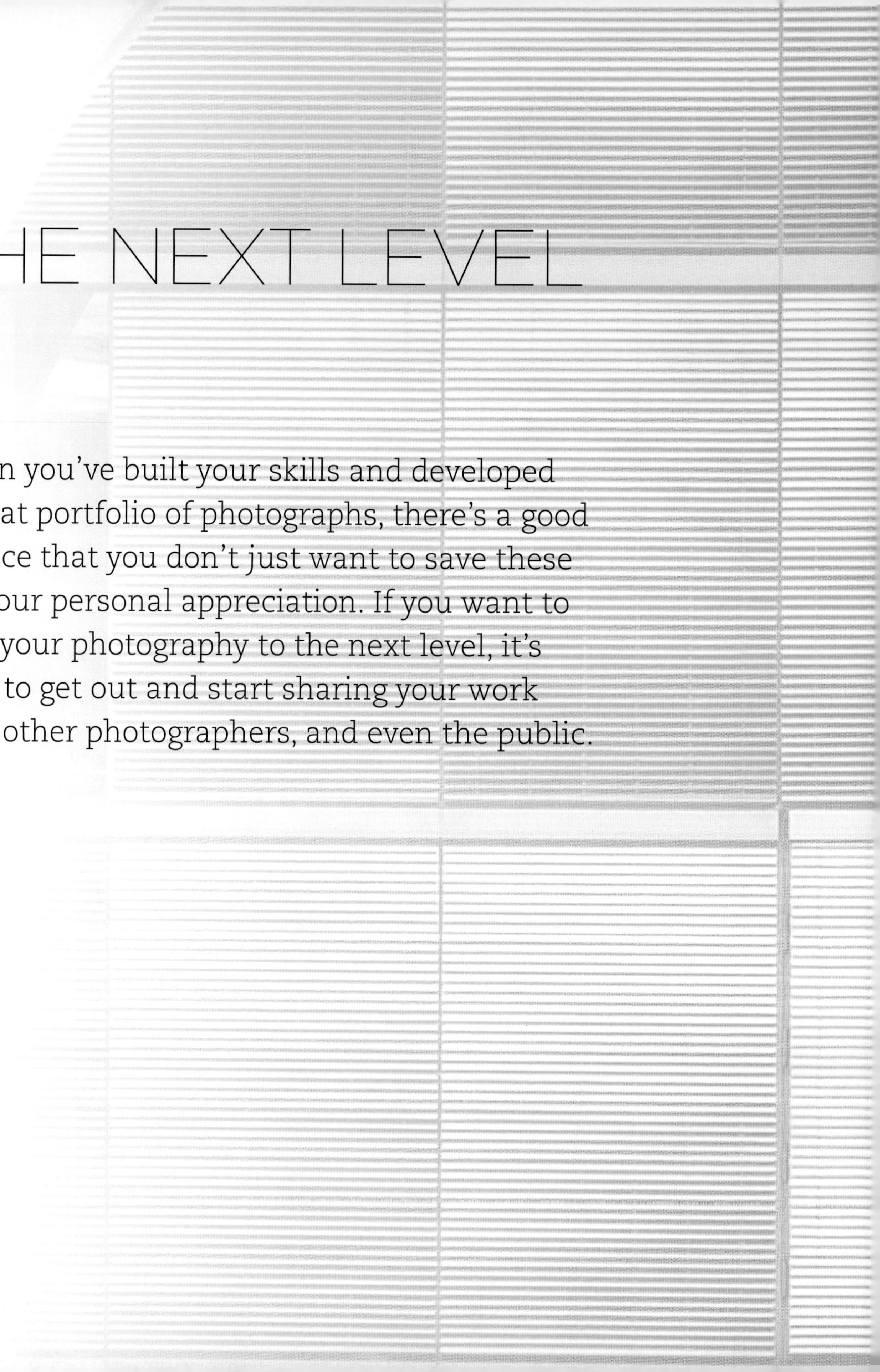

9 THE NEXT LEVEL

When you've built your skills and developed a great portfolio of photographs, there's a good chance that you don't just want to save these for your personal appreciation. If you want to take your photography to the next level, it's time to get out and start sharing your work with other photographers, and even the public.

DEVELOPMENT

A great way of developing as a photographer is to get feedback on your photos from fellow photographers. Attend a workshop where you can speak openly about your work and get honest opinions on your photographs. Don't be scared to put your work in front of others and don't be offended when people criticize your shots. This is how you learn what works and what doesn't, and these comments will enhance your development as a photographer.

You can even submit your photos to groups online, such as on the photo-sharing platform Flickr. Specific groups allow you to submit your photos and get honest feedback. Maybe someone will say they would have edited the photo differently, or would have stood two feet to the left to get more of the subject in. All feedback is good, and it will get you to see your photography in a different light.

If you really want to develop as a photographer, try to get outside your comfort zone. If you mainly take photos of buildings, try and shoot a few events or delve into street photography. As I hope this book has shown, you will learn so much by using your camera in a different way, or by putting yourself in a different situation.

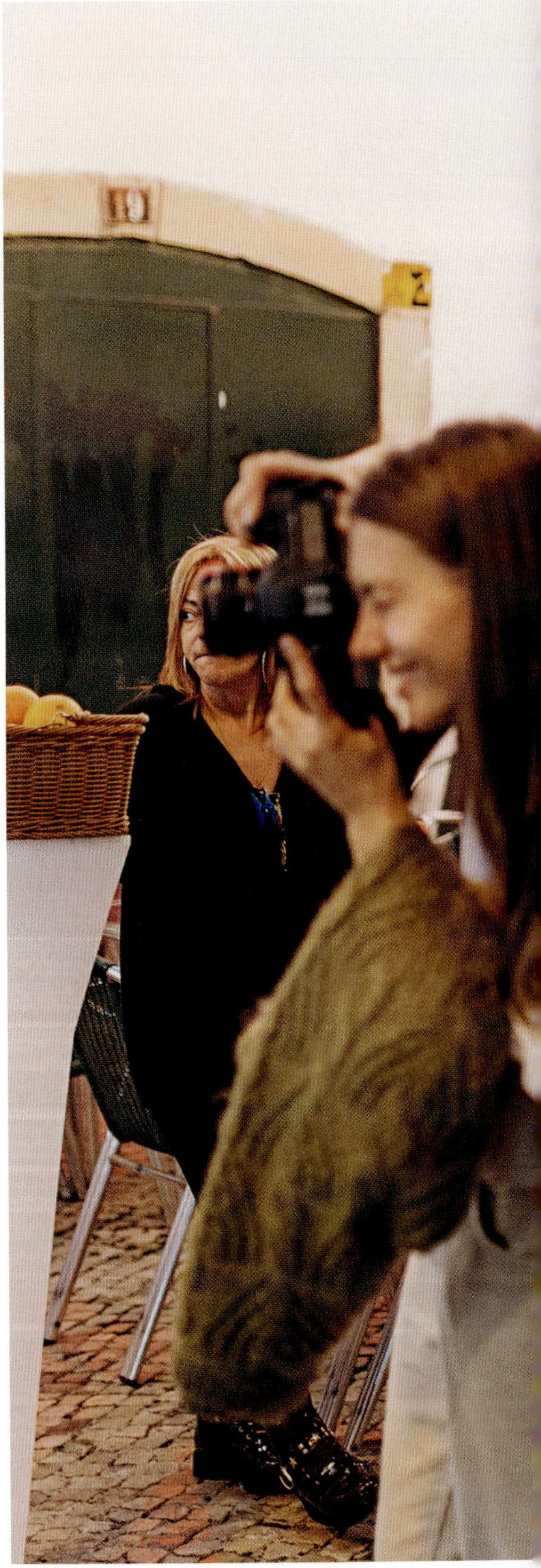

RIGHT
Joining a photography group is not only a great way to make your hobby more social, it's also a brilliant way to develop your skills.

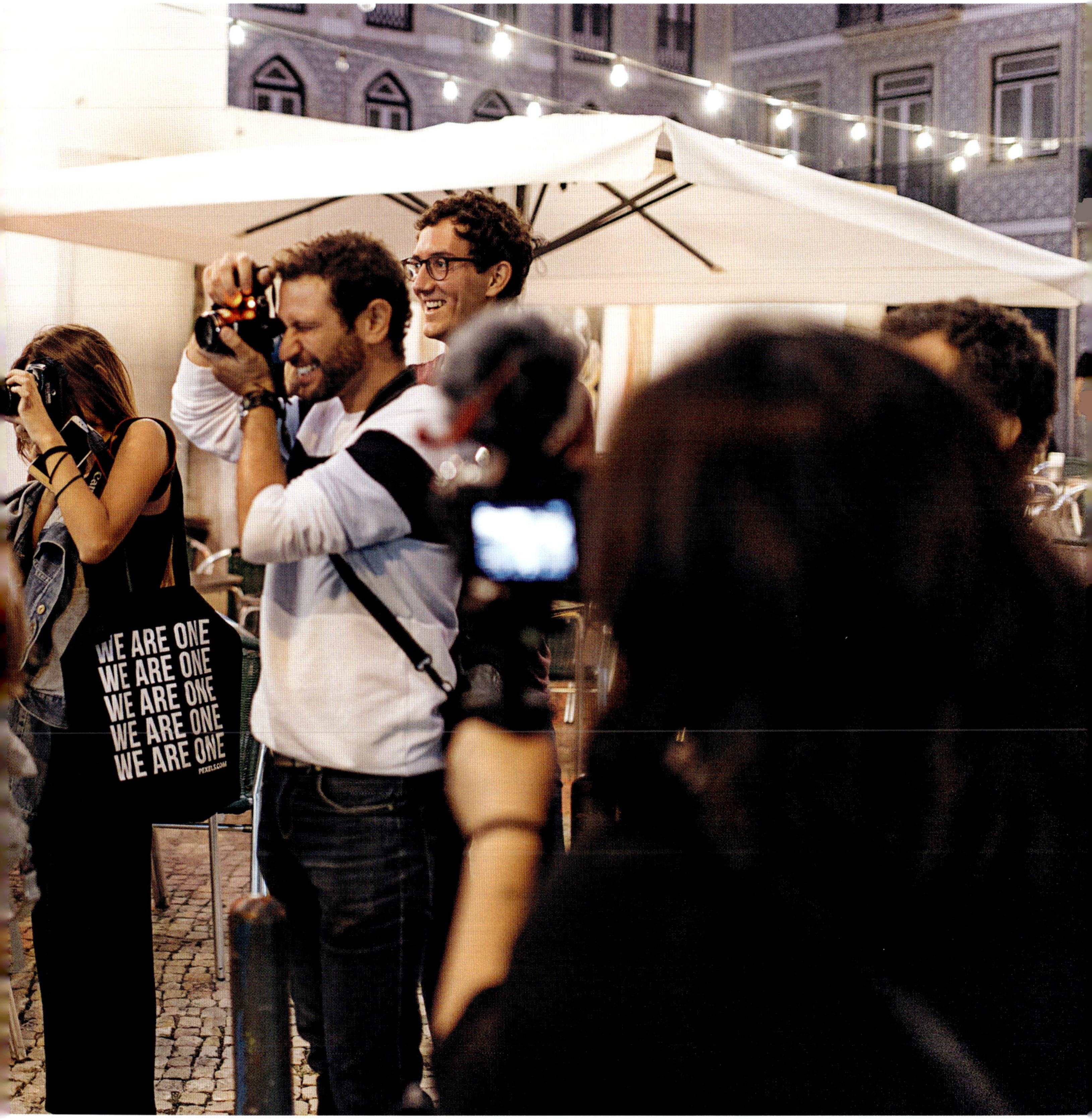
WE ARE ONE
WE ARE ONE
WE ARE ONE
WE ARE ONE
WE ARE ONE
PEXELS.COM

SOCIAL MEDIA

It is impossible to ignore the effect that social media has had on the photography industry. It is big business and it's also a great platform for showcasing your images and getting them out to a wider audience. Profiles on Instagram, Facebook and Twitter can be used to promote your work; here, I will compare the advantages and disadvantages of each platform.

INSTAGRAM

This is an image-based platform that is owned by Facebook and is currently extremely popular across the globe. The demographics of users are generally young, so the content tends to follow popular trends and movements. Because of this, brands and companies love to use the platform. They also seek out users with large followings and might pay them to use (and promote) their products, or send them on sponsored trips to demonstrate them.

Instagram is also great for inspiration. Because it uses hashtags and locations to catalogue images, you can easily locate content you are interested in and see what others are posting. The location tag is particularly useful for researching places before you visit them.

Many communities have stemmed from the platform. The Igers community has inspired groups across the world, so it is worth checking out whether there is one nearby you. In doing this, you can meet like-minded people and build a network to discuss photography.

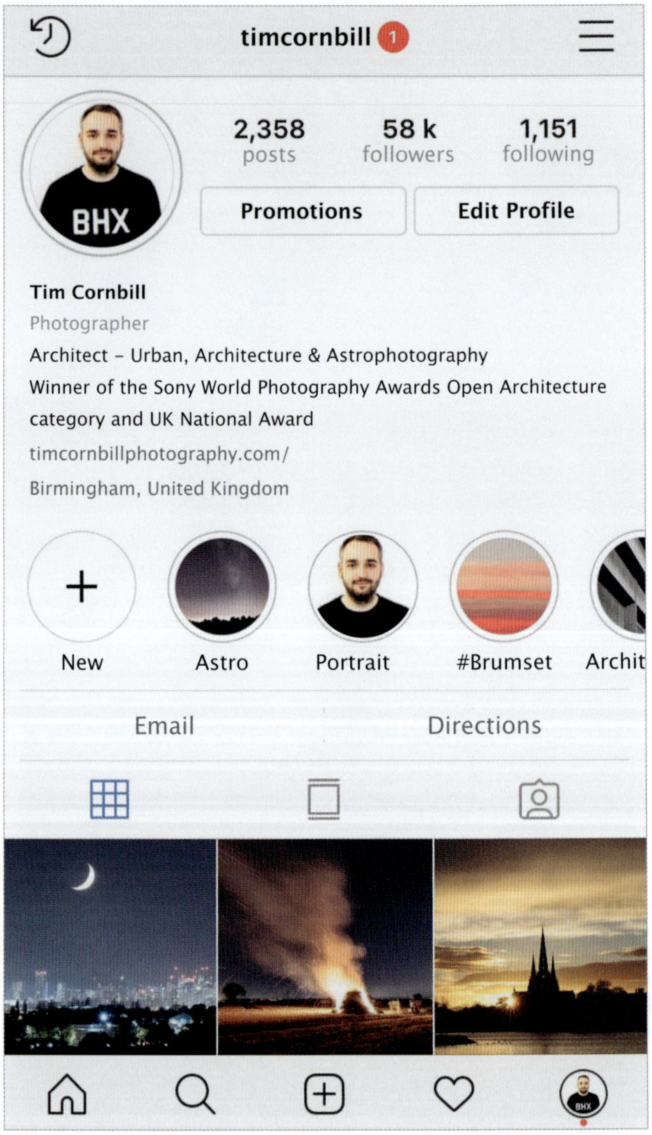

RIGHT
Instagram's profile view. If you want others to follow you for your photography, be sure to mention what you do in the editable text box at the top, in which you can also specify a website and location.

FACEBOOK

This platform was initially created for college students, but today it has a notably older demographic than that of Instagram. Here, you can create a business page for your photography, and add more in-depth posts. One of the big advantages of Facebook is that it is easy to have your content shared; people's interactions with your photos will appear in their timeline and those of their friends, too. This means that posts can get a large amount of interaction very quickly.

The disadvantage with algorithm-based platforms like Facebook and Instagram is that posts can be limited in the numbers of people they are shown to – requiring you to pay for advertising to reach more people. If you're serious about this, the costs can start to add up, so it's important to do the maths to see whether the paid-for advertising is worth the number of extra people you're actually reaching. A good thing about it is that it is set up quite well to target the people you want to reach. You can target people by age, occupation, or even the types of interests they have.

TWITTER

Twitter has many of the same sharing abilities as Facebook, but your posts are limited in both the number of characters they contain and the number of images you can post at once. This platform is more focused on real time, so generally you see content at the time it is posted, and posts can then get lost in the noise. Twitter also uses hashtags and displays popular tags at any particular time, so you can potentially add these 'trending' hashtags to your photos (when relevant) in order to try to reach more people. The hashtags can also help in finding other photographers to follow.

RIGHT, TOP

If you build a professional Facebook page, it will display analytics (on the right-hand side of the screen here) that show you how many people you are reaching over various timeframes, as well as how many people are actually engaging with your content.

RIGHT, BOTTOM

As with Facebook, you can add a 'cover photo' at the top of your Twitter profile page, as well as a short description of your work and any appropriate websites, plus link to other relevant accounts.

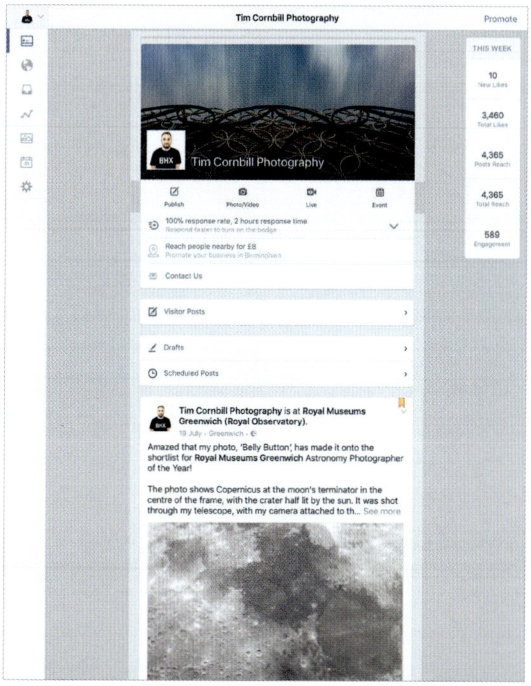

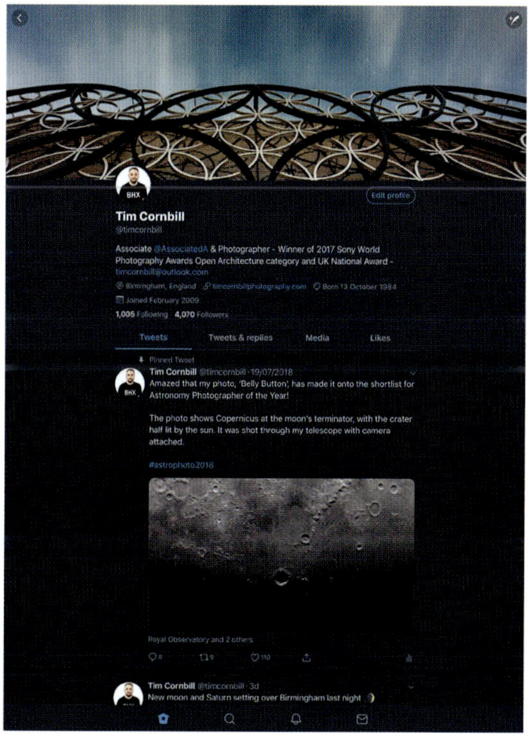

WEBSITES

In addition to using social media to build your profile online, you may want to consider creating a website. The advantage of having a website is that it looks more professional than a social media profile. You can pick out your best work to create an online portfolio and target the type of photography you want to concentrate on. Companies and brands will also tend to look for your website rather than seeking out your social media profile, so they are great for advertising and important for selling your particular brand to prospective clients.

The idea of building your own website can seem daunting. People tend to imagine that they will either need to learn to code, or have to hire a specialist to help them. Today, this isn't at all the case. There are a number of online, template-based website builders that make it incredibly simple to create something that looks highly professional, and the templates usually allow for a high degree of customization, meaning that your website will look unique. Some of the most popular website builders today include Wix, Wordpress and Squarespace (although there are plenty more), and all of these have free options for you to get started on.

The ins and outs of building a website really require a book of their own. Fortunately, however, all the web builders I've mentioned are fairly intuitive to use. Here are some tips that should help you to get started with.

Domain Name: If you're building a professional website, the name should match. Be clear and direct: your name, or your business name is ideal. If your first choice is taken, add descriptive words like 'photography' – but don't make it too long!

Own Your Domain: The next step in terms of looking professional is to pay to own your domain name. This means taking out the part of the URL that has your host's address in it (e.g. '.wordpress.com'). You will have to pay for this, but it makes a big difference.

Keep it Simple: There is no need to cram your website full of extra features. Stick to those you need: your name, your contact details and your photography. Don't add a blog unless you already blog. If you work across different genres, you might want to add separate pages for each, so that your potential clients can find what they're looking for easily. But as a rule, keep it as minimal as possible.

Black on White: If you're not sure which template to pick, stick with one that is mostly white, and uses black text. Black text on white is the easiest to read, and this will always look clean and contemporary.

Low Resolution: The photos you use on your website should not be uploaded at their full resolution. The website builder you're using probably won't let you do this anyway, but when you scale them down, think that they only need to be big enough to look good on a computer or phone screen. Keep them small to make them easier to load, and to discourage copyright theft.

RIGHT
This is my own website's front page at the time of writing. It has few different categories and puts the images front and centre.

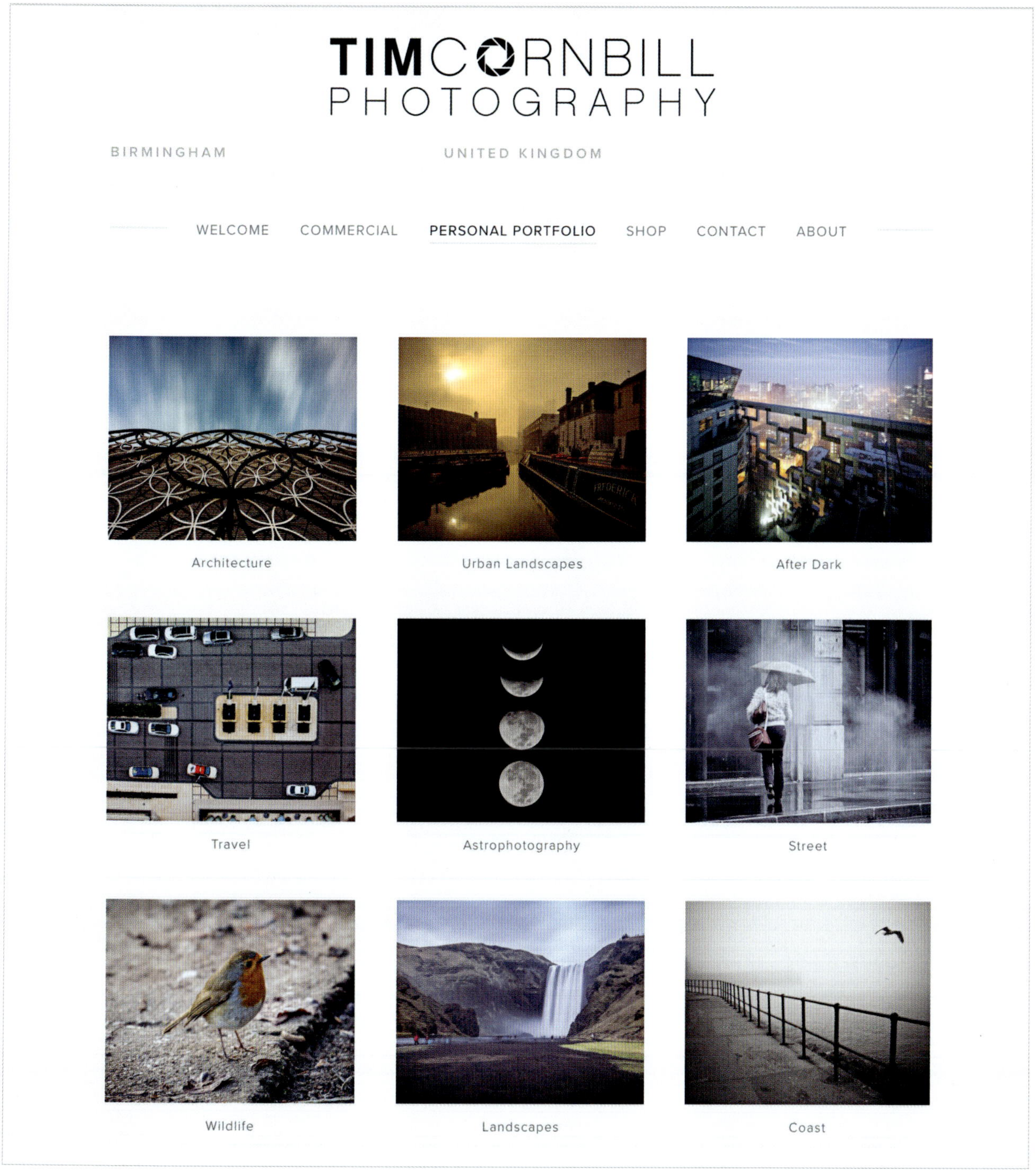
TIMCORNBILL
PHOTOGRAPHY
BIRMINGHAM
UNITED KINGDOM
WELCOME
COMMERCIAL
PERSONAL PORTFOLIO
SHOP
CONTACT
ABOUT
Architecture
Urban Landscapes
After Dark
Travel
Astrophotography
Street
Wildlife
Landscapes
Coast

ONLINE VS OFFLINE

We've talked about how you can use social media to promote yourself as a photographer, but the issue with them is that it is difficult to predict their future influence. People have built businesses around a single social media account but you have to ask, if that account were to disappear overnight for whatever reason, what would they be left with? It is also true that building a business through online networking is not for everyone. Building a following takes dedication and hard work, and comes with much frustration.

You also shouldn't be led to believe, just because everyone seems to be talking about 'influencers' and whichever social media platform is hot right now, that going online is the only way to build a business these days. This is just not true. Spending months building up a decent following on Instagram won't necessarily bring you any new clients, whereas if you can make a good impression in person, then you could (potentially) source and bag a client in one day.

ONLINE

There is no one sure way to build the kind of online brand that gets followers, exposure, engagement, clients and – what you're really working for – money. But if you've picked your platform and you're willing to give it a go, then probably the two most important things to keep in mind are regularity and consistency. Look at the brands or individuals you follow online. How often do they post? Every day? Every hour? Usually, the more successful accounts will be posting on a daily basis as a minimum. Think about how much you can keep it up, and don't overload yourself. There are ways of cheating, such as lining up a series of posts to be uploaded at certain times, which means that you can approach this task in one solid hit.

The other side is consistency: Do you have a clear and identifiable brand? Do your photographs have a recognizable style, or a particular feature that makes them recognizably yours? Be consistent to make sure that your identity sticks in the viewer's mind, if they like what they see.

OFFLINE

If you want to try to build your business offline, it may still help to have a website, so that people can find your details easily. As a starting point, try joining a photography meet-up group. There may well be people within this social group who have experiences or contacts to share, or even someone to collaborate with. Next, you need to locate your potential clients. Any business whose identity is connected with its location is a good lead for the urban photographer – town councils and local charities spring to mind, but you might also consider independent retailers and professionals. Don't be afraid to reach out in order to help a potential client visualize how your services can help their business in ways they might not have thought of yet. If they are located in an attractive building, why not show how they can use this in their branding? If a local business has some spectacularly unattractive photography on their website, show them how you could do it better.

RIGHT
Building a business from your photography might seem like a distant dream, but it can start with the smallest of things - building a website, approaching your first potential client - and who knows how big it might grow.

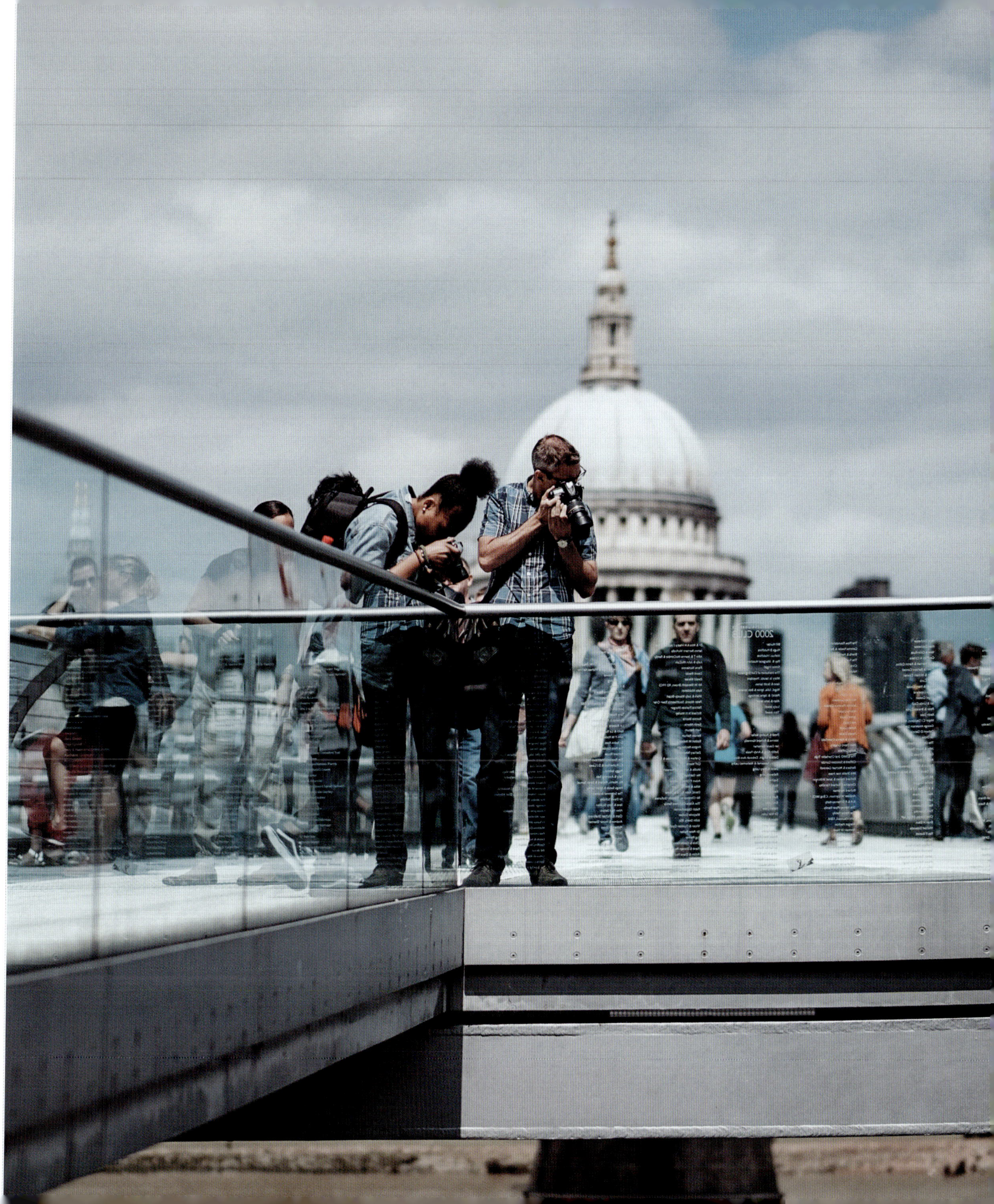

ENTERING COMPETITIONS

Oculus is the photograph that won the Sony World Photography Award for the Open Architecture category in 2017. Winning an award is an amazing experience, it's something that can give your name credibility in terms of approaching clients, it's something to brag about on social media, and it can put your name on the map.

Most importantly, entering a photography competition is something that anybody can do. You don't need to be a professional; you don't even need a lot of experience. The tips, techniques and approaches in this book will stand you in good stead for taking a prize-worthy photo, and then all you really need is a little bit of luck. To prove this point, here is my description of how *Oculus* came about:

'Having just arrived in Berlin on a bright summer's day, my wife and I decided to take a morning walk along the River Spree. We soon came across a large concrete building, and I was immediately struck by its geometry and scale. Across the river, I positioned myself for a single point perspective and waited for the right moment to capture it. A couple came into the viewfinder and I noticed the cyclist out of the corner of my eye. I waited for them to move into the frame and hit the shutter to try and balance the composition.'

Here, you can clearly see how it was a matter of chance, first impression, choosing the right position, considering compositional aspects, and then patience. It's true that experience helped me to decide when was the right moment to press the shutter, but it was pure luck that the three people in the frame were wearing a harmonious and minimal colour palette, and moved in just the right way.

When it comes to entering competitions, there are, however, a few things that are completely within your control. The first is to read the guidelines. Pay attention to the format, including size and file type; make sure you only submit photos that relate to the theme, if there is one, and don't submit more than the number specified. Is image manipulation allowed? Also note what personal information is required from you, and don't lie! If the competition is for a certain age group, or for non-professionals only, or specifically for any other type of demographic, then don't enter it if it doesn't apply to you.

How do you choose which photograph(s) to enter? You will have your favourites, but it can be helpful to introduce an element of objectivity. Find out more about the organization that is hosting the competition or the judges who will select the winners. Look up previous years' winners and analyze what you think it is that gave an image its winning edge. If the judges are photographers themselves, research their own work to learn what you can about their taste. When it comes to making your selection, ask friends and family which photos they like and why. It can help to involve others, if only because they may be able to spot a flaw that you hadn't.

RIGHT
Entering competitions is an excellent way to see your photography anew, and it is also an indication to yourself that you are ready to take the next step. I am immensely proud of *Oculus*, and the experience of winning will always stay with me.

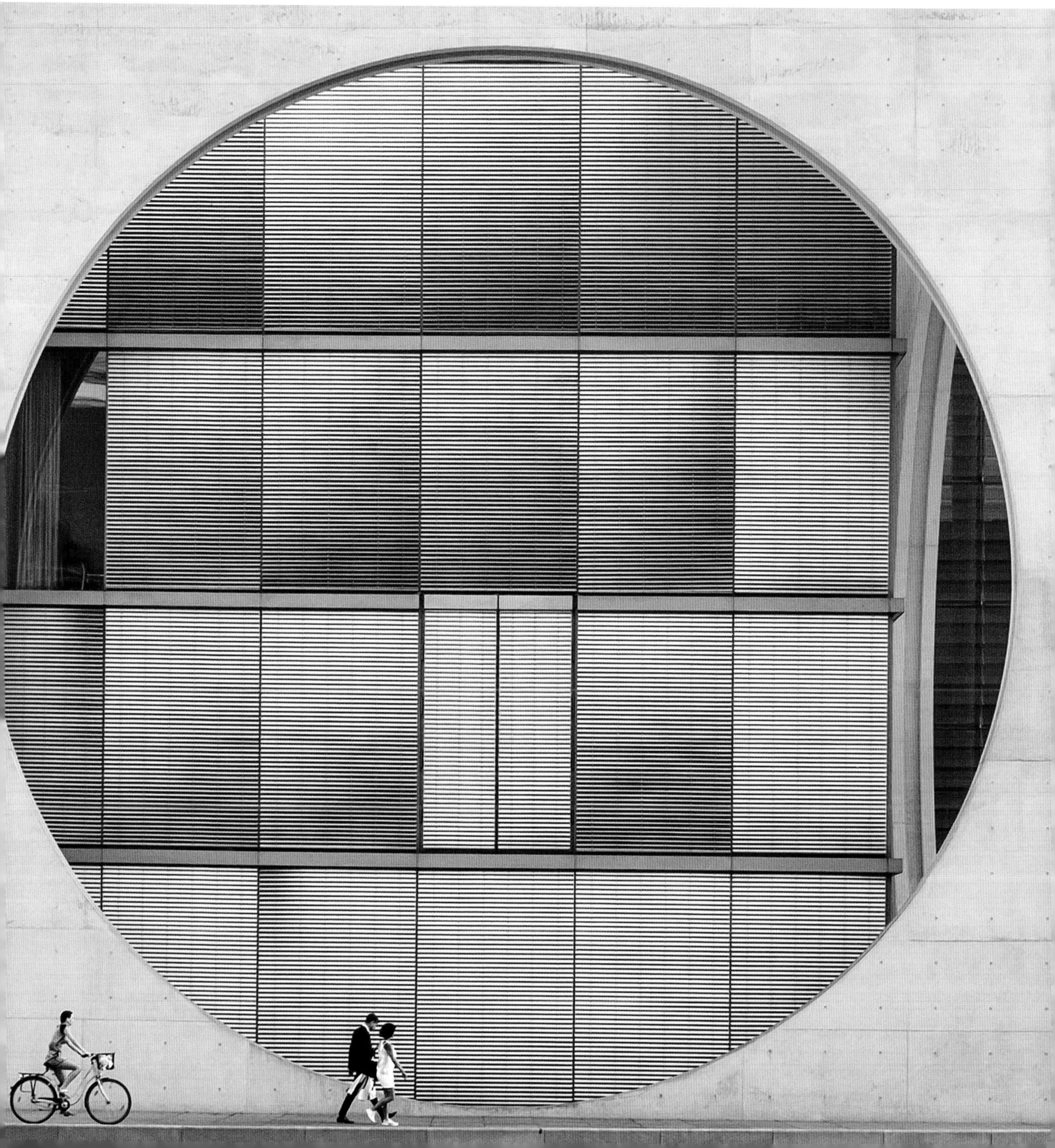

10 RESOURCES

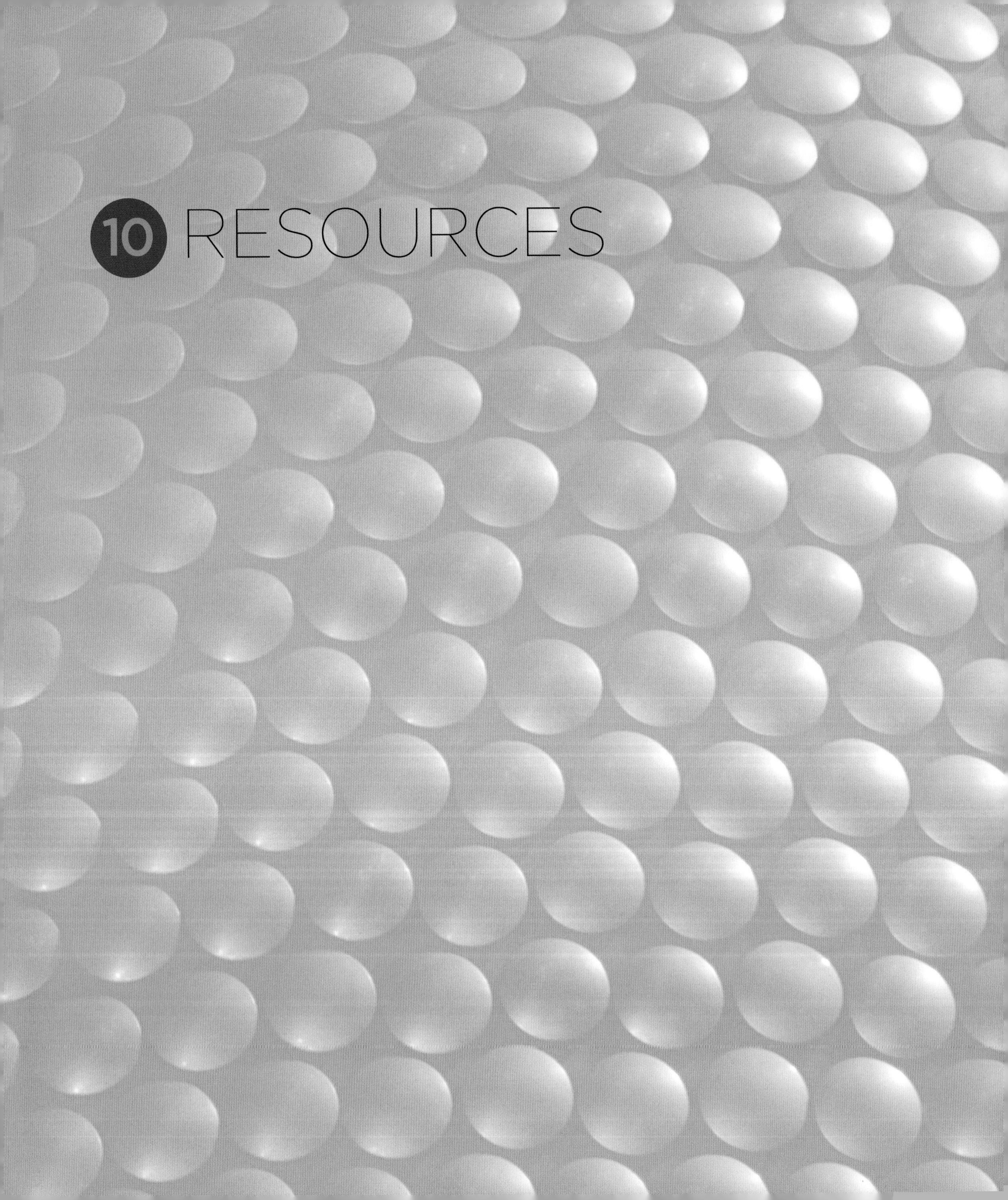

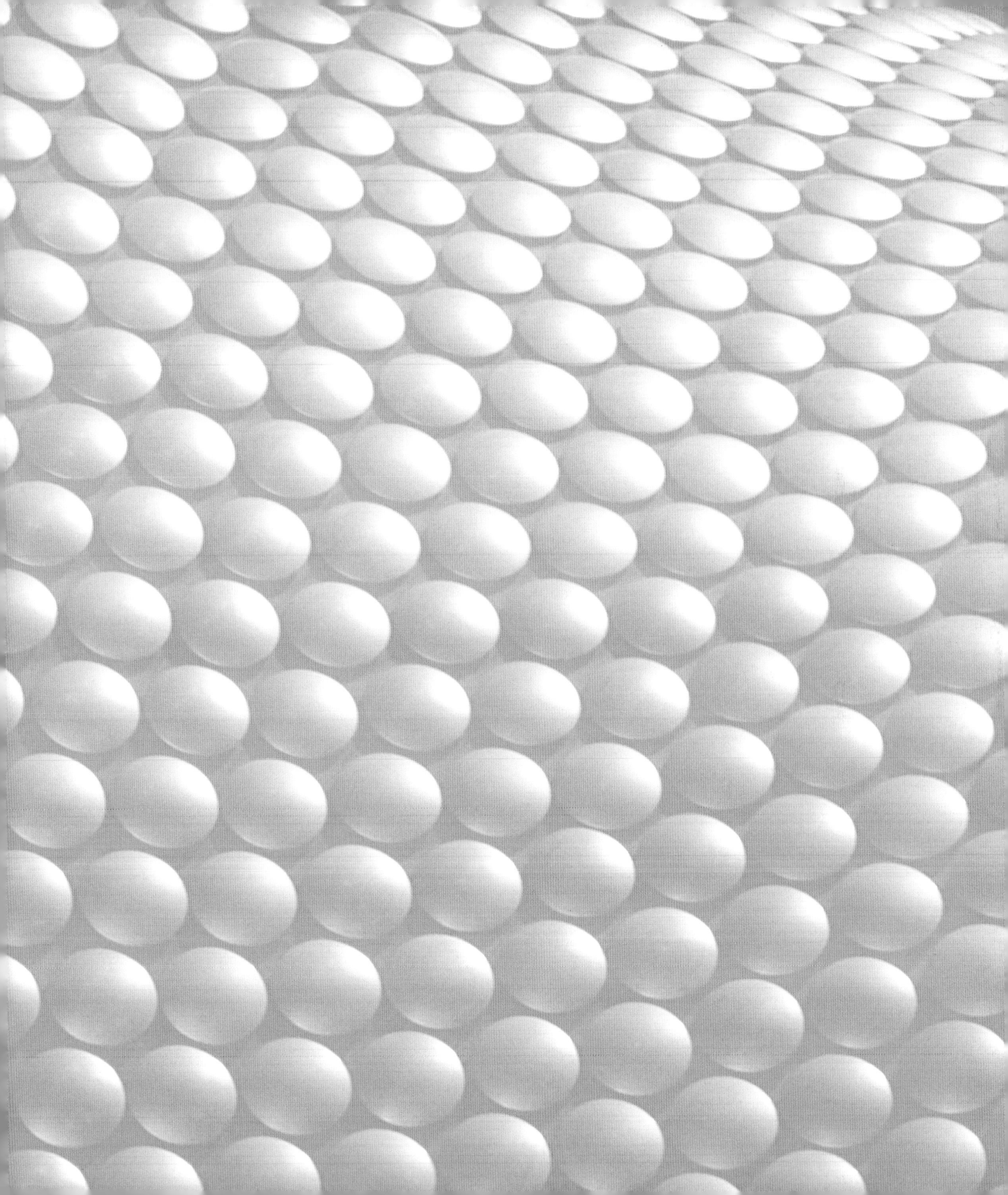

USEFUL WEBSITES

UNDERSTANDING ARCHITECTURE

ArchDaily
www.archdaily.com

Architects' Journal
www.architectsjournal.co.uk

dezeen
www.dezeen.com

RIBA (Royal Institute of British Architects)
www.architecture.com

The Architectural Review
www.architectural-review.com

WAF (World Architecture Festival)
www.worldarchitecturefestival.com

World Architecture News
www.worldarchitecturenews.com

URBAN PHOTOGRAPHERS

Hélène Binet
http://helenebinet.com

Dennis Gilbert
www.dennisgilbert.com

Vivienne Gucwa
http://nythroughthelens.com

Paola Franqui
www.instagram.com/monaris_

Roland Halbe
http://rolandhalbe.eu

Hufton+Crow
www.huftonandcrow.com

Rut Blees Luxemburg
www.rutbleesluxemburg.com

Cameron R. Neilson
www.cameronrneilson.com

Alex Roman
https://vimeo.com/7809605

Sebastian Weiss
https://le-blanc.com

URBAN PHOTOGRAPHY GROUPS & COMMUNITIES

Architectural Photography Meetups
www.meetup.com/topics/architectural-photography

Association of Independent Architectural Photographers
www.aiap.net

Photo District News
www.pdnonline.com

Street Photography in the World
www.streetphotographyintheworld.com

Street Snappers
http://streetsnappers.com

COMPETITIONS

The Architectural Photography Awards
www.photocrowd.com/photo-competitions

British Photography Awards
www.britishphotographyawards.org

Lensculture Street Photography Awards
www.lensculture.com/photo-competitions

Sony World Photo Awards
www.worldphoto.org/sony-world-photography-awards

Urban Photo Awards
https://urbanphotoawards.com

Urban Photographer of the Year
www.cbreupoty.com/en

GLOSSARY

aperture
The variable opening behind your lens that allows light to pass through it and reach the sensor.

aspect ratio
The ratio of the height to the width of an image.

auto white balance
A setting of the camera whereby the camera adjusts colour and exposure data towards neutral, removing what it considers to be anomalous data, including balancing colour temperature. For example, it will whiten the reds in a sunrise/sunset shot.

autofocus
The function of the camera to set the focus point itself, attempting to achieve the sharpest photo.

bracketing
A method of ensuring a correctly exposed photograph by taking three (or more) shots; one with the supposed correct exposure, one slightly underexposed and one slightly overexposed.

Brutalism
An architectural style popular from the 1950s to the 1970s, characterized by large-scale, blocky structures of raw concrete.

colour cast
A tint that colours part of or a whole frame, often caused by extremes of colour temperature, as well as certain types of artificial lighting.

colour temperature
A way of describing the colour of light, measured in Kelvins (K) according to a scale that ranges from dull red (1,900 K) through orange, yellow, white and blue (10,000 K).

complementary colours
A pair of colours that sit opposite each other on the colour wheel, namely: red and green, orange and blue, yellow and purple.

cropping
The process of removing unwanted areas of an image, to change the aspect ratio or composition to leave the only the most significant elements

destructive/non-destructive editing
Post-production work made using destructive editing software overwrites the original data; using non-destructive editing software preserves the original data.

exposure
The amount of light that reaches the camera's sensor when a photograph is taken.

fast lens
A lens with a wide maximum aperture, usually of at least *f*/4.

f-stop
The measurement of the aperture, ranging from a large or 'fast' aperture at *f*/1.4 (or lower on some specialist lenses) to a small aperture of *f*/22 or narrower.

field of view
The extent of a scene that is visible through the viewfinder and which registers on the sensor, dependent on focal length.

focal length
The distance between the mid-point of the plane of the lens and the sensor or film in a camera.

focal point
The centre of interest in a photograph; the area on which the camera is focused.

ISO
The measurement of the sensor's or film's sensitivity; increasing the ISO rating allows more light to register on the sensor, enabling the use of faster shutter speeds or narrower apertures, but can produce noise in digital photographs and grain on a film.

JPEG
A standard image file format that compresses data to allow small file sizes. Known as a 'lossy' file format due to the discarding of additional data.

keystone effect
An optical distortion effect whereby parallel lines appear to converge at a distant vanishing point. In urban photography, this is often apparent when the parallel vertical lines of a tall building's structure appear to lean towards a central point somewhere in the sky.

negative space
Areas of a photograph that do not contain any subject matter.

noise
A random pattern of small spots on a digital image, usually unwanted, caused by non-image-forming electrical signals.

leading lines
A rule of composition in which existing or implied lines in the picture suggest movement and/or draw the viewer's eye along them, often towards a focal point.

Lightroom
Non-destructive image-editing, organizing and formatting software developed by Adobe.

metering
The process by which the camera determines the shutter speed and aperture setting for a 'correct' exposure, dependent on the amount of light registered in the scene and on the ISO. Digital cameras commonly allow for matrix metering, in which the camera registers the whole scene and calculates the best exposure based on various 'zones' of light and dark; spot metering, in which the camera allows you to choose a small, specific point on which to base the exposure; and centre-weighted metering, which evaluates only the middle of the frame in its calculation.

Photoshop
Professional-standard, destructive image-editing software developed by Adobe.

post-production
The process of editing a photograph after the frame has been saved by the camera, i.e. edits made in the darkroom or using image-editing software.

prime lens
A lens with a fixed focal length. Does not allow for a magnification or variable field of view, but advantages include fewer distortions in the image and, frequently, a larger maximum aperture.

Raw
A non-lossy, proprietary image format that preserves higher levels of colour depth than standard 8 bits-per-channel image formats, as well as camera data including exposure and aperture settings, which can then be adjusted in image-editing software such as Photoshop.

rule of thirds
A rule of composition whereby the frame is divided into nine equal sections, and focal points or key compositional elements are placed along the dividing lines or on their intersections.

saturation
The intensity of colour, ranging from the palest hue to the strongest and least diluted with white light.

shutter speed
The amount of time for which the sensor or film is exposed to light.

telephoto lens
A lens with a long focal length, that enables distant objects to be enlarged. Results include a narrow field and angle of view, a flattening of elements within the frame and, due to the level of magnification, distant objects (such as the sun and the moon) can appear disproportionately large.

white balance
A digital camera setting whereby colour and exposure data is adjusted in order to remove colour casts.

wide-angle lens
A lens with a focal length shorter than 35mm on a full-frame sensor (24mm on a cropped frame sensor). Allows for a large field of view and immersive depth of field, but can introduce distortions whereby straight lines appear curved, and elements closer to the lens may appear disproportionately large.

zoom lens
A camera lens with an adjustable focal length, giving, in effect, a range of lenses in one. Disadvantages may include a narrower maximum aperture and increased distortion, in comparison with a prime lens.

INDEX

INDEX

ABOUT THE AUTHOR

Tim Cornbill is a self-taught photographer and architect who was born in Birmingham in the United Kingdom. His passion for photography centres on the urban environment.

Tim became interested in photography as a teenager, starting out using film and investing in his first SLR when he was 16. Studying Architecture at the University of Manchester, Tim used photography to help articulate his work, where he got involved with the photographic society, winning a university photography competition with a photo of the moon rising behind a lighthouse in St Ives, Cornwall (right). The photo was exhibited at the students union, giving Tim his first taste of photographic success and spurring him on to get more involved in the vocation.

In recent years, Tim has found a new outlet for his passion on social media, using his social platforms to portray his home city, with its evolving urban fabric proving to be an excellent backdrop for his chosen genre. His work has been picked up by local media, including the BBC, showing individual photos as well as features.

In 2017 Tim's work was recognized on a global scale, when he won Sony World Photography Award for Architecture for his photo of Marie-Elisabeth Luder's Haus in Berlin, titled *Oculus*.

RIGHT, TOP
This photo of the moon rising behind Smeatons Pier in St Ives won a university competition, encouraging me to pursue my photography further.

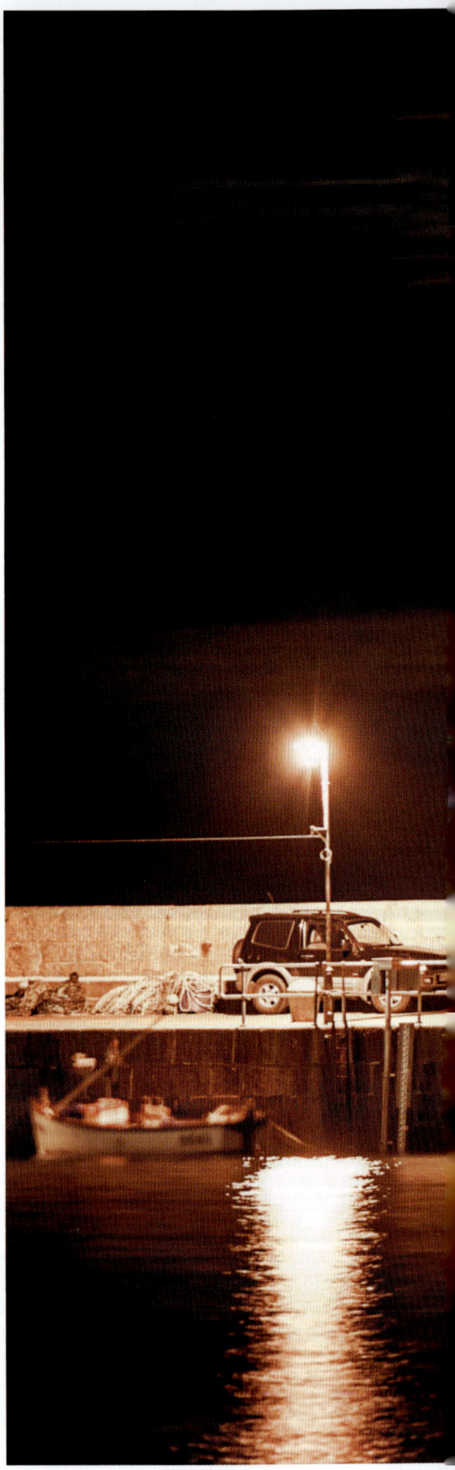

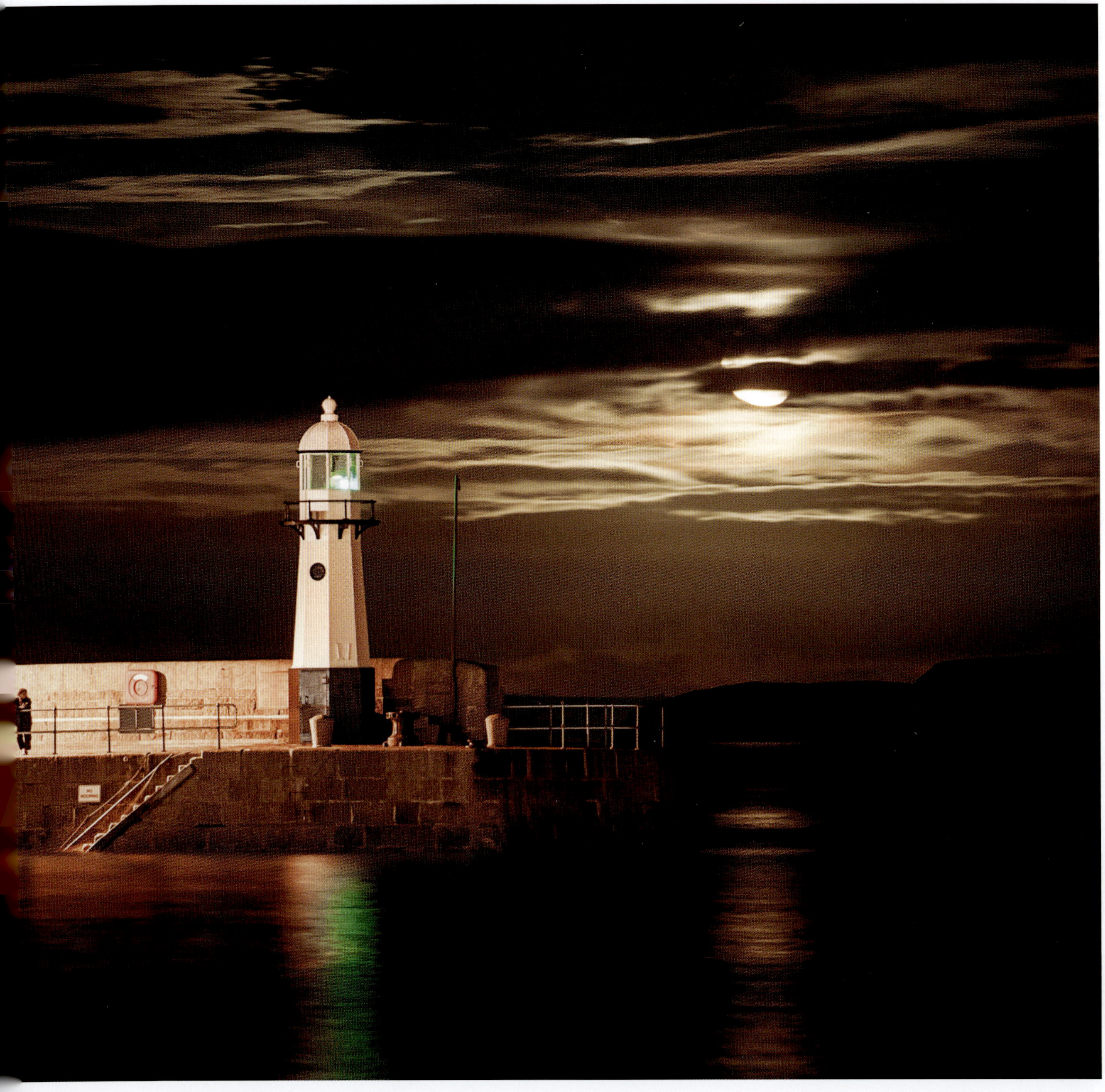

ACKNOWLEDGEMENTS

For Lucy and Seb.

I would like to express special thanks to my family, whose loving support and encouragement has helped me to become the photographer I am today; to the publisher who invited me to start this project; my friends, colleagues and fellow photographers who have pushed me to become the best I can be; and finally the city of Birmingham for its beautiful streets, architecture and people, which are a constant source of inspiration.

ADDITIONAL CREDITS

All photos are by Tim Cornbill with the exception of the following.

52 Banter Snaps/Unsplash; 53 Dan Freeman / Unsplash; 62-63 © Vivienne Gucwa / nythrough-thelens.com / @travelinglens; 72 Maxie Lebrun / Unsplash; 75 © Sebastian Weiss / le-blanc.com / @le_blanc; 90, 91 © Henri Cartier-Bresson / Magnum Photos; 102, 103 © Martin Parr / Magnum Photos; 107 a & b © Maciej Dakowicz / @MaciejDakowicz; 120 © Michael Tomas / @LondonViewpoints; 143 Photo RMN-Grand Palais / Gérard Blot © Estate Brassaï- RMN-Grand Palais; 170 Fox / Pexels; 177 Clem Onojeghuo / Unsplash